The Real LIFE OF BRIAN Barnes

Brian Barnes

Countyvise Ltd

First Published 2014 by Countyvise Ltd
14 Appin Road, Birkenhead, CH41 9HH

British Library Cataloguing in Publication Data.
A catalogue record for this book is available from the British Library.

ISBN 978 1 906823 95 5

I am dedicating this book to my eldest daughter Alison who just before she died in 2007 made me promise to finish the book, and to my family especially my wife Gill who has always been my reason for living, Cath and Gillian, my two other daughters as well as, James, Kate, Lisa and Leon my grandchildren, plus the latest addition to the clan, Mia my great-granddaughter.

To all my friends and work colleagues who find themselves mentioned somewhere thanks.

To Betty, a very good friend over many years.
I hope you enjoy the book.

Brian

CONTENTS

INTRODUCTION

Over a number of years many people including my close family have suggested that I should write about my life experiences. Especially after I have been holding court over a drink or two, I have always been able to tell a true story that I have personally experienced on almost any topic of conversation. I am sure that I have bored the pants of many people in the process. And yet they all appear to enjoy the stories and come back for more.

I was persuaded by my good friend and physiotherapist, Campbell MacIntosh, to record a series of talks for the Talking Newspaper for the Blind, about my exploits when I sailed my 34ft yacht Stratagem round the world. I had recorded a number of hours and reached Australia when Campbell died of cancer. I did complete the talks and since then I have gone on to record many aspects of my life over the past 70 years.

With the notes that I have produced for each talk I have amassed quite a lot of information all of which has surprised even myself. I had not realized just what I have experienced in what appears to me to be only a short period of time.

I have started to look at myself, my family and friends, and my way of life in a new light. I am now 79 years of age and yet I feel and think the same as I did whenever I recollect any aspect of my life whether it is at school, the war, the Olympic Games, or sailing round the world and setting off from Ecuador on my 65th birthday. I can recall them all as if they were yesterday.

I have now started to ask myself: why am I who I am? What made me into the person that I am today? What influenced me? What, if anything, would I have changed?

Can I, by telling the full story as it seems to me, influence my grandchildren? And if I can, should I?

If nothing else it will be a record of the past 80 years as seen by a young boy born in a council house in 1934 who grew up on Greenlands Estate Preston, and spent his first 21years there.

All in all an exciting time for me and my family who, at the time of starting this story, will be asked to contribute a chapter each at the end so long as they agree to write only the truth, the whole truth and nothing but the truth.

CHAPTER ONE

1934-1945 A Short Family History and Early Memories

My mother's maiden name was *Pullich*, which is a German name. *Rudolph Pullich* her father, my grandfather, was German. He came to England in the 19th century to work for the Catholic Jesuit College at Windsor. He later moved to Stonyhurst Jesuit College just outside Longridge.

He married Rose Ann Gudgeon, in Windsor in 1897; she was a sewing maid at Stonyhurst. They lived at Tan Yard, Dilworth and 113 Mersey Street Longridge. They had nine children: Louise, Agnes, Leo, Simon, Lona, Theresa, Rudolph, Wilfred and Wilfridus.

I have managed to trace the Gudgeon side of my family back to the year 1600.

At one time granddad was a quarryman at Longridge. My mum used to tell me that she remembered seeing the first motorcar in Longridge with a man walking in front of the car with a red flag.

When the First World War started my grandfather was interned as an enemy alien and sent to the Isle of Man. My grandmother died while her husband was incarcerated. He was let out to bury his wife and place the children in orphanages; the girls went to Moorfields Convent, Ribbleton and the boys to Saint Vincent's in Preston.

The local people in Longridge raised a petition to get him released, but the authorities would not allow it.

He died on the Isle of Man before the end of the war. In 2009 my daughter Cath found out from the internet that the POWs who died in the Isle of Man prison camp had been re- buried in a war cemetery in Staffordshire on Cannock Chase.

My wife Gill and I went to find the grave of my granddad. It was very moving to stand before his grave as I was the first and only relative to do so.

I know very little about my father's father, Jonathan Ralph Barnes, 1870 – 1908 who was born in Aylesford Kent, and was a soldier, saddler and dock labourer. He married Annie Maher 1880 – 1972 in 1887 and had four children, three boys and one girl: Jack, Alice, Charlie, and Billy, my dad.

He died and my grandmother married again to granddad Daniel Murphy in 1909 with whom she had a further six children, two girls and four boys: Danny, Pat, Joe, Doreen, Jim, and Maggie.

The Barneses lived at some time in Ulverston where they made good friends with the Breen's; Charley Barnes married Agnes Murthwaite who lived in Tarnside, Ulverston. Granddad Murthwaite was a blacksmith and wheelwright; there was also Jim and Lizzy.

My dad left home to live in Preston at 8 Dover Street with two spinster sisters called Maggie and Cissie Hall. He looked on them as his parents and I called them both Auntie Maggie and Auntie Cissie. As I grew up he asked me to visit them regularly which I did until they both died in the 1960s.

One of my mum's brothers, Leo, lived and worked in the Lake District, in the grounds of a large estate, Lingholme on the west side of Derwentwater, near Keswick. She told me that my dad used to take her on the back of his motorbike to visit him, and they used to take a rowing boat out on the lake at night playing records on a gramophone in the moonlight. It was this link with the Lake District that was passed on from my mum and dad that I still have today.

My mum left Moorfields Convent and went to work as a sewing machinist at Simpsons Goldthread Works in Preston, making epaulets and gold braid for officers' uniforms.

She had lodgings in Preston and she met my father who was the manager at one of Clarkson's five shops, the one in North Road at the corner with Saul Street.

The shop sold carpets, furnishings, jewellery in the front and had a pawnbroker business at the rear.

Pawnbrokers were very common in those days; people would pawn their belonging, that is, they would leave their possessions at the shop in return for a sum of money. When they collected their things they had to pay the money back plus interest. If the belongings were not collected by a certain time (12 months) the shop could legally sell them and keep the money.

I could not understand why people did this especially when it was often the same people who pawned their things on Monday who took them out on Friday.

My mum explained that in many cases people who had no place of their own, lived in lodging houses, and the safest way to keep their belongings was to leave them at the pawnshop.

For the same reason many people used gold coins or jewellery as currency because wearing it was easier to keep it safe, a good example being Gypsies, who wore a lot of gold rings and other jewellery. Others were genuinely in need of cash and so would raise the money by pawning a gold ring or a good watch. Although they had every intention of redeeming them at a later stage when money was available quite a few did not: this was where the shop made its profit, by selling the items from the pawnshop

I knew both my grandmother Murphy and also my stepgranddad Murphy.

My mum and dad married in 1932 and had a baby girl Barbara who died at birth.

I was born on 2nd March 1934 at 8, Dorman Road, Ribbleton, Preston which is on Greenlands Council Estate. (See appendix i).

Greenlands Council Estate (appendix i)

This council estate was built in the late 1920s/30s, on the east side of Preston off Ribbleton Avenue 2 miles from the centre of town going towards Longridge.

My mum and dad were the first to move into No. 8 Dorman Road. My mum had wanted to buy a house half a mile further along the road up the hill at Sion Close, but my dad had in mind buying his own shop so he would not purchase a house when they could get a council house.

Dorman Road backed on to the property on Ribbleton Avenue, No. 8 was at the rear of the Bowling Green Public House, which had a grass crown green bowling rink at the rear and was attached to the side of a row of old terraced houses. The pub used to brew its own beer; it had a building containing large vats in which the beer was brewed. When they were brewing and the wind was coming from the east you could not get away from the smell, even with the windows closed. On summer nights I could watch the men play bowls from my bedroom window.

I spent the first 21 years of my life on the estate living at 8 Dorman Road, until I got married. It had a big influence on my development. The roads in the estate were constructed in concrete. This was an ideal surface for playing all sorts of games both in summer and in winter when we would get watering cans to water the road and make super ice slides especially outside our house as Dorman Road was on a slight hill. The problem was that "old" people used to put salt on the slide and cinders and ash from the fire.

All the gardens had chestnut paling fencing which was ideal for making swords when we pretended to be Zorro like the man in the pictures. They also made good hockey sticks.

There were no shops actually on the estate but there were shops on Ribbleton Avenue.

There was a Co-operative store at the corner of Floyd Road. The shop had small canisters on overhead pulleys into which money was placed by the counter staff, and this was then sent on wires over to the cashier's office that was high up at the end of the store. Any change plus the dividend slip was returned the same way and given to the customer. The floor was tiled but always had a covering of sawdust on it.

Opposite the store was Shorrocks bakery and general store. Shorrocks bread was mouth-watering; it was not possible to buy a loaf without eating the crust at the corners and getting into trouble when you got home.

Two doors down in Floyd Road was the most important shop, the Chip Shop. They served hake and chips as well as cod, which was unusual. The speciality was Holland's meat pies and puddings. These are still made today.

On Ribbleton Avenue at the corner of Burnside Avenue were

a few shops: Doran's, another general store, a butcher, and a gent's hairdresser. 200yds closer to town was Southworth's post office and bakery, Lunts a newsagent, Cuffs an ice cream shop, and then a hardware shop. Next to the New Cemetery was a chemist and florist shop. All in all we had everything we needed. No one went into town to shop unless it was for clothes or furniture etc.

Every summer the Preston Council erected large tents on the field next to the Ribbleton Primary school in Downey Road. This was so that the people who lived in some of the houses in Cowley Road, Downey Road and round about could be temporarily housed in the tents while the council fumigated their houses to get rid of bugs, fleas, and other unpleasant things.

Our House 8, Dorman Road

No.8 was the left hand side of a pair of semi-detached houses as you looked at them from the front. We had three bedrooms, one large one at the front which was my parents' room, at the rear a double room which was mine and a single room. Downstairs the front door opened into a small hall at the foot of the stairs with a door into the lounge/dining room which was heated by a coal fire range containing an oven and back boiler for heating the hot water. It had a large bay window.

At the rear of the house was the kitchen with an electric cooker, and large earthenware sink with hot and cold taps. From this was a pantry with concrete slab then a door into the bathroom. The toilet was outside the back door in a porch off the kitchen opposite the coal house which was under the stairs. We had an outside door fitted to the porch which made the house much warmer and safer.

There was a very small garden at the front, side and rear. The wooden fence was covered with green privet hedge all round on the three sides. Cutting this hedge was the worst job I had to do; even when you had finished, the cuttings had to be collected and taken to the tip. One way I devised to get over the job of clearing away, was to hide a toffee or two in the leaves then get the smaller kids to pick up the leaves to find the toffees.

I made myself a promise that when I got my own house it would never have a privet hedge.

On a lighter note my father-in-law, Pop, always cut his hedge with a sickle on a very windy day. You live and learn.

Early Memories

1934 - 1939

My first memories are of my mum taking me to a photographic studio in Friargate Street Preston to have my photograph taken in a green siren suit which had woollen bobs on it. I was standing next to a chair. I was three years old at the time. About the same time 1937 the new King George VI and the Queen Elizabeth came to Preston. Crowds of people thronged the roads; we went to the top of Halfpenny Brow opposite the Deaf and Dumb School, to wave to them as they passed by in an open top coach.

I have very few memories of my dad. He was always at work. We did not often go out together as a family; I cannot remember any holidays which we had together. My only memory is of watching my dad play bowls on the "Bowling Green Pub" green from out of my bedroom window in the summer evenings.

There was one other memory that I have of a day out in 1938 at Fleetwood when my dad took me on the boating lake in front of the hill by the winter gardens. We had a small boat with a sail and my dad could not steer it or control it, I was scared and cried to be taken off as we drifted downwind to the other side of the lake.

My mum got me out; the boat could not be "sailed" back by my dad as he did not know how. The man at the lake walked it back. Who would have thought that 60 years later I would sail my own boat round the world.

The hours my dad worked at the shop meant that I was in bed before he came home. Closing time was 6pm with one late night closing at 8pm, half a day off on Thursday and open all day on Saturday.

1939 -1945 School

At Easter I started school at the Blessed Sacrament infant school when I was five. The Second World War started on 3rd September 1939. As part of the war effort all males over 18 years were called up for active service. The school starting age was raised to 6 years, due to the shortage of teachers. That autumn I was sent to live in Keswick with "Uncle" Ted and "Aunty" Dolly Able, in Wordsworth Street. Ted and Dolly were very good friends of my mum and dad from before they were married. I used to go up the road to Mrs. Ramsden's bakery; she had two boys Bunty, Wilf and a girl Anne. All of them were a lot older than me.

I was taken to Keswick in Ted's car, an old black Morris 8. As we went round the corner at Blackpool Road lights the door fell off and I would have fallen out if Ted had not grabbed me. We went back to our house at 8 Dorman Road, Ribbleton, Preston, and tied the car door shut with an old washing line. I took my little red kiddie car tied on the spare wheel at the back of the car. There was no motorway then so we used the A6 road through Lancaster, Kendal and over Shap Fell.

It was a slow journey; the top speed of the car was only about 40/50 miles per hour. To keep me occupied on the journey Ted kept saying that the little red car was just behind us no matter how fast we went. It followed us all the way to Keswick.

I enjoyed my time at Keswick and it started a lifelong love of the Lake District which I still have today. Keswick was a safe place to grow up, there were very few cars about and it was safe to play outside in the street. Keswick was then a small village where everyone knew everyone else. It is so different to the bustling town of today.

1940

Easter, I was six years old; I started school again at the Blessed Sacrament Infant School, Burnside Avenue, which was just 400 yards from our house. Other boys, who started at the same time and became lifelong pals, were Edward Walmsley, Peter Bradshaw, Terry Sergeant, and Ian Eccles. The school building included infants, juniors, and seniors, that is up to the age of 14 years which was the school leaving age in the 1940s.

My teacher Miss Ready was a young teacher and very bossy. She had red hair and a temper to match. Miss Sherrington, later Mrs. Green, was older and very nice.

I can remember learning to read. We had to say each letter of the alphabet and trace the shape with our finger on a card. Then there were reading cards with pictures on them: there was a dog called Rover and a cat. "The cat sat on the mat" was one we had to learn. There were 20 of them; you had to read each one to the teacher before going on to the next one. You were allowed to take them home to practise. (2006 March 21st Government reintroduced this method of teaching children to read).

We also had to learn our maths tables up to 12 times 12, by rote that is we sang them out loud in class each lesson. I still use my tables in my head today.

On the school playing field were built air raid shelters which were built of brick with a thick concrete flat roof. They built enough to house all the children who had to stay at school if the air raid siren sounded. Everyone who lived less than half a mile from school had to run home when the siren sounded. This included me.

We did not have the air raids that Liverpool and Barrow-in-Furness experienced; the Germans were targeting the docks there, but we did get a few. Because I lived near school I had to go home, but when I got home there was no one in of course, my mum was at work. Strangely as much as I try I cannot remember being afraid of being at home alone. I was supposed to go into the air raid shelter which every house had in the garden, but most were full of water (more about shelters later). I used to make something to eat and eat it under the oak table in the living room.

Now I am older and a father I have realised just how much my mum must have worried about me at that time and yet I was not at all worried. Why is it then that with this experience in my mind I still worry too much about my children and my grandchildren?

I stayed at Blessed Sacrament School until junior 4 class. Junior 4 was the only class in the school with a radio.

During the last week of the war in Europe, we all knew that it was about to end but not when. The teacher had the radio on quietly all day. When it was finally announced that the war was over we all began to cheer and run to all the other classes to tell them, then we were all allowed to go home.

I knew both my grandmother Murphy and also my step-granddad Murphy. My grandmother ruled the family with a rod of iron so my father told me; she used to hit the boys with a frying pan or other pots that were handy.

She was 6ft tall, a very large overpowering woman. All her children were afraid of her, except my dad. Granddad Murphy left his wife and went to live with his daughter, my Aunty Alice in Lancaster.

I remember him as a very old, fat but gentle man, who had a weeping eye; I used to sit on his knee while he told me stories.

He also taught me a lesson I will never forget. In 1938, I was about four years old and had been naughty to my Aunty Alice. Granddad took me on his knee and asked me to say sorry to my aunty which I did not want to do. He then said that it took a lot of courage to say sorry, more courage than most people had. I thought about it and went to my Aunty Alice and said sorry.

My aunty had a small dog called Scottie. It was a black Scottish terrier, and one day my granddad was planting some vegetables in the garden, everyone grew food during the war. This was not easy for him due to his weight; he was bending down moving along the row planting the young cabbage. As he moved to the next space the dog, following behind him, pulled out the one that he had just planted then waited for him to move to the next one. At the end of the row all his work was for nothing as the dog stood wagging his tail waiting for him to continue.

This was the only time I can remember a grown-up swearing.

Granddad died later that year, the funeral was to be in Lancaster starting from my Aunty Alice's house.

I can remember all the Barneses being in the living room dreading the arrival of their mother (now Mrs Murphy) with their step-brothers and sisters.

I sat on the stairs listening to them asking "how are we going to deal with mother?" I can hear my dad say very loud and clear "I will deal with my mother, leave all the talking to me". I could not understand how grown-ups could ever be afraid of anyone. I was sent out to the top of the road to tell them when I saw Grandma coming.

I saw Grandma and all the Murphys walking down the road; they looked like a posse from the cowboy pictures. I ran in the house told my dad and waited. My dad went to the front door to meet Grandma, told her that there was to be no trouble or he would not let her in the house. She said she had no intention of making trouble, they all walked inside in silence and the funeral went off without any trouble.

I was a little bit disappointed that my dad had not had to sort them all out. Over the years I only saw Grandma at funerals; she survived the three sons from her first marriage and lived for a time in Preston with Alice. She had the ability of the Irish to turn the water works on at a moment's notice, she used to call me "little Brian" even though I was 6ft 2ins and 18 years old.

The War

Most of the males were called up to the war and women had to take their places at work. My mum started to work at the shop where my dad had worked; he was the manager of a pawnbroker, jewellers and carpet shop, called Clarkson's. My cousin Molly later came to work for her. All males age 18 and over had to join the armed services; those who objected to the war were called Conscientious Objectors and were made to work in the coal mines. The coal miners were called "Bevin Boys" because that was the name of the politician who was in charge of recruitment. Some people were in reserved jobs, such as farmers, skilled people in factories making items for the war. Pop, Gill's dad, was one; he worked in Courtaulds factory making Rayon for tyres etc.

As the war progressed women were also called up to work on farms (Land Girls) and in munitions factories.

Home Guard

Those who were not called up had to join the Home Guard. They trained like the army and had a uniform. They also had rifles but no ammunition for it. They were called "Dads Army" by the press.

Evacuees

To keep children safe they were moved from areas that were dangerous such as Liverpool and Manchester, the big cities, to rural areas like Wales. Preston was considered to be safe so all the houses were visited to see what room you had: if you had a spare room you had to take an evacuee. Because we had a spare room but no adult to look after me we did not get a child but we had to have a Land Girl billeted on us; she was called Daphne and worked on a farm where we got our milk.

Anderson Shelters

All the houses had to have an air raid shelter put in the garden. It was called an Anderson Shelter. It was made from corrugated iron and had to be dug down into the ground three feet and the soil placed over the top of the shelter which was six feet tall i.e. three feet out of the ground. Almost all the shelters filled with water as it was below the water level of the ground. Ours did, the only ones that did not were those that had the man of the house still at home like the Shaw's at number 1. Mr. Shaw lined their shelter with a concrete floor and then duckboards; it also had an electric light and bunk beds.

We only went into ours once; the rest of the time we hid under the table near the stairs like most people in Preston.

Public shelters were built all over the place in towns and at every school. These shelters were brick built and we were told we would be safe in them unless it received a direct hit. Most of them smelt awful, they were damp and often used as toilets so the smell could be very bad.

In those days the bombs used were small and usually incendiary devices, that is, they set fire to buildings rather than blowing them up.

If the siren sounded, this meant that an air raid was due to start; you had to go home if you lived less than half a mile from school.

In my case I had to go home and be in the shelter on my own, if I went in it, as it was a foot deep in water. I did not mind but as I got to be a parent myself I realised just how worried my mother must have been. We all had gas masks and it was an offence to go out without it. At school we had to practise putting on your mask and keep it on for a set time. No one liked putting it on. The very young children used to cry and try to take it off.

There were E W S (emergency water supply) metal tanks at various places along the roadside. These were to be used by the fire brigade or the ARP people to fight the fires caused by incendiary bombs. In town and built up areas there were water pipes on the pavements that were painted black with white stripes so that you did not fall over them in the dark.

Every street had to have an Air Raid Warden and people had to do fire picket each night in turn, which entailed staying up all night looking for fires that may start due to the bombs. We all had to have a stirrup pump and a water bucket ready, plus sand as well. All the windows had to have brown paper sticky tape stuck on all over to stop the glass from flying about during a bombing raid.

There was a blackout which meant that you could not show a light through your curtains that had to be made of thick material. The street lights were very dim so it was not easy to see your way in the night time. Cars had special fixings to their headlights so that only a thin strip of beam shone on to the street. We all had to wear a band of light coloured material so that vehicles could see pedestrians.

There was only one bomb dropped on or near Preston and that was at Grimsargh. Everyone went to see the damage that it did to two houses. Many nights we could hear the planes going to bomb both Liverpool and Barrow-in-Furness docks. Some nights you could see the sky lit up with the fires that the bombs had started.

In 1940 my dad was posted to Saltburn-by-the-Sea on the north east coast and my mum and me went by train to visit Dad. All I can remember was Mum, Dad and me, standing on the cliffs overlooking the valley to the shore, which was covered with barbed wire and anti-invasion obstacles and seeing a line of ships on the skyline. My dad said that they were the convoys going to Russia to help them fight the Germans.

In June 2007 I visited Saltburn with Gill, my first return after 67 years and it was just as I had remembered it, but without the barbed wire.

Rationing

We all had ration books. When you went to the shop you had a coupon taken out of the book for what you were buying, e.g. meat coupon for your ration of meat, clothing coupons for clothes and so on, even sweets were rationed. The government set the allowance for each coupon that changed as things got better or worse in the war. Even if you had coupons you could not buy things if they were not in the shop. When a shop got a supply of eggs or meat, people would tell their friends to get to the shop quickly.

Due to the war some things were not available so people made do. Most children wore clogs that had wooden soles with either metal corkers for the boys and rubber ones for the girls, fitted to the soles. The uppers were made of leather. Peg rugs made from any old felt cloth or clothing had patterns woven into them and could be very nice. They lasted a long time.

No one in our road had a car; it was not until after the war that Mr. Mitchell who was an insurance salesman got one with his job. We all had coal fires; there was a fireplace in each room including the bedrooms although we only once had a fire in a bedroom. No one had a fridge, just a cold slab made from concrete and a meat safe, which was a box made from wood with a very fine metal mesh to keep out the flies.

There were no washing machines. The washing was done in a tub that was filled with water into which we put soap flakes, Rinso was one kind and Acdo was another. Then the clothes were put in and a dolly was used to agitate the washing: that is why the tub was called a dolly-tub. The dolly was like a three-legged stool on a long pole with a handle half way up the pole. The other thing used to do the washing was a posser, which was a brass or bronze inverted basin with holes in it fixed to a long pole.

Everyone had a washboard. This was made of ribbed metal in

a wooden frame. At the top was a place to hold the bar of soap. You used to rub the clothes with the soap against the ribbed metal to get the dirt free then plunge it into the water. If it was very dirty you had to scrub the clothes with a scrubbing brush.

To get the clothes dry you had a wooden mangle. This had two wooden rollers that squeezed the water out of the washing. It was turned by hand and could be adjusted to squeeze harder or softer.

Washing was physically hard work and took all day for even a small family. The water had to be heated and changed for each wash and rinse.

When my mum was ill I had to do the washing. I thought that I could improve things and make it easier if I did the washing in the bath and place the mangle at the opposite end to the taps so that I could mangle the clothes straight out of the bath into the rinsing tub of clean water in the dolly tub. It was like a production line.

I was very proud if my idea but my mum did not like me using the bath for washing clothes. Still I said that if I was to do a girl's job I would do it my way, and I did. (In 1961 I managed a laundry in Leicester employing 60 women.)

1943 My Dad Died

My dad was in the army, the RAOC (Royal Army Ordinance Corps) my mum had to go into hospital to have a serious operation (hysterectomy), my dad was on compassionate leave when it was my ninth birthday. He did not know what to do for me so when he asked what I wanted I said egg and chips and then we all went to the pictures at the Carlton cinema. It was the best birthday I ever had. All the lads thought so too.

In July that year my dad had another leave and after a week at home he went back to his camp at Bicester Oxfordshire. He left after breakfast in the morning; I can remember him saying to me "Look after your mum for me" and waving goodbye.

That evening he was cycling back to Bicester with his friend Mac when an army fire engine on a practices run went out of control, overturned and fell on top of them. My dad was killed outright and Mac escaped without a scratch because he fell in the ditch at the side of the road.

The following morning the police came to tell my mum about the fatal accident. I could not believe that it was true and thought that there must have been a mistake and that my dad would come home OK. My dad was 37 years old when he was killed.

I tried to look after my mum as well as I could but I did not like having to do all the things I thought were girls' jobs.

School Dinners

Our school did not have a kitchen so we had to go to Ribbleton Avenue School each day for our dinner. There was a bus but most of us boys ran each way and tried to race the bus which had to stop three times on the way.

I did not like the school dinners, we seemed to get a lot of cooked cheese which was like rice pudding. They used to pour it all over the potatoes and vegetables, it made me feel sick (that is what it looked like). The only way I could eat it was to cover it with a lot of pepper.

It was as late as 1968 when we went to visit Derek and Brenda that I ate cooked cheese again. I now enjoy it.

I do not know how I came to have piano lessons but I did. My mum bought a small upright piano and I started lessons, I cannot remember ever wanting to play, all I can remember was that I hated the whole thing, and having endless rows with my mum about it.

While I was still at junior school I decided to run away from home. Looking back I can see what I did quite clearly in my mind but I cannot remember exactly what the problem was other than I felt on my own with no one to care about me.

This was not true but that is how I felt at the time. I decided to stay off school and was going to build a tree house in a field up Ribbleton Hall Drive, which was way out in the country then.

I stayed away from school but it rained all day. I had climbed up the tree but I still got very wet. I had some sandwiches and a bottle of pop but I soon got hungry as the day wore on. At teatime I was still in the field, wet and cold. As it got dark I had had enough but I was afraid to go home knowing that my mum would know that I had not been to school.

Eventually, soaked, cold and feeling very sorry for myself I went home, dreading the meeting with my mum. To my surprise I got a big hug, a kiss and a cuddle, then a hot bath and some tea. My mum said that she was very worried and made me feel that I was all that mattered to her. I never thought about running away again even though we did have some rows over the years.

During the war sweets were in very short supply, we used to buy Rennies Indigestion tablets to suck. One day I bought some Bonamint Chewing Gum which was a powerful laxative, I placed it in an old Wrigley Chewing Gum wrapper, which was a well-known make of gum and gave it to my school pal Eddie Walmsley.

The next day Eddie did not attend school but in the afternoon the head teacher sent for me; Mrs Walmsley had been to school to complain of the trick I had played on her son. I was given a good telling off and told to go round to the Walmsley house to apologise. I knocked on the door dreading meeting Mrs Walmsley but it was opened by Mr Walmsley who was smiling as he asked me what I wanted. I said that I had come to say I was sorry for what I had done. Mr Walmsley said it was OK but not to do it again as Eddie was still sitting on the toilet where he had been most of the day. He also said that I should keep out of the way of Eddie's mum for a few days; with that I left and ran to tell the other lads what had happened.

Entertainment

The radio and record player was the only entertainment we had other than playing cards and board games. I often asked my mum what used to be on the wireless before the war started because at the time that was all that the news there was. She told me that you used to get the weather forecast which fascinated me to think that we would be able to know when it was going to rain so that we could plan our playtime and games.

Records were made of vinyl and played at a speed of 78 revolutions per minute. Because everything was difficult to get we used to make things out of the old records by melting the disc and making a plant pot or ashtray.

On the wireless there was a programme every night at 6-45pm

called Dick Barton Special Agent. It was only on for 15 minutes but everyone made sure that they were inside by a radio to listen to it. The adventures of Dick Barton, Snowy, and Jock were known to everyone in Britain.

Another favourite programme was "It's that man again" (ITMA) with Tommy Handly; Vera Lynn was a young girl singer who recorded a lot of sentimental songs that were very popular during the war. She became known as the Forces Favourite and I went to see her perform live at the Winter Gardens Theatre at Morecambe with my cousin Joan Woods.

In those days everyone smoked, it was the thing to do. I can remember friends of my mum and dad coming to the house to play cards in the evening and the room being full of smoke; we had ashtrays all over the house.

One night when I was about seven years old, I made an excuse to come downstairs: the room was full of smoke and there were four of them all smoking and playing cards. My mum wanted me to go back to bed but I would do anything to stay and watch. I offered to sing a song I had learned that day, and I was allowed to sing it then I had to go bed. I sang "My bonnie lies over the ocean, my bonnie lies over the sea, my father lies over my mother, and that's how my mother got me" I had no idea what it meant but it stopped the cards and the conversation.

Needless to say I was taken very quickly up to bed by my mum.

Cinemas

The local pictures were the Carlton cinema at Blackpool Road, a quarter of a mile away. Every Saturday morning there was the Saturday rush with a children's show for 2d (2 old pennies) with serial films showing each week, just like soaps on TV today. There were other local cinemas, The Guild near Skevington Road, and the Plaza in New Hall Lane. It was the custom when the sloppy bits came on the screen to throw apple cores and shout at them to get on with it. In Preston town centre there were five cinemas, Ritz, Empire, Palladium, New Victoria, and Theatre Royal. There were also two live theatres, The Hippodrome and another near the bus station in Tithebarn Street.

Health & Hospital

When I was at Primary school, Blessed Sacrament, I was running on the playing field behind the school brick shelters when I slipped and slid on a lot of broken glass bottles. I cut my right leg very deeply in two places just above the knee. I was taken to Preston Royal Infirmary (PRI) where the cuts were stitched. I remember that they did not freeze my leg or give me any pain relief. I cried and screamed while they were doing it. I can remember it as if it was yesterday.

There was the teacher with me as my mum was at work. I always seemed to be on my own. I was terrified of having the stitches taken out but in the end it was OK, it did not hurt. The only problem was that they took the stitches out too soon and the scar opened up. I still have two scars on my right leg 64 years later.

The other bad memory I have of PRI is having my tonsils out. I was always getting a sore throat and catarrh so it was decided that I should go into hospital to have them removed.

I can still remember and see in my mind the mask being put over my face and the terrible smell of chloroform just before they did the operation.

Dentist

Once a year the dentist caravan came to school and everyone dreaded it. First there was the inspection when everyone in the class went one by one to let the dentist examine your teeth, this was bad enough but if you got called back it meant that you were going to have treatment which usually meant having teeth taken out in those days.

I was 10 when I last had any teeth taken out. After the examination the dentist sent me for an x ray of my mouth. It would seem that just like my father I had too many teeth so that they would not grow straight. It was decided that I should have seven healthy teeth removed. I was petrified. I can still remember that occasion because I dreamt of Hitler. The war was still going on. I am now 80 years old and I have not had any other teeth removed.

As a child I used to get severe pain in my groin area and stomach. It often came when I was climbing up trees or lampposts or lifting things. It was so bad that I used to go home and lie down on the couch and cry. The problem for me was that it used to go away after a time.

So when my mum came home from work it had disappeared. She used to say I was putting it on. I got no sympathy at all.

It was only in 1952 when I was 18 years old that I had a medical for National Service and a month later one for the Olympics that the doctors said I had a double hernia, each doctor found one at each side, left and right. They said that I had been born with them and that this is what the pain had been over the years. So I was not soft after all.

I was allowed to compete in the Olympics but was said to be unfit for National Service. I went into PRI (Preston Royal Infirmary) in the autumn of 1952 to have my double hernia repaired and started my National Service the following February, 1953.

Growing up

I was always very tall for my age; I was 6ft tall at 14 years of age. This was more of a handicap than you might think. All boys fight, it is part of growing up, the problem for me was that if I fought boys my own age and won I was called a bully because I was bigger than them, but if an older boy, my size, fought and beat me I was soft for crying. I could not win.

The toughest boy at school and the best fighter was a boy called Harry Bishop; he was the "cock of the school". After leaving school I never saw Harry Bishop again until I was a policeman on nights in Preston town centre. (More of that later).

This did not mean that I did not get my own way with my mates, just that I developed a different and better way of achieving it, persuasion. I soon learnt that the person who suggests playing a game first usually gets his way, also if you organise something you can pick the job or part you want to do, then let the others sort out the rest, or you can even organise the lot, which is what I used to do.

The only perk I can remember that being tall gave me was my ability to get into the cinema without an adult. I was once stopped by the commissionaire at the New Victoria Cinema and was asked if I would take in a boy with me, when I looked who it was I was amazed. It was one of the prefects from school who was two years older than me but very small. I agreed and took him in; as soon as we passed the ticket collector he was off and so was I, in a different direction.

Looking back the image that sticks in my mind is one of being alone. It had a good side as well as a bad side, I had the house to myself I could do as I pleased, I did not have an adult bossing me about all the time, I could play out more than my friends but there was not always someone to play with. I also had plenty of time to think, I did a lot of thinking and planning. I used to imagine what I would do when I was older and grown up.

How I would not allow my children to get away with what I did, how I would look after my family and love them as much as I could and always tell them that they were special because they would be. Perhaps it was because I missed those things that I attached more importance to them. I don't know.

I could eat what I wanted, but I had to make it myself, I had to make the fire if it was cold, if I did not do my homework I was punished at school. It was this cause and effect that taught me a lot. I valued things more than others especially little things that they took for granted, but I envied those who had brothers or even sisters, but most of all those who had both a mum and a dad when they went on holidays.

I was looked after, my mum arranged for neighbours to make my meals and let me stay with them until she got home but I always had a front door key and used to go home alone most of the time.

We bought a small black Scottie dog and called it Mac. Mac was a friend but also a pain; with us both out all day during school term Mac had to go with my mum to work. He had a basket under the counter in the pledge shop, and after school I had to go to the shop to collect Mac and take him home. This added three-quarters of a mile to the walk to the bus and an hour to the time it took me to reach home.

The bus stop for the Ribbleton bus was outside the Miller Arcade opposite the New Victoria cinema. It was always the longest queue of all the buses that went from the Miller Arcade; many times it was round three sides of the square. In winter when Mac was wet he had to be lifted upstairs on the bus because he was so little, all in all he required a lot of looking after. Because of the lack of time he had outside he developed eczema, I had to take him to the RSPCA to be put down. It was a terrible thing to have to do; when I got home my mum and I both cried and cried.

I started to do things about the house, I wanted to do boys' things not cleaning and washing which I thought of as girls' jobs.

The first job I remember doing was to replace part of the doors into the bathroom and pantry which were made of wood, with frosted glass in order to let more light into the kitchen. I was so proud of the work when it was finished especially when neighbours saw it and copied the idea.

Being alone was worst when I was ill; we all need plenty of TLC (tender loving care) then. Like all my pals I caught measles, mumps, chickenpox, German measles, and scabies but missed scarlet fever and whooping cough.

Scabies was the most embarrassing, everyone thought that only dirty people caught scabies which are spots caused by a parasite which spread all over your body and itch and itch like mad. It seems that it spreads very easily and goes through a family like wild fire. I caught it and gave it to my mum and Cousin Molly who was working with her at the time. Once diagnosed by the doctor we had to attend a special clinic in town to be washed down and then painted with a white substance all over and I mean all over by a nurse. Your clothes were burned and you had to go home in fresh ones that had been washed at very high temperature or boiled.

This did the trick but we were all embarrassed and told no one about it until you found out that all your friends had had it as well.

These were the times when I felt all alone and it seems like it was only yesterday.

Football

This was the main game for me and all my pals: to be good at football was the best you could get. I was not good at it, even though I loved it. I was even worse at cricket.

I could not get in the school team or the church team or any team, so I formed my own, Greenlands Athletic football club.

I picked the team and so I played: it was as simple as that. My

Aunty Theresa brought home a leather "T Ball" from Germany, so called because all the pieces of leather were cut in the shape of a letter T. I was the talk of the estate; no one had seen a T Ball before. This was the kind that Preston North End (PNE) football club played with. The ball had a replaceable inner bladder which was pumped up, and then the ball was laced up with a leather thong. It was important to get the laces tight and the ends tucked in so that players did not get hurt when heading the ball. As the ball was used it got wet, absorbed water and got heavier and heavier. It is totally different from the ball used today, and so is the game of football.

As I said although I was tall I was not as rough or tough as many other boys my size, who were usually older than me. One afternoon I was playing football on the Ribbleton Hall Drive football pitch for the Church Junior team when I got fouled by one of the other side, something inside me snapped and I decided that I was going to get my own back on the lad who kicked me. Each time I went for the ball I charged into the other side as if my life depended on it, and to my surprise I got every ball. All my team mates said that it was the best game I had ever played.

The church team managed to get into the final of the local league cup, which was to be played on the Preston Catholic College football ground using the first team pitch. I had never managed to get into any of the college teams, not even the class team so I was thrilled to be chosen to play for the church team even if I was only picked to play outside left because no one else was available. I was not a left foot player, I was not very good with my right foot either, but I was willing to play anywhere just to say I had played on the first team pitch.

The game was a typical schoolboy match, everyone chasing the ball and no one scoring. In the second half with the game heading for a draw everyone was over on the right side of the pitch when somehow the ball came over to me standing in front of the goal with only the goalkeeper to beat. I can remember thinking I must not miss this. I stopped the ball, kicked it and in it went past the goalkeeper. We had scored, that was the only goal and we won the cup; I was the hero, it was the only medal I ever got for playing football.

After the war I used to go and watch Preston North End FC who played in the first division. Their star player was Tom Finney, who played at outside right. He was the best player I have ever seen, he played for England in every forward position from outside right to outside left. He was never booked for fouling anyone but defenders were always fouling him, for it was the only way they could stop him. Playing at right half, behind Tom was another great player Bill Shankley. Bill used to protect Tom by going after any player who fouled Tom, even to the other side of the pitch. Later when Bill left he was replaced by another Scot, Tommy Docherty, who was in the same mould.

Tommy and his wife Agnes lived close by us; we used to baby-sit for them, and became good friends. Although we could walk to Deepdale, the football ground, we used to cycle there and leave our bikes at any of the numerous houses in the vicinity for 6d. The houses with gardens made enough money from this to pay for their summer holidays.

Games we used to play

During the 40s, the ten years from age six to sixteen was spent mainly on my own. This is how I felt but of course I was not literally left alone; Mrs Hall across the road would keep an eye on me, and during the school holidays a lady close by would cook my dinner; this was arranged and paid for by my mum. I always had a door key and I used to spend a lot of time on my own thinking and planning in my mind what I was going to do. I still do to this day.

Playing was a serious business and had to be planned to get the most out of it. Many boys including me used to get severely constipated because you could not waste time going to the toilet, playing was too important for that. Even though we only had a small garden I used to pitch my tent in it and sleep in it with my friends Jackie Brown and Derek Price. We also had a wooden shed which my Uncle Dick made on top of which he stored wooden planks for future use.

These were great for pretending to be ship's planks that pirates used to make people walk off the boat. I was always getting into trouble for climbing on the shed. As I got older I used to fight as most boys do. Our estate, Greenlands, used to get into a war with the Holm

Slack Estate which was down the railway line to Blackpool Road, by the sand works.

About once a year we would get together and go and raid them. We were armed with dustbin lids, railings and stones. We would go down the railway line and charge at them. Sometimes they would come to our estate and both gangs with about 20 - 30 lads would chase each other. The only difference then was that if only one policeman appeared we all split up and ran away.

Life for me was great and my main thoughts were on what games to play; my favourite game was "relievo".

Relievo (A more sophisticated game of tag)

I liked this game because it involved thinking and running, and I was good at both. It can be played by any number of players but three-a-side is the least that can be enjoyed. Players are divided into two teams of equal ability, i.e. size and running speed, one being the keepers the others had to stay free.

At the start a "prison" was marked out on the pavement with chalk or privet leaves, usually under a lamp post. This square had to be large enough to hold all the players from one team.

The side being free had five minutes to disperse anywhere within the set boundaries agreed at the start of the game, but it could be over an area larger than the estate and had been known to cover a number of miles.

The chasing team only had to touch a member of the other side to capture them, and then they must go back to the "prison". One of the chasing side would be the guard. When all the free side were in "prison" the game was won by the chasers. A time limit was often agreed at the start.

It was possible to get your team members freed from "prison" by touching them inside the marked area. There are many ways of doing this, one being to send a team member back on their own to say they have been caught when they had not, and then when a number had been caught they let them out. Of course the guard should touch all new prisoners but you could distract them if you were clever.

Another way was to climb into the garden next to the "prison" and touch your team members through the hedge. When it got to the stage of all but one member being caught you had to judge how many you sent out to chase and how many you left to guard the prisoners.

It could last for hours and you ran many miles. All good clean fun which is more than you could say for the next game, "climbing over backs".

Climbing over Backs

Greenlands Estate consisted of semi-detached and terraced houses, all with a garden front and back. All had a chestnut paling fence but most had privet hedges as well.

Two parallel roads Dorman and Derry Road had rear gardens that backed on to each other. The game was to have a race climbing over all the fences between the two roads. It sounds easy but the person who got far enough in front made a noise so that the householder would come out to see what was going on and catch those still climbing over the fence. It has been known to break a greenhouse window or the glass of a cold frame to get the house owner out and mad enough to chase the lads at the back.

Knocking on Doors

This is another unsociable game but at the time it was looked on as great fun. The idea was to knock on a front door then run away when the door was opened. Variations on this included tying a piece of cotton on the door knocker and hiding across the road, so that as soon as the door was opened then closed you "knocked" again and again until you were found out, then you ran. I had the idea that instead of running away with the rest I stood there and told the owner that some lads had done it and had run that way down the road. My street cred went up for having the nerve to do it.

Slides

In winter, because our road was made of smooth concrete and on a slight slope it was perfect for making a long slide. As soon as it was freezing we would get a watering can and water the road to make a super slide. Kids from other roads that were flat would come and use the slide. Because there was no one in our house only me I was the one to get the water. As the slide got better some adult would notice and come out with either salt or hot cinders from the fire or even both to spoil our fun.

These last three games were played without malice at the time and yet now I would be appalled if they happened to me. The difference between then and now is that we knew that if we were caught we would get a good hiding first from the owner then when we got home we would get another from our parents. We also knew that we deserved and expected it.

As I said there was no malice in it even when caught. I cannot remember anyone being taken to court for an offence in all my ten years. During the 40s, we were dealt with on the spot and it worked. Park keepers, bus conductors, householders, shopkeepers, teachers, all gave out physical punishment as well as the local policeman but we respected them for it. We did not enjoy it but we knew the rules which we decided to ignore and therefore expected the punishment.

Other games were more sociable and went in and out of popularity, such as:

Marbles

We had good surfaces on which to play marbles, we played in the street gutter and also on the pavement. This was called puggy when you had to get the marble into a hole.

Roller Skating

Again due the concrete road it was ideal for roller skates. We also used to play hockey on skates, using railings for sticks. Another variation was to sit on a board or thick book on one skate and race down the road.

Trolleys

These were made from old pram wheels, fixed onto a plank of wood 6 feet long. The large pram wheels went at the back. They were fixed by nails about 12 inches from the back of the plank. The front wheels were smaller and were fixed by one bolt in the middle of the plank through the axle so that they could turn from side to side and so steer the trolley. To make it steer better the front 2 feet of the plank was made narrow. A rope was fastened to the front axle near the wheel from this the trolley was steered.

The better versions had a wooden box nailed to the rear of the plank just over the rear wheels, leaving a platform at the back for the person pushing the trolley to stand when he got the trolley going fast enough.

Races between trolleys were very important events and some even went to the extent of putting 6 inch nails at the front to ram the opposition.

Pram wheels were cadged from families who had children growing up or collected from the council tip which was on the edge of the estate.

Bicycling

As soon as you could, you learnt to ride a bike. No one had a new bike; you could only get second-hand bikes, so as you grew larger you sold it to get another one the right size. There was not a lot of traffic on the roads which were much safer than they are now.

Hockey

This was our own version played with a tennis ball and railings for sticks. Sometimes we played on our bikes and in winter we made a rink with frozen water until the grown-ups stopped it.

Conkers

Every autumn we climbed horse-chestnut trees to get conkers, the bigger the better. The conker had a hole drilled in the middle and a piece of string with a knot at the end was threaded through it. The object was to hit your opponent's conker with yours and smash it to bits. You tossed to see who struck first and you kept going until you missed, then the other lad had a go at hitting yours. Sometimes both broke at the same time. One trick was to bake the conker in the oven so that it dried out and was very hard. Or place one in a drawer and save it until next year.

Tappit

This was a game played like football with a tennis ball across the width of the road. The goals were very wide. You could only tap the ball with the side of your foot, and you could not touch it more than once, then your opponent had to stop the ball with a tap back to your side as well as trying to score himself. To score you had to hit the kerb at the other side. The skill was to be able to tap the ball to the far end of the goal so that your opponent had to go to one side then place it at the other side on its return.

Cricket

We played in the street and in the gardens often with boxes as wickets. Many is the time I have hit a good ball straight through the window.

Dodgers

This was played in the street within set boundaries, annul number of people could play. The person "on" had a tennis ball and had to throw it at someone if hey hit them then that person was "on". Again it was all about running and dodging.

Skipping

This was usually played by the girls but sometimes the boys joined in, especially the one where the rope stretched across the road and as many as possible jumped at the same time.

Swings on a lamp post

This was great fun: the swing would be tied to the top of the lamp post and wrapped round and round until it was tight to the post. Then you would swing round as the rope untied itself.

Top & whip

The tops were made of wood often by dads who worked in the weaving factories, although you could buy them in the shops. The whip was made of a leather thong. If you put a drawing pin in the bottom of the top it went faster for longer, we also used to make patterns on the top with chalk so that it looked great when spinning.

You could start a top going by wrapping the whip round the top tight then you threw it in the air at the same time pulling the whip. The spinning top would land on the road spinning and you kept it going by whipping it. Competitions were judged on how long the top was kept going.

Sledging

When the snow fell we had a super time and we made sledges out of anything we could get. I was very lucky, my Uncle Dick was a joiner, and he made me a proper sledge with metal runners, which was the envy of all my pals. At the bottom of our road was a valley with a stream running along the bottom. It had steep sides: part of the valley was the corporation tip which was being filled in but the rest was ideal for sledging.

Some of the older lads got part of an Anderson shelter, the metal bent at the end like a letter J. Four or five lads would get on together and slide down the hill, but you had to jump off before it went into the stream. The stream was a problem for my sledge because it went so fast I ended up getting wet most times. My mum was not at all pleased, not only because I was getting wet and dirty but she said it was also dangerous.

Hopscotch

This was played a lot because again we had a good surface to play on. The game was played by marking out nine squares on the road in a pattern of a single, then two, then single, then two, single, then two. The singles were 1, 4 and 7 doubles 2 and 3, 5 and 6, 8 and 9. You had to slide a flat stone into the squares in sequence then hop up and down them all without touching an edge.

Schooling

Playing was the most important thing in my life; school was something you had to put up with in between playing, eating and sleeping.

The last year at junior school when I was 11 years old we started to have tests each week ready for the eleven plus exam. I was at the bottom of the class, or at least in the bottom two. After the first test I thought about going to the grammar school which in my case would be Preston Catholic College (PCC): they had their own swimming pool. I decided I would like to go there and decided to start learning my tables and other subjects, and for the first time we were given work to practise at home.

A new test called an intelligence test was introduced; really it was about general knowledge. I immediately loved it.

The second week when we were tested I came second. A girl was first, Maureen Swan, she was the best in the class. From then on I was either first or second in the tests, no one including me could understand why, but for the first time I was trying hard to achieve something I had decided I wanted to get. That has been the way it has worked for me all my life.

"If you want it enough and you work at it you can get it" is my lesson from life

I passed the eleven plus exam and started at PCC on 17th September 1945, my dad's birthday.

Holidays and visits

Some of my best memories are of going to the River Ribble near the Halfpenny bridge where the Tickled Trout Hotel is situated now. A few of the mums used to take as many kids as wanted to go down to the river in summer. It was a good walk, up Ribbleton Hall Drive, past the hall, past the dog kennels where they trained and kept greyhounds for racing (all the roads were just cinder tracks). Then to the woods which had a steep path down to the farm at the bottom and on to the riverbank. There was a very large old tree that had its roots on the surface of the path that made it hard to walk over. The very small children and the prams had to be carried over these roots. We all carried bags with sandwiches and water or Tizer to drink.

The river at this point meandered to go under the Halfpenny road bridge and this caused the bank to crumble away which made a sandy part on which we played for hours.

We called this place "Little Blackpool". Because there were so many children to play with we spent hours there; it was an all day job for the mums.

The funny thing was that the same way home was twice as long and took four times as long to walk home, but it was worth all the aches and pains that we all seemed to get.

Many years later I used to go with my friends from the Preston Amateur Swimming Club, the Banisters, Jean and Jim, Kath Bowen, Keith O'Melia, Leslie Carter, Ken Shaw, Barbara Simpson, Jean Burns and others to swim in the river against the current when I was training for the Olympics. It was at this place under the road bridge that I asked Gill to marry me and gave her the engagement ring, in 1953.

The towns in the north of England developed because of the cotton and woollen mills that dominated all the towns. The owners all agreed to close the mills for a week at the same time for maintenance. This is when the workers had to take their holidays and it became known as "Preston Holiday Week" and the whole town closed down. It was the last week in July, the schools were closed and if you could afford it you went away for the week.

We either went to Keswick to stay with Ted and Dolly, which was most of the time, or we went occasionally to Fleetwood or Morecambe and stayed in a boarding house, just me and my mum. I liked Fleetwood; there was plenty of sand to play on and the fishing boats went out each day on the high tide. The wives of the fishermen used to wave goodbye as the boats passed close to the promenade on their way out to sea.

I used to love to watch the marionettes (a puppet show) near the paddling pool on the promenade where we went every day. As I grew older we used to play putting on the green and later even pitch and putt which was much harder; I think my mum let me win but she never said so. Fleetwood was at the end of the tram line which went into Blackpool. Blackpool was much busier and noisier, and so by staying in Fleetwood we could go into Blackpool for a show on the pier and yet have the quiet of the fishing town during the day.

A favourite part of staying in Fleetwood was the ferry to Knott End. This was only a short trip across the river when the tide was out but much longer across the sea when the tide was in. In my mind I was crossing the ocean on a large steamer; I never thought I would do it for real some day in a small yacht.

Sometimes we would stay at Bare, a place just outside Morecambe. We travelled by train and I used to wait to see if the guard would shout out "All change bare please" but he never did. Very soon after the war ended in 1945 the illuminations were resumed at both Blackpool and Morecambe. In Morecambe Happy Mount Park was the centre of the lights, this was more concentrated in a smaller area while Blackpool was spread out over the miles of promenade, from South Shore to Bispham.

For me holidays could be lonely because I had no one to play with, but my mum did her best and as I got older, about 10 years, I was able to take a friend with us.

I had twin cousins both seven years older than me, Molly and Marjory Whaley who lived at New Longton. Their parents Uncle Tom, a builder, and Aunty Agnes lived in a house that had a very large garden, almost a smallholding, at Saunders Lane. They kept geese, chickens, and ducks. They had a lot of wooden buildings with all sorts of tools in them but the memory that sticks in my mind to this day is that of the house being in a constant untidy mess. There were always pans in the sink in the kitchen and potato peelings cooking on the stove, these were for the livestock.

It was to me so bad that I promised myself that when I got a house of my own it would always be kept tidy and clean. (Kids this is why I am like I am). I used to go and visit from time to time and enjoyed it but I was always glad to get home to an orderly house.

Occasionally I would go to stay with my Uncle Charlie and Aunty Agnes at Burton and Holm. Charley Barnes was my dad's brother; he had two daughters Margaret the eldest and Mary. Uncle Charlie was a signal man on the railways and his signal box was just north of Carnforth at Burton and Holm. The village in which they lived was next to the Lancaster canal and it was there that one of the local lads taught me how to catch trout in the canal by tickling them. I did not believe him at first but we all went to the canal side just outside the village. There were reeds growing in the water and the fish used to lie in-between the reeds. We were told to lie down, keep still and not to talk. The lad then slowly placed his arm in the water and very slowly brought it close to the fish, and then to my amazement he started to rub the underside of the fish with his fingers. The fish seemed to like it because it never moved, after a few minutes he scooped the fish out of the water onto the canal bank.

It was unbelievable. Next it was my turn: we walked further up the canal and found a similar spot for me to try. I did as he had done and slowly placed my arm in the water then I moved to the fish and to my surprise it did not swim away when I touched it. It felt cool and smooth as I rubbed the underside of the trout, after a time the lad motioned for me to scoop it out, I took a deep breath and scooped the fish and a lot of water out onto the bank. The fish came out and was still wriggling, it was about six inches long, I thought that it was large enough to eat but when we got it home Aunty Agnes said it was not fit to eat. When I got home to Preston and told my pals that I had tickled a trout and caught it by hand they would not believe me.

Fuel

Coal was the only source of heating and indeed cooking when I was born in the 1930s; all the houses that we lived in until we moved to Hoylake in 1967 only had coal fires. Then in 1968 we had oil fired central heating installed for the first time in my life, I was 34 years old.

Coal was delivered by the coalman in 1cwt (50.8 Kg) sacks on a cart pulled by a horse. It was only after the war in the 1950s that lorries replaced the horse and cart.

The coalman had a square piece of leather on his back and shoulders to stop the wear on his clothes. He would carry the sacks to the coal shed or drop it down the coal hole which went into the cellar in some old houses. It was very dirty and dusty work and we used to close all the widows and doors when we had a delivery. The coalman was black all over apart from his eyes and mouth.

The best coal was nutty slack which was about the size of an orange or lemon. During the war coal, like everything else, was rationed and you had to take what you were offered even if it was in very large lumps and had slate in it. The lumps had to be broken down with a coal hammer. This created a lot of dust and very small pieces of coal which we called "slack." You used to put a shovel full of slack and vegetable peelings on the fire when you wanted it to stay lit over a long time, say at night or if you were going out.

Some people mixed the dust with cement to make coal bricks to be able to burn all the coal, even the dust, it was so precious.

Each town had a gas works. The gas was made by extracting it from the coal, and the result that was left was called coke. This would burn without making smoke and was cheaper than coal.

At Dorman Road our coal hole was under the stairs off the porch at the side of the house opposite the toilet. Uncle Dick Wood, who was a joiner, made an outside door on the porch which made the house a lot warmer and as it could be locked stopped the coal from being stolen. It also meant that you did not have to go "outside" to the loo. Even so the water pipes in the loo were often frozen solid in winter; we used to place a paraffin lamp in the loo to keep the temperature above freezing.

You had to get coal when it was available so to be able to store more coal under the stairs wooden boards were placed across the doorway up to about 5feet high. The bottom board had a hole in it the width of the shovel to allow you to get the coal out. The coal was tipped in over the top board.

Burning Coal and Lighting the fire

The living room had a coal fire place and so did 2 of the 3 bedrooms.

First the fire grate had to be raked clear of the ash and non-burnable left overs from the previous day which fell into the ash pan under the grate; these were then placed in the dustbin (in those days dustbins were made of metal) and if they were still very hot the bin could and did set on fire. The sides and back of the fire place were also brushed to get rid of the soot.

To start the fire old newspapers were screwed up, and then small pieces of fire wood were placed all round the paper, also on top to make a triangle with all the pieces touching in the centre. The coal was placed all round the paper and wood with smaller pieces on top so that they did not squash the wood and paper.

The paper was then lit which in turn set light to the wood which when it was hot enough set fire to the coal. You needed a good draught up the chimney to draw in the air underneath the wood and coal to get a good hot fire. If the wood or coal was damp it was more difficult to get the fire started: you then used a "Fire Blower" this was a piece of galvanised metal the size of the opening in the fire place which you put in place so that it covered the whole of the fire opening and forced the air to be drawn up underneath the fire grate, this acted like a bellows and had to be removed as soon as the flames started to roar up the chimney, if not you set the chimney on fire (this is when the carbon soot starts to burn) and this could mean the fire brigade turning out. It was a common occurrence.

Our house had a fire range until after the war when my mum had it removed and a tiled fireplace installed. Aunty Cissie and Aunty Maggie who lived at 8 Dover Street in Preston, (this area has been demolished and the new road and bus station has been built) had a fire range until the house was demolished.

A range was made of black cast iron and consisted of a fire grate, with one or two ovens, a large and a small one. Ours also heated a back boiler to give us hot water.

The fire grate had a metal shelf at the front on which a large kettle stood; this could be swung over the fire or pulled back so that the kettle was over the hearth not the fire. The kettle was always hot so if any one arrived who wanted a cup of tea you just swung the kettle over the fire for a few minutes and it would boil.

There were dampers by the fire grate which could be opened or closed to allow the flames and heat to go under and round the oven to increase the temperature. The same applied to the back boiler if you had one. The range was kept clean and black by painting it with "Black Lead" which withstood the heat.

Every day the ashes had to be taken out from under the fire grate to let the air get under the fire so that it would burn well.

Gas lights

Prior to the 1930s most houses had gas lighting; this was the case at Aunty Maggie's in Dover Street. The light came from a mantle that was made of cotton like material which was placed over the gas burner. When it was lit for the first time it burned, went white and glowed very bright, but from then on even the lightest touch made it turn to powder even if it was not lit. My problem being so tall meant that I was always accidentally catching the mantle with my head. These houses all kept a good stock of matches.

The downside of coal fires was that when it was cold weather and you had the fire burning well you had all the heat coming at you from the front but the back of the room was as cold as ever. Many older women had mottled skin on their legs from sitting in front of the fire.

When we lived in Wombwell, Yorkshire in 1962-64 my job as Baths and Entertainment Manager included as part of my salary a house next to the baths, with free coal and electricity provided. Wombwell was built on top of a coal field which had one of the richest coal seams in Britain. The coal was delivered to the house by the ton in a council lorry. The quality of the coal was such that in the two years we lived there we burnt out three fire grates due to the excessive heat produced.

In the 1950s a new invention came out which had a fire grate that could be made air tight under the main grate. This made it possible to control the speed at which the fire burned; you could in fact keep the fire burning slowly all day or all night. Then when you wanted to increase the rate of burning you opened the control on the front of the grate, let in more air and the fire roared. This grate was called a Baxi Grate.

With the shortage of fuel even after the war there was an effort by the government to have better insulation in houses by cutting out draughts at windows and doors. Fires need air to burn so Baxi's next development was to have the air for the fire delivered under the floor from the outside of the building directly to the underside of the fire grate with a mechanism for controlling the air flow from almost nil to a full flow. This idea together with a large metal tin below floor level for holding the ash and cinders meant that not only was it possible to have full control over the fire but it was only necessary to empty the ash box once or twice per week. Some houses kept the fire going for days at a time, this together with full draught-proofing of the house made a big difference to the comfort of the home and at the same time conserved fuel. Until central heating became widely available in homes this was the way most people kept warm.

Street Traders

In the days when I was growing up 1930s and 40s it was common to see traders visiting the street either with a hand cart or usually with a horse drawn cart. All the names were about men, because no women did these jobs, it was not until the war that women started to do men's jobs because the men had been "called up" (to fight in the war).

Milkman

Our milk was delivered each morning by the milkman with his milk float. This was a specially built cart for holding milk kits or milk crates. The kits were made of metal and held gallons of fresh milk which was scooped out with a measure which held a gill ($^1/_4$ pint). The crates had glass milk bottles large size 1pint or small $^1/_2$ pint.

Rag and Bone Man

Also with a horse and cart, he would visit every other week or so and collect old clothes and any old pans etc. If you gave him enough he would give you a goldfish in a glass bowl.

Coalman

As mentioned previously the coalman came every week with his horse and cart if he had coal.

The three trades above had regular rounds which the horses knew as well as their masters. When they left the cart to deliver their goods the horse would walk to the next house and be waiting for the man to return the empties and collect the next delivery. The horses also knew which houses would feed them carrots or bread, and were part of the life of the community. When horses were replaced by vans and lorries the tradesmen took longer to complete their round.

Knife Sharpener

This man usually had a hand cart which was also his workbench. This contained a stone grinding wheel that was turned by a pedal. The man used to sharpen knives, scissors, and any other tool that needed sharpening.

Ice Cream Man

In summer he was a regular visitor to the estate but he had either a hand cart or a bicycle on which was a cold box to keep the ice cream cold. The man on the bike used to have a sign on the front which said "Stop me and Buy one".

Soft Drinks Vimto - Tizer - Sarsaparilla

After the war vans toured the streets selling "pop", usually Vimto or Tizer but also sarsaparilla in a large earthenware jug with a stone stopper. These large jugs were often used as hot water bottles when it was hard to get rubber ones. The shop keepers used to give ½ d or 1d for empty bottles taken back to the shops; this was one way for us to get extra spending money.

Telegram Boys

To get in contact with one another you either visited or wrote a letter. Only shops and offices had telephones, none of the people I knew had a telephone. Urgent messages had to be sent by telegram, and these were delivered by boys in uniform on bicycles. The only time you got a telegram was for important events such as a wedding, but more often for news of a death during the war. People dreaded seeing the telegram boys coming down the street.

Lamp Lighters

In parts of Preston and other towns they still had some street lights that were lit by gas. A man used to go round with a long pole with a flame on the end to reach the street lamps and light them each evening and put them out in the morning.

Knocker-upper

It might sound strange but people who worked in the factories worked shifts and started very early in the morning. Those who could not get up early, used to pay a man to call at the house with a long stick who would tap on the bedroom window to wake them up.

CHAPTER TWO

1945 - Preston Catholic College

1945

This was a big year for me: I passed my scholarship to go to Preston Catholic College (PCC), the war ended and a new chapter began in everyone's life. The blackout was over and you could have lights on without closing the curtains. The first neon light that I saw was over a tailor's shop next to the New Victoria Cinema in Fishergate. Rationing was still in place and things took a long time to get back into the shops. The first time I saw a banana and a pomegranate I did not know how to eat them.

I was told by older boys that PCC had a swimming pool in the grounds; they also said that new boys got thrown in, so as I could not swim I decided to learn. My uncle Dick Woods said he would teach me; we went every day to Saul Street baths and by the end of the week I could swim a width breast-stroke. I felt safe.

The day the war ended in Europe was called VE day (Victory in Europe), but it was still going on in the Far East against the Japanese. In the summer of 1945 my mum took me to Bicester to see where my dad had been killed. We were on the train going to Oxford but when we stopped at Crewe, all trains stop at Crew, there was an announcement that the war with Japan had ended (VJ day). Everyone went wild, most of the people were in the forces, and they got off the train and danced on the platform, it was some time before the train was able to start its journey again.

I started school in September on my dad's birthday after a long holiday; grammar school had six weeks, two more than the other schools.

I was put in Form 1B in the first year and at lunch time on the first day could not wait to go for a swim in the school pool. It was only a small pool but it was great. I met another boy who seemed to be just a keen as I was to get a swim: his name was Harvey High.

Harvey High

My best friend of all time, we met on the first day at Preston Catholic College when we both went for a swim in the school pool. Harvey lived on a farm outside Blackburn, called "Higher Twistfield Farm"; I often stayed there at weekends and holidays. Harvey had two sisters one older Marie and one younger, Ann; sometimes Harvey stayed at our house.

The friendship between us was a bond that was only surpassed when I met and married my wife, Gill. I used to go and stay on the farm which to me was a different world. I liked getting stuck in, helping with any of the jobs from mucking out the cows to feeding the hens, collecting the eggs from the nests. I even learnt how to harrow the fields with the two horses they had. When they eventually got a tractor I was able to drive it in the fields. The muck from the cow sheds was kept in a heap in the yard to go rotten and ripe; it was then spread on the fields by hand before they got the tractor.

Piles of muck were dropped off the cart around the field. Then we all had to spread it out by hand using a fork. I was always able to do things both right and left handed and still can. Harvey's dad thought this was great because I could spread more than the others because by changing hands I did not get as tired as the others.

Harvey's dad was always playing practical jokes on people, especially me. One time when they had got the tractor, muck was spread by the machine towed by the tractor. He asked me if I wanted to have a go at driving and muck spreading; I jumped at the chance.

He did not tell me that he had made up an especially watery mix of muck or that I was going to spread it going down wind, or that I should have had an old sack over my head and shoulders. The result as you can guess was that I was covered from head to toe in shit. Harvey and his dad just laughed but his mum was very annoyed because she made me strip off all my clothes and get into a tin bath. It was in my hair and took some time to get rid of the smell.

Another party piece that his dad caught me with was balancing a cow's tail on my head.

Harvey's dad was milking the cows by hand, as they did in those days, when he asked me if I could balance the cow's tail on my head. He got up from his milking stool and stood behind the cow put its tail on his head, left go of the tail, and put his hands out wide. The cow waved it off straight away. Each time he tried the cow did the same thing. He bet me that I could not do any better.

I got ready to have a go and he gave me his cap so that I would not get my hair dirty.

I stood behind the cow with my arms out wide and his dad placed the cow's tail on my head. He asked me if I was ready and when I said yes he pushed my face forward into the rear end of the cow. I did manage to get someone with the same trick months later.

My visits to the farm are my fondest childhood memories. I learned to shoot a .22 rifle, ride horses bare back, drive a tractor, work the fields with the horses and later drive the tractor, all things that my friends back in the town could never imagine.

When my Aunty Teresa returned from Burma she was in the Royal Women's Volunteer Service (RWVS) she gave me some water purifying tablets; they had to use them in Burma. One summer Harvey, his sister, Ann, who was about 6 years old, and me decided we were going to camp out in the top field, out of sight of the house. We did not want little Ann to be with us but we were given no choice. We had a primus stove to cook on and got the water from a stream. Although we did not need to we decided to use the water purifying tablets and put a handful in the water. That evening we began to feel drowsy and little Ann fell asleep. It was lucky for us that Harvey's mum came to see if we were all OK and saw Ann sleeping in the tent. A doctor was called and we were taken back to the house the following day and the tablets were thrown away. We all recovered with no ill effects.

The only toilet was outside in a wooden hut next to the house at the rear. Inside was a wooden bench with two holes in it on which you sat. The results of your efforts dropped down to a hole that was cleaned out every so often and spread on the land with that from the cows. I never shared the experience but I suppose that is why there were two places so that you could do if you felt inclined to do so.

At that time in the years 1945 to 1950 rationing was still in force. When I returned home I was usually given some meat or bacon or eggs to give my mum although it was illegal to do this.

I kept in touch with Harvey after school. We both did our National Service but when Harvey was demobbed he could not settle back to farming much to the dismay of his dad.

A year might go by, and then a phone call or a visit out of the blue, and we would carry on as if it was only a day since we last spoke. It was an incredible friendship.

Harvey had a number of jobs, from delivering bread to running a processed meat canning factory. Then the United Nations, who was looking for someone to set up a factory in Africa to process farm products, approached Harvey to see if he would do it. He did and made a success of it before returning to England where he lived with his family at Great Harwood. He died suddenly of a brain tumour driving back home from London.

No one has, or ever could, replace this friend.

Preston Catholic College (PCC) was in town off Winckley Square, a good walk to the bus stop outside the Miller Arcade opposite New Victoria Cinema where I caught the P2 or Ribbleton bus home. The longest queue was always the Ribbleton bus queue. Getting home from school seemed to take forever. On cold, dark winter nights, arriving home to an empty cold house did not encourage me to sit down and do my homework. My first job was to light the fire then make something to eat. Like all other teenage lads I was always hungry.

It was conditions like this that made me a better cook than a scholar. I did not like homework or for that matter school. At the end of the first year I came 30th out of 32 in the class. I was put down a class to Form 2C. I stayed in the C stream until I left.

The school buildings were built on a slope in the shape of a square, the playground being in the centre. In winter, and 1947 was the coldest winter on record, we made a super slide the length of the playground, from corner to corner. I as usual was in full flow going down the slide when the lower school headmaster, "Bobbie" Brooks walked out of a door with his arms full of books, right on to the slide as I was descending at full speed. I could not stop, and hit him square on. The books went up in the air as did the headmaster; I landed on top of him to the delight and shouts of everyone in the playground.

Then it all went quiet and boys just melted away: I was left with Mr Brooks to pick up the books, and then he said "Follow me Barnes". I knew I was in for it and I was right. I got caned, six stokes on each hand.

Discipline at PCC was strict, but only the headmaster and lower school headmaster could administer punishment. We were hit with a ferula, a piece of whalebone 2 inches wide and 18 inches long. In the first form you could not get less than three strokes on each hand, in the second six strokes on each hand, nine in the third form, twelve in the fourth and fifth.

The teachers used to put up with a lot in class but at a certain stage they would say, "That's enough: the next one to do that will go down". That was the phrase used to send you to the headmaster for your punishment.

I got the cane many times in the first and second forms then I said to myself I was being stupid; all I had to do was to stop when the last warning went out. This I did and I never had the cane again.

By this time I was getting taller, I was 6 foot tall at 14 years. I was full of energy and getting more cheeky at home with my mum. It got to the stage when even if she hit me she could not physically hurt me. I used to say some awful things to my mum.

At night I would lie in bed and cry because I knew it was wrong and that if my dad had been alive I would have received the good hiding I knew I deserved. I made a promise to myself that if I ever had children I would be very strict with them for their own good.

I believe more than ever now that lack of discipline is the cause of most of the trouble today.

Girls

It was while I was at PCC that I realised that girls could be good friends. My first girlfriend was Edna Fisher. She was a quiet girl and lived with her mother who had a greengrocer's shop at the top of

Gammul Lane. She was a member of the C of E Church at St. Mary Magdalene and used to go to church twice on Sundays. I used to wait for her in the doorway of the Co-op store opposite the church, and then I would walk her home. I never got to the stage of taking her to my home or going to her house, although my mum knew all about her. I went out with Edna for 2 years or so, and at the time I thought it was very serious.

It was not until I joined the swimming club that I went out with my second girlfriend, a swimmer, Barbara Simpson. This was short lived but then I met Dorothy Moulding, also a swimmer who lived in Blackburn but joined PASC because she went to college in Preston. This was my first serious relationship, I was 16 years old, and even so it was always second to my swimming. I was truthful about it; Dorothy knew that my swimming came first and always would.

We trained together at the baths. Dorothy was a backstroke swimmer and reasonably good, although she did not make the County team. If we had a swimming fixture Dorothy would stay at our house because it was not easy to get back to Blackburn at night.

We went out together for a number of years but had a lot of arguments because she was never on time.

We would be getting changed at the baths and agree to go the cinema that night in Preston. Dorothy would say a time to meet me, when I checked the arrangements, she had to go home to Blackburn, shop, get ready, travel back to Preston, and she was already late. I used to give her a maximum of 20 minutes then go home. It did not happen too often. When Preston played Blackburn in a swimming fixture my mum had to sit with Dorothy's mum and dad who caused a bit of a strain for my mum, or so she said. I went out with Dorothy until I met Gill just before I went to Helsinki in June 1952. More of this later.

I was still poor at playing football and cricket, the two main sports at school. I could not get in the school team, house team or form team, the only thing I could do was swim.

CHAPTER THREE

1948 - 1953 Swimming - Tom Banister Olympic Games

Swimming

I enjoyed swimming but I could only swim breast-stroke, taught me by Uncle Dick in August 1945. I splashed about at the other strokes. One day three years later, I was at Saul Street Baths in Preston when Tom Banister, the Assistant Baths Superintendent who was the town's swimming coach asked me to swim a length for him. I did and he asked me if I wanted to join his classes on Saturday lunch-time. This was the chance of a lifetime and the start of a sport that literally changed my life.

I did not know when I joined Preston Amateur Swimming Club (PASC) that I would join a group of people who would become lifelong friends and very close friends at that. At first I was not only the new boy but the poorest swimmer as well, but that soon changed. I had found something that I enjoyed doing and the more I did the better I became. To me it was not hard work but very enjoyable, when Tom Banister told us to swim ½ a mile although we all started, if he had to leave the bath side because of work, everyone stopped but I carried on because I wanted to.

We all spent a lot of time together, in summer we would go to the River Ribble where the "Tickled Trout" is now and swim against the tide for strengthening exercises, and in winter the round of Christmas parties was superb with the one at Banister's being the highlight.

Especially the games of "truth or dare" with the girls all fearing the forfeit of having to light a candle by striking a match on the nearest gravestone. The house backed on to the old cemetery, and it was a must for someone to hide with a white sheet covering them, and then jumping out on the unsuspecting girl. One girl kept running and arrived home without returning to the party.

I joined Preston Amateur Swimming Club (PASC) at the same time as I started in Tom Banister's Saturday coaching classes.

Tom was the Amateur Swimming Association's (ASA) Northern Counties Senior Coach. His job at Saul Street Baths meant that he was at the baths every day, but on Saturday lunchtime he had the small pool to himself for 1-2 hours from midday. Only the top swimmers were invited to attend these sessions, not only from Preston but from anywhere in the North West. I loved the training from the start, I could not get enough of it, and the more Tom asked me to do the more I enjoyed it.

Tom's children, Jean and Jim, were very good; both swam for the county team Lancashire, at breast-stroke and backstroke respectively. From time to time Tom would be called away from his coaching to deal with something at work. He would set us all some training to carry on with but as soon as he left the bath side everyone stopped training except me.

It was not for any other reason other than I enjoyed training so I kept going. The results paid off; I improved every month, every week even, I just got better and better.

Tom introduced me to the butterfly stroke, which at that time was a variation of the breast-stroke but was much faster. You used the same breast-stroke leg kick but brought the arms out of the water on the recovery stroke which enabled you to get a very long two handed pull through the water which propelled the body much faster than the original breast-stroke movement. The problem was that it was very strenuous and could only be used for short races i.e. 50 yds. Even then not many swimmers used it.

As I have already said I was 6ft 2ins tall and like a bean pole weighing 11 stone 11lbs. It was said that I did not cast a shadow if I stood sideways. This stroke suited me just fine so I practised every day.

The first swimming gala I ever swam in was the P.A.S.C. Clarkson Cup 1948, in the 200 yards breast-stroke. There was an old man who had swum in this race for many years; he was the only swimmer to finish behind me. I was next to last.

The records show that I won the Clarkson Cup every year after that so I didn't mind losing the first one.

Targets

One day Tom Banister put a poster on the swimming club notice board; it was a target with a series of coloured circles and the wording said pick your target.

The outside circle was the Club Championship, the next the County Championship, then the Northern Counties Championship, with the inner circle being the British Championship. Of course, me being me, I asked "What was the dot in the middle where the compass point had been". Tom said it was the Olympic Games. I said "That is my target".

Each Easter there was a Northern Counties Training Course at Blackpool. Only the best swimmers and coaches in the north were invited to attend. We stayed in boarding houses just off the prom at the north end of Blackpool behind the Derby Pool where we did our swimming. It was a week of hard training but a lot of fun; you got to know all the other top swimmers. Tom, who was chief coach, used to get us to run on the dry sand to loosen up our ankles. Each day we had to walk or run to the south shore and back before going to the pool.

One day when the tide was in and waves were crashing over the promenade we deliberately stopped Tom to ask him about some aspect of training, keeping him talking with his back to the sea. We could see a large wave approaching and at the last minute ran off leaving Tom to be thoroughly soaked right to his skin. He was not amused though later he used to tell the story himself, so it was looked on as just high spirits.

The one trick we pulled that was not appreciated was the time we placed a cod's head that we obtained from the fish market in Jean Wrigley's bed. She got into bed that night touched the fish with her feet, screamed and ran out of the house crying. We quite rightly got into trouble for that one, but it was worth it.

Training involved swimming every day and for me at least doing exercises to gain strength and suppleness. But I know that I was the only one doing what Tom Banister had told us all to do. I was soon in the town swimming team doing the breast-stroke in the league fixtures. Because I had a good leg kick I was put in goal for the junior water polo team. This for me was a relaxing sport; my swimming was serious, water polo was a game.

With long arms and being very tall I was quite a good goalkeeper. I soon made the county junior team (under 18 years) where most of the team came from Preston A.S.C..

We managed to win the County championship and the Northern Counties championship as well in 1949 beating Birkenhead 6-4 at Lancaster Baths.

We got into the English Junior Water Polo final against Plaistow from London; they had three full international players in their side even though they were under 18 years old.

The game was played at Preston and at half time we were only one goal down with the score at 2-1 to Plaistow. In the second half they threw everything at us and won 8-2. The press reported that "it would have been many more if it had not been for the superb goalkeeping by a young Brian Barnes".

I continued to play for my club junior team and was picked for the County senior team but I could not get into Preston senior side. This was my first taste of politics in sport.

I was winning most of my races with the exception of one person who I just could not beat. Derek Snelling came from Darwin which meant that I had to compete against him in the local league, County races, Northern Counties races and the British National events.

Every time he won; even if I had broken the record in the heats I could not repeat it against Derek in the final. He won every time, fair and square. In 1951 at Lancaster I did the fastest time in the heats of the British Championships, yet in the final against Derek, who won, I came third even though he did not manage to swim as fast as I did in the heat.

One week later at the Northern Counties Championships we were due to compete against each other plus the swimmers who came fifth and sixth in the Championships the week before.

The venue was Darwin, Derek's home town. No one turned up other than me and Derek: they waited half an hour then decided to hold the race with just the two of us competing. Prior to the start they presented Derek with the British Championship trophy he had won the week before.

We lined up on the bath side just the two of us, eight lengths of the 25 yard pool for the 200 yard race. The gun went and I flew down the first length, I was in front by a yard. We turned, pushed off under water, came up and we were level. I had lost a yard on the turn. At the end of the second length I was in front again by a yard but when we surfaced after the turn we were level again. This happened each of the seven lengths, by now the crowd were on their feet shouting, the noise was deafening even in the water, I put all I had into the last few yards and felt the side of the pool. It was over, I looked at Tom Banister, I knew it was close. It was, Derek won by a finger nail. We were both given the same time but Derek won the race.

The time 2mins 37sec.was not as fast as mine the week before in Lancaster where I had done 2mins 34sec.

I did not realise it but this was now psychological. My brain was telling me I could not beat Derek Snelling. Tom Banister and I agreed that I would never again be beaten on a turn. I would do all my training in the pool by swimming widths not lengths.

We trained by diving and turning under water with my eyes open so that I could judge my speed by seeing the tiles on the bottom of the pool go past my head. There is a maximum speed that you can go through the water so there was no point in using my arms to propel myself until I had started to slow down, this meant that I could use the energy from the push to rest and wait before pulling to keep my maximum speed longer, that way I improved my turns.

You have to repeat techniques in training so that they become the norm and you do it without thinking, because in the excitement of a race you don't have time to think about technique. I did so many widths that I could perform perfect turns in my sleep so much so that I never again lost out on turns again in any race.

I trained every day and loved every minute of it. I was good at it and I relished it. At school I was far and away the best swimmer, but I was still no good at the other games we had to play. The big difference now was that no one took the mickey out of me any more.

Each year we had the school swimming gala in the school pool.

It was so small, about the width of the large pool at Saul Street baths. To me it was so easy, I could enter any race and win it, even the fun games like collecting money thrown into the water by the headmaster at the end of the event: I was able to stay under longer than anyone and in the end I gave the money to my friends. I was at last looked up to by my peers.

As I said earlier if I put my mind to it I could and did succeed against all the odds. In my last year at school (1950) I was still in the C form; our year was the last to sit the School Certificate Examination which was replaced in 1951. To pass this exam you had to pass in at least five subjects including English, any less than five meant you failed. I managed to pass in four OK, but read the question wrongly in one and just failed; fortunately they decided to pass me because what I had written was correct though it should have been on a different subject.

Only one other beside me in our form passed but some in the A and B forms failed so I was very pleased with myself. I had done it again, just.

Work - The Lancashire Evening Post

I left school in 1950 and had no idea of what I wanted to do. I thought of all sorts of wonderful jobs but I did not have a chance of getting them. One was to be a Forensic Scientist but I did not have the qualifications.

Four of my friends in the swimming club had joined the Lancashire Police Cadets, but when I tried all the places had been filled. My mum did not want me to join the county police because it could mean that I would have to move away from Preston so I got a job in the advertising department of the *Lancashire Evening Post*, as the office boy at £1-10s per week, £1.50 in today's money.

At that time newspapers used to print by making lead rollers that had ink on which transferred the print to the paper. In the works, compositors, who were always male, used to sit at a machine which had a keyboard like a typewriter: each time the operator pressed a letter on the keyboard the same letter dropped down from large fan shaped holders in which all the letters, commas and other print items were stored. These were all made of metal, each letter and space dropped down to form a group the width of a column in the newspaper. Each line of words was made up for every line that was written in the paper, the story or item was then placed on a wooden block inked over and a piece of paper placed on top so that the print showed up for the sub-editor to check what had been printed.

When it had been checked it was taken to the person responsible for making up the page in the paper where the article would go.

This person also used metal blocks that had been made for display adverts and metal blocks that had been made from photographs that were going to be used in the paper.

The whole layout of each page was laid out on a table. At regular intervals it would be inked over and a roll of paper pressed on it to get a rough copy of what the page would look like. When the editor was satisfied, a special cardboard was pressed on to the page: this was used so that it could take up the indentations of the metal and then bent over large rollers into a half moon shape. This was to be the mould for the lead which was poured into it to make a lead roller. These rollers fitted onto giant printing presses; ours were made in Germany by Goss.

Every page was constructed in the same way. When all the pages were in place a bell sounded and the presses started to roll. The noise was tremendous; you could not hear anyone speak. The very large drums of newspaper were fed into the press at one end and the newspaper came out printed at the other end, folded and cut and ready for the vans to take it out to the shops in the town. To see a paper "put to bed" was an inspiring sight.

1951 – Olympic Training

I was training very hard at swimming now. With all my energies going into my sport I was kept out of trouble that I would surely have got into in my teens.

In 1951 the Amateur Swimming Association set targets for entry into the trials for the following year's Olympic Games to be held in Helsinki, Finland.

The time set for the 200yds breast-stroke was 2mins 30 sec. This time had never been achieved in Britain, but the year before I had swum the best time of 2mins 34sec.

Tom set me a very strenuous training regime: I was to swim three times each day as well as doing strengthening exercises including running and fell-walking in the winter.

The problem I had was getting time in the pool with room to swim my lengths without someone getting in my way; it was, after all, a public swimming pool.

I used to get up in the morning at 6am to do half an hour of exercises, have a bowl of cereal and then run two miles to the baths. I used to run a lamp post distance then walk a lamp post distance.

I arrived at the baths before they opened at 7am. I was first in the water and swam 1 ½ miles butterfly, split up as follows: 1 mile full stroke, ½ mile legs only and ½ mile arms only butterfly.

I would then go to my auntie's who lived in Saul Street for breakfast, a full fry up with plenty of toast.

I arrived at work for 9am. At 11am I had a snack of sandwiches and tea then I had a lunch break of 1 ½ hours. I finished at 12 noon and could be in the water at 12.15pm. I would swim three or four 400yd races, or as we got closer to the trials changed them for four 200yd races at faster speed. There was a small café round the corner from the baths were they placed the dinner of the day on a reserved table for me, and at precisely 1.10pm I ate my dinner and was back at work for 1.30pm.

Again snacks at 3pm then after work depending on the use the baths had at public swimming I would either go back to train swimming 100yd sprints at 5.30pm when I finished work, or I would go home and return to the baths at 8pm if it was club night.

I trained like this 7 days each week.

Most evenings the baths were hired to swimming clubs such as the Preston Amateur Swimming Club, a competitive club, and works clubs that were more social clubs. Every night was taken, so when one works club decided not to renew its booking I suggested that P AS C should take the extra night for training. The Club said that they could not afford to pay for the extra night, so I got most of the competitive swimmers together and said that we should hire the baths that night and raise the cash ourselves, which we did.

Officials

The Club said that we could not do that according to the rules of the Amateur Swimming Association and put in a complaint to the Lancashire Branch of the A S A. In the meantime we, the swimmers, booked the baths and collected the money from our supporters.

A few weeks went past and a meeting was called to sort out the complaint against the swimmers. I was the leader and so we attended a meeting chaired by Mr Wilding the chairman of the North Lancashire League Swimming Association. Mr Wilding was also the Registrar of Births Marriages and Deaths for Preston. He was a very tall man and a quiet man who looked very authoritarian.

At the meeting the Club put its case and then I was asked to put the swimmers' case, which I did saying that we needed all the time we could get to do our training, and added that if the P A S C would not help us we would form our own club.

This caused a furore with both sides getting agitated, then Mr Wilding stood up and said something that I shall never forget and something that I have used myself on many occasions.

He said "It is possible for swimmers to run a swimming gala without officials, it would not be very good but it is possible. However it is impossible for officials to hold a swimming gala without swimmers." The room went quiet as his words sank in.

"I suggest that the Club rethink the hiring of the baths for an extra night and the swimmers could donate the cash they have raised to help the Club finances."

With that he closed the meeting and the problem was solved. I have often reminded sports officials at the most senior level of that meeting with Mr Wilding, including the Sports Council at National Level.

One of the main problems with British sport is the fact that too many officials think that the sport is run for them and not the competitors.

In comparison the Belgians had picked their water polo team and were touring the country playing games in order to improve their chances of a medal. They had beaten the English National Team but were touring the regions and were due to play a team from the North West at Southport in the summer of 1951. I was picked to play in goal at the large open-air pool at the resort.

The weather was a typical English summer's day, cold and wet. The game started and I was the first player on our side to touch the ball as I picked it out of the back of the goal. We lost 18 -0.

The Olympics would be held in a 50m open-air pool but the nearest one to Preston was at Grange-over-Sands. Dick Reynolds, a club member, who owned a bakery at Penwortham just outside Preston, said he would take some of us to train at Grange in his two-seater MG sports car. Three got in the front Dick driving, Kath Bowen in the middle and Jim Banister. I was sideways in the very small rear section. The car had a soft hood covering the passengers.

Off we went up the A6 road but after an hour I got an attack of cramp and shot my leg out straight. It went through the canvas hood before Dick could stop the car to let me out to stretch my legs. The rest of the journey was done with the hood down and my legs sticking out at the side. When we arrived it was so cold that we only did one length then returned home.

One Friday lunchtime I arrived at the bath side to be told by Tom that a newspaper wanted to do a piece on my training for the Olympics. They wanted to know if I had done the qualifying time of 2min.30sec. They said no one else had managed it. Tom said I would just go over the ten lengths (200yds) at 7/8th speed: this was his way of saying I was to go flat out but tell myself I was not flat out if I failed. He often used this phrase during hard training sessions.

There were only the three of us in the small pool hall at the baths that lunchtime. I can clearly remember standing on the side of the pool waiting for the start.

I dived in and felt as if I was flying over the water not swimming through it.

I reached the end of the first length with ease and performed my by now perfect turn, then back down the second length; I was going so well. Tom as usual walked up and down the pool side at a pace equal to what I should be doing to achieve the time set, but he seemed to be going so slow, I was in front of him. I kept going because I felt good and it was so easy. Five lengths, 100yds, half way and still not feeling at all tired. Eight lengths, only two more to do and yet still feeling as if I could go on for ever. I decided to cruise the last two and finished relatively fresh. "How was that then," I asked Tom. 2min.28sec. he said without even a smile. The reporter looked amazed: "So Brian has done it," he shouted.

Tom had to explain that it would not count as an official time for qualifying for the Olympic Trials because there was only one timekeeper. For times to be recognised officially there had to be at least two.

I was not bothered by all that, I knew that I had done it with a lot of energy to spare and so did Tom.

The reporter went to town with his story of seeing the only person to date swimming the required time for the Olympics. The really nice thing for me was the fact that all my friends at the club were genuinely pleased for me, so it was back to training as before.

Disabled Children

Twice each week at lunchtime I shared the small pool with 3 or 4 disabled school children who received one-to-one swimming lessons at this quiet time. We got to know each other as they saw me doing length after length flat out as they struggled in a rubber float; most of them had no use of their legs but they seemed to enjoy the lessons. As time went on they followed my progress and I watched theirs, it was painfully slow but their achievements counted more than mine.

I later gave each one, one of my Northern Counties winner's medals for their achievement which I thought they deserved more than me.

I was not to know at the time but these disabled swimmers started me on the road to becoming the first Chairman of the British Sports Association for the Disabled (BSAD) some 25 years later.

Tom Banister was the Northern Counties Chief Coach; swimmers came from all over to be trained by him. At first I was upset when he allowed Peter Entwistle, a lad from Bolton, to join his elite training squad. Tom explained to me that if I wanted to be the best I had to beat the best and the best way to do that was to train with them.

Peter was a very good swimmer; he was a faster sprinter than me and almost always won in the 50yds and 100yd races, but I could go on after the 100yds race and swim another 800yds as I did in training.

I learnt a very important lesson competing against Derek Snelling. I had developed a feeling that I could NOT win against him and I used that in my training sessions with Peter Entwistle. I always finished in front of him no matter how much training we did together, even if Tom sent us off on a slow one mile warm-up swim I made sure that I finished first.

I had a problem finding other swimmers to train with other than Peter because I was so much fitter than the rest. The swimmer who could give me a good race was Kath Bowen who was the Ladies Northern Counties 200yd freestyle champion: the problem was that Kath did not want to train as hard as me and used to say "Barney go and swim with someone else, I'm tired." But on occasions we did swim side by side and it made me go flat out to keep up.

In the winter of 1951/52 two of the Scottish swimmers Doug Welsh and Ronnie Burns, were both in the RAF doing their National Service, stationed at Lytham close by. They both joined the Preston Amateur Swimming Club (PASC) and trained with me. This was a great boost to the training levels as the pressure increased to qualify for the games.

Athol Still, another Scot, soon joined us for the same reason; he was also in the RAF locally.

The lads often stayed at our house with my mum cooking for four hungry wolves, or so it seemed. In the winter we went hiking over the hills round Chipping and Longridge as part of our training to keep fit and the lads joined in with the rest of the club.

Part of Tom Banister's job as Chief Coach was to run coaching weekends for other coaches in the North West.

In the spring of 1952 one such weekend was at Victoria Baths in Manchester. Tom used his top swimmers for these sessions so that the other coaches could learn his techniques. It was a long day with swimming for us and lectures for the coaches.

At the end of the day with all the Northern Counties Officials present including the timekeepers Tom announced that I would have a go at the 2min.30sec. time trial for the Olympics. I was amazed and so was everyone there. The other swimmers including Peter Entwistle said it was impossible. Tom came over to me and said this was my big chance, he said that I could do it with plenty to spare.

The other swimmers agreed to swim or at least to start the race but did not think they could finish 200yds.

We lined up for eight lengths of the 25yd pool. We had all been in the water training for a number of hours off and on all day so I was a little apprehensive myself.

The gun went and I set off at a fast pace which I knew that no one else could keep up with, or if they tried they would not last the distance. The first length most of us were in line but some had dropped back after the 50yds mark. At 100yds, half way, only Peter was within sight: some had stopped. After the next two lengths I was on my own, this gave me a boost and off I went on the last 50yds.

I finished alone and I was very tired but when they announced the time of 2min.29sec a loud roar went up from everyone present.

I was officially picked for an Olympic trial.

Doug, Ronnie, and Athol also qualified for the trial which was a tribute to Tom Banister's training, getting four through.

Training continued and the pace increased. Tom was sure that no one else would qualify for the 200yds butterfly and he was correct. I was the only one, but to make a race of it they let the next best swim against me at Blackpool where the trials would be held.

1952 - Gill Gorst

It was at this time that events happened that would change my life for ever. I began to notice a girl in the swimming club, also a backstroke swimmer, called Gill Gorst, still only15 years old.

She was beautiful, radiant, quiet, slim, and full of fun, with dark curly hair. I fell in love with her and immediately knew that I would spend the rest of my life with her. This time swimming would not take first place in my life, Gill would.

I told my mum who asked me not to finish with Dorothy until after the fixture with Blackburn Swimming Club to which I agreed. But I was already totally committed to Gill.

The break-up with Dorothy did not go down too well, she gave Gill a hard time at the club even hiding her shoes and silly things like that, but we were together and that is all that mattered.

Gill lived with her mum and dad and her brother Barry at 42 Sulby Drive, Ribbleton about half a mile from our house going away from town.

The Trials

The Olympic Games Trials were held at the Derby Baths, Blackpool. This was a 50yd pool the only one in the country at that time. Ronnie was in the 400yds and relay team trials, Doug and Athol were in the 100yds and relay team trials.

I only had one other swimmer to swim against and I won so at the dinner in the Cliffs Hotel after the trials, where the team would be announced, mine was a formality but for the others it was a nail-biting time.

The team was announced and all of us were included. Tom, my mum and Gill were, like me, unbelievably happy, it was a dream come true.

The town was also celebrating because a member of the shooting team had been picked from Preston.

At 18 years of age I was the second youngest member of the British swimming team; Angela Barnwell was the only one younger than me.

The newspaper wanted articles and photos of me in my blazer, the whole event was carrying me along at a very fast pace. Then two things happened that nearly ruined it all.

First, I had been deferred from being called up to do my National Service until after the Olympics but I still had to have my medical so that I would be ready to enlist as soon as I returned from Helsinki.

I had to attend the medical centre for a full examination and to my surprise and that of the doctor he said that I had a hernia in my right groin and that made me unfit to be called up.

I was mortified but there was still a further medical that I had to undergo for the trip to the Olympics. At this medical, performed by my own doctor, he said I had a hernia in my left groin. I told him that the other doctor had said the other side then he told me that I had one at each side.

There was immediately the problem of whether I would be allowed to travel to Helsinki.

It was explained to me and the Amateur Swimming Association that I must have been born with both hernias and as I had managed so far to the age of 18 I should be OK to compete. It was suggested though that I should get both repaired as soon as I got back from Helsinki. This was agreed and that hurdle was overcome, and then came the second bombshell.

I had used all my holiday entitlement from work for training sessions so I had to ask for time off from work. My boss, the Advertising Manager, was sympathetic but said that he needed me at work and could not give me two weeks off. I was devastated.

The father of one of the girls in the office where I worked was the Editor of the paper, and she told her dad that I could not go to Helsinki. The next day the Editor sent for me. I had never been up to the top floor in the building where I worked; this was the holy of holies.

I was told that if I agreed to send daily reports back to the paper I could have the time off to go as a reporter for the paper.

This was just up my street and it is the only time that I have been praised for my essays, because at school I was always told that they were too short: this time the Sub-Editor said that my reports were the only ones he did not have to cut, they were just the right length. One in the eye for my English teachers.

It took a long time for it to sink in that I was going to the Olympic Games and to a foreign country as well. The fact that we would be flying was also a first for me.

I was now a celebrity with my picture in the press regularly; people would stop me in the street to ask how my training was going.

My mum was very proud and so she should be, because she had supported me as much as she could. She had taken over the role of treasurer at the swimming club and came on all the away fixtures.

In those days swimming was very popular, most swimming pools had been built in Victorian times at the start of the 20th century. They had the changing cubicle on the side of the pool. When a gala was taking place iron stanchions 3 ft high would be placed along the side of the pool and a curtain hung from them, spectators would then sit on chairs behind the curtain to watch.

We travelled in a corporation double-decker bus taking the team and supporters who followed us to away fixtures.

Bolton was famous for its fanatical supporters, the bath side would be packed full of women with their handbags shouting support for their team.

The bus driver dropped us off then took his bus a long way away from the baths to park it in a safe area.

Ronnie Burns was swimming for us at the time; Ronnie had a straight arm action as he swam freestyle which meant that he made a considerable splash which soaked the women on the bath side. We thought it was funny but it upset the Bolton fans.

When we were playing water polo if you committed a foul you were sent out of the water until the next goal was scored.

It was usual to leave the water at the nearest place to the foul then go back to your own goal area to sit it out. As Ronnie was sent out for a foul, the women all started to hit him with their handbags as he passed them, so much so that he had to dive back in the water and swim to our own goal area and then climb out.

To give Ronnie support we all started to splash the spectators as we swam past. It got so bad that crowds waited outside for us to board the bus shouting and jeering.

It was at Bolton that I had to learn that even though I was picked for the Olympics I could still be beaten. The race at club level was only

50yds and I was against the local boy Peter Entwistle. They announced that I was soon to go to Helsinki prior to the start of the race. I knew that Peter might win and so did all our team, even Peter knew that he could not win over the 200yds distance but at 50 yds he could.

He won, just, and his home crowd went wild. Looking back it was not a bad way to keep my feet on the ground and my head out of the clouds.

I always tried to remember something that I had read which said:

"Be nice to the people on the way up for you will meet them again on the way down".

Training continued and so did the arrival of our uniform, trilby hat, blazer, white trousers, tie, track suit, and nylon swimming trunks. The nylon swimming trunks were the first I had seen (they were not on sale to the general public) and the effect on performance was incredible, due to less drag compared to wool or cloth. We were issued with a pair of under slips or small trunks also made of nylon, the girls also had a pair of these but they were the size of our swimming trunks.

It immediately crossed my mind that the women's slips would make good trunks for me. I made arrangements with 4 members of the women's team to give me their slips after the games. It was only when they were handing them over that any of the other males realised the value of my deals, but they were too late.

We were all invited to meet the Queen at Buckingham Palace prior to the games. This was a highlight of my life. We arrived at the palace and went through the gate inside the courtyard and up a large staircase. We were all introduced to Her Majesty and the Duke of Edinburgh; we had a buffet with all the food set out on a long table. Jean Wrigley asked one of the butlers if the crisps were Smiths. "Of course they are madam" he replied.

It was here that I met John Davies, the Australian butterfly swimmer for the first time. The Australians had picked their team months ago and travelled up through Asia and Europe, swimming as a team against various countries: we had only just picked our team.

The British team was to assemble in Hastings for a farewell gala then fly to Helsinki. I was going to travel by train from Manchester with two other swimmers Jean and Roy Botham from Manchester where their father was the Baths Superintendent. I was seen off by my mum and Uncle Ted, who was living just outside Manchester at the time. He gave me a five pound note. This was the first time I had ever seen a £5 note, it was the old fashioned type on large white paper (6ins x 4ins), worth a week's wages.

Helsinki

The flight was in a piston engine plane; there was no pressurised cabin so we were limited to how high we could fly and the journey took nine hours. At one time you could see a very black cloud which we had to fly round, and as we did so the plane started to pitch and roll, everyone was sick except me but I had my bag ready just in case. I was sat next to John Disley the steeplechase runner; we were both OK until they served cucumber sandwiches then John was sick.

When the Duke of Edinburgh visited the games he flew in the new jet powered plane that was the envy of the world, the Comet. We were among thousands that went to see it land. It was only a few years later that two Comets fell out of the sky and it took months before they found out that it was metal fatigue, a new problem that was caused by the new technology.

The games were held over a two week period, the swimming was in the second week which meant that we could train at a smaller pool in woodland, a bus ride away from the Olympic village. I used to train with John Davies: we would travel out and back together after our swimming. It soon became clear to me that John was not doing anything different in his training other than he was doing four times as much. I was swimming three miles each day, John was doing twelve miles.

John had taken part in the 1948 games in London, and at the games he was offered a sports scholarship at Michigan University in America for four years. He explained that they had their own pool to train in, no public to contend with. The squad he was in trained three times per day; the first was early morning, then back to bed, a second session late morning and a third in the afternoon. In total he swam twelve miles each day. As I have explained earlier I had to work, train in a public baths and fit in when I could. I thought I was doing well swimming three miles per day.

The Race 200m Breast-stroke

Although it was a breast-stroke event no one swam breast-stroke, everyone swam butterfly because it was much faster. At each Olympics the governing body sets the rules for the next four years and Helsinki was the last time that butterfly was allowed to be swum in a breast-stroke race. They made a new event for butterfly with only the traditional breast-stroke allowed to be swum in a breast-stroke race.

The pool was 50m long and eight lanes wide, it was outside but it was heated. The rules were that the fastest 16 would progress to the semi-final with the fastest 8 of those competing in the final.

I lined up with encouragement from the team captain Bert Wardrop. To hear my name over the public address system "Brian Barnes Great Britain" was a memory that I shall always treasure.

The starting blocks at the end of the pool seemed a long way from the other end. The gun went, I was flying down the pool and at the turn we were all in a line. At the next turn, half way, we were still all in a line abreast, the third length was as if someone was hanging small pieces of lead on my arms, by the time I was at the last turn with 50m to swim I was dropping behind. I knew what to do but the lead weights seemed to get heavier and my body began to hurt all over.

I finished all in; I could not have gone any faster.

I did 2min.39 sec, my personal best and better than any other British swimmer had ever done, but all the 18 semi-finalists broke the old Olympic Record.

This proved to me that as a country we were so far behind every other country. John Davis went on to win and set a new Olympic Record. I was offered a scholarship at Michigan but turned it down: from now on swimming would take second place to Gill.

After I had finished I still supported the other swimmers as we all did, but as a team we only won one Bronze Medal in the Ladies 200m Breast-stroke with Helenor Gordon.

In the first week during the athletics we all had competitor passes to allow us to watch any of the other events if there was room.

The most memorable event I have ever seen in my life was the 10,000m in which Emil Zatopek won one of his three gold medals. He was up against Chris Chataway from Britain, the crowd shouted and chanted Zatopek, Zatopek, Zatopek until the whole stadium appeared to be vibrating in time with his name. It was a moving occasion which no one who was there will ever forget.

In the second week after we had finished our races we decided to have some fun and go for a swim at midnight, it was the land of the midnight sun and it never really got dark.

All of the swimmers had finished which meant that 20 of us went to the training pool and climbed over the gates to have a game of water polo. After a while someone suggested a game of tag and off we all ran up the diving boards, chased by the others. I am not a diver and don't like heights but I had to go with the others, 3 metre board, 5 metre board, then to the 10 metre high board. As we got chased the lads began to dive or jump off the end, it looked a very long way down but I could not back down. I took a big breath closed my eyes and jumped. I seemed to be going down for ever, I needed a breath so I took one just as I hit the water. Down and down I sank; I wanted to get out so I started to swim to the surface, when I hit the surface I shot out of the water gasping for air. Never will I do that again; in fact I will not even go on to the 5 metre board.

It was in Helsinki that I experienced my first sauna bath. In Finland they are used by everyone, whole families use them together then they go out into the snow to cool down, everyone is of course naked.

As my career progressed I installed many saunas, but in the UK if they are mixed you have to wear a swimsuit.

Preston Guild

1952 was also the first Preston Guild since the war; it only takes place every 20 years. The Council Baths Department had a float with two swimming club girls in swimming costumes on each side of the float with a Bath Attendant, and in the centre was an Olympic Emblem with me stood in a track suit. I was only just warm enough; I don't know how the girls managed to keep going.

1952 English National Championships

We returned home and I had the English Championships at Brighton & Hove to compete in and then I was due to have my hernia operation.

By this time it was official, I was going out with Gill Gorst and wanted everyone to know about it.

The championships were held in a pool that was an odd length which meant that we had to swim 6 ½ lengths.

Most of the swimmers who had been to Helsinki won their events as you would expect. In my heats no one managed to get near to the time I recorded. In the final Ronnie, Doug and the others said I would win it easy.

I remember standing on the starting blocks then nothing else until the start of the 6th length. Everyone was shouting and waving at me. I looked round and saw that I was in last place, I was not tired, I was full of energy but I was last. I started to swim as fast as I could and overtook them all except one. I was catching him with every stroke but the finish came too soon for me. I was second. The time of the winner was seconds down on the time I had done in the heats.

Every one wanted to know what had happened, so did I. I could not explain because I did not know, to this day I have no idea why I swam the way I did. The press had a field day, all the reporters jostled me for a quote, I just wanted to go away and hide so that I could cry in peace.

I still had to phone home and tell Tom Banister, my mum and Gill. I told them but could not explain it.

I did learn one lesson; nothing could ever be such as big a disappointment as this in my life again.

Hospital

I returned home and in September went into the Preston Royal Infirmary (PRI) for my hernia operation, with the maximum publicity, not that I wanted it. "Preston's Olympic Swimmer Enters Hospital" said the *Lancashire Evening Post*. In those days you stayed in bed for two weeks for this operation. I was in a large men's ward just behind the door to the left. I had a lot of attention but the visits I longed for were from Gill. The lads from the club brought me a pile of girly magazines, the last thing I needed with this op. One of the jokes that the patients used to play was to try and make you laugh which was most painful.

I enjoyed my stay in PRI; I got special treatment from all the nurses. I got the lads to bring me a water pistol and I would "shoot" the nurses as they went passed. One nurse got her own back by pulling back the bedclothes and pouring a full bottle of orange squash over me.

As she did this the other patients shouted that Matron was coming on her rounds, as she entered the ward they called her to the other end while the nurse covered me up and straightened my bed over the pool of orange squash in which I was lying.

Matron came to ask me how I was and I told her that I was enjoying my stay in hospital; she looked at me and said that I must have been up to no good if I was enjoying it, and walked on.

The nurse gave a sigh of relief and all the lads in the ward cheered as the screens were placed round my bed and I was stripped along with the bed, washed and re-dressed.

When I left hospital I thanked everyone for looking after me. I really did have a good time

Gill had her 16th birthday on 4th October; we were now totally committed to each other; Gill came to see me each day in hospital and continued to do so when I got home. We were made to be together, I was 2 ½ years older than Gill at 18 years. but that did not matter. When young people now go out at such an early age adults say it won't last, but I never had the slightest doubt that I was meant to spend the rest of my life with Gill.

I was a devout Roman Catholic and Gill was even more committed to her church, the Church of England. This could have presented a problem but the fact that Gill's grandmother and Aunty Dorothy were Catholics made it easier to sort out. At that time there was no question of me changing so I asked Gill if she would become a Catholic in the future and she agreed.

The fact that I would be going in the RAF and be away for two years would be a test to see if our love would last. It did and I knew it would. Gill would write me a letter every day; she even wrote and posted a letter on a Sunday when I was at home so that I would get it on Monday morning. The lads at camp could not believe it, in the end Gill addressed the letter to "AC Barnes RAF Cosford," nothing else, no section or number but I received every one. I was loved by the person I was totally in love with.

CHAPTER FOUR

1953 - 1955 National Service - Royal Air Force

19553-1955 - National Service

When I came out of hospital I was off work for a few weeks then I went back to work and started swimming, gently at first with no diving or jumping in. By Christmas I was passed fit to join the Forces.

This also caused problems. The RAF had an arrangement through the Air Ministry to get all the Olympic Swimmers into the RAF. At that time it was not easy to get in unless you signed up for three or more years, so recruits were normally placed in the Army. There was a war going on in Trieste and the Army needed men.

A civilian called Jimmy Sefton, who was a former officer in the RAF and now worked in the Air Ministry, contacted the recruiting office where I was to register and fix it so that I was entered in the RAF. The same day that I registered two professional footballers from Blackpool FC and Blackburn Rovers also joined and the press printed our photograph.

The following day a mother wrote in saying it was not fair that her son had to go into the Army and fight in Korea.

I joined the RAF on 1st February 1953 (1/2/53) but the clerk entered (2/1/53) I did not know this until five months later, which is another story.

All recruits had to attend RAF Padgate near Warrington to be kitted out then they were sent to another camp to do their 8 weeks basic training, called square bashing because of all the marching and drill that you had to learn. We did ours at RAF Hednesford on Cannock Chase, near Stoke on Trent.

It was bitterly cold, we were housed in wooden huts containing 20 beds which had one coke-fired stove to heat the whole hut. I had been told to keep my head down and not let the corporal get to know your name, that way you did not get picked on.

For many of the lads it was the first time away from home and they did not know the least thing about looking after themselves. We had been issued with all our kit and had to iron the uniform and polish our boots to shine like a mirror.

One lad ironed the crease down the side of his trousers instead of the front and cried when the corporal made fun of him. At least I could look after myself.

When Friday arrived the footballer went off to play for Blackpool FC, the rest of us had to stay on camp. When he returned on Monday morning I asked him how he managed to get off:, he told me that his club had written to the Commanding Officer.

I immediately phoned Tom Banister to get him to say that I was required home every weekend to train for my International Duties which he did. Every week there were now two missing from camp.

Because of my swimming and being off camp I missed the issue of part of my kit called webbing, this is the straps for carrying kit and is used on parade especially on ceremonial occasions. I also missed a lot of basic drill.

I had permission from the CO to go swimming whenever the camp sent any recruits to the baths which was three or four times per week.

I was also told by Jimmy Sefton at Air Ministry that if I was prepared to just be an ordinary airman and not go for promotion they would get me off duties to swim throughout my National Service. I readily agreed to this.

This meant that I never learned to drill properly or fire a gun, and was not issued with all the necessary webbing for doing those things.

In all my time I only went on one parade. This was when the present Queen's Grandmother, Queen Mary, died. I had no idea what to do so I followed the two lads on each side of me; I was just a fraction of a second behind. All went well until we had to put our rifles down and do some marching without them then we had to pick the rifle up and start marching with them again.

I missed picking mine up, but had the sense to carry on as if I had. When we marched off the parade ground my rifle was left there on its own.

I was told that I was never to go onto a parade ground again and to keep out of sight. So I did.

Everyone had to fire a rifle and a Bren gun, which is a machine gun. I was told that I must fire them even though I had not been to any practices due to my swimming. I went to the firing range got hold of the rifle took aim and pulled the trigger. The gun kicked up into my face and cut my lip, which made everyone laugh because they were expecting me to do it. Once again I was told never to go near the firing range, which I didn't.

After we finished training there was a passing out parade, which I was not allowed to attend so I sat in the bus which was to take us home to Preston, and waited for the lads to be dismissed. When they all ran to get a seat for the journey home, I had the seat at the front by the driver.

School Of Physical Training RAF Cosford

After a week's leave I was posted to the RAF School of PT at Cosford near Wolverhampton as a clerk organisation in the Headquarters offices.

The CO had been briefed by Jimmy Sefton and was proud to have another international sportsman at the camp.

The School of PT had international competitors in every sport, for example; Ronnie Flowers International Footballer, Wolverhampton FC, Higginson Twins, Cyclists, Brian and Jack Harper Boxing, Brian fought under his professional name London. Myself and Eddie Burnet a Scottish International Swimmer, Internationals at Judo, and Fencing.

The facilities were excellent: there was an indoor and outdoor track, a superb gymnasium and we had a large 100ft swimming pool in which to train.

I was able to swim ever day as often as I wanted to with only myself and Eddie who was in charge of the pool keeping it clear of other users. I had an arrangement with a lad in the cookhouse that he would serve me anything I wanted, when I wanted it. The best was a pint mug of cream to put on my cereal and in my Ovaltine at night.

Next to the pool was a very large hangar in which was the boxing area and gym. The Warrant Officer (WO) in charge of the school was WO Berrage who was a black belt 3rd Dan in Judo.

Every day I had to go through the gym to get to the pool, WO Berrage would call me over put both hands on my shoulders and try to get me to take up boxing, he would say I could be the next "Bruce Wells"; Bruce was a Golden Gloves champion of USA and the English ABA champion, he was also 6ft2ins tall.

I used to decline his offer and later told the WO that even if I was beaten in swimming I would be in better condition than if I had won at boxing. He never gave up trying to get me to box though.

One of the International Boxers was Brian London who fought as a professional for the world heavyweight championship; his real name was Brian Harper. Brian's brother, Jack was also at camp with him. Jack was arrogant and lived on his brother's reputation; it was surprising because Brian was such a nice lad.

One day I was training in the pool with only one other person in the water. I was being timed by Eddy over 100yds which was three lengths of the pool. This other swimmer started to swim widths across the pool as I was doing lengths. After the second time he got in my way I threatened him if he did it again. When I finished Eddy asked me if I knew who it was. It was Jack Harper, but he never did it again.

I was the nearest thing to a professional swimmer. In total there were six members of the Olympic Swimming team in the RAF so you can imagine the effect this had at the Interservices competitions. The RAF won everything.

That year, 1953, was the first year of the new race for the butterfly with its separation from breast-stroke. I had been 3rd then 2nd in the previous years when I should have won so I wanted it badly this year.

1953 English National Championship

The championships were again at Blackpool Derby Pool. Because of the change in rules it was now legal to keep both legs together and swim like a dolphin rather than kicking the legs apart as in breast-stroke, which was much slower. I still used the old breast-stroke leg kick. In the heats I was once again the fastest time until a 38 years old Jack Hale, a former 200m international freestyle swimmer turned in a staggering 2.48sec. He swam under water most of the time only surfacing to breathe just like a dolphin. He was the talk of Blackpool; no one could beat this man.

Tom Banister took me to one side, looked me in the eyes and said I could win if I did as I was told. I had only swum one way and that was to go out in front and stay there. Tom's plan was that Jack Hale's technique was such that if he lost his smooth rhythm he would not only go slower but could even stop.

I was to go slow at first, let Jack get in front then on the last length go after him, he would panic, according to Tom and I would win.

My trust in my coach was such that if Tom had said swim with your hand behind your back I would have done so.

The day of the race everyone was looking forward to watching me against Jack Hale. We lined up for four lengths of the pool, the gun went off and Jack disappeared under the water, not to reappear until he was over half way down the pool, then under water again.

At the half way stage Jack was way out in front with me second and the rest a long way back. I could hear the crowd shouting for me because I was a local lad, whereas Jack came from down south. As I approached the third and final turn Jack had already turned and surfaced on his last 50m.

I then decided to give it all I had left and that was plenty. As soon as I began to improve on Jack's lead the crowd went wild. It had two different effects: I knew they were cheering for me and I was gaining on Jack, and Jack knew the same but the result was as predicted by my coach Tom Banister, he panicked and lost his smooth rhythm.

The result was spectacular: I was catching him as if he was going backwards, I passed him with plenty to spare and won my first English

National Championship in a new record time. Thanks to my coach Tom Banister.

Back at Cosford I received my extra increase in pay that everyone was entitled to every six months i.e. 6, 12, 18 months, only I got mine after 5 months. I was on my way to the pay section to tell them their mistake when I thought about it so I asked to see my records instead.

I started on the 1st Feb (1/2/53) the clerk had entered 2/1/53. I said nothing and took my pay a month early each time, in the end I only did 23 months National Service.

Starting pay was 27 shillings a week (£1.35p). I managed to live on this with the help of my mum baking cakes etc and each time I got a rise I put it away as savings. When I was demobbed I had £100 saved for our wedding.

At camp everyone played jokes on one another, e.g.

- In the middle of the night picking up a person's bed while he was asleep and placing it with him in it, on the parade ground.
- Taking out a lad's bed when he was away so that on returning late at night he would count the beds, his being for example the third on the right but it would be occupied, and so were all the others.
- Painting the corporal's windows black, so that he did not wake up or get up on time.
- Blocking the chimney in another hut so that the stove would not light.

A regular airman called Jack, who was a very big tough guy and was afraid of no one befriended me, stopped any jokes happening to me. He thought that it was great to have a pal who was a British Champion

The Queen's Coronation was a big event in 1953. Not many people had TV so neighbours shared a TV. Jack told me to volunteer for Fire Picket that day, which was strange because it is an unwritten rule, you never volunteer for anything.

But I did as he said.

When the entire camp was on Parade to celebrate the event Jack and myself were in the NAFFI (a canteen) with two large armchairs set immediately in front of the large TV. After the parade hundreds of airman ran to get into the NAFFI to try and see the TV. We had the perfect places all day. When I told Gill she was surprised I had seen it as she and her mum and dad, along with other friends had all crowded into my mum's place to watch it on a small telly.

Whilst at the School of PT I made my first blood donation. The Blood Transfusion Service came on camp and the whole of the school of PT was paraded and were told that a blood donor session was to take place. The parade ground was told that volunteers to give blood would take one step forward, and then the order was given "Parade one step forward march". We did, and all volunteered. That was the easy part: men were laying head to toe on camp beds and some, the biggest and toughest included, saw the blood and promptly fainted. What a sight, some never lived it down.

In the summer of 1953 it was decided to move the School of PT to South Wales to RAF St Athan. There was no way I wanted to go that far away from Preston. After trying all the wangles I could think of, including the fact that I was an only child and my father had been killed in the war, I could still not get a compassionate posting.

I even asked the Soldiers Sailors and Airforce Families Association (SSAFFA) to help; they thought I had a good chance but no luck. I went to see the Padre, he tried unsuccessfully. I then thought of Jimmy Sefton at Air Ministry. I phoned Jimmy and his reply was "which camp do you want to go to?"

RAF Weeton

Within three days I was posted to RAF Weeton about 12 miles from Preston. This was a dream: I was given a living out pass and permission to train with my own coach each morning before going into camp. It also meant that I could see Gill each day. There were no cars to get around so you either walked or went on a bicycle. We spent many hours walking round what was then countryside in Ribbleton.

I got a normal bus into the village and the milk van which delivered to the camp used to wait for me and take me directly to my place of work, HQ building.

The camp was the Motor Vehicle training camp for the RAF but they gave me a job in the office.

I was given a list each month for the dates and venues that the RAF wanted me to swim. The CO was informed that I had to be given all the time off I needed. He seemed to be proud of the fact that I was in his office.

The Adjutant, called Clive, was an officer who is like the secretary or assistant to the CO; he was a young officer whose father was the Managing Director of Fords GB. He did not like the fact that I was always going away and he could not do anything about it. He was used to getting his own way.

At Christmas most of the lads were given leave, just a few Scots stayed on and took their leave at New Year. Every person was entitled to railway warrants which were exchanged at the station for a ticket.

Four RAF camps all used the railway station at Kirkham to travel home, so to save time and to help the flow at the station, Clive the Adjutant had this bright idea of issuing warrants weeks before and then collecting the tickets from the station at Kirkham and giving them out to the lads on pay parade just before they left on leave.

There were some 2000 personnel on the camp so Clive decided to have a number of different venues for pay parade, A to G, H to M, and N to Z. Unfortunately he did not have the correct tickets at the right parade so no one received a ticket.

You have to realise that this was less than an hour before the lads were due to go on leave for Christmas, they had no ticket and wanted to go home. The HQ offices were suddenly under siege with hundreds trying to get in and more outside. The CO came into the office and when he saw what was happening he ordered all of us in the office to issue warrants to everyone. It took hours to get all the lads away and we had no idea who had got what, other than we had signed hundreds of warrants and had thousands of tickets to places all over the UK.

Everything was locked away until we returned after Christmas. In January an inquiry was set up to look into the fiasco of the tickets, it turned out to be so big that at high level a decision was taken to forget the whole affair and write it off.

That was OK with us but we had thousands of tickets locked away in a safe. It was decided to lose them which we did, that is until someone wanted to go somewhere then they came to us and for a small fee received the ticket of their choice. They were even exchanged for extra leave with the other offices and so the tickets were eventually put to good use even if it took a long time.

One of the lads in the office, Reg Billington, was also from Preston. He was an engineer but the RAF made him a clerk. He used to clean the lino on the floor round his desk and polish it so that it shone and stood out against the rest of the office. When the Adjutant saw it he would order everyone else to do the same, much to the delight of Reg who would sit back and watch the rest of us hard at it.

Because Reg was also living out he was the first to get into the wooden hut which was the HQ building. His first job was to light the stove, the only source of heating. Reg used to bring in some paraffin to get it going.

One day the lads changed the paraffin for petrol and when Reg put a match to it he blew the stove to bits as it went through the roof. Luckily Reg was OK but it was a close thing.

Again all the time people were playing jokes on one another e.g. answering the phone in the office saying "C of E Padre" the phone would be put down with the person apologising for the mistake

One of the corporals used to greet the new recruits and get them to fall in groups by religion and shout R Cs, C of E, O Ds and Church of Turkey. We only got a few in the last group. Now it would be an offence.

There were five members of the 1952 British Olympic Team in the RAF at the same time, plus other good swimmers, the RAF team won everything there was to win. We would often get asked to swim at galas in the London area so a phone call would go out for me to go to London for a week's swimming. We would be put up at the US Air Force base at RAF West Drayton because this camp was not subjected to normal rationing of food as it was flown in directly from America. I was often given advanced warning of such arrangements so I decided to take some leave and get Gill to take her holidays and we went to stay at her Auntie's in London near Wembley. We had a great time; Ronny Sefton fixed it up for Gill to accompany the team to all the receptions afterwards.

I had arranged for my travel warrants to cover the longest journey from Keswick to London and back, plus Preston to St Athan return.

When I returned to the camp I was met at the Guard House and arrested on the orders of Clive the Adjutant for fraudulently claiming £48 pounds, 17shillings and 6 pence (£48.86) in expenses.

I was marched into the Commanding Officer's Office, all the time my mind was in overdrive thinking how to explain myself.

I started by saying that I was in Keswick when I was told to report to London to swim, which I did, returning home at the weekend. Clive immediately said I was not on camp, I told him that I had a living out pass and was at home with my widowed mother.

Then I said I had to return to London again to swim for the RAF the following week and needed living expenses, again I returned home to see my mother.

All the time a clerk was totalling the amount as I explained it; in the end I had explained all but 15 shillings and 6 pence (77p).

The C.O. said "Barnes I do not believe a word, but for your cheek I will write off the rest. Dismiss."

I was marched out, but it was a near thing.

While at Weeton I met up with Dave Toft a Northern Counties Backstroke champion. Dave was quite a character who was into anything and everything. He suggested that we could get a Swimming Team from the camp to enter the RAF Championships at St Athan, when I said that I did not know any swimmers on camp he said it didn't matter so long as they lived in South Wales. They would pay to get a week's leave and expenses which would make us a nice profit if we used his dad's car to transport us all from Weeton to St Athan and back.

Both Dave and I would be getting our own expenses anyway.

Dave soon had three lads signed up for the trip and Dave went home to collect his dad's car.

The day we were due to leave we would meet in a pub outside the camp so that no one would see us use the car; we had all claimed rail fare.

Time passed but Dave did not show, after a few hours Dave arrived saying that the car had broken down close by, but it would take the rest of the day to get it repaired and was going to cost over £100. Panic broke out we had to be in St Athan by noon the next day and no one had £100.

In the end Dave persuaded his dad to pay for the repairs and my mum agreed to let everyone sleep on the floor at our house.

We left at 4am the next day to drive to South Wales; there were no motorways just local roads.

As Dave was the only driver we took it in turns to sit in the front passenger seat and keep watching so that when Dave shut his eyes to sleep we shook him to stay awake. It was an exciting journey but we made it in time, just. The "Team" booked in and the lads went off to their homes. Dave and I both won our races and we got three other swimmers to stand in for us so that we won the team race as well.

On returning to Camp we were all congratulated on the results and Dave and I made a few bob.

1954 Empire Games - Vancouver, Canada

I was still the British Champion and when the trials were held at Blackpool I was there with most of my pals from Helsinki. I won my race and so was expected to be picked as did the other winners; others who finished second or even third could still be chosen for the relay races.

The team was to be announced at an official dinner at the Cliffs Hotel. We all sat together, Ronnie, Doug Walsh, Athol Still, and The

Wardrop Twins. Then the bombshell dropped: Dick Hodgson from Blackburn, The President of the ASA, said that it had been decided not to send anyone to compete in the 200m Butterfly event. I had trained, I had won, and then the officials decided not to send me.

I walked out in tears and vowed never to swim again. Sod the lot of them at the ASA.

In 1954 I was still the British Champion until the next person won the event, but I would not swim again. The press and some members of the ASA put it about that I was afraid of losing, as the reason for my not competing. It got so bad that I decided to enter.

I went to Blackpool for the Championships and when my heat was due I lined up on the bath side at Derby Baths. Dick Hodgson was on the bath side when the gun was fired to start the race, everyone dived in and I just stood there. There was a gasp from the crowd, I waited until the swimmers were almost at the end of the first lap of four, then I dived in. I swam as slow as I could, all the other swimmers in my heat had left the pool when I finished. I climbed out of the water, went up to Dick Hodgson and said "Now are you satisfied? You can f**k your swimming I've finished with you".

I never swam competitively again. It was not until the 1970s when Ernie Warrington, President of the ASA, apologised on behalf of the ASA that I made my peace with them.

My feelings for Gill were like nothing I had ever experienced before; it was as if all the love songs ever written were about Gill and me. My life was only about being with Gill, nothing else mattered even though we were apart quite a lot of the time, and I never stopped thinking about her, day and night. I never for one split second thought that I would not marry and start a family with her. Nothing could stop us, age, religion, money all could be sorted out and they were.

We were meant to be together for always. The one thing I could not explain was how I could be so lucky to find such a wonderful, beautiful girl who also loved me as much as she did.

It was during that year that I plucked up courage to ask Pop (Gill's dad) and Gran (Gill's mum) if they would mind if Gill changed her religion to marry me. In those days Catholics were not allowed to marry non-Catholics. They said it was all right with them but it was up to Gill to make the decision.

That was all I needed. I asked my mum to look out for an engagement ring at the shop. She produced some for me to look at and I chose one and a nice ring box. I took Gill for a walk down by the river by the Halfpenny bridge, we sat by the river and I asked Gill to marry me. She said yes and I gave her the ring.

The place where this happened is where the Tickled Trout Hotel and Restaurant is now at the M6 junction.

In November 1954 Clive was determined to get his own back on me and make me attend the Remembrance Sunday parade. As I only had two months left to do I decided to put up with it. The problem was that I did not know how to drill nor did I have the webbing necessary for the parade. I was told to go and draw out webbing but when I asked at the stores the Officer contacted the CO to see why I needed it after all this time. The CO went wild; he sent for the Adjutant and cancelled my parade.

As I have said I was going to be released a month early i.e. after 23 months not the full 24 months due to the cock-up by the clerk when I joined.

When anyone arrives at a RAF camp they have to get an arrival card filled up and signed by all the different sections to make sure that the camp records are up to date for example pay section, padre, stores admin, section head, police etc.

The reverse side must be signed for you to be able to leave the camp. Because my last day was 1st January 1955, the CO signed me off the camp before he went home for Christmas and so did all the other parts of the camp. I was even paid up to my last day before Christmas. Everyone thought I could go before the Christmas holidays except the Adjutant

He made me return between Boxing Day and the weekend. So I did. I was joining Preston Borough Police Force and had already been sworn in so that I could start Police training at Bruche on 3rd January 1955.

I came back in to the camp and sat at my desk with nothing to do as I had given in all my papers and someone else had taken over my work.

At 10am the CO arrived and asked what I was doing as he had signed me off the week before. I told him that the Adjutant had said I must come in. He hit the roof, sent for the Adjutant and told me to leave wishing me all the best. I could still hear the CO going on at Clive as I left the camp for good. I joined the Police Training course at Bruche, and two weeks later I received a letter in an RAF envelope and I thought that I was going to be called back to do my 24th month. To my relief it was from Clive apologising for being such a prat and wishing me well for the future.

So ended my 23 months of National Service.

CHAPTER FIVE

1955 - 1957 Police Constable 69 Preston Borough Police Force

1955 – 1957 Police Constable No. 69

My mother had wanted me to work with her in the shop and then take over, even buy it from Clarksons. The idea was good but I had got engaged and wanted to purchase a house. I had an interview for the job at Clarksons, they offered me £6 per week. The police pay was £13 per week with a uniform and housing allowance.

The decision was made for me. I applied to join Preston Borough Police Force while I was still in the RAF. I was sworn in as constable 69 in December 1954 and was due to start training on January 3rd 1955.

I started at Bruche Police Training College, Near Warrington for 13 weeks initial training. 48 years ago there was still respect for people in authority, Park Keepers, Bus Conductors, Police and Firemen. Not everyone was a good person but almost all respected the law.

I learned the Definition of a Constable:

"A constable is a citizen appointed by the Crown for the protection of life and property".

Time at Bruche was spent learning about the law and whether you had power of arrest or not. At that time everyone had the power to arrest anyone who had committed a felony, i.e. a serious crime. Less serious crimes were called misdemeanours, for which you could only report someone.

The instructors would not tell us what to do if you had no power of arrest and the person would not give you their name and address. They kept just to the law. We had to learn how to deal with this sort of situation as it arose.

Only after we had been on the streets for 12 months and we returned for our second course at Bruche did we discuss how we had managed this type of situation.

Traffic Law. This took up a large amount of time due to the number of laws that motorists could and did ignore. Bruche had its own road system with traffic lights, crossings, halt signs etc. plus a number of old bangers that were pushed into accident positions so that we could pretend that there were traffic accidents. Instructors and constables acted as drivers, victims and witnesses, while we attempted to gather all the relevant information necessary to write a report on the incident. We all forgot something, either about the car or a witness or the driver.

There was also a very good mock courtroom with defendant's box, witness box and an imposing judge's bench, which could frighten even the best of us. This proved to be of immense benefit in preparing us for the real thing.

By the time we left I could attend an accident and obtain name and address, age, occupation of driver, and any passengers, Reg No, make, colour, type of car, Road Fund details, insurance of car, witnesses' full details, and draw a sketch of the incident.

Now I believe they have a booklet to fill in the answers to all the questions.

48 years ago there was a lot of traffic control duty, called point duty, now there are more traffic lights.

Traffic Duty

Because there were no personal radios, contacting constables in an emergency was not easy, but you could always take one off point duty. You knew where they were. At busy road junctions there would be two or three constables allocated to point duty so that they could have a rest every 40 mins. Some constables could not care less whether the traffic moved well or not, they were there for eight hours so what?

Others, me included took a pride in getting the cars moving as fast as we could. The difference could be seen and was appreciated by drivers and the public who in summer would sit on the seats by busy junctions and watch for hours at a time.

Some even brought us drinks and biscuits and had been known to applaud when we changed over for a rest.

One old man was a regular and came every day in summer to sit and watch the policemen on point duty. I got to know Tom; he lived in a small terraced house off Ribbleton Lane. He was poorly dressed but always clean. That Christmas, Gill and I decided to take him a Christmas dinner complete with all the trimmings including a small Christmas cake.

His house had no carpets and there was only one chair by the table which was covered with newspapers. When he opened the door he was amazed that we had thought of him, he was almost in tears and so were we.

The first motorway in the UK was the Preston Bypass opened in 1957. This was because of the congestion caused at the junction of the main north south road A6, and the Blackpool road, east west, A59.

I have been on duty at this junction when the county police would drive up and demand that the A6 be given a long run as the traffic was backed up for six miles south. We did this then we had the same demand from the other county police in Blackburn because they had a queue back there 10 miles to Blackburn in the west.

In summer and during the illuminations at Blackpool this junction would be policed by officers all day, starting with the morning shift from

6am when the traffic lights would be manually operated,

8am point duty by three constables to be relieved by the afternoon shift at 2pm,

7pm or dusk the traffic lights would again be operated manually,

10pm the night shift took over the lights and it could be 2am before this junction could be left to run itself.

This was the worst junction in the UK.

I was on duty at this junction one day, I had switched the lights off, most of the traffic was going to Blackpool and they were given the longest run. A queue of traffic had built up on the north-south road, when I heard a fire engine bell (no sirens then). I stopped the east-west traffic and signalled for the fire engine to pull out of the queue and go on the outside lane across the Blackpool Road. This went OK then I saw an ambulance and signalled it to do the same. I was in the middle of the road junction with all the traffic stopped with the ambulance going north across Blackpool Road. The traffic on Blackpool road was also stopped with most of it going to Blackpool. A motorist coming from Blackpool saw the cars and bus in front indicating their intention to turn right. He could not see me in the middle of the road with my hand in the stop position and overtook the stationary vehicles on the inside just as the ambulance crossed the junction. There was a big crash with the ambulance spinning round twice before coming to a stop on the grass verge on the other side of the road.

No one was hurt but there was a lot of damage to both vehicles. A police car brought the Inspector from the station; he took me to one side and asked me what had happened. I explained that it was a pure accident and no one was to blame. I said I would do the same thing again if the same situation arose.

He looked at me and said "69 there was a bloody accident so you would NOT do the same again". I had to agree and that was another experience to learn from. "Never make the same mistake twice"

My first week on the streets of Preston was quite an event. I felt that everyone was looking at me and of course they were. I was in the centre of town when I was told a woman had collapsed outside M & S. I went there and found a lady on the floor with a crowd round her. As I wondered what to do another woman said she was a nurse and that it looked as though the lady was having a fit. I immediately asked her to take charge and called for the ambulance. After getting witness details I went with the lady to the hospital and contacted her relatives. After this I felt I could deal with anything.

First Arrest

The next day I was told there was a man lying in the street at the rear of the shops. When I got there he was struggling to his feet and shouting at the crowd. He was drunk.

I had no option but to arrest him. When I got him to the police station the sergeant was not at all pleased with my first arrest, as the drunk was well known to him. This was his 102nd appearance and my first time in court.

In Preston we had a number of streets named after people, e.g. Smith Street, James Street, and Thomas Street.

One morning I was told to go to 22, Smith Street and inform the family that Mr James had died that night in hospital. He had been ill for some time.

When I informed the family they did not understand because I had been given the wrong information it should have been Mr Smith at 22 James Street. After apologising I went back to the Station and checked the information.

Sudden deaths are never easy and informing relatives is one of the most difficult tasks that constables are asked to do. The other is attending to an attempted suicide.

At the time I was a constable suicide was a criminal offence like murder. It was changed before I left.

I was called to a house where a man had attempted to gas himself using the gas oven. I managed to get him out, called the ambulance and went with him to the hospital. When he came round he was placed under arrest. You can imagine how he felt: he was so depressed that he had failed in his attempt to kill himself. I felt drained being with him and trying to get him back his will to live.

There is a happy end to this incident in that I was able to find out that his problem was at his workplace; I talked to his employer who was very sympathetic and was able to solve the problem.

As I said before there were no radios so at the beginning of each shift the sergeant gave you places that you had to be at given times called "points", usually one each hour.

One constable would have a point on the hour, the next at 10 past, the following at 20 past and so on. The sergeant and the inspector could meet you at any of your arranged points. This was for them to be able to contact you and also for your safety. If you missed one point you got a telling off but if you missed two it was a search party out looking for you. You could be lying in a pool of blood. Radios have made a big impact on the way constables work.

Inspector Stone was a character, he had been in the army fighting in Ireland. On a Saturday night he would come up to you and say

"Constable when were you last in court" and whatever you replied he would tell you to walk behind him. Then with the sergeant by his side he would walk right into a group of people who had just been put out from the pub at closing time and place his stick into the heel of one of them and as they fell down he would turn to me and say "Constable lock him up, drunk and incapable" The rest of the crowd would disperse at once.

In 1955 the police worked three shifts, 6am to 2pm, 2pm to 10pm, and 10pm to 6am. You had to be on parade in the police station 15mins before the start of your shift, but prior to that you had to read up all the incidents from the day before and any new orders that may have been issued. To do this you had to be in the station 20 to 25 mins before the time you officially started and were paid from.

One Sunday night I had been sent home early at 2am because I felt sick. The following morning I was not fit for work, I was due to start at 6am. At 5-45am, Gill went to a phone box at the top of our road to inform them I would be going off work officially sick. At 6am the sergeant arrived and forced his way past Gill into the house to make sure that I was indeed in bed sick. How things change.

As soon as I could I sat and passed my Sergeant's examination, then started studying for the Inspector's exam. I was introduced to all sorts of life that the average person not only does not see but does not believe goes on.

During training at Bruche we were told that a good sense of humour was essential and that was soon proved to be a necessity. In Preston at that time the public houses in the area round the Ribble Bus Station were the place where all the villains hung out. It suited the public who did not frequent these pubs and also the police who knew where to find the villains.

Saturday night at the bus station could be relied on to have at least one or two arrests, along with incidents of a more humorous kind, like the time I was called to the gent's toilet at the bus station where a man who was drunk had been peeing against the urinal wall when he dropped his keys. He bent down to grab them and got his fist stuck in the open top drain still holding his keys; he could not let go or get his fist out of the drain. He was on his knees asking for help with all the other users carrying on peeing all round him with the water level rising with every visit. I took one look and decided to leave him to it. Half an hour later I sent for the fire brigade to get him out and by then he was sober and wet through.

New recruits were each paired up with an older more experienced bobby for the first month. The first time I was on duty on Saturday night in the area of the bus station I was paired with Rocky, a bobby who loved a scrap: if it was quiet he could start one with ease. Our job was to see that all the pubs closed on time 10-30pm, so we started at one end and went into the first pub. "All out", shouted Rocky and got hold of the nearest bloke and pushed him through the door, then he went for the next and so on.

Most of the drinkers knew Rocky and did not argue, but then he got an awkward one who wanted to debate the issue. Rocky got hold of him and told him to get out. The chap swung at Rocky who was waiting for it then he grabbed him and arrested him for assaulting a policeman. We arrested two more that night, and were in court on Monday morning.

The next time I was on nights in the same area I was with a totally different bobby. Charlie had been in the force 20 years and reckoned he knew most of the villains by name. Closing the pubs with him was an example of how to do it without any effort. In we went with Charlie talking to the punters by name telling each one that his Mrs would be waiting for him or asking some woman if her kids were going to school or was it prison?

At the end of the night we had the job done and no trouble. This is the way I wanted to police from now on.

The funny thing is though; later on when Preston got its first police dog unit, Rocky was one of the first dog handlers, and what a combination that was.

I remember being with him in an area that was being demolished but was being used by prostitutes and their clients. Rocky, the dog and

I walked into the area quietly and in the dark. When we were in the centre we shone our torches on the couples and let the dog go.

The nearest two were up against the wall with the man with his back to us and his trousers round his ankles; the dog jumped and sank its teeth into the bare buttock. As the man shouted out in pain, Rocky yelled to the dog "Put it down you don't know where it's been". I nearly fell over laughing, as the dog let go and both of them ran off, the woman in front with the man following trying to pull up his trousers. Again illegal, but effective.

My second arrest after the drunk was a girl called Barbara; I will never forget her name. I was on duty in Church Street when a man came up to me and said that there was a girl round the corner who had stolen his money and watch. I went with him and arrested the girl, Barbara.

She was 19 years old and a prostitute: the night before the man had been with her and she left with his money and watch. Barbara admitted it and I locked her up overnight. The following morning we were in court with Barbara pleading guilty or so we thought. I gave my evidence and she was asked by the magistrate if she had any questions for me. She said it was all a pack of lies and that I had made it up.

The witness had not been required to be in court because of the guilty plea. I thought I was in trouble but evidently the magistrate was used to this and knew her from past appearances in court. He found her guilty.

Barbara still managed to embarrass me each time she saw me with Gill going to the pictures: she had her "pitch" outside the Empire cinema and always said in a loud voice "How are you Brian love, nice to see you again".

Another lesson learned "Never presume things are going to be smooth and straightforward: they never are".

There was a Sergeant 6ft 5ins tall with a round red face who was called Baby Face by everyone but not to his face. Brian Blackledge and myself, both new recruits were stood in a doorway near Manchester Road at 10.30pm one Friday night when a lady came up to us and said "there is a fight outside the Ritz Cinema they are killing him" she pointed 200 yards up the road.

Brian and I were just about to run in the direction of the fight when the sergeant grabbed hold of us and told the lady that we would deal with it and suggested that she went home and left things to us.

As soon as she had gone we asked the sergeant why he was holding us back. "Let the buggers knock hell out of each other then we will arrest the lot", he said. With that we all three began a slow walk towards the fight, which by this time had stopped the traffic and one of the men had crawled under a bus to escape being kicked.

Baby Face stood there all 6ft 5ins of him and pointed to each man in turn. "Arrest him, him and him", he said. By this time the police van had arrived and some of them were thrown inside while Brian and I took one each and frogmarched them through the town to the police station.

As soon as we entered the police yard they began to shout "Don't hit me, don't hit me". You would not recognise the same men who had been kicking hell out of another man, minutes before. They were locked up and given a lesson in humility before going to court the next day.

When they stood in the dock looking all meek and mild pleading guilty to being drunk and not remembering anything of the fight, I thought that if the magistrate had been with his wife at the scene and witnessed the trouble caused by these bullies they would have received a harder sentence.

Because there were no radios to contact policemen there was always a constable or two patrolling the main shopping centre in Preston at night. This beat was called Fronts, as it was the front of the shops.

One night I was on Fronts when I could hear a loud noise which turned out to be a gang of six lads shouting and singing at 3am. I walked up to them and told them to shut up or else. As they got nearer to me I recognised one of them as Harry Bishop, the top fighter at school. I wondered what was going to happen but they all apologised and walked on quietly. I breathed a sigh of relief.

Another night in the middle of summer I was stood by the traffic lights at the junction of Blackpool Road and London Road at 4am in the morning, it was daylight with no traffic about when a cyclist approached me from the direction of Blackpool.

The traffic lights were red but he cycled past on red towards me on the other side of the junction.

I thought that this was a bit cheeky and stepped out into the road to stop him. I asked him if he had seen the red light and he said yes, I asked him if he had seen me, he said yes. He was stood astride his bike, when I asked him his name he got off his bike threw it at me and ran off across the park. I started after him and caught him with a flying tackle. I arrested him and marched him back to the road.

I had a dilemma, no means of communicating with the police station which was 2 miles away and a prisoner, who wanted to do a runner. I stopped the first car to come along and explained the position to the driver who agreed to take us both to the police station. I left the bike behind a hedge to be collected later.

After a lot of enquiring at the station we eventually found out the man had escaped from a mental institution, stolen the bike and had been to Blackpool.

My first fatal accident was also the worst. I was on nights at about 11pm when I heard the sound of a crash on the bridge over the River Ribble at the bottom of Fishergate Hill. I was about 200yds away. I ran to the scene and found a motor cycle lying on the ground with the driver by the side; a car was crashed into the bridge wall on the wrong side of the road with the driver still inside. To my surprise a police car was also involved and had been hit by the same car, two policemen still in the police car were badly shaken but unhurt.

The motorcyclist was asking about his passenger, it was dark and I could not see anyone else; I walked further on and found a young man dead with his head split open and contents of his skull all over the road. I took off my cape and placed it over the body. It took hours to free the car driver and clear the debris from the scene. I was left with the traffic section to help in measuring up and taking statements. It appeared that the police car was behind the motorcyclist going out of Preston over the bridge when the car with no lights came in the opposite direction on the wrong side of the road and hit the motorcyclist head on, then hit the police car. The car driver was drunk; he was arrested after going to the Preston Royal Infirmary for a medical check-up and later charged.

One summer morning I had just started my 6am to 2pm shift and was checking the pavilion at Fishwick Golf Club. All such buildings are vulnerable to break-ins because they are away from other buildings. As I went round the rear of the building I noticed the door had been forced open. As I entered two men ran out of the front door across the golf course. I telephoned Police Headquarters and gave a description of the men; they would send a police car to the other side of the course near London Road.

I called the key holder to identify what was missing and make the building secure then I made my way back to the police station.

The two men had been caught and were in a cell. I was told to go and identify them. There was only one man in the cell; the other had gone to the toilet. As I identified the man as one of the two who had fled the pavilion two policemen burst into the cell knocked me aside and grabbed the man and pinned him to the floor. They then searched him thoroughly, this was because the second man had been caught trying to hide a revolver in the toilet cistern. In those days firearms were not as prevalent as they are today. Thank goodness.

Pranks

There were lighter moments though; someone had left a tailor's dummy at the rear of a shop in the town centre. One of the bobbies placed it behind a shop propped up so that when the next bobby came round that night it would fall over on top of him. Those of us in the know waited to see the Bobby run out from behind the shop, his face white with shock. It was such a good trick that the dummy was moved from site to site over many weeks. I got caught out one night, and it was not funny when it happened to you.

The prank went wrong when someone had the bright idea of taking the sign off a hotel near the station and hung the dummy there instead. It looked as if someone had been hanged and the person reported it to the police station.

The best trick was played on a policeman call Rodney. The Harris Public Library and Museum is a very large Victorian building many storeys tall in the centre of Preston. Because of the valuable collection the police had the job of inspecting the premises each night; it was a very spooky place in the dark. When I first had the job of going into the building I was shown round by an older bobby who asked me if I wanted the grand tour or just go to the staff room on the top floor and make a cup of tea.

You were supposed to go into every room from basement to the staff room on the top floor where you signed your name and number. To get into the building you obtained the keys from the police station, and you were allowed 45 minutes for the task. The door was a large oak door with a mortise deadlock. Rodney was afraid of going into the museum and used to leave the door unlocked but closed.

The plan was for Tommy to follow Rodney inside with an old chain to rattle and a white sheet with which to cover himself with. Rodney went inside, left the door unlocked and Tommy followed. The rest of the night shift came from all over the town to watch. Rodney went straight to the staff room to sign in then he heard a noise, it was Tommy moaning and rattling the chain. Rodney suddenly ran two at a time down the stairs past the white sheet and out of the building locking the door as he departed.

All the lads were in hysterics at the site of Rodney still running down Lancaster Road.

Then we saw Tommy at the window telling us he could not get out. We all ran off to our own beats that we should have been on and left Tommy with the task of telephoning the station and explaining to the sergeant how he came to be locked in the museum.

Tommy was a true larger than life character. In summer at night during the hot weather couples could be seen lying in the park doing what comes naturally: one of Tommy's tricks was to go up to them without disturbing their actions and collect their clothes and hide them. Then he would return making a noise and shining his torch saying "Hello what's going on then". The couple would be all flustered looking for their clothes to put on.

Another lesson that I learned as a policeman happened when I was on point duty at the top of Lune Street and Fishergate. Most of the traffic coming into Preston up Fishergate Hill turned left into Lune Street because Fishergate became a no entry 200 yards further along the road. The junction was in the shape of a Y with the foot of the Y being Fishergate Hill and Lune Street being the left section of the Y.

There was a white box in the road for the policeman to stand on and most of the time the traffic was stopped from coming down the other arm of the Y so that the main stream of vehicles could go up and down Lune Street into and out from Fishergate Hill. The only thing the policeman had to watch out for was the odd car that wanted to go straight on up Fishergate and not turn left into Lune Street. They had to be stopped until you decided to stop the flow from Lune Street to let them proceed straight on up the other arm of the Y into Fishergate.

On the day in question there was an Army convoy coming up Lune Street to leave Preston by going down Fishergate Hill. I signalled to the convoy that I would give them priority by stopping all the other traffic except those who wanted to turn left down Lune Street. There was a very large tank transporter slowly making its way up the hill in Lune Street while the traffic from the other direction was all going left. Just as the tank transporter reached the police box, with me in it, a small A35 car with a learner driver in it came straight on even though he was signalling to go left, which is why I had waved him on. I could see the car disappearing under the large tank transporter, when there was a sudden hiss of air breaks and the army vehicle stopped at the same time as the small A35 car, only inches apart.

I rushed to the driver of the car as the passenger shouted "It's all right officer I'm the examiner, I shall fail him." I was so livid that I shouted back, "Think yourself lucky I don't book you as well for dangerous driving, you should have signalled me. Now get out of here". The car left and the convoy got on its way. Five minutes later a police car arrived with the Inspector and a PC in it. The PC took over the point duty and the Inspector took me to one side. "Do you know who that was in the A35?" he said. Before I could answer he said it was the Chief Driving Examiner and a friend of the Chief Constable.

I told him I could not care less and that he should know better. "Listen lad," said the Inspector, "You should always find out who you are dealing with before you shout at them."

It was good advice that I still use.

Holidays

Prior to our wedding Gill and I went to Keswick for our holidays, we stayed in a B&B in Wordsworth Street, in two single rooms.

The landlady delighted in giving us a hearty breakfast every morning before we went out walking, her speciality was Cumberland sausage which was not as nice as it could have been, and we made the mistake the first morning of wrapping the sausage in a paper hanky and disposing of it outside. The problem was that she thought that we liked them and served them every day for a week.

We decided to walk over Grisedale Pike which was quite a walk, especially for Gill who had had her kneecap removed. We reached the summit and decided to go down to Crummock Water but could not find a path.

We could see where we wanted to go so we took a direct rout down, the ground was full of bilberries all ready to eat and full of juice, soon we were a purple colour from our waists down. We slid more than walked but eventually arrived at the lake, had a drink and caught the bus back to Keswick.

Another occasion which nearly went wrong was when we decided to walk from Seatoller at the foot of Honister Pass along the ridge of Cat Bells back to Keswick. It was raining very fine rain which lasted all day, in those days the only waterproof clothing was all ex army which we reproofed with tent proofing; unfortunately mine needed proofing again and was letting in rain down my shoulders and back.

After an hour or two I was wet and cold yet Gill was fine. As I got colder I got more tired and sleepy, I just wanted to lie down.

We could not see exactly just where we were but we knew that if we went down to our right we would reach the main road.

It was a good job that Gill was with me otherwise I would have stopped then and there.

We reached the road and stood shivering waiting for the bus back to Keswick and when it arrived we must have looked awful because the driver was most concerned about us and me in particular.

All ended OK but it taught me that you need the best equipment and clothing in the Lakes.

First House

It was during my time as a policeman that I got married in the autumn of 1955. We had wanted to get married in the new church being built at Gammul Lane but it was not ready so we were married in The Blessed Sacrament Church where I had started school. Our best man was the footballer Tommy Docherty, the Preston North End and Scotland right-half. We had met Tommy and his wife Agnes and used to baby sit for them. At the time I was far fitter than Tommy even though he was a professional footballer.

We had saved up over £150 which was a lot of money, and on my 21st birthday my mum gave me £500 that had been awarded to me after my dad's accident. My mum had not used this money even though money must have been tight for her over the years, and as she gave me the money she also gave me all the cuttings, letters and papers to read in connection with my dad's fatal accident.

I read them and cried: it was the first and only time I had seen them. The papers where all disposed of by my mum at some time because when she died I had nothing at all belonging to my dad.

Houses in those days were a lot cheaper than now and because of the extra money we had we bought a semi-detached house at 17 Lauderdale Road, Ribbleton, which cost £2000. It was up the hill where my mum had wanted to buy one in 1932.

We bought the house from Mr and Mrs Watmough; Mr Watmough had been a decorator so the building was in very good condition, even though we did not like the decor.

We had the house before the wedding and used to go there and do some decorating and curtain fitting.

To have our own house in a very nice area was a dream come true. We were like two big kids playing at house but it was for real.

Gill was 18 years old and I was 21. When I look at my grandchildren now they appear very young even when they are 22 and older. We never even thought that we were too young to get married, I was absolutely sure that Gill was the person I wanted to be with for the rest of my life. I wanted to make a home full of love, with our children wanted and loved like no one had ever loved before. I felt so happy and lucky to be alive.

We used to go for walks or ride our bikes together, anything that did not cost money. We were saving up for our life together. We used to ride round the pubs and country places to see which we wanted to use for the wedding reception, I could not believe that many were all ready booked for the date we had in mind. Although we wanted a small wedding the list soon grew when we started putting names down on paper.

We started with immediate family, plus uncles, aunties, cousins etc. then friends; the list must have been about 30 people.

The final list was as follows;

Gill's mum and dad, Barry; Leonne and Barbara Redfern bridesmaids; Roy and Hilda Gorst. Leonne's parents, Bill and Edna Gorst, Dorothy Gorst, Joe and Doris Ashton, Joe and Aunty Madge Ashton, Bill and Doris Moon from work, and Ken, Barry's friend. (17)

Brian's mum, Tommy Docherty (Best Man) and Agnes, Margaret and Mary Barnes bridesmaids, Charlie and Agnes Barnes, Aunty Maggie and Cissie Hall, Molly and Frank Singleton, Marjorie and Harry Gillette, Auntie Agnes Platt, Jacky Brown, Brian's friend, Father Clegg, the priest who married us. (16) Total 33

We finally settled on a pub in Longridge called the Duke William Hotel for the reception. We did not tell anyone our plans for the honeymoon: I was learning to drive and the firm I was having lessons with said that if I passed they would hire me a car, an A35. The problem was that I could not take my driving test until the Wednesday before my wedding, so we planned a weekend in Blackpool in case I failed the test, then we would take the car if I passed and go to the Lake District for a week.

To help me with my driving lessons one of my pals, a policeman in the Lancashire County force, who was in the traffic division and used to be on the same shifts as me, would meet up with me in a quiet part of town and he would let me have a go at driving the police car. It was not easy with large police boots on but I will always remember the advice he gave me. "Anyone can drive fast but a good driver can and does drive slowly" I have passed this on to all my family; it is still true today 52 years on.

On the day of my driving test I had to start in Winkley Square and then drive towards Manchester Road. The roads are narrow with terraced houses and no gardens. I had only gone 200yds when a dog ran out of a house in front of the car, I slammed on the brakes, the car stopped and stalled but I missed the dog which ran off. I was instructed to start the car and proceed with the test. Somehow I felt a lot better because I knew I would react quickly in an emergency. I passed my test.

As the day of the wedding got closer both families started to get annoyed that they could not find out about our plans. Friends of both Gill and me tried to get it out of us.

1955 - The Wedding

Gill's mum was going to make all the dresses for the wedding so gran, Gill and I had a day out in Manchester to look for suitable material. We ended up at Affleck & Brown, a large department store; I was used as a mannequin to drape the material over to help the ladies to choose. The cost was £10, a week's wages, but it was worth every penny, just look at the photograph of the bride.

Gill carried a prayer book and white carnations. Gran also made the bridesmaid dresses, blue for the older ones, Barbara and Margaret, and white for the younger ones, Mary and Leonne.

Pop, my best man Tommy and I had rose buttonholes, and the others wore carnations.

Barry, Gill's brother, was in the army but managed to arrive at the church just in time for the service.

The church was only 400yds from my mum's house. My relations and friends gathered there and most walked to the church; people did not have cars as they do today. I had arranged for the wedding car to take my mum and the older guests, then return for me and Tommy. The car arrived very early and I refused to go then and told the driver to come back later. He did just that, much later, so much so that when Gill and her dad arrived they were told to go round the block as I had not arrived.

Eventually I arrived just before Gill got there and the wedding went off OK.

The press took photos but we were relying on Uncle Bill who was supposed to be a good photographer to do the wedding album; we never got one. The pictures you see in the book were taken by all different people but the one that is a classic is that of Gill on the stairs inside the hotel looking like a film star but more radiant and beautiful than any ordinary film star. I took a copy of this with me round the world.

We had soup, followed by roast turkey and then trifle: food was still short after the war. The cake was a round three tier one.

We only told the guests where we were going for our honeymoon after the reception when we were getting into the taxi to take us to Preston Railway Station.

There was a mad rush to get cars to follow us which they did; they caught up with us just before the train left the platform and duly covered us and another young couple with confetti as we left for Blackpool. After we waved goodbye we shook the confetti from our clothes and left for a clean carriage; the young couple did not want us to leave them with all the confetti in the carriage in case people thought that they were newly married.

We had booked a room on the front at North Shore. It was a cold October day and we walked round then went to the pictures.

On Monday we went back to our own house, hired the car as I had passed my driving test, and drove up to Keswick for the rest of the week. It was strange having our own house with just the two of us all the time, no one to disturb us, no one to ask permission from. It took a bit of time to get used to it but it was the best thing in the world, Gill and I in our house in our own world, perfection, all that I had dreamed about for many years had now come true.

1956 - Olympic Games Melbourne Australia

While I was still in the Police Force I swam for pleasure and fun, I swam in the Police Championships and won the event, which for me was easy. There was only one person who had beaten my old British Record and as there were three places to be filled in the 1956 Olympic Games at Melbourne Australia, Tom Banister, Gill and my mum suggested that I should get back into training to see if I could make the grade.

I was now a married man with a mortgage and a wife who was expecting a baby: I was also a policeman who would have to get six weeks off work since the team would be travelling by sea, so I decided to ask the Chief Constable if I could get time off work if I was picked.

I was marched into the Chief Constable's office, I saluted him and he said that when I was on mornings I could train in the afternoons, when I was on afternoons I could train in the mornings, and when I was on nights I could train all day. Then I was dismissed. Just as I turned to leave he said I had a piece of loose cotton on my gloves and I should get it seen to.

I did do three weeks of training and to my surprise I got back to my best time, which meant that I was still the second fastest butterfly swimmer in the country, but I was so tired. After talking it over with Gill I decided that my family was more important and decided not to resume competitive swimming.

1956 - Alison Mary Barnes 30th August.

After two months Gill was pregnant and we were more pleased than we could say; for me it was all coming true. I am not sure if Gill's mum agreed but we could not wait. Early in the New Year 1956, Gill caught a bug and the doctors thought we might lose the baby so she went into hospital. All the neighbours thought that we had been forced into the wedding until she came home still pregnant.

I was on nights when Gill phoned the station to say that she was going into hospital in labour. I was on my bike and at 2am signalled the ambulance to stop so that I could see Gill. She was OK but I thought that the baby would be born before I finished duty at 6am.

Of course it took longer than that, and as we did not have a phone and mobiles had not been invented, it was arranged that I would go to Tommy's house to sleep that morning because they had a phone. I woke up at 12noon but there was still no sign of the baby. I went round to Pop's house in Sulby Drive to wait for events to happen.

I phoned from the phone box every two hours, still no news, then at 4pm I was told to ring back in an hour. I decided to leave it an extra hour so I rang the hospital at 6pm. I was told that both were fine and well, I thought we had had twins until they said they meant mother and 7lb 1oz baby daughter, born 30th August 1956.

I ran all the way back to Pop's and gave them the news that we had a daughter. Off I went to Saint Joseph's Hospital in Mount Street, Preston, where I found my wife in bed but no baby: all they would let me do was to look at her through a glass window.

It was not until I took Gill and Alison home by taxi ten days later that I was allowed to hold my baby.

Alison was beautiful just like a little pixie. From the start I washed her nappies and changed her; I wanted to be involved in looking after my baby daughter.

I even invented the "Barnes Nappy Pooper Cleaner" this was a method of squirting the water from the tap by squeezing the rubber tube at the end of the tap so that a strong jet of water removed even the most impregnated poo from the nappy., and very successful it was too.

Pop and Gran bought us a grey Silver Cross high pram, and I was so proud to be out pushing the pram with Gill. We walked everywhere, we did not have a car, and Alison looked as if she was enjoying being the centre of attention which she was.

I bought myself a new cap made by Christie's, and for me it cost a lot of money; I came home in it and went to see Alison who was sat in the pram outside the rear door. She grabbed the hat from my head and I let her hold it: as usual she put it to her mouth and was then sick in it.

I can see the result swilling round inside my new hat as she gurgled and smiled at me. What could I do other than give her a big love? She can still twist me round her little finger, but I like it and would not change things even if I could.

Pop and I got on very well. He taught me how to decorate, wallpaper, paint and do odd jobs; it was his brain and my brawn. He also taught me subtle tricks like the time we papered the dining room: it was late at night when we put on the last strip in the corner by the fireplace. As we were cleaning up I noticed that the last piece, a narrow strip about 4 inches wide, was upside down. I told Pop who confirmed my worst fears, and then he said I was to tell no one and if we kept quiet no one would notice. We did and no one noticed for three years, then the day we moved to Leek I pointed it out and both Gill and Gran laughed because they had not seen it.

The house had only a single path from the road but there was room for a double drive to take a car. Pop and I decided to make a double drive and mix the concrete ourselves. Again my brawn and Pop's brains, so he used to tell me. We started by moving the concrete posts to the width we wanted, then we ordered the wrought iron gates from Reg Billington's firm, the lad I was in the RAF with.

We set the gate posts and fitted the gates, a week later Mr Brown from next door but one asked why we had different patterns on the two posts. We thought that he was winding us up, but when we looked we had got one post back to front. Again I was sworn to secrecy, again it worked.

Another incident occurred when we were concreting the double drive from the gates to the house, the last section. We had been at it all day and only finished the last bit as it got dark; we placed wooden planks across the wet concrete to stop anyone walking on it until it had set. We were in the house having a cup of tea when the front door bell rang, it was dark outside but as we opened the door we could see Geoff, the policeman, had stepped over the planks and walked the full length of the wet concrete leaving his size eleven footprints all the way from the gate.

I cannot print what was said by Pop or myself, suffice to say that Geoff left very quickly while Pop and I rigged lights so that we could see as we trowelled the surface to repair the damage.

Smog

During the early 1950s the air pollution in Britain was at its worst. Smoke from coal fires, mixed with fog to create smog was a killer. Alison's first winter was so bad that one day when I was cycling home from work as a policeman I missed the turning into our road. Visibility was down to a few feet at best.

One day when Gill was out her mum was looking after Alison at her home in Sulby Drive, half a mile away from Lauderdale Road were we lived. The smog was so bad that you could not see across the road. I was worried about crossing the junction of Longridge Road with Gammul Lane, because this was where the buses turned round. Gran decided to come with me; she pushed the pram with Alison in it and I went into the middle of the junction to see if it was clear for Gran and the pram to cross. I could not see Gran so I had to shout that it was OK then take a risk that it would stay clear until they managed to cross safely. I have never seen anything like it before or since, thank God. It was weather like this that prompted the government to introduce the Clean Air Act, after thousands of people died as a result of the pollution.

We did not own a car nor did any of the family but one of the men Gill worked with, John Abraham, said we could always hire his for a day or so. It was a large Humber Hawk, an old one but it had plenty of room. It did not do many miles to the gallon but it was worth it to get out for a day. The first time we borrowed it we had a puncture: I changed the wheel and said that I would get it repaired when we got home, which I did.

The second time we took the car out, and the third time, we also had punctures. I was getting very good at changing wheels but the news from the garage was that there was no more room for another patch as there were more patches than tyre. We offered to get a new tyre but John said he would see to it.

The next time we had the car Aunty Dorothy, Gran, Pop and Alison were all in the car when we went to the Lakes for the day. Coming back we had just gone through Burton on the A6 when we felt a knocking at the front of the car. Dorothy had been saying for some miles that there was a noise but no one took any notice of her.

I thought that it must be a puncture but no, the tyres were all OK. We set off but stopped after a hundred yards with the knocking much worse, the tyres look fine but when Pop got hold of the front nearside wheel it almost came off in his hands. Only one of the four nuts was still on the wheel. Dorothy thought that it was so funny when we had to walk back to the village to get spare nuts, but it could have been serious. The problem was made worse when we could not find any nuts so we took one nut from each of the other wheels to get us back home.

Eddie Walmsley, my school friend, had a scooter which was all the rage at the time. I never fancied a scooter or a motorbike, I always wanted comfort. Eddie was constantly trying to get me to go on the scooter, so one day he took me for a ride. When we returned to our house I asked if I could have a go at driving, I got on the front with Eddie on the back; Gill stood watching holding Alison who waved as we set off. Our road was still unadopted which meant that it was unmade. As we approached the main road there was a large articulated lorry coming from our right. I know that I should have stopped but I was not sure which was the brake so I accelerated out of the road in front of the lorry with Eddie shouting at the top of his voice that I was a silly bugger, or words to that effect.

The driver of the lorry was not at all pleased and showed it by revving up the empty vehicle and chasing after us. The only thing I could think of was to get away from the lorry, Eddie was shouting for me to stop, but I knew that it was going to Courtaulds factory half a mile away so I just kept going. Faster and faster with the lorry doing the same, it must have looked funny to anyone watching but not to me or Eddie. As we passed the gates to the factory the lorry turned in as I knew it would then I heard Eddie's voice. "For God's sake stop", he shouted. I still did not know how to so I just slowed down and then turned off the key, we slowed and I ran into a hedge by the side of the main road.

After many words and a long rest we went home with Eddie driving and me sat on the back. I have never been on a two-wheeled machine since.

CHAPTER SIX

1957 - Schools Swimming Instructor

1957 Schools Swimming Instructor

One night in the spring of 1957 I was sitting in the police car with my pal Geoff from the Lancashire County Police force who was telling me of a job he had put in for: School Swimming Instructor with the Preston Education Department. I had not even heard of the job or seen it advertised. Geoff said that it was the same salary as the police but had school holidays and hours, with no nights.

I asked Geoff if he would mind if I put in for the job also. I could tell that he was disappointed but said that he did not mind. I found out that the present instructor, Ray Scholy who I knew very well, lived in Blackburn and had been appointed to the same job in his home town.

I applied and got the job: it was a dream come true, no nights, 13 weeks holiday a year and the same money, but best of all I knew more about swimming than anyone else, quite the opposite of being a policeman and all the laws of the land. The press made great play of the fact that the local Olympic Swimmer was now teaching local children to swim. The kids thought it was cool too.

1957 Catherine Ann Barnes 5th November

Because I was working at Saul Street Baths, next to the shop where my mum worked, she thought it would be a good idea if she bought a car so that we could go to work together. I thought this was a great idea and so we, or at least my mum, bought a 2 litre Standard Vanguard. It was a large blue car and Alison used to sit on the pull down arm on the rear seat. I started to teach my mum to drive but the car was far too big so she changed it for a new Austin A35 which cost £550. At the age of 55 my mum passed her test at the 2nd attempt which I thought was brilliant seeing that she was so nervous that I could not tell her I was going to give her a driving lesson until she got into the car.

It was great to see more of Gill and Alison, and soon we would be adding to the Barnes family as we both looked forward to the birth of our second baby. Gill was getting bigger and bigger as she got to the end of October into November and, after staying in most of the time, we decided to go to the Empire to see a horror film, Frankenstein. While we were there Gill said she thought it would be a good idea to head home as soon as possible: we did and Cath was born at 9-30pm that night, bonfire night 5th November 1957 in St Joseph's, Mount Street, Preston.

Once again I had to wait to hold my daughter until we left the hospital when she was a week old. We thought that if we had any more children they would be born at home.

Catherine was 8lb 3oz, a large baby, so cuddly and lovable. Alison loved her sister and could not wait to be able to play with her. Alison had slept reasonably well as a baby but not Cath; she was and still is a night bird. We tried everything to get her to sleep at night, we even gave her tots of brandy but still she stayed awake.

Both my mum and Gills' mum thought that we did not know how to deal with Cath so we suggested that they stay for a night or two, which they both did in turn. There was no change and neither of them could stand more than a few nights each without sleep. They went home leaving us at least with the satisfaction of knowing that it was not just us.

We had a good young doctor called Dr. Scarret, who also had small children like ours. He gave us some strong medicine but when that did not work he said that we would just have to take shifts because there was nothing more he could do. He said some children need very little sleep.

We decided to take sleep when we could; while one stayed awake the other tried to get some rest. On the 6th December 1958, exactly 13 months after Cath was born, Gill and I both woke up in the night and said at the same time "Have you been to Cath?" When we realised that neither of us had been we rushed into her bedroom to find her fast asleep: for the first time in her life Cath had slept through the night. She was 13 months old.

We now had two beautiful daughters. Alison was prim, always clean, very upright, so that when you went to pick her up she jumped up in your arms. Cath was the opposite: cuddly, floppy, and when you tried to pick her up she just melted in your arms and went like a dead weight, but a loveable dead weight.

The two girls played together and when we all went out I felt like a real dad with a real family.

I had all the school holidays, 13 weeks each year. One of the teachers used to work part-time on the docks at Preston as casual labour unloading bananas. He asked me if I wanted to earn a bit of extra cash, which I did so I joined him and stood in line on the dockside with all the other casual labourers waiting for the foreman to pick out those he wanted to work that day. When I looked around I recognised many of the men I had locked up as a policeman, but no one said anything. If you were picked out you worked that day for a set amount for a number of hours. The work was all labour, moving bananas from the hold to the dockside. You could find very large spiders called tarantulas about the size of your hand. They would be dead having been in the refrigerated hold for a week or more, but I did not know this, so when one of the lads threw one for me to catch I caught it then screamed and dropped it. They all laughed; it was what they did to all the new boys.

We were allowed to take home off the docks as many bananas as you could carry, you just had to pay 2s 6d (12½p) to get a receipt. We were the only two to pay for a receipt but we had a reputation to think about as well as our jobs; the rest had nothing to lose.

I enjoyed teaching swimming. I was full-time but there was a part-time instructor called Mrs Lea, who was excellent at getting timid children into the water and teaching them to swim. I learnt a lot by watching her with the young ones. If we had one large class between us I took the better swimmers and Mrs Lea taught the very beginners.

We used the public baths which meant that others were in the pool at the same time; this presented a very difficult environment when the Catholic schools were on holiday while the Protestants were not. On summer days there could be over 100 swimmers playing in the pool when we were supposed to teach a class of 30. It was a day such as this that I had a visit from a Government Schools Inspector, who came to observe me at work.

I lined up the 30 children, counted them and said that when I blew my whistle they had to come out of the water and line up again, as they were now. Then I told them to go and play. Half an hour later I blew my whistle and 30 children lined up for me, and then I sent them to get changed. The Inspector was impressed and agreed that there was no alternative given the current situation; at least they had all enjoyed themselves and were safe.

1958 Trip to France

We used to baby sit for our friends Stan and Marge Taylor when they lived in a detached house with a large garden and paddock. Stan used to live next door to me in Dorman Road.

Stan was a self-made business man who was building houses and also had an estate agency business.

In 1958 they asked us to go with them to the Mediterranean in Stan's car, a large Jaguar saloon.

We had no money but Stan said he would pay for the trip and I could work it off by working in the holidays on his building site. I had 13 weeks off each year then because of the school holidays.

It was all last minute: Gran looked after the two girls and off we went, no bookings even on the channel ferry. We were last on and first off.

We drove and navigated in twos, Stan and Gill, Marge and me. We left Preston and drove overnight to the ferry at Dover, no motorways then. The journey through France was much longer than we thought. Each country, England, France etc had a full page on the map, but the scale was totally different, so it took far longer to drive a page in France.

To keep costs down we had tents and camping equipment in the car. We drove day and night until we reached the blue Mediterranean at Frejus. Gill and I had never seen such blue clear water before. The campsite was stony, the weather was very hot and we found that ants love jam and sugar. Next to our tent was a campervan which appeared to me to be far more civilised. (I later bought one).

We moved along the coast through Nice to Monte Carlo where I was left on the beach while the others went shopping I ended up overcooked but that was the least of my troubles as we went to a very nice restaurant for a meal. At the end of the meal Marge grabbed Gill and left leaving Stan with me wondering what was going on. Stan said he had no francs only pounds sterling.

He offered the waiter English pounds who immediately shouted for the manager and we found ourselves surrounded by four very large waiters. I was frightened but Stan said it was all he had. Negotiations started and Stan even managed to get a better rate of exchange than he should. We left with all our limbs intact but it happened every time we left a country.

We never did erect the tent again; we just slept in the open. We would look out for a long drive to a hotel or villa, then go back after midnight, park the car and sleep on the ground. As this was hit and miss especially for the girls we decided to book into a hotel when we got to Alassio in Italy. I say hotel: we did a deal with a member of the staff to let us sleep in the staff quarters if we ate in the hotel. This was the first night in a proper bed since we left Preston; the celebration resulted in our littlest, Gillian.

We travelled up to the Italian lakes and stayed in Como, then into Switzerland and back to Paris. While we were in Switzerland we stopped one early morning by the roadside all feeling very hungry. We got out the primus stove and had a great fry-up, bacon, eggs, tomatoes, sausages, the lot. Gill had her plate on the grass when she stood on the edge and flipped the contents onto her shoe: she was so hungry she just flipped it all back and ate the lot.

We arrived in Paris early on Sunday morning. We visited the Sacre Coeur, Notre Dame, the Eiffel Tower, the Arc de Triomphe, and left to get to the ferry in the afternoon. When we arrived back in Preston we were exhausted after driving over 2,000 miles in 10 days but it was worth it.

Stan and Marge used to have very good parties at their house which was larger than most.

Stan was a party person, Marge was great at organising, and the food was always excellent. One New Year's Eve they held a fancy dress party: Gill wore my mum's wedding dress (1930s) and I went as Hilda Baker's stooge wearing my mum's real fox fur. One person came in a full hunting pink outfit. As the night wore on and the drink flowed the party was in full swing when the "hunting pink" got a pony from the paddock and rode it through the house chasing me and the "fox fur" shouting "tally-ho-tally-ho". It was a good job that Marge had gone to bed.

As time went on I realised that if I wanted to progress I would have to move into management. I talked to the Baths Superintendent, Mr Goodlad, who advised me to sit the examination of the Institute of Baths Management. I also realised that if I wanted to be a manager I would have to move away from Preston. I talked it over with Gill and we both agreed that I should take the exams and apply for jobs wherever they came up. This did not please my mum.

The nearest course of training was at Burnley organised by the Baths Superintendent, Tom Anderson. Every Tuesday night throughout the winter of 1958 I travelled to Tom's classes and studied the rest of the time. In the spring of 1959 I passed the intermediate examination of the Institute and started looking for jobs in baths management.

Mr Goodlad took me into his very small office and gave me some of the best advice I have ever heard. He said "Most people think that Tom Banister is the superintendent and runs the place, which suits me because he does the work but I hold all the purse strings". He went on to explain that whoever controls the money or resources is the one in charge. It is true even in government. He then showed me how he kept the records of all the expenditure and income for every single event that took place in the building, all hand-written by him in a large ledger. He had ledgers for every year that he had been there. No one else, not even the Borough Treasurer, had so much information. You cannot have too much relevant financial information in business.

I have always followed this method of working throughout my life and I even use it at home for running the house and keeping Jamie's sailing campaign expenses.

CHAPTER SEVEN

1959 - 1962 Management Leek UDC & Leicester City

Baths Management

Jobs were advertised in the journal of the Institute of Baths Superintendents, "*Baths Service*", which came out monthly but the weekly publication "*Municipal Journal*" was the most useful. I saw an advertisement for a baths manager at Normanton in Yorkshire, which I had to look up in the atlas to find the exact location, so I applied. I got invited to attend the short list of six applicants.

I was to find out that most interviews were conducted in alphabetical order which meant that I was usually in first. After we had all been in we talked to each other and all thought that Sid Handforth, who was very untidy and sloppy, had no chance, but to everyone's surprise Sid was offered the job. Just as I was leaving the chairman of the interviewing panel called me back to say that they had been most impressed by me but as I had not managed a swimming pool they could not appoint me. He strongly advised me to get management experience. With that in mind I asked Sid where he was currently the manager, and Sid said Leek in Staffordshire.

After talking it over with Gill I decided to apply for that job when it became vacant.

1959 Gillian Mary Barnes 19 June - Leek

Leek was an old pool built in 1853, and was 106 years old. It had only one small pool, 6 slipper (private) baths, a small laundry and a flat on the first floor over the offices, which went with the job. It had a staff of two plus the manager.

I applied for the job but Gill did not go with me as she was expecting our third child, so Gran, Gill's mum, travelled with me for the interview. I was appointed to my first Bath Manager's position.

There was a flat with the job so we had to sell our house as well as get ready for Gillian's arrival. This enabled us to buy our own transport, a New Bedford Dormobile campervan. My mum was not at all pleased at my leaving Preston, and Leek was 60 miles away.

We expected Gillian to arrive prior to my taking up my new position for I had to give a month's notice. In the event, due to Gillian's late arrival, (nothing has changed over the years) I moved to Leek on my own with a camp bed and a bureau, and I had a cooker which was part of the flat. The local newspaper was full of the fact that the new baths manager was an Olympic swimmer but also covered the fact that my wife was still at home waiting for our baby to arrive.

I was very excited to have my own baths and to be in charge at last. I had an arrangement with the town hall switchboard that if there was any information from Preston it was to be passed to me as a matter of urgency. A week went by, then a second week, with no news; I went home each Sunday but no Gillian. The third week I travelled home on Sunday then Wednesday after a phone call, then again for the real event on Friday, when I was able to be present at the birth which took place at home. It was the most wonderful experience I have ever had and I was able to immediately hold my daughter and not have to wait for 10 days.

When I returned to work the day after, (no paternity leave then) the whole town had the news: it was like a Royal Proclamation. Gill joined me three weeks later, and I was so proud. We converted one of the ground-floor rooms into a lounge in order to save us going up and down the stairs during the day. Gillian used to be in the high pram in the entrance because everyone wanted to see the cause of the delay.

Leek U D C 1959 - 60

My move to Leek was an important milestone in my life; it was my first job as a manager, the person in charge, the person who takes all the glory and all the blame. 'The buck stops on my desk', as a famous American President once said.

Leek is a small market town in Staffordshire on the main road to Buxton from the Potteries.

At that time, 1959, the baths were situated in the centre of the town by a roundabout, in the middle of which was a large clock which chimed every ¼ hour (more of this later). The building was 106 years old; over the entrance running the full width of the building was a first floor flat for the manager. The flat, plus the cost of electric, heating and water was included in the salary package. This was a common practice in those days.

I was required to attend council meetings and meetings of the committee that dealt specifically with the swimming pool, where I would make my monthly report and answer any questions the council members wanted to ask me. The proceedings were fully reported in the local newspaper, and I loved every minute if it.

I was amazed to find that there was no swimming club in the town since it had been disbanded many years earlier, and no provision for teaching swimming to the general public other than the school children who attended in formal classes.

I found that there were many large solid silver trophies stored in the Council vaults which had been presented to the former swimming club. I told the council that I intended to restart the swimming club and introduce swimming lessons for both adults and children. The press immediately took up the idea and soon I was able to call a public meeting which agreed to re-form the Leek Amateur Swimming Club. I was in the press, both local and regional, talking about the revival of the Swimming Club and what I would do for the town.

Because of the publicity we made many good friends, which was especially good for Gill and the girls who felt as if they had been living in Leek for years.

All the council members were elected as independents, although you could tell who supported the various political parties. Gill made a good friend of Isabel Smith, the wife of Stan Smith, a prominent councillor who had a very large building business in the area. She had young children and a large garden in which all the girls could play.

Her husband's business was converting an out of town old barn into a restaurant; the building had been derelict for many years and without a roof. This had weathered the old oak beams so that they appeared to be white. These oak beams were to be the centre of attraction in the conversion. One day Stan came home in a foul mood cursing his incompetent staff; and after a few whiskeys he told us that the painter had painted his oak beams and ruined the whole scheme.

Life for me was different, with new problems and challenges but very enjoyable. I learned much from mistakes and achievements, and the former will always stay in my mind. Gill on the other hand had to cope with being away from home for the first time as well as being mother to three daughters and a husband. No one could have done it as well because it was impossible to do it any better. I only had two staff but every night after the baths closed I cleaned the pool surround and the changing cubicles with bleach then hosed it all down, so I knew that the place was clean. On the night that I had a meeting Gill would do the cleaning for me even though I had asked her not to. We were a very good team and still are, the "A team."

The baths were very popular which meant that on Sundays, when we were only open until 12noon it was always difficult to get the public to leave the water at 11-30am. Gill had a solution though: she started to cook bacon and eggs in the flat upstairs but opened the window so that the cooking smell filled the pool which made every one hungry, so off they went home for a bacon sandwich.

The filter for the swimming pool had not been emptied for many years; nobody at the council could remember it ever being done. I decided to empty it, clean it out and refill it with fresh graded sand. There are two manholes to allow a man to get inside and to shovel the sand out, which is a tiring, hot job but I did it. To refit the manhole covers I needed a special washer. I could not get one from the manufacturers so I asked a firm to provide me with a piece of fabric from which I could cut 2 washers to fit the filter. When the fabric arrived there was enough to make washers for every filter in the country. I got on to the manufacturers who told me that they had sacked the salesman who had ordered too much in order to boost his commission. They agreed to take half back but even so we were left with enough to last the council for 50 years. From then on I have been very wary of salesmen advising me on amounts to order: once bitten, twice shy.

The boiler was oil-fired; there was a maintenance agreement for the servicing of the burner. I sat with the fitter all day as he dismantled the burner, cleaned all the parts and reassembled them, and after that I cancelled the agreement and did the job myself. This is the best way to learn. While I was working on the boiler one day I saw a very large rat. I shut the door and sent for the council vermin controller. The man came and we saw the rat climb into a dustbin in the passage by the boiler house. We pushed the lid on tight, and we could hear it scratching inside. The controller said it was better to take the bin with the rat away and I agreed with him. I was glad to see the end of that, but we still had bait put down which must have worked because that was the last we saw of them.

The only time the baths were closed to the public was on Sunday afternoon, when we used to have a quiet swim with the girls and sometimes friends. One afternoon both Gill and I were doing something around the building, Alison and Catherine were playing with their dolls and prams, when we heard a scream and a splash. We both rushed onto the bath side to see Cath standing screaming at the water and Alison in the water holding on to the rail making her way to the shallow end. Alison's pram with teddy, her beloved Rupert, was at the bottom of the deep end. We got Alison out of the water and comforted both her and Cath. It was a very near thing, and affected Alison for the rest of her life: she never liked water and did not want to learn to swim though she was only three. Later when she was ten she swam a mile then said she would never swim again. And she didn't.

We had both my mum and Gill's mum and dad to stay with us but none of them could sleep because of the chiming of the clock outside; we could not understand because we never heard it. The only time it woke us both up was one night when it stopped. It was hard, physical work for both of us and we were glad to get to bed. Having three young daughters though meant that we had a lot of broken sleep. One night we woke up and could not find Catherine: we had a look round the flat and found her with her teddy under her arm and the lavatory brush in her other hand standing by the toilet. When we asked her what she was doing she said "Dus bushing". We picked her up gave her a big kiss and a hug and off she went back to bed.

Because we had sold the house to move to Leek we were able to buy a car. We bought a Dormobile campervan, which was great for the kids and we could even get the large pram in it.

It was in this van that Gill took her driving test; it was not easy to drive, much larger than a car. I taught her and said that she must not reverse this van without making sure that the back was clear because you could not see from the driver's seat. On her test Gill asked the examiner to get out to see if the rear was safe to reverse; he refused but did not ask her to reverse and she passed first time. Gill was now mobile which made a lot of difference to both our lives.

1959 was a very good summer with many dry sunny days; it was great to be able to plan a picnic a week ahead knowing that it would be fine weather. Our favourite place after the park was Rudyard Lake, a man-made lake which was used to fill up the canals in the area.

I received a phone call from Tom Anderson, the Baths Manager at Burnley, who had coached me through the exams. He had just been appointed to the post of General Manager at the City of Leicester, his wife's home town, and he was looking for a deputy and asked if I was interested. I was thrilled to be asked and said I would like to work with Tom. I had only been at Leek 12 months when I left to go to Leicester.

Gill had agreed to move but it meant that I would have to find a place as there was no housing with the job.

We decided that Gill and the girls would move back to Preston and stay with my mum, I would get lodgings on a temporary basis, and the house contents would go into storage. The new job paid more than I was getting at Leek but we had to find a house and pay for our light and heating.

The day we left the flat Mrs Salt who lived across the road from the baths offered to make a meal for us before we left. We all went to her house and sat down for the meal when both Gill and me asked "Where is Gillian"? We looked at each other each of us thinking that the other had brought her, then we realised that she was still at the baths sitting in the pram as happy as can be smiling at anyone who looked at her.

We also realised that the Dormobile was not going to be as useful as we thought so we exchanged it for a new Simca, a fast sporty French Saloon car.

Leicester City 1960 -62

Tom Anderson was also in the same position as me at first; we were both on our own in B&Bs. After a month living away from my family, only seeing them at weekends I decided to look for temporary accommodation. During my lunch break I would visit estate agents in the city centre but I could not find anything. As I became more desperate I decided to rent a terraced house at the corner of Ash Street in the centre of town. The estate agent was reluctant to show me the property as he thought that it was not good enough for me and my family.

It was a Victorian terraced house with steep steps to the front door and even steeper steps to get upstairs. It had two handrails just like those you see on ships which look vertical. The plot of land on which the house was built was shaped like a triangle, the widest part at the front going to a point in the yard at the rear, where the only toilet was. I explained to Gill that this was all I could get so it was Ash Street or carry on living apart. Gill as usual said we must be together and so we moved to Ash Street, all five of us. The furniture was brought out of storage and we made a home out of a property that I would never have thought of living in before we were married.

I had an office in the baths in the centre of the city in Vestry Street, which was next to the old indoor market. The boilers for the baths also heated the market. The Vestry Street Baths were old and waiting to be demolished when the planned new baths were built.

There were two pools in the building and many slipper baths which were in constant use, especially at the weekend. The department consisted of other baths at Spence Street, Cossington Street, and Aylestone where there was a very large laundry employing 60 women and two men. The laundry washed 30,000 articles of clothing each week. (More about this later).

1961 saw a large influx of Asian immigrants who were concentrated in Leicester. The first thing we noticed was a problem in the slipper baths; most Asians wanted two lots of water when using the slipper baths and used to oil themselves down prior to leaving the cubicle. This caused problems with other people waiting in the queue as it took twice as long to bathe and the staff refused to clean out the oily baths left by the Asians. We decided that they could only have one bath of water and they were not allowed to use oil.

While I was at Leicester Tom introduced vending machines, the first time they had been used in a public baths. We had chocolate bar machines that dispensed a bar for 6d (2 ½ new pence) and I had the job of supervising the trial. I put in the machine 100 bars of chocolate and when I came to refill it I expected to have 100 sixpences. This never happened, as the kids soon realised that if they told the receptionist that they had put 6d in but did not get any chocolate they would be given another 6d. When we stopped this we found the machine full of metal washers the same size as a 6d.

The auditors came along and to my surprise asked me how long it took me to check all the filling and counting of the machines., When I told them they said that I was not to bother but just keep filling the machine and over a 3 months period see if we made a profit or a loss, because it was costing more to check it than we were making. The results over many months showed a profit so we not only kept the machine but installed many others in all the baths. 40 years later they are everywhere. Lesson learned: don't spend more on checking things out than they are worth.

At Spence Street Baths there was a steam room in the Russian Baths which was very popular, but we started to get complaints that homosexuals were using the facilities and embarrassing customers. Tom approached me and said, "You were once a policeman so go and sort it out." As I arrived at Spence Street a regular customer solved the problem for me: I walked into the area outside the steam room to see the door burst open and a body fly out horizontally and land against the wall at my feet. At the door to the steam room was a large, tough looking man aged about 30 who said, "If you come back in here again I will really sort you out." That was the end of the problem.

Life at Ash Street was awful; the only good thing was the fact that we were all together. We decided to sell the car and purchase a house, just at the time the government removed the purchase tax on cars which knocked the bottom out of the second-hand market. We could not afford to sell the car, nor could we afford to run it.

My mum lent us £500 to put a deposit on a two-bedroomed bungalow in Thurmaston, just outside Leicester on the Nottingham road. The price was £1800. We had a garden, a garage and a greenhouse.

The girls all slept in one bedroom with Alison and Cath in bunk beds, Alison in the top bunk. One night Cath was not very well and after getting up a number of times in the night we moved Cath into our bed with Gill and I got into the lower bunk. At about 7am I was woken by being hit on the head with something. I immediately sat up and banged my head on the top bunk, and as I shouted out a terrified Alison looked down at me from above saying over and over again "Sorry Dad, sorry". It was a routine of the girls to annoy each other by Cath kicking the underside of Alison's bed (forever after referred to as 'striking the bunks') and Alison hitting Cath with her cold hot-water bottle.

In order to help with the finances Gill taught swimming at the baths each Sunday morning for £1-10shillings, (£1.50) while I made the Sunday lunch. I stopped using the car to get to work and used my bike instead.

We did not have the money for us both to go to the cinema so we took it in turns; we were hard up but very happy to be together as a family.

Alison started school at Leicester. She was terrified and so were we, but after the first day she managed. It is always harder for the eldest child because the others had a big sister to show them the way.

Bradgate Park was a large park on the outskirts of town where there were deer roaming around. It was one of the favourite places the girls liked to go. During one visit in the spring the girls were eating ice creams when a young deer came over to see if there was any food to spare; Gillian was in a pushchair eating her cornet when the deer went up to her, she held out the cornet for it to see what she was eating, and it took the lot. Poor Gillian, she cried while Cath and Alison laughed, so we bought her a second one.

Laundry

As I said the laundry was a commercial one, washing 30,000 articles each week. We did the laundry for the remand homes in the county, the university halls of residence, the ambulance service, the county cricket club, the Leicester City football club, and all the council departments including social services homes.

We had our own large laundry van with driver so that each day the washing arrived, was sorted, washed, ironed and packed ready for delivery the next day. The only day we did not wash was Sunday.

Part of the training and examinations for being a Baths Manager included laundry work and management, but because I had never worked in such a large laundry I decided to work full time for two weeks in the laundry alongside the workforce, even though I still had my own job to do as well. I got a pair of overalls from the stores and started work at 7-30am on a Monday morning.

There were three large 100cwt washing machines then a bank of smaller capacity machines; at about 9am when I was attending to one of the large machines the men emptied all the machines simultaneously. As the water flowed out the drains would not take it and the floor flooded. I was not wearing wellingtons and got my feet very wet. I had been set up, all the staff knew what was about to happen and had a good laugh at my expense. It seems that they had been asking for the drains to be fixed for over a year but nothing had been done. I arranged for it to be sorted at the weekend in order not to disrupt the laundry.

On the first Friday I had to go into my office for a meeting so I did not get to the laundry until 11am. As I entered the main room where the women worked their shop steward said aloud to one of the girls, "If he works here he can keep our hours." They started at 8am each morning Monday to Friday. I said nothing but got to work with the machines.

On Saturday only the men worked, washing towels for the department.

Monday morning I was at the laundry as the women arrived, and as soon as the shop steward came in I said "Where were you on Saturday and Sunday?" "What do you mean?" she shouted, "We don't work at weekends." "Well," I said, "I worked all Saturday and all day Sunday so if I have to work your hours you can work mine," and with that I went back to work. From then on I had a good relationship with all the women and especially with the shop steward.

Another reason for going to Leicester baths department was the entertainment that they promoted. It was always part of the baths manager's job to cover over some of the swimming pools in winter to provide a large hall for various activities from sport to entertainment.

In many towns the main or only hall was the converted swimming pool.

In Leicester, Spence Street baths used to promote professional wrestling which was very popular in the 60s. Joint Promotions had the television rights with Kent Walton the presenter and commentator. Wrestling is entertainment and although bouts are fought, it was not who won that decided the payment but the level of entertainment that the fans got. Usually there is a "good guy" and a "bad guy": two of the best at that time were Mick MacManus and Jackie Pallo, with Mick being the bad guy.

Out of the ring they were two really nice men. Pop and Gran had never been to a wrestling match before, so I arranged for them to have ringside seats, and I also told both Mick and Jackie where they were sitting and who they were.

The bout started and Mick soon started "fouling" Jackie and "breaking the rules". The spectators started to shout at the referee and began booing Mick; with that he threw Jackie out of the ring so that he landed on Gran's lap. Gran helped Jackie to his feet and started to hit Mick with her handbag as he came out after Jackie; other women helped Gran to have a go at Mick. I could not believe what I had seen: little Gran having a go at a big wrestler believing that it was a serious fight. Although I tried to explain it all to Gran I don't think she believed me.

While I was here I studied for my final exams in Baths Management and used to go to Nottingham Tech with some of the other staff. We also let as many of the branch managers as possible attend Institute of Bath Manager's meetings in the Midlands area. We took the department car. The problem was that Tom Anderson, the General Manager, was always late for any meeting we set so in the end we used to tell Tom that we would meet half an hour sooner than it was, and it worked.

1961 was the year of the Asian Flu epidemic with most of the country going down with it. The department was no exception; Tom caught it, as did most of the managers, and then the laundry van driver got it. I was told that I was the only one left to drive the van. I called at the council depot to collect what to me seemed a very large van. I was given the keys and told to move it as there was someone behind waiting to get out. I climbed up into the driver's seat and looked round: it was huge. I could not see behind other than through the wing mirrors, which I was not used to. I very slowly moved forward to the shouts of the men telling me to get on with it. As I got out into the city centre I realised that I could see over all the cars and most of the other vehicles.

When the police on point duty recognised the van and waved me on, I felt much better. I had to go to the laundry to collect the washing to be delivered then pick up a load on the return journey, and as I did not know the route I had arranged for the trainee manager to come with me to show me the way.

As time went by I got used to driving the van and actually began to enjoy it. Out we went into the countryside to a remand home. There was a main gate then a circular gravel road off which was a side path into which I had to reverse the van up to the door for the laundry crates to be loaded. In the centre of the circular drive was a beautiful lawn with white posts with a chain link all round. I started to reverse the van; I was doing so well until someone shouted and I could see these white posts with the chain appearing from underneath the front of the van as I ran half on the lawn. I have never been so embarrassed in all my life.

We quickly loaded the crates and left to the shouts of the staff and inmates. I managed a full week driving and still doing my own job as well as doing Tom's, then I went down with the flu but by this time Tom had come back to work.

After 18 months Tom asked me to sack a woman who worked in the laundry. She was an alcoholic who had been given numerous warnings about not being fit for work but this time she had to go. I spoke to the shop steward who was expecting the decision and who reluctantly agreed that it was necessary. It is not pleasant sacking anyone even if they do deserve it, and unknown to me she went to headquarters and saw Tom who after listening to her pleading reinstated her. I was livid and told Tom that he would have to sack people himself in future. He agreed that he was a soft touch but that was the time I started to look for another job.

CHAPTER EIGHT

1962 - 1964 Wombwell UDC

I had been at Leicester 20 months when I managed to get the job as Baths and Entertainments Manager at Wombwell in South Yorkshire. We sold the bungalow for £2,000, a profit of £200 but that went in fees and removal costs. However I had an increase in salary and there was a house with the job with free rent, coal, and electricity. We were rich at last.

Wombwell U D C 1962-64

Wombwell is a mining town. There were seven active coal mines within the council boundary and everyone had connections with the pits. The Coal Board's policy of taking out a complete seam of coal and then paying compensation for the damage to property that this caused was evident throughout the town. If you lived directly over the seam you were OK, because the land just lowered itself by two or three feet: it was the property on each edge of the seam that suffered the most damage as part of a building would slip or crack away from the rest.

The baths consisted of two pools one large (25yds long) and a small teaching pool; there was a separate café area as well as slipper baths. The heating was of course provided by two coal fired Lancashire boilers. In the winter months both pools were covered over; the main pool was the dance hall with full stage facilities while the small pool became the bar. The large café area served both facilities summer and winter.

The hall catered for everything in the town from the Civic Ball to Ideal Homes Exhibitions, and both council-organised dances and private functions. It was the centre of the town's social life. The building had only been open for 50 years when I arrived yet I was only the third manager; each of the other two had served 25 years.

The house provided for us was a semi-detached council house 50 yards from the baths, separated only by allotments. There was a garage for my car at the baths.

From previous experience with three children we knew that the first thing we had to do was to find a good doctor and this proved no exception. As we packed the car to leave Leicester that morning Alison had a high temperature and was not at all well, we thought she had German measles. She got worse as we travelled but it was Gillian who had a fit just as we arrived.

The staff at the baths called out Dr Bell who took all her clothes off to get her to cool down. What a way to start a new life and job.

There were five permanent staff: three women, Jessie, Elsie, Abby and two men, Jim and Ken. The men looked after the plant and Jessie the office, with everyone working on the baths side in summer.

All the record books were large ledgers which when opened gave a complete record for each month; the writing was all in copper plate. Jessie not only knew every child that came in for a swim but also knew equally well their parents, having worked at the baths all her life. Jim Tabener was a gem: older than Ken who was in his twenties, he had a lot of experience with the plant and the operation of the building. Between Jessie and Jim there was all the knowledge I needed to call on.

When I was appointed I had to give a month's notice to Leicester Council and during this time the Civic Ball was to be held at Wombwell. As it was always organised by the manager I was invited to attend as the council's guest to see how it was run. I left Gill and the girls and went up to Wombwell by car, and what an event it was! I was shocked by the very low standard of the meal and by the whole event. I left early knowing that I could not fail to improve on the event next year.

I officially started work on 1st April 1962. My first week was the last week of the winter dancing season: this was the time of rock and roll but the council still had an 18 piece dance band on the stage, which no one wanted. There were more people on the stage than were dancing on the dance floor.

My first reaction was to ditch the dance band and get groups for the winter season, but to my horror, Harry Swift, the leader of the band told me that he had signed a new three-year contract just before I had started. I was amazed and annoyed that I had been left with this mess.

I told Harry Swift that I would not open the dance hall next season so the fact that he had a contract did not matter. This made Harry realise that I meant business and that changes in the entertainment industry were here to stay. After much discussion I made Harry an offer: I would open the hall but we would have rock groups on stage which I would get through Harry so that he got his commission. Harry agreed but admitted that he knew very little about rock groups. "No bother," I said, "we will go out this summer and ask around."

We found an agent in Sheffield and went to see him. He told us that he had the contract for the Winter Gardens in Morecombe and that last winter (1961) he had four groups on which cost £12 each, a total of £48 for the night. They were The Beatles, Jerry and the Pacemakers, The Merseybeats, and Billy J Kramer.

We agreed to get our groups through him for the winter season. Harry told his band that they would not be working on Saturday nights at the Baths Hall; it was as simple as that.

One day that summer I was called to the bath side because a male swimmer had dislocated his shoulder in the pool. We got the man out and managed to get him into the boiler room where it was warm, sat him down and waited for the doctor to arrive from his surgery just up the road. The doctor was Dr Norman Piercy, who was to become one of my best friends.

Dr Piercy had only one leg, he had lost one during the war when he was a pilot flying bombers, but he got around with a false leg which matched his good one. The swimmer was in agony but Dr Piercy told him to look away as he put his artificial leg under his arm as he gave a pull and the shoulder went back in place. We were all amazed; the doc asked the man how he had travelled to the baths; when he said that he had driven the doc offered to take him home in the doc's car if I would drive the man's car home. We delivered the man back to his wife and Doc Piercy drove me back to the baths: it was from this first meeting that we became great friends.

Norman's wife Shirley was also a doctor; they had four children and lived about 50yds from us up the hill. Because they were not our GPs it was easier to make friends with them. Our girls loved to go and play in their garden and I used to let them come to the baths on Sunday afternoon when it was closed to the public.

Norman's stump used to cause him problems. He liked to keep fit and played golf but the walking often caused ulcers when the artificial leg rubbed. I asked him why he did not swim for exercise and he said he could not swim.

When I first offered to teach him Norman was not too sure so I started with just the two of us when the baths were closed. Norman was a great one for driving himself to the limit and often got annoyed with himself thinking he should be doing better. I used to tell him that I was in charge and he would have to do as he was told. Norman swam seven days each week, sometimes twice a day. I got him to swim crawl, backstroke and then tried breast-stroke which he found hard. I used to swim arms only and say if I can do it so can you.

Swimming suited Norman; he was getting good exercise and it was doing his leg a lot of good as well. He swam a mile and could do it on all three strokes, so it was time to teach him to life save. The first time I gave Norman the heavy rubber brick to train with he sank straight to the bottom of the pool, but he persevered and eventually got all the Royal Life Saving Society awards including the Diploma. It was an outstanding achievement, and many years later he took up scuba diving and became the official police underwater diver in Montrose where he had moved to.

The Wombwell Swimming club water polo team had finished bottom of the 2nd division and had to seek re-selection, so they asked me if I would train them and play as well. I enjoyed the training and the playing; it was the first time in a number of years that I had played water polo. They were a great group of lads, all worked down the pits and were as tough as they come, but so was the opposition, and I soon realised that if you did not stand up for yourself you got hammered. It was a great way for me to relax, and that first season we won the league and the cup as well. The presentation party for the County Trophies was held in Barnsley, and both Gill and I had a super time even if we were older than most of the others.

One fixture I will never forget was our visit to Normanton; we used to travel by a hired coach with wives and girlfriends. When we arrived we were told that there was no referee, one of the Normanton Swimming Club Officials agreed to stand in.

The start of a polo match in those days was by both teams racing from opposite ends of the pool to the ball that was thrown into the middle of the baths.

As I was the fastest swimmer I used to go for the ball then resumed my place as the centre half back. I got the ball then felt a sudden pain in my face, I was startled as I looked down and saw blood in the water, my blood, from my broken nose. Their swimmer had deliberately hit me in the face. As soon as I realised what had happened I went after him but before I could get to him one of our side had hit him hard, and a fight started, we all joined in and gave better than we took.

Both sides had players sent out of the water but by the end of the game there was a broken nose, cut eye, bruised face, black eyes and that was only our side. The game was a farce, I cannot remember who won the game but we won the war.

On the way home it was the custom for the coach to stop off for fish and chips. We all got of the bus and walked into the fish and chip shop. The owner took one look at the lads with all the cuts and bruises and refused to serve us, so we left and drove to another shop where only the girls went in to order the chips, and then we went home happy.

One of my staff, Ken, was always taking a day off at the weekend. I warned him about it and threatened him with the sack if he did it again. At one of the Council Meetings I was sat next to the treasurer, Harry Sager and told him about Ken and his malingering. Harry, much to my surprise asked me not to do anything about Ken until after the next meeting. I was very surprised as I thought that the treasurer would have been all for saving money, but anyway I agreed. Harry then asked me to meet him in the pub opposite the Town Hall on Tuesday night the following week at 7pm.

I arrived at the pub just before 7pm to see Harry sat at one end of the room with two pints of beer; at the opposite end were five of the council members including the Chairman. They had placed four tables together and had a large chart which covered the tables. Harry waved me over and as I sat down he gave me a beer and told me to drink up.

"Apart from the beer, why are we here?" I asked Harry. "Have another drink then go over and ask the councillors what they are doing," he said. As I walked over to the five councillors they said, "Hello Brian, we'll be with you in a minute, we are doing important business."

Intrigued I asked them what they were doing. "We are arranging us sick leave," they said. "We each have 16 weeks and it takes some planning to get it all in as well as the holidays." You see they all worked for the Coal Board. I could not believe what I had just heard, I went back to Harry the Borough Treasurer who said "And you thought you could sack your staff for malingering." I just sat there and drank my pint and then another one as well.

I took on a young man as a trainee manager, his name was James (Jimmy) Hart, a quiet lad but very keen to make a career in Baths Management. He had to work at all the jobs in the building from the boiler house to the office work.

It was during the winter after he had been with me six months that I was told that some of the youths that had been excluded from the hall for causing fights had threatened to wait for Jimmy after work and beat him up. One of the youths, a red-headed lad, was outside the front door. I went out and asked the youth if he would come into my office as I wished to talk to him.

He was not too keen but eventually I persuaded him. I asked him to sit down and I sat at my desk. I told him that I had heard that someone was going to attack my assistant manager, Jimmy Hart; the youth said that he knew nothing about it. I said that it was a pity because if anything at all happened to Jimmy he, the youth, would end up in prison.

At this the lad was shaken and asked how that could happen as he would not have done anything. I explained to him that I would get a knife, cut myself with it and then inform the police that he, the red headed youth had attacked me. "You can't do that," he said, " no one will believe it." "Won't they," I said, "I am a Chief Officer with the Local Authority, you are a troublemaker. I am prepared to swear on oath that you did it and I guarantee that you will do time inside." "That's not fair" he said, but now he was starting to realise I meant what I said. "What if someone else gets Hart?" "That's your bad luck," I said, "so you had better make sure that nothing happens to any of my staff or you will do at least six months in jail. Now get out of my office and don't ever try and come into this building again." The red-headed youth left and we never had any trouble with him or his mates.

That first winter when the baths were converted for entertainments was the most successful in the history of the building: every month the income was over 300% more than the previous year. The maximum limit in there was 800 and we had more than this number trying to get in every Saturday Night. Fights would start when someone inside would open the emergency exits to let their friends in, and there was only Ken, Jim and myself to sort out the fights. Most nights I had to put my shirt in cold water to get the blood out of the material, and it was not often my blood, but I decided to employ some extra doormen.

I knew from my police days that it was essential to get the local constabulary on your side. I had an arrangement with the police, and if I called them we would prosecute and go to court. There is nothing worse for a policeman than being called to a disturbance and then the complainant backing down.

I asked around and found that there was a family of five boys who were the tearaways of Wombwell, the Fleming lads. Mick had been Coal Board boxing champion until he was convicted of causing trouble and fighting. I told the police that I intended to employ Mick Fleming as my doorman: they said that it was up to me but he was more than capable of sorting anyone out. Mick was married and had a young baby but was out of work, so I said I would give him a trial and he would work every Saturday night.

It worked wonders. No-one would take Mick on: if he said they had to leave the building, they did. We still had fights but not as many, Mick asked me if I would also employ his older brother who was a male nurse at Rampton High Security Mental Hospital, as it would make things easier. I did and as it got closer to Christmas I also took on two other brothers as well. We had stopped the fighting on Saturday night but it was now happening on other nights when we hired the hall to outside organisations, and in the end I made it a condition of hiring that my door staff must be employed.

The only time we had a problem was on New Year's Eve night. Everything was going well with a maximum attendance when two women started fighting over a lad in the café. My staff went to sort it out but did not know how or where to grab the women. If they had been males they would have sorted it out quickly but as they picked up both women and took them to the door they were kicking and scratching the staff so much so that I decided to lock them up in separate rooms and send for the police. When the police arrived they had a job getting the women into the police van but in the end they took them away. That was our only incident over Christmas.

The first Civic Ball I had to organise was to be held in February on Valentine's Day.

I persuaded the Chairman to go upmarket; I promised him that it would be the best Civic Ball ever seen in the town. All the chief officers and business people wanted it but some of the chairman's colleagues thought it would be too posh.

During the time I had been in the job I had been on the look-out for a first class catering company, and I found one in Rotherham. I told them that I wanted Silver Service at a price that I could afford; in return I would see that they got all the publicity they could handle.

There was a small committee that ran the Civic Ball with a separate account in my name; it consisted of the Chairman and Vice Chairman, Town Clerk, Borough Treasurer and me. I said that I was going to have a Valentine's Day theme, which was agreed. The invitations to set individuals were free, and the rest were sold to members and the public.

When I said that my wife and I would be on the top table with the guests I was told that my predecessors never sat down as they were organising the event. I soon put them right by saying that when I organise anything it goes like clockwork and that I would be enjoying the evening like them.

I had four 6ft polystyrene hearts painted red with arrows through the middle, hanging over the top table which was covered with flowers and silver candelabra. The hall was a mass of flowers from the parks department. I had set Ken to stand opposite me at the other side of the hall with instruction never to take his eyes off me so that if I wanted anything I would signal and he would come to see what I wanted. I never needed to call him: the evening went off like clockwork and was the talk of the town for weeks to come.

Winter 1962/3

That winter of 1962-63 was one of the worst in living memory; it snowed but never melted so that we had layers of snow piling up at the side of all the roads. This went on for months including Christmas. I used to carry a sack of salt and grit, plus a spade and two sacks to put under the rear wheels when I went out in the car.

Over the Christmas holidays we had dances at Christmas Eve, a children's dance and party at 2pm Boxing Day then a dance each night to New Year's Eve. The only time off was Christmas Day, and because of this I decided to take Gill and the girls over to Preston to stay with my mum the week before Christmas then I would follow as soon as I could get away on Christmas Day, picking up Aunty Dorothy in Blackburn before returning for Boxing Day lunch-time.

The arrangement I had with the staff was we could stay behind after the Christmas Eve dance and clean up ready for the Boxing Day party or come in early on Boxing Day. They always chose to stay late on Christmas Eve. This meant that it was 2pm or 3pm before I took the staff home on Christmas Day, and only then could I set off for Preston.

It had been snowing all night and most of the main roads were covered in virgin snow with no other vehicles about. There were no motorways then, just the A roads over the Pennines. The first car I saw was a police car in Halifax. I had to go as fast as I could go down hills so that I could get up the other side without slipping. I knew that if I stopped I would not get the car going again. When I was past Todmorden there was a snow covered electricity pylon with a broken cable dancing about and sparking every time it touched the ground. I had to get past it as best I could on the wrong side of the road, but there was no-one about.

I got to Blackburn at 6-30am but did not risk going down Aunty Dorothy's road; I left the engine running and walked to collect Dorothy and all her presents. We arrived at my mum's house about 7-30am to be met by my mum who said "Where have you been? The girls have been awake ages." I could have cried but Gill and the girls had been worrying about me not moaning.

We had a good Christmas with Gran and Pop joining us for dinner. I stayed the night and left early the next morning to get back to work for lunch time. I collected Gill and the girls after the New Year when things at work settled down to normal. That is what it is like to work in the entertainment business but I enjoyed every minute of it.

During that winter it was reported in the local newspaper that two brothers had been sliding on the frozen canal when they fell in the water. The eldest boy managed to save his younger brother who could not swim and pulled him to the canal bank.

I asked the Chairman of the Baths Committee if we could offer the young boy free swimming lessons, it would help the boy and be good publicity for the Department? He agreed and I arranged to teach the boy myself.

The parents were very pleased and arranged for him to attend the baths the following day.

After talking to the little boy I got him in the water, there was no one else in the pool, he did everything I asked him to do. I was tempted to ask him to swim without using the armbands but instead I let all the air out and said we would discard them the next day.

The following day he swam a width of the pool without any aids, he was now a swimmer. His mum and dad and his brother were so proud and so was I.

I informed the newspaper about the achievement and they sent a photographer and reporter to see him swim. The story got into the national press and then the Yorkshire Television Company sent a team to film him towing me in a life saving mode the length of the pool. It was not as hard as it looked as I floated easily and all he had to do was pull me along, but the publicity was first rate.

My second year at Wombwell saw me double the income that I had trebled the previous year. I introduced swimming lessons in summer and in the winter we held the Ideal Homes Exhibition as well as Professional Wrestling which I managed to get televised. I was the talk of the town and was promised a substantial pay increase by the councillors.

I should have known better than to believe any councillor, for all of them I have ever met in any council are only there for their own good.

When I managed to get the Ideal Home Exhibition, the organisers wanted to provide a private room with bar so that they could entertain councillors and other VIPs. On the opening night the councillors drank the entire stock which was supposed to last the week, promising all sorts of things to the organisers, none of which materialised. The wrestling was a similar story. Joint Promotions the company who had the TV rights wanted to promote wrestling on a Sunday for commercial reasons. All 15 councillors promised the company that they would agree to it at the next Council Meeting; this was promised when Joint Promotions took them all to Leeds by limousine and wined and dined them. At the next meeting it was refused.

It was here at Wombwell that Catherine started school, and at least she had Alison to go with. That left little Gillian at home on her own so she spent many hours with me at the baths especially in the winter when the floor was down, and it made a perfect place to ride her bike. The bus stop was just outside the steps leading up to the baths entrance; Cath used to stand on the steps and make faces at the boys getting off the bus, and when they chased after her she ran into my office just inside the door. The staff at the baths loved all the girls and at times spoilt them. Whenever there was an exhibition on in the hall any freebies were available for the girls.

On wet days in winter the hall with its stage was the perfect place for Alison to organise her sisters to be the Beatles and pretend to play their toy guitars, Gillian had to play left- handed because she was Paul. We had some good acts and groups and some awful ones, the worst always wanting to make the loudest noise possible, which was probably to mask the poor playing. We had George Melley, Russ Abbot and the Black Abbotts, Dave Berry, the original Eagles, Clinton Ford and many more.

We visited Preston as often as possible travelling by car; we had an Austin Cambridge and took a different route sometimes to vary the journey. During one trip we were passing through Accrington town centre with Gill driving with Cath and Alison in the back and me in the front with Gillian on my knee. All of a sudden Gillian said she wanted to be sick, and at the same time she was, all over me. I was sat in a pool of sick: Gill stopped the car, the smell was awful. I looked at Gillian and saw that she had something in her mouth. "What are you chewing?" I asked her. "A sweet," replied Gillian, and carried on eating it. How she managed to keep it in her mouth and still deposit a load on me I will never know. I had to open both the front and rear doors to give me some privacy while I changed my trousers and Gillian's dress. Then with all the windows open we drove off. Unfortunately this was a scene that was often repeated in later years!

Living next door to us was a family of three boys and a girl called Carol, the same age as Gillian. They used to play together a lot but Carol was used to getting her own way being the only girl at home; she was also used to fighting and often hit Gillian and made her cry, so I told Gillian that if Carol hit her she should hit her back. One day they were both playing in our garden in the sand pit when Carol fell out with Gillian and hit her in the face. Gillian stopped, rubbed her face, thought a while, and then with her arm outstretched, swung round and hit Carol with her fist, knocking her to the ground.

At first Carol could not believe what had happened, and then she began to cry and ran home to her mother. Carol's mum said it was her own fault and left it at that. That was the last time the two of them fell out.

Bude. 'The Lobster Pot'

We now had enough money to think about taking the family away for a holiday, we decided to try a self-catering cottage that was advertised in the Sunday Times, called the Lobster Pot which was about a mile north of Bude in Cornwall. The property was built of wood with a tin roof; it had three bedrooms and a veranda from which you could see the beach. It was set in a large field with its own well for water which had to be pumped up to the sink. There was a single track to the property from the beach which made it very safe for the girls. We had such a great time that we went there for the next seven years, always in the Whit holidays. The beach was perfect, with miles and miles of golden sand. The first year we had Gillian in nappies and had to carry all the girls over the rocks and pebbles to the sand.

The farmer who owned the land all round the Lobster Pot made a place to sit by the beach from which his wife sold cakes and drinks; the girls loved to go there on their own (we kept watch) to buy a drink and a cake.

Bude became the perfect place for us to take our holidays, we all liked the sand, and sea and surf, over the years there are many tales to recollect.

Making sand castles became a serious business, we even took a garden spade to help with the construction, and it was especially useful when trying to hold back the tide. Most of the time we spent outside regardless of the weather, there was a swimming pool which was filled by the sea at high tide but we preferred playing in the surf, we even made our own surf boards.

One year we were playing in the surf when I noticed a man and two boys much further off shore than myself, I always kept within my depth even though I could out swim everyone there, I kept watching and saw that they were in difficulties.

I told the girls to stay put and I walked and swam to the man and boy. The man was the boy's dad and although he was holding his son he was in the worst condition, I asked the boy if he could swim he said yes, so I towed the dad back to shore in a life saving hold.

The girls had been watching and waiting, I told them to go for the Life Guard, I was going back for the son. The boy had drifted further out and was very tired, I got to him and held him close to me as I swam on my back with the boy's head close to mine.

It was slow progress with the surf lifting us up each time a wave passed underneath us, then we reached the area where the waves broke over us, I had to clasp my hand over the boy's mouth and hold my breath until we surfaced again. It was a very tiring experience, eventually my feet touched the sand and I could stand up, I handed the boy to a man on the beach and set off for the last boy who by now was a long way out, as I swam out I could see that a youth on a large surf board was also going to help the lad, then I heard the Life Guard shout to me that he would get the boy so we swam together. The Life Guard was attached to a rope held on shore by his team mates but it was not long enough so he untied himself as we both swam towards the surf board and the boy.

When we got hold of the surf board the Life Guard placed a life jacket on the boy that was fastened to him, after a rest we all decided to swim back to the shore but still holding on to the board. All went well until once again we reached the spot where the waves broke, suddenly we were picked up and thrown in the air, then taken under the water, when we came up we were all ok but the surfboard had carried on up the beach.

The other Life Guards were waiting to take the boy to the first aid centre and clouds of people stood watching as we waded ashore.

Gill and the girls were there and I said I was all right but I could not stop shaking and shivering, but after a cup of hot tea I was soon OK.

We had another incident when we were on holiday in Bude when Steve and Maureen came with us. Steve who is also a good swimmer and younger than me, was surfing when the tide started to take him towards the rocks; he was able to swim away but was still being taken back. I had to call out the Life Guards who only managed to pull him away because of the rope that they had attached to the beach.

It was on the same beach that a young married couple on honeymoon, the man with his trousers rolled up, where paddling along the sand at low water, when a wave knocked them over. The man could not swim and was taken out to sea, his wife raised the alarm and the Coastguard helicopter turned out. This happened during our holiday and his body was not found until after we arrived back home.

We also had a holiday in Bude without the girls, when Lance and his wife Marlene from Wombwell came with us; we stayed in The Burns Hotel near the golf course. It was a nice change to be able to go out for a drink at night, something we did not do when the girls were with us.

One day we both took a rowing boat on the canal, Gill and I, Lance and Marlene, we soon challenged each other to a race up the canal, the lads rowing the girls steering, we won by a good margin when Marlene shouted that we would race back.

They had about 50yds start on us but Gill kept egging me on saying I could not lose now. It was a long way back but we were catching up, faster, faster, Gill shouted as I tried as though my life depended on it, and it did.

We did in fact win, just, but my hands had blistered and then burst so that both of them were covered in blood.

I was unable to hold my pint in the pub after but Gill said it was worth it, I think she thought she was Queen Cleopatra on the Nile and I was Anthony (or was I a slave).

CHAPTER NINE

1964 - 1967 Highgrove Baths Eastcote

The winter of 1962-3 was one of the coldest on record, and the snow stayed on the ground for weeks and weeks. During this winter my Aunties, Maggie and Cissie, who I looked on as my grandmothers, died. I attended both funerals but on each occasion I had to make difficult journeys through the snow. At the close of the winter season we had the most successful season in the history of the building, all the councillors individually promised me a substantial rise in my salary, but when the time came to vote at the council meeting I did not get it. That was typical of the elected members regardless of which party they stood for. I decided to move on and looked for other jobs.

I wanted to get the chance to open a new building; there were many being built in the 60s. I got an interview at Ruislip Northwood just outside London.

Highgrove Baths Eastcote 1964-67

When applying for a new job I always looked up the council in the "Municipal Journal" so that I could get as much information as possible about the political composition of the members as well as the size and complexity of the services the council operated. I also ordered the local newspaper for a month prior to going for an interview. In those days the bank manager was also very helpful in contacting his opposite number to find out about schools, house prices, and locations to live in or avoid. By the day of the interview I was as well prepared as anyone and much better informed than most.

The Council was 95% Tory, just the opposite of Wombwell which was 100% Labour. The leader of the council was a barrister, Lesley Freeman, a very nice person; the Chairman of the Finance Committee, who was also chairing the interview committee, was the opposite, and we locked horns at the interview. Candidates are always asked if they wish to ask questions of the committee at the end of the interview. My research told me that there was a special school for disabled children in the area so I asked if it was intended that the children should use the pool. Of course, replied the chairman, as if I should have known. "Why do you ask?" said Councillor Freeman. "Well," I said, "the pool is built with access on the first floor and there is no way you could get a wheelchair or a stretcher on to the pool side. The room went quiet; I was the first of the applicants to be interviewed, as usual being a Barnes.

I finished the interview and went back to sit with the other five candidates. One by one they came out and asked what was behind all the questions about disabled swimmers. I just smiled and said nothing.

After a few minutes the clerk came out and asked me to go back into the interview room where I was offered the position of Baths Manager. I accepted and straight away I was asked how soon I could start. I had to give three months' notice so they asked me if I would be prepared to come down to meet the architect and the senior council officers the following week to see how the building could be adapted to cater for disabled swimmers. I readily agreed and was given a set of plans to take away with me.

The building was not due to open for at least six months so I made a number of visits during my three months' notice, the result of which was the construction of a completely new changing block with direct access to the pool side with ramps in place of steps to cater especially for disabled swimmers.

The building was the most sophisticated swimming baths to be built, no expense had been spared. The pool had been built without excavating a hole, but by building it up from ground level. This meant that although the entrance was at ground level with all the plant for heating and filtration, you had to climb stairs to get to the bath side, and changing rooms.

The standard of the finishing was a joy to behold. There were three types of heating in the changing rooms, which were on the first floor level: radiators, under-floor heating and a warm air conditioning system. The air in the entire building could be re-circulated 100% or have 100% fresh air and any percentage in between.

There were two pools, a teaching pool which was shallow all over and a large 110ft. long competition pool with a deep end of 12ft.6ins. which enabled divers to use a 5m fixed board and 1m and 3m spring boards.

The water was circulated in both pools using the Surflow system, whereby the water was introduced into the pool by inlets along the length of the bottom of the pool, and was extracted by the water overflowing the side of the pool into a channel then returned to the filters. It was a new method of water filtration, the old way being to introduce the water at the shallow end and extract it at the bottom of the deep end.

The advantage of the new system was that clean treated water was on the surface where most of the bacteria is and can then be taken into the mouth.

The council was building two detached and a row of four terraced houses for staff, but they were not ready when we moved from Wombwell so we were given a semi-detached house in Eastcote at Woodlands Avenue.

The move from Wombwell was once again a big event in the girls' lives. It meant leaving their friends and starting a new school for Alison and Cath. We packed the removal van and off it went; we would catch it up and arrive before they would. On the motorway we spotted the removal van and Gillian started to cry, because tied on the rear of the van was her little blue scooter. Gillian thought she would lose it but it arrived OK.

Next door to us were Peter and Josie; they had two little girls called Julie and Pat. Peter worked for the council as well. We liked the house, and it was not far from the shops or the tube station. As time went by Gill wanted to stay in the house and not move to the detached house by the baths. I asked her to mention it to Mrs Freeman at the next opportunity, Gill did and Mrs Freeman spoke to her husband and we stayed put (wheels within wheels).

One of the first things I did was to organise a public meeting to inform local people about the progress of the baths and to form a local Swimming Club if there was enough interest. The response was staggering: the venue for the meeting was overcrowded and spilled out onto the park outside, there were literally hundreds attending.

We formed a committee, one of the members; an American called Al Williams, had been an international diver and was now a coach. He said that the diving boards, although made by a well-known firm in Lancashire, were not up to the latest Olympic standard. The council would not replace them so the swimming club bought new ones from America and gave them to the council who installed them. A number of years later Al's daughter, Beverley, became the British diving champion and represented GB at the Olympics.

Prior to opening the pool the councillors asked to be shown round the building and to be able to have a swim afterwards. One of the councillors who I did not get on with was quite a show-off and thought he could dive. I asked him to try the new Olympic diving board, and I had adjusted the fulcrum to give it maximum spring, which he was not used to and did not know about. He had taken a few paces to the end of the board to get a good bounce, when the spring of the board catapulted him up in the air; he was out of control, somersaulted, and landed on his back with an almighty splash. Everyone laughed; I just looked away then asked if he wanted to try again: he didn't.

The new accommodation for disabled swimmers was being built but was not yet ready Nevertheless we formed a swimming club for them which was a great success, so much so that I managed to get on the committee of Sir Ludwig Guttman at Stoke Mandeville Hospital which was promoting sport for the disabled throughout the UK (more later about BSAD).

The day we opened to the public there were queues round the building, with all the clothes storage full we had to limit the time people had in the water. It was a great success. The deep end was 12ft 6in. deep and each day we swept it with a very large heavy brush to get any bits off the bottom. I was using this brush after we had closed for the day when I felt my back crack. I could not stand up straight, the pain was unbearable. I could hardly walk and I could not get into my car. I set off to walk through the park but I had to keep stopping to lean against a tree because of the pain. A passer-by asked if he could help, so I stayed still and he went to get Gill. I managed to get to the doctor who was close by; he took one look at me and sent for the ambulance. I was taken to the Northwood Hospital were I was given an anaesthetic to enable the consultant to put back a slipped disc.

I had a few days off work but I was told that swimming was the best thing I could do which was great for me. Eventually I had an arrangement with the consultant, he sent me patients to have swimming sessions and he treated me privately.

The baths were so popular that we had record numbers attending. One Sunday morning I counted seven Rolls-Royces with chauffeurs waiting in the car park.

It was another Sunday, I was not on duty but at home, when I received a phone call asking me to go in. When I got to the pool it was full, but the trouble was that about 20 men, about 18 to 30 years old, were causing trouble and would not leave. I told them who I was and asked them to leave; I got a mouthful of abuse so I called the police.

The Metropolitan Police arrived, including an inspector, a van of officers and two vans with police dogs. The inspector recognised the gang and asked me to empty the rest of the people from the premises. When everyone had left other than the gang of men he asked me to go onto the side of the baths and again tell them to leave, which I did and got the same response. The inspector then told them to leave; they said "make us". With that some policemen came on to the bath side carrying armfuls of clothes, their clothes. "Are these yours?" asked the police, and threw the clothes into the water. As the gang swore, the dog handlers arrived and let four dogs go into the water. "Get them," said the handlers. You should have seen the look on the gang's faces as the dogs went for them. As the gang tried to climb out of the water the police stood on their hands with their large boots.

One by one the police let the gang out of the water, handcuffed them and marched them off to the changing rooms to put on wet clothes before being put into police vans. The gang threatened to return and do the same to me but the Inspector said all we had to do was call the police and they could and would deal with them. We never had any further trouble from that gang.

The ABC Murders

Later in the year I was approached by a film company who were making the film ABC Murders with Anita Ekberg and Tony Rendell. They wanted to film the opening sequence at the baths and they required the building all Sunday; they would pay for it of course. The film crew arrived complete with their own mobile kitchen. The scene was that a drunken clown was practising his high diving act at night when he was shot in the neck by Anita Ekberg who then left an ABC guide to London at the site. This was the first of many murders of people whose names began with A then B and C and so on.

The Film Director was Frank Tashlin who had directed all of the Jerry Lewis/Dean Martin films; he was a great man but his assistant director was arrogant. When the clown was shot he had to fall off the 5m high diving board, which had been raised to 20ft. He was then supposed to float face down on the surface.

They shot the film from five different angles, and each time the stunt man had to fall into the pool from 20ft. He was exhausted so I suggested that one of my staff could do some of the preliminary work while they were setting up the lights and getting the right focus. Frank thought this a good idea but it did not please the assistant director.

A problem arose because they wanted the clown to float up to the surface after he had been shot; he could not do this because he had enormous clown's boots on with long toes. I pointed out to the assistant director that a body does not float until it has been in the water for days, but he insisted that he wanted it to float. He would not listen so I sat next to Frank and watched as they tried in vain to get the clown to float back to the surface.

After many failed attempts, I said I could get him to float if they wanted him to. Frank said go ahead do it. I sent for two sets of arm bands that we used for teaching children to swim, I placed two bands on each leg and the others on his arms underneath his clowns uniform. "Go ahead and try it now," I said, and sure enough the clown floated to the surface. "Each to his own," I said to Frank as he thanked me for my help.

Both Gill and I were invited to Elstree Studios to see the rest of the film being made, and we were also shown round "the lot" and saw part of the Danger Man Series being made with Patrick McGowan.

It was at this time that my belief in God and religion was fast leaving me. I could not go along with all that I had been taught as a child and young man, including the belief that Catholics should eat fish, not meat, on Fridays. One Friday I said to Gill let's have a plate full of mortal sin and chips and with that I bought two steak pies and chips; it was the best meal I could remember.

Gillian started school in Ruislip, so now all three were at school. Gill started to help at the school and thought of training to be a teacher.

When I moved down to Eastcote I asked Steve Goodwin if he would be interested in coming to work for me as the engineer. Steve was a qualified engineer and worked down the mines in Wombwell. He jumped at the prospect, he was about to marry Maureen and they would have one of the houses built for staff at the baths. It was a dream come true for Steve and Maureen. I went to the wedding and Steve's family were so proud that he was able to leave the mines and get a house and job in London. Tony Dagget came as my deputy manager and the three of us made a very good team.

As I had said all the fittings and fixtures were of the very highest standard. The lamp posts in the drive up to the baths building were made of aluminium and looked futuristic; they cost the earth. One morning as I arrived for work I saw a number of the lights had been smashed, and it happened the next day as well. We had reported it to the police but it still went on: each morning a light was smashed. I asked Steve if he was prepared to stay behind all night to see how it was done and by whom. We settled down in the café area at first floor level, and round about 10-30pm we saw three lads walk up the road until they got to a lamp that was still intact, then they started to push at the post until it vibrated, the more they pushed the more it vibrated, then the light shattered.

We phoned the police who said they were on their way; we went down to the front door and waited until the police car turned into the road than we went out. "Got you!" we thought, but the lads started running, leapt over the fencing into the next road and away. We got into the police car and cruised around the area, thinking we would recognise the lads if we saw them but we did not.

A short time later after the police had left, Steve and I decided to visit all the pubs in the area, and in the third one we visited were the three lads.

We called the police back who questioned the lads, but their mates all swore that they had been in the pub all night. We did not believe them but the police could do nothing.

The police left but Steve and I decided to stay and watch the lads. They were not at all at ease and when one got up to leave we decided to follow him. He went up the main street to the tube station and onto the platform and we followed. There was no one else on the station so we went up to him and said that we knew it was he who had damaged the lamps. He denied it of course but we said that if he came anywhere near the baths again he would find himself under the next train. He was terrified that we were going to do it that night, so we let him sweat for some time then we left saying that he was a very lucky man, but he would not be so lucky next time. We never had any more vandalism at the baths.

At the time Highgrove Baths was the most popular in the country, and we had more swimmers than any other pool. I had a visit from a lady who said she was from Social Services: I was sure that one of my friends was setting me up, because she came to warn me of a young girl, 15 years old, who was a nymphomaniac. This girl was reportedly using the baths quite a lot. I just did not believe this happened, but the lady from Social Services said she was addicted to sex, (I have never come across this since) and thought she was seeing one of my staff. I promised to look into it and she gave me her card. I told Steve and Tony about the visit and they also thought it highly unlikely but agreed to keep an eye on things.

That night I got a phone call at home asking me to return to work; on arriving I was told that the girl had been seen hanging round the entrance with the supervisor. I asked the supervisor to be brought to my office but no one could find him. I went out to look round the building but there was no sign of him. I realised that the café on the first floor was not in use, so I went upstairs to find the café door locked and the lights switched off. I used my master key to get inside and I could hear noises from behind the counter: I went round the counter and switched on the lights, and there on a pile of swimming towels were the two of them naked. "What are you doing?" I asked which with hindsight, was a stupid question. I let them get dressed then sent for the lady from Social Services. The girl was taken back into care and I dismissed the supervisor for gross misconduct and reported him to the police. The supervisor was given a caution due to the girl's history but he would never work with children again.

1965 Skiing

Stan who used to live next door in Preston was by now a successful businessman and we still kept in touch. Stan asked me to go to Switzerland skiing with him, but I had to tell him that although I would love to go I could not afford it. Stan said he had some business in Switzerland and he could pay for me out of the business account, so all I had to do was to get my own kit.

I had a very good friend in the swimming club who worked in the stores at the American Airforce Base at West Drayton. He could lend me all the kit I needed for the two weeks holiday. Stan drove down to our house in his large Jaguar and Gill took us to Heathrow then took the car back and parked it on our drive.

As we were getting the car ready with all my stuff Stan asked me to carry a holdall that he had with him, I thought nothing of it and off we went. I even took the bag through customs both out of England and into Switzerland. We were staying in a very posh hotel in Davos, the heart of the skiing country. As we got to our rooms Stan asked me if I had any idea of what was in the bag. I had no idea, and then he opened the bag and emptied the contents onto the bed: there was £35,000 in used notes. I was amazed. Stan said that if I had known what was in the bag I would have been nervous and it would have alerted the customs. In those days you were only allowed to take £250 out of the country. The following day we went to a bank and Stan deposited the cash in a numbered account, and said that we could now enjoy the skiing. I kept thinking what I could do with that amount of cash.

We booked lessons every morning and afternoon and had a packed lunch so that we could practise during the quiet lunch period. The first time we put on our skis was on the road to the ski lift, but we could not stand still, and started to roll downhill until we fell over so that we could stop. We took off the skis and carried them to the nursery slopes for our first lesson.

It was belittling to see small children aged six or seven going down the slopes without a care in the world while we struggled to stay upright. With all the lessons and practise we began to improve, but we still fell over as the pace increased, though it was great fun.

On Friday at the end of the first week I sprained my ankle, and as we had medical insurance I went to see the doctor. I was given treatment twice each day and I was able to ski again on Monday, three days later. The second week we were in a medium ability class and our instructor was going out with the girl in charge of the advanced class.

On the Thursday we were told that we were going to attempt the Parsene Run, and it was a good job that we had no idea what it was or we would not have agreed. The idea was that the two classes should join together for the day. That morning the fog was down over the mountain, most classes decided to cancel all except our two love-sick instructors. Most of our class backed out so we had two instructors for twelve skiers. We went up the mountain in the cable car unable to see anything, and when we arrived at the summit it was still like pea soup.

It was agreed that the girl would lead and the class would follow in line with our instructor bringing up the rear. We had no idea what to expect, and if we had it would have stopped us there and then. The girl started down the mountain zigzagging to keep the speed down so that the rest of us could keep up. It was my turn next and off I went into the mist: I could see the person in front and also the one in front of him.

It was exhilarating, and all I did was to concentrate on the two in front of me, even to the extent that when one fell over so did I. No harm done, up we got and set off after those ahead, then we suddenly came out of the cloud into bright sunlight. The scene was dramatic and breathtaking: we were in a valley with white snow all round us, you could see for miles in the cold crisp air.

The mountains appeared to go on for ever, down and down for miles; if I had seen what we were going to ski down I would never have left the cable car. From time to time we stopped for a break and to take photographs, then down again. By this time everyone's confidence had grown in leaps and bounds. There was an alpine hut half way down where we stopped for lunch, and looking back that was the worst thing we could have done, because we all relaxed while the two instructors went off together.

When it was time to leave my legs were like jelly, and the others felt the same. Off we went and soon we all started to fall over: one ran into the other so that we all piled up laughing but unable to keep our legs from giving way. It was a wonderful run down through the woods to Cloisters for the last part of the trip where we had a bus waiting to take us back to Davos. It was a magnificent achievement to have finished the trip; none of the others in the advanced class could believe that we had only started skiing ten days previously, and neither could we.

We had two days left before we left, so I decided to just play around but Stan kept on with the lessons. That night we decided to try out the local sauna, so we walked into Davos. The temperature was 15 degrees below zero, and there was a stream which although the surface was frozen over underneath it was still flowing. This water was piped into the sauna to fill the plunge pool so you can imagine just how cold it was.

The idea of a sauna is that you go into a log cabin which is heated to 100 degrees centigrade with dry heat, you stay as long as you feel comfortable and then you jump into a cold water lake or bath. We had the water from the stream running into a large plunge bath about 8 feet x 4 feet and 4 feet deep. No one wore clothes in the sauna cabin, and just outside the cabin door was the plunge area with loungers placed all around it.

The game that everyone seemed to be playing was to try and guess the nationality of the people going into the water by the language they used once they got in, since it seems that we all swear in our own tongue. This was only explained to us after they had all had a good laugh at our expense.

The last day before we left I decided to have some fun on my own on the slopes while Stan had more lessons. I used the chair lift to get up the mountain and then skied down zig-zagging from side to side to slow myself down and sometimes I even stopped for a rest. As I grew in confidence I began to miss out some of the stops and did a jump turn, this kept my speed up and I found that I was going faster and faster.

I then realised that I was going too fast and that I could not stop just as I saw a class under instruction ahead of me. I tried to shout but no one saw me until I hit the class and lost control: over and over I went, skis lost, and I rolled on and on until I eventually stopped. I felt OK, no bones broken but I could not see. I panicked and tried to wipe my eyes, but I still could not see then I realised that the snow had got inside my goggles.

What a relief. I had broken my ski binding but I found my ski. I had to walk back to the hotel. Stan came back to tell me that some idiot had run into the class and could have killed them. I laughed and so did he when I said the idiot was myself.

At that time I smoked a pipe, my favourite tobacco was Balkan Sobranie which was expensive in the UK. I bought eight tins to take home but I forgot them and left them in the hotel. On the plane I realised what I had done, so Stan said that I might as well take my allowance in cigarettes for him, which I did.

On the plane back we had been drinking duty free spirits which we started in the hotel hours before so that when we landed at Heathrow we had drunk more than we should have. We stood next to the carousel waiting for our luggage but it did not arrive. Everyone else got theirs but we were left with an empty carousel. Feeling very annoyed we demanded to see someone in charge to complain about our lost luggage, and when we did we were told that we were in the wrong area. Still feeling fed up we went into the next room where we saw our bags on their own with just two customs officers stood by them. We went up to the bags and took them to the exit when we were stopped and asked if we had anything to declare: we said we only had our duty free allowance which we then produced. I was smoking my pipe, and the customs officer asked me if I had purchased any pipe tobacco. I replied that I had. "Where is it then?" he asked. "On the hotel table in Davos," I replied.

"What were you doing in Davos?" was the next question, and by this time we were both fed up, so I said, "Smuggling." That was it! "Empty everything out," they said and then they went through all our things. It was our own fault; we should not have tried to be cocky with them. I never went skiing again but Stan went on a regular basis.

We did not go into London every week but we did take the girls in to see the sights. We only drove in on a Sunday and even then it was busy. Cath asked if it was "Rush Hour" and that was in the afternoon. During the week we would get the tube, and one day we took them to see Buckingham Palace. Standing outside the gates Gill told the girls not to put their heads through the railings, but too late! Cath had already got her head through but could not get it out. It did not help that both Gill and myself were doubled up laughing while Cath started to cry. We had visions of the fire brigade arriving with bells sounding, though we did realise that to Cath it was no laughing matter. All of a sudden out her head popped to everyone's relief, especially Cath's.

In 1965 there was a reorganisation of Local Government in the London area. I was the highest paid Baths Manager in the area which was to be called Hillingdon, and at my interview I was told that although they could not promise me the top job I was almost certainly going to get the position of General Manager of the new Baths Department. When the day finally came, out of 34 new London Boroughs 30 created a position of General Manager while the other four absorbed the baths department within another discipline, Hillingdon being one: I was placed in the Borough Valuer's Department. I was devastated. I went to see the Borough Valuer who was a nice person; he said that he did not want to be in charge of the baths and he understood how I felt. I told him that I would be looking for another job but until I left I would do my best. I started looking and found one in the North West, at Birkenhead.

CHAPTER TEN

1967 - 1973 Birkenhead Borough Council

Birkenhead 1967 - 1974

They wanted someone to be in charge of the Baths and Indoor Recreation Department with suitable experience to open a new complex that was being built at Woodchurch. The previous manager was Tom McLennan, a past President of our Institute. I applied and got the job. There was a detached house at one of the baths in Byrne Avenue which went with the job, but I had no intention of living on the job again. I declined the house and started looking around the various parts of the Wirral. Gran, Pop, Gill and me drove round with a map to see the districts first hand; we called in the Half Way House, a pub in Prenton and had liver sausage sandwiches.

We finally agreed that Hoylake was to be the place to live, but we needed a 90% mortgage. We went into many estate agency offices: one called Moscrop in Birkenhead was owned by John Moscrop, and he told us that his own house in Hoylake was for sale, a four bedroom semi-detached. Off we went to look over the house in Ferndale Road, No 67. We liked it at once, and when John said that he could get us a 100% mortgage we agreed the price £4000. We had many happy years in Ferndale Road. The hall was built with a landing above giving a height of 20 feet to the ceiling at the top of the stairs, and each year we had a Christmas tree that was over 16ft tall, which looked super when the lights were lit in the evening.

I was determined to learn from my experience in the London Government Re-organisation, it was not who you were, but who you knew that counted. With this in mind I set out my stall; I worked in Birkenhead, lived in Hoylake and joined Wallasey Golf Club.

The department consisted of Argyle Street Baths, Livingstone Street Baths, Byrne Avenue Baths and the new complex being built at Woodchurch. There were laundries at Argyle, Livingstone, and Byrne Avenue, and the last two each had two pools, one of which was turned into an indoor hall used for sports and other events. All three had slipper baths (private baths). The three earliest baths used the salt water which was pumped out of the Mersey Railway Tunnel; this water was also used to wash down the streets in the centre of Birkenhead.

Woodchurch Community Centre

Once again I was a chief officer with my own department reporting to the Baths and Markets Committee. The Woodchurch complex was nearing completion; there was a 25m pool and a teaching pool, adjacent to a health centre and youth club which were linked to the theatre. Outside were hard-surfaced tennis courts and a 400m running track with an all-weather pitch in the centre.

My staff cleaned and controlled the building but the Education Department ran the youth club, Health Department ran the health centre and the General Purposes Committee ran the theatre. This was causing chaos with the staff and the Director of Education and Health Chief, so a meeting was called by the leader of the council, Alderman Platt. The chairman of each committee and their chief officer had to attend, and each one wanted to be in total charge of their space. Alderman Platt asked me to show him round and when we came back he announced that I would be in charge of the building and all the staff. He walked off and left the others wondering what had happened. That is the way that Alderman Platt ran the council; he was in total charge.

Prior to opening the pool I arranged for 100 children from nearby schools to arrive at the same time so that we could check out our procedures for managing crowds of swimmers once we were open. It all went well; we opened to the public on a Friday and we had many customers throughout the day.

At about 6pm when everything had settled down I decided to go home for some tea. At 7.30pm I had a phone call asking me to return as the crowds of people were too many to handle. As I drove up to the baths all I could see were hundreds of people outside the building trying to get in, and as I arrived so did the police. I told them who I was and together we fought our way to the entrance. I shouted at the top of my voice that I was the manager and that if they formed an orderly queue I would guarantee that they would get a swim that night. That seemed to do the trick. I went inside and could not believe what I saw: there were clothes everywhere on the floor and in the corridors, but it was in the pool that I felt very scared.

There were so many people in the pool that you could have walked from one side to the other without getting wet. I did not know if there was a body lying on the bottom as it was impossible to see the bottom of the pool. I ordered everyone to leave the water but not many took any notice, so I placed an attendant at each exit on the bath side and I and other members of the staff grabbed people and pushed them out of the pool area into the changing rooms.

As the numbers reduced we looked to see if the worst had happened, and thankfully it had not - there was no one on the bottom of the pool. Once we had cleared the building I went outside and let in those still waiting as I had promised, it was after midnight when we finally closed the building. When I looked into how it had happened it was because the manager and staff had panicked when the crowds started to push their way in, and they had lost control.

It was at this time that there was a large fire in the leisure centre in Douglas, Isle of Man, with many deaths. As a result fire regulations were tightened up with exits being made larger. This affected the opening of the theatre where we had to install extra exit doors.

Because I was in control of the building we had a rule that if any person caused trouble in one part they would automatically be excluded from the whole of the centre.

The Building had a liquor licence and I was the licensee. We had numerous occasions when we had to evict people but one person called Wood was a pain in the bum: he caused problems wherever he went so I had him barred. A few months later at the Baths Committee meeting a councillor for Woodchurch Ward raised the question of Wood being barred: he said that only the council could exclude people, not officers. I immediately told the committee that as I was the licensee I could and would exclude anyone who caused trouble, but if any member of the committee wanted to have their name on the licence then it could be arranged.

All the councillors looked at the legal representative, who calmly said that the manager was right as it was his name on the licence, and that was the end of that.

We were having trouble when we were closed at night so I decided to change the cleaning arrangements. Instead of employing a number of part-time cleaners early morning we would have two permanent staff work all night, which would increase the security of the building at the same time. It worked well and reduced costs and vandalism.

Birkenhead was twinned with the French town of Genevilliers, the port of Paris. The Mayor Counsellor Eileen Keegan and I took a party of sports people on a visit. The age range of the team ranged from 16 years to 38 years, the older ones being in the judo team. We were accommodated in a leisure centre, and after competing they all wanted to go out on the town in Paris. There was no way I was going to allow the youngsters out so I struck a deal with the older members, that if they stayed in that night until the young ones went to bed I would take them into Paris.

We set off for the city after midnight with our own interpreter, one of the French organisers. We did a couple of night clubs and at about 4.30am, on our way home we went into a café to order a few drinks but we were told that it was about to close. We pleaded with the owner who was admiring my matching flowery tie and handkerchief. I said he could have them if he served us, and he did so wearing my tie.

On the last night the French organisers took the mayor and me out for dinner, and it was several courses long with a different wine with each course. Their Mayor made a speech then it was the turn of Eileen to speak, and she did so in English which was interpreted by our host. Then there was an announcement to which everyone clapped. I looked at Eileen but everyone was looking at me, then I was told that I was supposed to sing a song: I could have died. Eileen said that I could not let the town down, but I could not think of a song to sing other than "Nellie Dean", so off I went with Eileen joining in. It was a great success with everyone joining in the chorus.

Each year there was a conference organised by the Institute of Baths Managers, and it was customary for a councillor to attend with the chief officer. This year it was a lady councillor. She thought that I was going to arrange everything for her but that was not what I was used to, having attended several times previously: I would be staying with Gill at the conference hotel, the Imperial Hotel, Blackpool. The Councillor did not want to spend so much on the hotel and I thought that I had managed to get away from her, but no, she decided to book the Imperial.

I was well known at the conference as was Gill.

The Councillor only drank hot water, not tea, just hot water. She could put a damper on anything and anyone, and all she could talk about was herself. At a reception given by the town council the other managers could see that the councillor was following us about demanding attention. Nick from London said that he would dance with her which he did, he also got her drinking something that was very potent because she could hardly stand up by the end of the reception. The following morning Gill and I had breakfast on our own for the first time.

There were many firms who supplied local authorities with equipment who regularly attended the conference. One was a Scottish company who sold washing machines: their representative always wore his kilt and full regalia and Gill and I had got to know him well over the years. Gill and a few friends were sat in the lounge talking when the rep entered in a normal suit; Gill did not notice him and kept on talking. "Aren't you talking to me now?" he said to Gill, who looked up and realised who it was. "I didn't recognise you with your trousers on," she said. The whole room went quiet.

When I got back I told the Town Clerk that I was not going to any more conferences with councillors. The Councillor complained to Alderman Platt who took no notice at all and said that I had done the other officers a huge favour.

Grange Road West Sports Centre

In 1969 the council had the opportunity to purchase the old army drill hall in Grange Road West. It had been used to hold the North

West Badminton Championships for a number of years and I was asked to report on the potential use and conversion costs if we bought it. I did a detailed report with a drawing of the main hall showing all the different sports that we could cater for.

It was Christmas Eve when I got a phone call from Ian Holt the Town Clerk saying Alderman Platt wanted to see us both about the Drill Hall scheme, at his house at 11am. Ian was not at all pleased as he was about to drive to Nottingham to see his family for Christmas. Alderman Platt lived in a terraced house in Slatey Road near the Williamson Art Gallery.

We arrived at his house and were shown in to the living room, and his wife left us to make some tea. "Tell me about your plans for the Drill Hall," said the Alderman. I produced my report but he said, "I'm not reading that. Tell me how it will work and what will it cost and is it worth it." I told him and said it would be very good value for money and that there would be no other place like it in the north of England. "Right," said the Alderman, "that'll do, we will have it," and we did. Just like that. We had some tea and biscuits and left. I went home jubilant and Ian drove to Nottingham.

We obtained the hall immediately but it was a further year before we started the conversion. When it was finished it was used by the Sports Council as an example of good value for money in sports provision.

The county badminton association continued to use the hall but now many other sports also played there. Les Macklin was the badminton representative on the sports council, and he and I used to travel to meetings together. One day he was playing in the hall with his daughter, when he stopped and went to the café to get a cold drink of water. He did not return and his daughter went to look for him and found him on the floor dead. It was a terrible shock to his daughter but it was also a shock to all the staff including myself. When we completed the conversion of the sports centre we called the new bar "The Macklin Room" in memory of Les.

The Sports Hall was the first on Merseyside catering for all the indoor sports; many such as Handball and Volleyball were new to the area. I was the licensee so when our French Twin Town sent a sports team to compete with us the events were held there. The café fed them and the bar provided liquid refreshment that is until 10.30 pm, when I had to close the bar.

Our French visitors could not understand why we had to close so the Mayor asked me what I was going to do for no one wanted to stop drinking at 10.30. There were about 60 people, both teams and the VIPs. I phoned the owner of the Golden Guinea Club in New Brighton, John Stanley, and asked him if he would allow 60 visitors to his club: it was a Tuesday night which was a very quiet night so he was delighted.

A coach loaded with high spirited people, half French, arrived at the club, John took me to one side and said I did not have to pay for any drinks all night.

I was asked a number of times by the French why we could not drink at the Sports Hall but we could at the Golden Guinea. I could not explain, that was just British licensing law.

I was now on the North West Sports Council. I had gone to a public meeting in Liverpool about starting a Volleyball Association, and the room was packed but no one seemed to have any idea about running a meeting. I made a number of suggestions after which someone said I should be the Chairman. I told them I did not play volleyball but they said they could all play but could not manage meetings. I was voted in as Chairman that night and represented volleyball on the Sports Council.

Galway County Council, Ireland

There was a job advertised in Galway for someone to manage a multi-million pound sports and leisure complex which was to be funded by the Irish Government, The Tourist Board, and Galway County Council. It sounded like a perfect job. I applied for the job and was invited to attend for an interview in Dublin; I booked into a hotel and flew from Liverpool. When I arrived at the venue I was amazed to find about 60 other candidates, some I knew and one who had worked for me until a few weeks ago as a bath attendant. Either he should not have been there or I should not.

Three other colleagues of mine, from Wolverhampton, Edinburgh and Gateshead all agreed that it was a farce. We were all given a paper with multiple choice questions and told to tick the appropriate answer. The four of us just ticked any box and left to have a pint of Guinness in as many pubs in O'Connell Street as we could manage.

The following day I flew home. That night I had a phone call at 11:45pm from a Mr Fitzpatrick asking me if I would attend a second interview in Dublin and then Galway the following week to which I agreed. When I contacted my three colleagues they had all been invited to Galway but not Dublin. I arranged to meet the lads in Dublin after my interview; they were all meeting there and driving in one car, Joe's, to Galway so saving on expenses. The Council did not realise that we all knew each other, so we all claimed, then shared the money.

I had to be at No. 22 Fitzwilliam Square in the centre of Dublin, which I thought would be the HQ of the Tourist Office. When the taxi dropped me off I went to 22. There was a brass plate with 7 names on it but as I did not know any of them I thought that I must have got the number wrong. I went all round the four sides of the square but no Tourist Office or anything like it.

I returned to No.22 and was just about to leave when the door opened and an old lady said "Mr Barnes, Mr Barnes". I looked round and she said she was expecting me. "Come in," she said. She just looked like Margaret Rutherford, the actress who played eccentric parts. I followed her upstairs thinking it must be a joke or candid camera.

We went up to the top floor and in she went in to a bed sitting room. "Would you like a cup of tea?" she called out as she went behind a curtain. I was certain this was a set up.

She obviously knew me but I did not know who she was or even her name, but I decided to go along with the "game".

She appeared from behind the curtain with a tray of tea and biscuits. "How are your girls?" she asked. Then she realised that she had not introduced herself. "Do you know who I am?" she asked. I said that I had no idea and I was looking for the Tourist Board. She told me that she was the Professor of Psychology at Dublin University and she was to interview me prior to my attending the meeting in Galway.

She had read my application which is how she knew about my family. After a chat she said that she wanted me to look at some cards and say the first thing that came into my head. The cards were about a foot square that had been folded in half with black ink blobs on it and nothing else.

The first one looked like a large moth so I said "a woolly bear". The cards were thrown on the floor in front of me and I said whatever I could think of because nothing was easily identified until the tenth card. She threw it at my feet, I looked at the ink, and it was a perfect example of an erect penis entering the place it was made for. "A train entering a tunnel," I said. She looked at me and said nothing. "That's the first time I have heard that description," she said, then we finished.

I was by now fully back to my normal self so I asked her how on earth that had any connection with my ability to manage a Leisure Complex. She said that was only part of it and that she had a lot more to write up before she sent in her report. I agreed to leave her to it and I left to meet the lads.

When I told them of my meeting they all laughed and said the job must be mine. When the job was advertised there was no mention of the salary, and I had been asking around about schools and cost of living from the Irish Government and, as they did not reply, the Irish Embassy in London. I had a friend who worked in the Inland Revenue in Liverpool, who was able to get me information. He warned me of the Income Tax which rocketed over £2000 pa; it was called Surtax and was levied at 90% over this amount. I was advised therefore to get as much in kind as possible, like a house, a car, medical insurance, etc.

When we got to Galway they had put us up in four different hotels. Joe dropped us off and we all agreed to meet in my hotel for dinner that night.

The hotel was owned by the man who served us at the bar. I asked him what the cost of living was like and what sort of salary you would need to live quite well in Galway, £2000 to £2500 was his reply. I could not believe it bearing in mind the tax position. "What about the Income Surtax?" I asked. "You don't pay the tax," he said. "Are you sure?" I said. "You don't pay the tax because you don't fill up the forms" he replied, and he was speaking the truth.

I went for the interview and present were members of the Irish Tourist Board, the Government, Galway County Council, Local Councillors the Bishop's Representative and the Town Clerk. I was not at all sure that I wanted the job but I did want my expenses. I asked about a house and a car, and both were agreed, then I asked about the salary and the Income Tax position regarding Surtax. Not one of the panel had any idea about the tax or that it existed. I left thinking I was well out of it.

We were all told that we would be informed by letter of the outcome. Once again I was phoned late at night and told that I was being offered the job and they had agreed to all my requests. I said that I would need to bring my family to see the area, and this was also agreed. I did not know how to turn the job down, but then Gillian developed appendicitis and was rushed into Clatterbridge Hospital late at night. This was the excuse I needed which enabled me to withdraw from the job. Not long afterward the troubles started in Ireland which made me very pleased that I had turned down the job.

At Livingstone Street baths we had two long rooms which used to be full of slipper baths but were now empty, I realised that the area would be ideal to turn into a sauna suite. I got the architect, Peter Finney, and the works manager, Tom Liniker, to draw up a scheme, after taking them on a day out visiting other saunas in the north west. This was then priced and I submitted a report to the council showing that we could make a profit on the scheme and pay for it out of the income. The council agreed and so the best sauna suite in the north west opened a year later. Arthur Rimmer, one of my staff, was also the Physio at Tranmere Rovers FC; he was put in charge of the sauna which was the perfect arrangement for everyone. The conversion was a terrific success.

The oldest of the swimming pools was Argyle Street Baths. This was no longer used as a swimming pool, but the laundry and slipper baths were still in use. The building was in need of a lot of money for repairs so we carried out a survey to see who used the facilities and where they lived, as we had the same facilities at two other establishments. The results showed that the majority of customers only bathed every other week and that many could be catered for at Byrne Avenue Baths. It was decided to close the building, which was to be the first of many that I would close over the next 20 years.

Ibiza

I was asked by a construction firm who were well-known in the leisure industry if I would advise on a sports complex they were going to build. I did such a good job that they said I could use an apartment they had in Ibiza for two weeks which included the air fare for Gill, the girls and myself. The girls thought that this was the holiday of a lifetime, they had never been abroad, and we were all excited. On the plane we flew over the Pyrenees Mountains which we could see out of the window. I told Gillian that she would get a better view in the toilet; I said that if she looked down as she was sitting on the toilet she would see "the pair of knees" (Pyrenees). Gillian came out complaining that she did not see the mountains but when the others explained to her what I said she cried.

The apartment was at San Antonio Abad. The weather was hot and sunny with white sand on the beaches and clear warm water. We had a super time. One day when we all had been trying to speak a little Spanish I said that I would order lunch in three languages. The girls all said I couldn't do it. In we went to the bar and I ordered "Dos oeufs and chips", two eggs and chips.

It was that day we let them have a taste of wine, but what we did not notice was that Catherine was downing some of mine and Gill's. As we walked back to the apartment Cath said that it was like walking on air, and it was then that we noticed that she was a little drunk. We had so many laughs, especially when looking round a gift shop Gill got her finger stuck in the top of a goatskin leather water bottle: she was doubled up laughing so we all went out and left her in the shop. After much pulling and trying Gill managed to get free; but she has never again tried out water bottles.

Mum's Move

One morning at 6am there was a telephone call from the Preston Hospital saying that my mum had been taken in having suffered a heart attack. I drove to Preston convinced that I would be too late to see my mum but to my great relief she had survived though was very ill.

It was February and very cold. I stayed that night in my old home, 8 Dorman Road, and I have never been so cold in all my life. There was no central heating, to which I had become used to; I slept in all my clothes, a hat and still I was cold. There was ice on the inside of the bedroom windows. The next day I decided that my mum would have to move into sheltered housing.

Back in Birkenhead I saw my colleague, Cliff Darley, and Dr Phillip Nicholson the Medical Officer and arranged for my mum to have a place in a new development in Birkenhead on Woodchurch Road.

When my mum came out of hospital she told me she did not want to move after she had agreed to do so. I realised that it was a big decision to leave the only house she had lived in for 40 years. I said that the arrangements had been made and that I would carry her in my arms to my car if necessary, but she was going to move.

In the end she told me she was glad I had insisted and she moved into a ground floor apartment. It had a lounge, kitchen, bathroom and a bedroom, all with central heating. There was a warden on hand and I had a phone put in as well. I believe that the move added 15 years to her life. My mum had to give up driving so the Austin A35, which she had bought new for £550 was given to Gill to use for work.

Driving Tests

I have always believed that the second largest expense after a house is a car, so in order to get the maximum benefit from the car everyone should be able to drive it. With this in mind as soon as the girls reached 17 they started to learn to drive. Alison was the first, then Gillian because Cath had left home at 16 years. All of them said that it was much easier to take the test than to have a lesson with me, but they all passed first time. I used to do hill starts on Argyle Street South the steepest hill in Wirral, and we used to go into town at the busiest times. I was not bothered about long journeys, they were easy.

I was at work when Alison passed her test: I came back into my office to find her L plates on my desk and my car gone - she had taken it for a drive. When Gillian started her test at the Test Centre in Cleveland Street, Birkenhead, there was limited parking outside because there was a zebra crossing with zig zag lines leading up to it. I got Gillian to park at the start of the no parking lines so that no one would park in front of her and she would be able to set off easily. We went into the office along with a number of others waiting, one of whom was a BSM instructor.

They called out for Miss Barnes and Gillian went out with her examiner. To my dismay someone had parked their car on the zig zag lines within inches of Gillian's car. She had to go back and forwards 8 times to get out but she managed it. The BSM man said "she will be OK; mine could never have got out of that space".

Both of us went to a local café in Market Street for a cup of tea, and 30 minutes later we went back to the test centre to wait for our cars to return. The BSM pupil arrived but there was no sign of Gillian; I walked up and down the road and 10 minutes later I was getting worried, when I saw the examiner walking back to the centre. "Where is my daughter?" I asked. "Is she all right?" He said that he could not discuss an examination with me, and walked inside. I was now very worried for Gillian and my car, when I heard a toot toot, and saw Gillian driving on her own waving as she passed by. She had only gone for a drive on her own.

Cath was 21 when I taught her to drive; it was not easy as Cath and I tended to clash at times. One day she stopped the car and threatened to get out of the car if I shouted at her again. She hasn't changed.

In contrast Pop never took a test and yet he had a full licence to drive any vehicle because the national driving test only came in 1934, and prior to that you just asked for a licence and he did.

Aunty Dorothy

After my mum moved I suggested that Aunty Dorothy would be better off in sheltered accommodation in Blackburn: she lived in a terraced house in Hargreaves Lane with an outside toilet in the yard and only a sink with no hot water. There were two rooms upstairs and two down. The only heating was an open coal fire. Dorothy had not been upstairs for two years at least. When Uncle Bill told us that he could not get Dorothy moved I had a word with our Medical Officer, Phillip Nicholas, who in turn spoke to his opposite number in Blackburn and we managed to get Dorothy a council bungalow in a sheltered accommodation block. This was to change her life forever.

Pop and I got a skip delivered to Hargreaves Lane and we filled it with all her old belongings.

It was the only way to do it, even though we must have thrown out some valuable antiques. Dorothy loved her new accommodation; she was warm with modern facilities, and it was the best thing we could have done for her.

Each summer and every Christmas we brought Dorothy to stay with us for 4-6 weeks; this included filling the car with all her belongings which now included Kim, her small dog.

Dorothy was by now very large and could only get about on crutches; if we wanted to keep her in one room we hid her crutches. Aunty Dorothy was someone once met you never forgot or never wanted to forget: everyone loved her.

I used to brew my own beer which was very, very strong. One night I was having a beer when she asked for a sip. I gave Dorothy the glass and she downed the lot in one go. "That was nice," she said, "Can I have a glass?" "Only if you sip it," I said. I poured her a glass, handed it to her but before I could sit down she had drunk the lot. Gill and I looked at her and wondered how she would get upstairs to bed. As the night wore on Dorothy began to giggle and could not stop. "She's drunk," said Gill and I agreed.

The time came for Dorothy to go to bed; she usually went upstairs on her hands and feet. I stood behind her ready to catch her if she fell but Dorothy stood up and with one hand on the banister walked up the stairs, one leg after the other, completely upright. I followed behind hoping that she would not fall back onto me. She went to the toilet and then walked unaided to her bedroom. She said goodnight and went to bed. Gill and I started to laugh and could not believe what we had just seen.

In the morning I took Dorothy a cup of tea and asked if she had slept. She said it was the best night's sleep she could remember. "How did you get into bed?" I asked. "I waited until it came round the third time then I jumped in," she said. That sums up Aunty Dorothy.

Birkenhead Council was developing land at Noctorum and Ford Estates. When the plans for Ford were being drawn up the Planners asked me what I wanted in the way of recreation facilities, I said a swimming pool and sports hall, and so this was added. No councillor input was involved but at least the residents would have something, unlike on the Noctorum Estate where nothing was included.

As usual the houses were built before any of the amenities, which meant that there was nothing for people to do. The residents of the Ford Estate were up in arms; it was decided to hold a public meeting in the school hall to try and calm things down.

The night of the meeting was electric, the hall was packed with people standing, and I was on the stage next to the Chairman who was having a rough time trying to explain why there were no amenities.

The people did not want excuses and shouted him down. He then stood up and shouted to everyone that "I will have a temporary erection on the estate within a few months". I could hardly believe what he had said and had to bite my lip to stop laughing. Others had no such qualms and many people started to laugh. The chairman left the meeting still not knowing why the people had laughed at his promise. The outcome was that he didn't, but we did erect a temporary building on the estate which remained until the sports centre opened.

When Cath was 14 years old she and I decided to have a few days walking in the Lake District. We drove up to Keswick and booked a B & B. I decided to take Cath up Borrowdale and then climb Great Gable if we could manage that far. We parked the car in the valley and started the long hike to Sty Head Tarn. From the tarn you cannot see the summit for it is almost straight up, and Cath kept asking how far it was to the top. I said just over the next hill but after an hour of this she did not believe me. When we did reach the top it was raining and the cloud was low so we did not see a thing.

On the way home we stopped at an old pub called the Drunken Duck near Coniston. We sat outside and ate our sandwiches; both Cath and I wanted to use the loo so in we went.

There were a number of locals at the bar so I went up to them and asked where the ladies toilet was, thinking Cath was right behind me. "It's over there mate but it's full of bloody women!" said one of them and they all burst out laughing. I looked round and Cath was nowhere to be seen. I went into the gents and could hear them still having a good laugh at me. I was so embarrassed that I climbed out of the toilet window so that I would not have to face them again, and when I saw Cath she was bent double laughing and crying at the same time.

CHAPTER ELEVEN

1973 - 1984 Wirral Metropolitan Borough Council

1973 Local Government Re-Organisation

For a year or two all the councils had been preparing for re-organisation which would take place in 1974, but the appointments and elections would start in 1973. Everyone was jockeying for position. There were five Local Authorities: Birkenhead, Wallasey, Bebington, Hoylake, and part of Cheshire County Council

The elections resulted in no party having overall control but the Labour party was the largest party. Alderman Jack Roberts, the leader of Birkenhead Council, was the most prominent politician with Councillor Billy Wells and Councillor Malcolm Thornton, both from Wallasey, close behind.

We had no idea how the new council would organise itself. Would there be separate indoor and outdoor departments, plus libraries and entertainment? No one knew, which meant that all the discussions were about making sure that everyone had a job, but which job was the burning question for each of us.

I felt that I was in a good position being in charge of all indoor sport and entertainment as a Chief Officer, that is I was not subordinate to any other officer, bur reported directly to the committee. The only other Chief Officers in our discipline were Walter Briggs, Birkenhead Parks, and Bert Arthur Birkenhead, Chief Librarian. All the other departments in the other authorities were not chief officers. In total there were parts of 15 departments in 5 different authorities, all vying for position.

As I have already pointed out I had learned from the re-organisation in London that I needed to get known in as many different areas as possible. I was a chief officer in Birkenhead, and I lived in Hoylake and played golf in Wallasey. I also got involved in HIPO, the Hoylake Indoor Pool Organisation which was campaigning for an indoor swimming pool in the Hoylake/West Kirby area, and the Council asked my advice on the plans which were being drawn up by Cheshire County Council. There were many basic mistakes with the plans such as not being able to get a stretcher on to the bath side in emergencies, the lights in the sports hall were in the wrong place for badminton courts, the walls were white coloured which would not show up a shuttle cock in play, there was no lift for disabled participants. Altogether there were 4 pages of mistakes which needed to be corrected, and this did not go down well with the architect in charge of the project but Hoylake Council were very pleased to have my comments.

Everyone was on edge that year, and no one wanted to go on holiday in case they missed the interviews. I was talking to one of the councillors who said quite innocently, "Nothing will happen while Jack Roberts is away." Quite so I thought: when is he away? Once I had the date I went home and told Gill that we could go away for two weeks holiday.

We went to the travel agents in Prenton and asked what was available for the two weeks in July. They had a cabin on Thompson's new cruise ship *Ithaca,* on its maiden voyage, but they could only hold the cabin for 6 hours. We thought about it and said yes; we had never been on a cruise before.

We flew to Brindisi in southern Italy and cruised for 14 days all round the eastern Mediterranean, stopping at Athens, Istanbul, Beirut, Cypress, Rhodes, Crete and Corfu. On our visit to Jeruselam we visited the Church of the Holy Sepulchre just as the priests were changing over; it seems that the church is looked after by three religions, Christian, Greek Orthodox and Byzantine, and we saw the priests fighting over the money in the collection plates.

It was this and other events that we saw in the Holy Places that turned me from a Catholic to an Atheist. Even including this, it was a wonderful trip and just what I needed. On returning home I found that there had been information given out about the organisation of the new Wirral Authority. There was to be a Chief Executive and eight other departments with directors, all of equal status and salary.

Director of Leisure Services 1973

This new authority was the first to include all the leisure activities: libraries, theatres, entertainment, sport, swimming, parks, and beach patrol, including publicity, plus the addition of cemeteries and crematoria into one department. The latter would report to the Housing and Environmental Health Committee.

This was such a bold move that it made the appointment of the Director of Leisure Services attractive to many more people, such as the Town Clerks, Engineers, and other Chief Officers in the smaller authorities.

The first appointment was the Chief Executive, and Ian Holt, the Town Clerk of Birkenhead, got the job. Next was Director of Finance, Norman Rothwell of Wallasey was appointed. Director of Education was next: Reg Price, Birkenhead Education Chief was successful. Director of Engineering Services saw Frank Roget, Wallasey, and then Director of Development was Roger Shaw also of Wallasey. The Director of Admin and Legal Services was given to Gerald Chapel, from Bebington, and Director of Social Services was Douglas Jones.

By this time both me and my friend and colleague in Birkenhead, Cliff Darley, who was the Environmental Officer, were convinced that one of the unsuccessful town clerks would get the last two directors' jobs.

It was such a shock when Cliff was appointed as Director of Housing and Environmental Health; he phoned me and said that it proved that I had a good chance of being appointed.

Cath was going on a school trip to the Isle of Man and would be away when the interviews were to take place, so, this being the days before mobile phones and email, we devised a scheme where I would send a telegramme saying "Water wings" if I was successful.

The night before the interview I lay in bed thinking what questions would I ask if I was on the interview panel? I knew I could do the job and that I was the best qualified but I had to convince a committee of eight people.

There were 15 people to be interviewed: town clerks, engineers, deputy clerks and engineers, as well as parks, baths and library chief officers from all the authorities.

The interviews took place in the town hall at Birkenhead and everyone was on edge. When I was called in I sat down facing the panel and the first question was as expected, "Why should we offer you the job?" I explained that while no one had the experience of all the disciplines that were to be managed I had experience of most of them and certainly more than any of the other applicants. I was on the National Sports Council and a member of the Entertainment Managers Association; I had been in charge of entertainment as well as indoor and outdoor sports provision. They then asked me about my previous positions and my experience of opening and commissioning new buildings.

The third question was asked by Clr. Bill Wells of Wallasey. He asked "What would you do about developing New Brighton?" I smiled but before I could answer Bill Wells said "What's so funny?" I replied that last night I had thought about what I would ask if I was in his place, and he had just asked the third question I had chosen.

"Well go on then, what is your answer?" said Bill Wells. "If anyone gives you a quick slick answer to this question they are not the person for the job. I would make it a priority to look into problems facing New Brighton and then submit a professional report for the Council to consider."

There were no more questions so I retired to sit with the other applicants. A few minutes after the last person came out I was called back in and offered the job. I could not speak at first, and Bill Wells said, "Are you going to accept the job?" I said yes and thank you very much.

I had just doubled my salary from £4000 to £8000, but more importantly I had achieved my dream, for this was the most important job within the leisure field in the UK.

Gill and the girls were so pleased, and I telephoned the operator to send Cath a telegramme. "What do wish to say?" asked the telegramme lady. "Water wings," I replied. "Is that all?" she said. "Yes, she will understand thanks." The fact that I had been appointed as Director in Wirral, on equal footing with all the other Chief Officers, spread round the country like wildfire. I was asked to write an article for Bath and Indoor Recreation, the journal of my institute, and to give a talk at the autumn conference.

At 39 years old I was by far the youngest of the directors. The first job was to sit in on the appointment of my deputy and the third-tier officers, recreation, libraries, entertainment, etc. A number of my former colleagues in Birkenhead were disappointed at not being successful in getting the director's job, even to the point of being jealous that I had been appointed, and this was a problem like many that I would be faced with over the next 12 months.

A short list for the deputy director's post was drawn up with many of the same people who had applied for my job included. The interviews were conducted by the panel of Councillors and me.

It was an insight into the attitude of those who thought they should have had the director's job that surprised me most. A Birkenhead Chief Officer was almost arrogant towards the members, so much so that not only did he not get the job but it was said that he would not get the next one either.

The choice of the panel was Brian Lucas, Engineer at Hoylake. I knew Brian but he was not my first choice. We discussed the issue and I agreed that Brian would be appointed; it turned out to be the best decision that I ever made. Brian was totally loyal, a very good administrator and his strengths were my weaknesses. Not only did we work well together, we became lifelong friends.

The whole detailed structure of each department was to be put before a special meeting of the Council the day after Boxing Day 1973. The chief officers had all presented their staffing structures to each other the week prior to Christmas in order to get feedback on their suggestions.

I was told that there was no way that mine would get the agreement of the Council. I spent the whole of the holiday going over the structure and my reasons for it, so much so that it spoiled my Christmas, but at least I knew all the arguments to support my case.

On the day of the meeting I was told that the Council would kick off with Leisure Services. I had a flip chart; set up and of course all the councillors had had a copy of my report prior to Christmas. Soon after I started to speak, Clr Wells had a question which I answered easily, then another and another until I said to the Chairman, "If Clr Wells had read the report he would know the answers." Clr. Wells jumped up and said he had read the report and did not accept my reasoning.

I carried on, and in all I was speaking for 45 minutes without even looking at any notes. When I sat down the other directors knew that I had taken the sting out of the opposition and my recommendations were accepted.

From January to April 1st 1974 everyone had two jobs, their existing one and the one they had been given with the new authority. In many cases lower down it was going to be the same but for the top tier of management there was double the workload.

During these three months the Leisure Services Department and me personally had a rough time at council meetings, so much so that I spoke to the Director of Administration and Legal Services, Gerald Chapel, a truly great man. He did not know of any reason for the aggression but asked me to sit quiet while he phoned the Leader of the Opposition, Clr. Bill Wells.

The phone rang and he said "Chapel here sir. Is there any reason why you have been giving Brian Barnes and his department a hard time recently?"

"Bloodeeey Hell No, we picked on him because we thought he could take it. It will be someone else's turn next" The conversation went on for a short time then finished. "You heard that did you?" said Gerald, "I wonder who will be next."

1974 - Wirral Metropolitan Borough Council.

The morning of April 1st I received a telephone call from the Chief Executive, Ian Holt, to say that at midnight the old Wallasey Council had done a land swap and I now had Leasowe Castle and adjoining land added to my department. I had to secure it and put a caretaker in immediately. "And by the way," he said, "the Wallasey Parks staff have gone on strike." What a start to my new job!

There were two parts to each director's job, one was to manage a department, and the other was to collectively manage the whole of the Authority. I found this a wonderful challenge and opportunity. Although I had to get used to seeing the bigger picture and doing a lot of homework, it was much easier for me to move up, than for the likes of the Director of Finance to have his opinions challenged.

I had a lot to learn about collective responsibility and loyalty, or lack of it. It took me over a year to realise that the Director of Education would always agree that we should share sports and recreation facilities with the public when not in use by schools, but it never happened. He said yes to me and the other directors then went away and did his own thing.

The Social Services Director never agreed with anyone but still did his own thing. He would never agree at any review of spending or prioritising of his department's services; all he wanted was more and more resources at the expense of anyone and everyone.

The financial climate was getting worse each year with the government seeking more and more cuts in Local Government spending. In the old days the big three would have started with cutbacks in the "minor departments" of parks, baths, libraries and health. Now those services were on equal terms with the big boys and could and did argue their case.

Education, Social Services, Engineering, Finance and Adimin and Legal Services all had to justify "their" expenditure so that the whole authority was under scrutiny, as it should be. Even then Douglas Jones would go to any lengths to keep us from looking into his department.

A trick both Education and Social Services Departments used, was to find out which Councillor was wanting to make savings, then they would pick a school or care home in that Councillor's ward and suggest closing it. Neither of them used management assessment.

With the exception of these two officers the rest of the management group got along very well, and after a meeting we would meet in the Magazine Pub in Wallasey for a drink to wind down before returning home. This followed on from the past practise of the Wallasey Chief Officers. It became a great way to bond together and was very enjoyable as well; I made very good friends with them all.

My new department consisted of fifteen parts of five former Councils. The first task was to try and get them all to feel part of the new Department of Leisure Services (Tourism came later). It was not an easy task and was made more difficult by some senior staff still smarting over not getting the job they thought should have been theirs, but most of the staff felt that they were part of a new beginning.

To help with the bonding I took a leaf out of Frank Roget's book and asked Gill if she would make a meal for about 12 -15 of the senior staff prior to the Christmas break.

It was also cheaper to buy in the drinks and food than to pay a pub or restaurant.

Over the years it became the talk of the department, and the aim of all staff was to get on the list for Barnes's Christmas Do. Gill never failed, even making an especially hot curry for Walter Briggs after he complained the previous year that it was mild.

I had appointed a person from outside local government to be Head of Entertainment and Special Promotions, David Lee previously with British Airways. Dave suggested holding a "Christmas Do" in a local nightclub away from any specific part of the department in 1974.

We took over the whole of the Hamilton Club in Birkenhead.

Unknown to me Dave Lee had special "Banknotes" printed (by photocopying a £1 note and superimposing my head on it in place of the Queen). While this went down well, it was of course illegal.

This was one of many schemes Dave came up with and although he was a breath of fresh air to Local Government most of the time not even the Council had the authority to do the things he did. In the end

I had to advise Dave that he was not the sort of person to work in local government so he returned to the private sector, but I will never forget working with, and worrying about, Dave Lee.

Ray Wood a Wallasey man, who had been his second-in-command was promoted to head the section and proved to be one of my best and most successful appointments, as well as becoming a good friend.

The financial situation did not help morale. The National Government kept squeezing more and more out of Local Government. One day in the town hall cloakroom as I was putting on my coat Clr Wells remarked that it was a wonder that I could get my coat on over all the knives in my back.

He would not say who he was referring to but he advised me to watch out for some of my senior staff. I did know who they were but there was not much I could do about it other than let the individuals know that if they did not like the set-up they had a choice retire, leave, or get used to it. It was not until many years later when most had moved on that things could function as they should. The same problems were evident in all the other departments of the Council.

Each of the five local authorities had started or had just completed building a major sports complex prior to reorganisation in 1974. Wirral could not afford to open them all and I was told to put the Leasowe and West Kirby centres on hold.

Each Director had a separate private telephone on his desk which did not go through any member of staff. One day I was contacted by Clr Wells the Labour Leader on the private phone while I was on the other phone to Clr Thornton the Tory Leader. I never told either of them about the other, but I am sure that it was a test to see if I could be trusted.

These were troubled times with the council having no party with an overall control, although the Tories were the largest party.

Council Meetings started at 6.15pm and usually adjourned at 1am to recommence the following day at 6.15pm. All committee meetings started at 6.15pm.

In a six-week cycle there were five meetings I had to attend, plus the Council Meetings.

In 1974 we had a number of very good orators on the Council: Clrs Wells, Thornton and Porter (the latter two became MPs), and Griff Evans (later Lord Evans). All could hold the council chamber spellbound with sparkling wit and quick remarks.

There is not the same talent now in any of the politicians from any party. I believe that this is partly due to the very low esteem that councillors are now held in by the general public and the poor standard of Chief Officers who do not have the confidence, backbone or ability to exert their rightful authority to manage their departments within the political objectives set by councillors.

One day I had a phone call from Clr Wells on the private line asking me when the Leasowe Centre was going to open. I told him it was confidential information, to which he replied that running the Leisure Services was far easier than controlling the Labour Group, and he needed the information promising that he would never let me down. I did not give him the actual date but just enough information to allow him to make a very accurate guess.

He never did let me down and on many occasions supported me when others attacked my department, which was just as well for he was a formidable opponent in the council chamber.

As I was the only Chief Officer in the UK in charge of both Sport and Leisure and also Arts and Libraries I was an adviser to the Association of Metropolitan Authorities on both the Sports and Arts Committees. These Committees advised the Minister for Sport and the Minister for the Arts, and I used to travel to London regularly for both.

London Car Bomb

One meeting was at the Arts Council of Great Britain in Piccadilly. We finished about 1pm and Roy Bee from Manchester, myself, and a few others left the building and turned left into a side street to find a pub that did food as did most did in central London.

As we sat eating we heard sirens and police cars passing at speed with lights flashing and horns sounding, not an unusual situation at that time with all the IRA bombs going off.

After about an hour we got up to leave for home but we were stopped at the door by a policeman who told us that there was bomb scare close by and all the roads were closed. We all thought nothing of it and settled down with another pint. As time went by I realised that Gill might be worried knowing that I was in London, plus we were hours late for the train.

We all decided to seek a back way out of the pub to try and get to Euston Station. The gent's toilet was outside in a rear yard, and there was a door through which we could see a narrow passage. There was no one about so off the five of us slowly walked to the end of the passageway. There was a helicopter hovering which was very low overhead, and as we reached the end of the passage we were at Piccadilly 150 yards east of the Arts Council building where we had been for our meeting.

There was a single car parked outside and a robot machine was approaching it. There were no police, only army bomb disposal personnel keeping well away from the car.

William, one of our group suddenly said, "That's my car!" just as the robot machine fired a shell into the boot. There was a bang but no large explosion, and the car was destroyed. We all looked at William who was usually full of himself; he was devastated.

William had always boasted that he never bothered about parking his car he just left it and paid the fine if they managed to get it to him, but this time his luck had deserted him. We all felt it was justice and wondered just how he would explain the incident to his insurance company. Roy and I left William and the rest as we made our way to the Liverpool train and home.

1975 Cath leaves home

I came home from a Council meeting one night and Gill and the girls said they wanted to tell me something. We all sat down and Gill said that Catherine wanted to leave home. I could not believe what I had heard, the first thing I thought of was what had I done wrong, so I said, "Why leave? You have your own room." Gill said that she wanted to have more independence; she had the chance to move in with a friend in Birkenhead.

That night in bed Gill tried to explain just why Cath felt she needed to move. I still could not understand but as Gill said it is better to let her go with our blessing than to fall out over it. On 4th January 1975 we helped Cath to move to an old Victorian house on the edge of Birkenhead Park. It looked a mess; Cath had a bed-sit with a shared bathroom on the first floor. As we left her there Gill and I could not believe that she preferred to live there more than with us in Hoylake.

It took me quite some time to get used to Cath leaving home, and one evening after a meeting I was feeling fed up when one of the directors told me to snap out of it and asked what was wrong. When I told them about Cath moving out most of my colleagues smiled and said that their kids had done the same years ago. That put things in perspective for me and helped me get used to the situation.

York Avenue

1976 I was advised by my bank manager to move house and take out a large mortgage to help offset my income tax. We moved to a four-bedroomed bungalow 31, York Avenue, West Kirby. The property had been advertised at £27,000 but the agent said they would take less. It was a super place but we had set our limit at £19,000.

I asked the Borough Valuer to advise me, and he said that it was worth the £27, 000 but why not offer £21,000 which we did, and to our surprise it was accepted. Although it was above our limit we could manage the payments if we cut down on other things. The girls were as excited as Gill and I; they each had their own bedroom again.

It was now an established thing that everyone came to us for Christmas dinner, even when it meant that I went over to Preston for Gran and Pop then to Blackburn for Dorothy, taking them back at night. One Christmas Gill cooked for 17 people, I will never know how she did it, but it is very good as well as on time. What a wife!

Sailing – West Kirby Sailing Club (WKSC)

I joined the club in September 1979.

I decided I would like to learn to sail now that we lived in West Kirby which had a marine lake $^1/_2$ mile long. I bought a second hand Enterprise dinghy that I saw for sale in Heswall but I could not keep it upright, so in early spring the following year I went on a week's sailing course at Windermere run by the RYA.

Gill came and stayed in the accommodation but did not take the course; instead she acted as a helper to all who needed things bought from the shops in town. Cath was on the course but relatives were not allowed to sail together so I was paired with Margaret, a nurse who was married to a doctor also on the course.

It was bitterly cold, and one morning we had to clear six inches of snow off the boats before we launched them. There were three in the boat, Margaret, me and the instructor. Halfway through the week we had to practise man overboard drill, and we should have known when the instructor turned up in his wet suit. He was helming, when he suddenly fell backwards over the side and shouted, "Man overboard!" I grabbed the tiller, turned the boat round and Margaret grabbed him.

The instructor pretended to be unconscious and just lay in the water; we could not get him into the boat: although we had his arms over the side of the boat we could not lift him out of the water. I told Margaret to hang on to him while I reached down into the water and grabbed him between the legs. He jumped into the boat and said, "That's not fair." "No," I replied, "but it's bloody effective."

We all had a good laugh and sailed back to the shore. I learned a lot on that course, and on the last day we had a race between all the boats from the top of the lake at Ambleside to Windermere. There was very little wind so we all sat there wondering what to do, when out of nowhere we had a gust of wind that overturned many boats. We were lucky that due to our combined weight we managed to stay upright and we won the race.

When I bought my boat, Dennis Butler, my neighbour, said he would sail with me. I thought he was a competent sailor but he was not much better than me. We had many a good laugh as we tried to sail on the marine lake; the boat was too fast and lively for us at that time in our sailing career.

We used to capsize regularly but over the year we managed to improve a little. We entered the West Kirby Sailing Club (WKSC) handicap races but tried to keep out of everyone's way rather than race.

One day we were racing when we capsized; I stood in the water holding the boat head-to-wind, while Denis bailed out the water from inside the boat. The lake was only 5ft deep.

There are two openings at the stern of the boat, and the idea is that if you get water in you sail off as fast as you can, put your weight at the back of the boat and the water empties itself. Unfortunately we had the weight at the front of the boat, so that the water went to the bow and we sailed down under the water like a submarine.

This happened at one of the marks on the course. Sailing rules state that you must give way to other racing boats so that they can get round the mark if they are on the inside of you. We were in no fit state to do anything when Blair, the club secretary, racing at great speed, shouted, "Water on the mark," telling us to get out of the way. I replied by shouting "Rule 49," and did nothing.

When we eventually got back to the club house drinking a pint, Blair came up to me and asked what Rule 49 was. I said "Piss off; we're out of control and sinking." (There is no rule 49).

One of the local class boats sailed at West Kirby is a Hilbre, which is 19ft long, clinker built and made of mahogany. Denis and I bought No3 Hilary, and we had many happy times sailing and racing Hilary although we never won a race.

We raced the boat to Rhyl and took the boat to the Menai Straits a number of times. To race a Hilbre you have to have three people in the boat and it is not always easy to get the third crew member. In order to get as many boats sailing as we could I would often sail with other boats and others would sail with us.

No 20 Hilda with Tony Goodwin, Dave Graham, and Dave Jones sailed together a lot especially at the Straits. One year I stayed at the Black Bull Pub in Beaumaris while Hilda's crew camped at the local campsite. The weather was typical Straits weather, wet, cold and raining.

We had been on the boat for hours going nowhere due to lack of wind so we decided to put the engine on and go back to Beaumaris. I went on the foredeck to unhook the jib when Dave pulled on the halyard which slipped from my cold hand and managed to get hooked up my left nostril. I shouted for Dave to let go and stood up as the halyard went higher, before he realised that I was stuck on the end. Blood rushed from my nose and all the shouts were, "Don't get blood on the sails," from the others on board.

By the time I got back to the pub I was cold, wet and bleeding; I went straight into the hot shower, clothes and all, and stayed there until I got warm. On other occasions Gill came to stay and we hired a cottage for the week; the lads enjoyed this as they were better fed than normal.

All the races start at Beaumaris, then move to the southern end at Caernarfon for the second week. The race through the Straits themselves is a truly great experience, at low water but the current is so strong that it takes the boats through the rapids, forwards, backwards, even sideways, until they emerge at the southern end when you can really start to steer the boats and race each other.

Gillian

Gillian left school and was successful in being accepted at Bradford University to read Modern Languages. After a year she decided that she did not wish to be an interpreter or teach children, and she just didn't like being a student, so she decided to leave. This was also the time of the "Ripper" Peter Sutcliffe who was killing a number of women in the area over a period of time, and that had certainly given us something to worry about.

After leaving university Gillian got herself a job with George Henry Lee in Liverpool, but soon came home and announced that she was going to join the Merseyside Police.

Gill and I had many sleepless nights worrying about our youngest patrolling the city centre late at night. I told her I thought she would never stick at it but she did.

Gillian thoroughly enjoyed her job and was promoted to Sergeant; amongst other things, she joined the Mounted Section which is where she wanted to be. Seeing my daughter sat on top of a very large horse called Sean, a real scouser who looked after her well, made me a very proud dad indeed.

Many years after abandoning her studies at university, while in the police Gillian obtained her degree in Police Studies, by studying in her own time.

1977 Cath and Mike

Cath was now living in Aigburth Liverpool, and told us she was going to get married to Mike Murphy, a lad she had been seeing for some time. Mike worked with a band but wanted to have his own private-hire car, so I sold him my Ford Cortina E, quite a posh car at the time, which he used.

They got married in the registry office in Liverpool. Mike's brother and his mum Aggie, Gill and I, Gillian and Alison, attended with the "reception" after in the Grapes Pub in the city centre.

Most Sundays Gill cooked lunch and the girls brought their current boyfriends round, along with Cath and Mike and Grandma plus Gran and Pop some weeks. At first the boys held back when the food was passed round but they soon learned that if you did not get it first time round there was nothing left.

I had now got myself an allotment next to one of my park staff, Ron Dransfield, who showed me how to plant and grow the finest vegetables. We grew enough to feed all my family plus Grandma and Cath and Mike as well.

Over the next few years the department took over responsibility for tourism and was re-named Department of Leisure Services and Tourism. Things began to settle down but there was so much going on that I was at work every day and most evenings as well. I was licensee as we had licensed bars at all the Leisure Centres as well as the theatres and public halls.

Royal Visits

We had four Royal Visits, the first being when the Duke of Edinburgh visited the Oval Sports Centre, arriving by helicopter. As the helicopter circled the athletics track prior to landing it flew low over the Civic Reception Party, and the downdraft blew the Lord Lieutenant, Sir Douglas Crawford, off his feet which was an embarrassment although he was not physically hurt.

We also had Princess Ann who came to open the Community Centre at Livingstone Street; she was the nicest and easiest to get along with. I had to introduce the Princess to all the VIPs including Gill my wife, and then I took the Princess round the building. When we were having tea and biscuits she asked me if she could meet the ladies who had made the refreshments. We went to the kitchen and the Princess spent some time talking to all the ladies, a thoughtful act that made their day.

The second time the Duke visited the Department was the opening of Leasowe Leisure Centre. I had been approached by the Lord Lieutenant's Office nine weeks prior to the opening to see if we could carry out the security checks with the Special Branch in case the Duke performed the opening of the centre. Having done this a number of times in the past we provided details of all the staff, councillors, participants etc to Special Branch. It was the time when the IRA and others were bombing buildings and events throughout Britain.

A number of weeks later I received a call from our Mayor informing me that the Duke of Edinburgh is to open the centre; but that this information was top secret and no one must be told for the time being. I smiled as I told the Mayor that the secret was safe with me.

On the opening day it was my job to introduce all the staff to the Duke and to explain the philosophy of the centre while walking round the indoor and then the outdoor facilities. At one point the Duke remarked sharply, "You have told me that already". Suitably rebuked I carried on. On all these occasions Gill was with me sharing the moment. The fourth Royal Visit was that of Princess Alexandra.

At this time the Government put the squeeze on Local Government finances, so much so that all pay was frozen so that even though I should have received yearly increments I did not get them, this put a severe strain on our cash flow at home. The council would not let me open the newly constructed West Kirby Centre which was to be called the Concourse, a name chosen by John Shepherd, my Assistant Director Administration. The fact that the building was finished but closed was a cause of much disquiet amongst the residents.

I suggested to the Council that if I could keep the cash taken at the till I would open the Concourse one part at a time starting with the most profitable so that it would be self financing (bearing in mind that the loans and security costs were already being paid).

I started by opening the squash courts and bar, then the sports hall, café and finally the swimming pool. A year later I converted an area into a sauna which was paid for out of profits. (It is now closed. Why?).

Special Promotions
New Brighton Rock

The department was now running at a hectic pace and there was always something happening in Wirral. The Publicity and Special Promotions Department managed to attract a number of television shows: It's a Knockout, Sports Family of the Year, Superstars (twice), Swap Shop, televised professional snooker and wrestling, European Golf Tournament, The Transplant Games (twice), English Schools Athletics Championships, County Cricket with Cheshire v Yorkshire, international netball with England v New Zealand, and The Antiques Road Show.

Because of our contacts and our past co-operation with the media, Granada Television approached us to make what was, at the time, the largest outside broadcast show in Europe; they called it "New Brighton Rock".

The venue was to be in the New Brighton open-air swimming pool which seated 10,000 people. A stage would be built in the middle of the water and the event would be recorded over four nights in the autumn. All the top artists in the music world both here and in America would be performing. No charge would be made for entrance to the recording sessions but tickets would be distributed to the Council and the general public.

On the day the tickets were made available the result was chaos, with the police having to be called out to disperse the crowds. The police recommended that we distribute the tickets through organisations and youth clubs. The mayor and the councillors all asked for allocations as did the chief officers, but many were given to youth organisation and voluntary bodies.

The first evening of recording was quite an event; many mayoral cars arrived as guests of our Mayor, along with a host of VIPs. In conjunction with Granada Television we laid on a reception area with drinks etc. and the whole atmosphere was electric with every seat taken and people standing all round the back of the seats. My daughter Gillian was on duty with several of her police colleagues.

Once the VIPs had been shown to their places the show started and I relaxed. I wandered round the swimming pool drinking in the great atmosphere; everyone was enjoying themselves.

On the far side of the pool standing at the rear of the crowd was Gillian in her uniform. I went up behind her and grabbed her with my arms and said, "Its great isn't it?" To my horror the officer who turned round, with her arm raised ready to hit me, was not my daughter but another policewoman. I put my arms up and shouted, "Sorry I am Constable Barrington's dad." She slowly lowered her arm and then laughed and I joined in. It was a close thing, and something Gillian and the other officer had a good laugh about.

Some of the artists taking part were:

Gloria Gaynor, Flying Pickets, Frankie Goes to Hollywood, Eddy Grant, Helen Terry, Madness, Spandau Ballet, Nick Kershaw and Weather Girls

Chariots of Fire

Ray Wood who was in charge of Special Promotions and Publicity was also a very good friend of mine. One day he came into my office and said that a film company wanted to use the Oval sports centre to make a film about the 1924 Paris Olympics; the director was David Putnam.

Having been involved with the film industry before in Eastcote where we were taken for a ride on the amount they paid for the facilities they required, I told Ray to negotiate down to the fine detail of their requirements and then involve myself.

The film was called Chariots of Fire. The oval track and stadium was built at the time of the Olympics, 1924 and was just what they wanted. After some negotiating Ray thought he had a deal but I was not happy with the amount of money they were prepared to pay. I entered the meeting with David Putman and others who thought that we would be overawed by the fact that a major film was to be made at our centre. I refused to allow the use of the centre unless the offer was greatly increased. To help them out I said we would provide the catering for the film crew at the same cost they would pay an outside caterer, and we would also take up and re-lay the running track and provide a cinder track as was in use in 1924, also for the same price as an outside contractor.

This sealed the deal to everyone's satisfaction especially when many of my staff acted as extras as well. We were also able to help in obtaining other venues locally, such as Birkenhead Ferry Terminal as the Dover ferry, and Liverpool Town Hall as the Palace at Versailles.

All in all it was something that helped to put us firmly on the map.

As part of the publicity programme we had a department tie designed. It was felt that we should have it made in three colours: blue, red and yellow, one for each political party.

They would sell for £3 each.

I took a few samples to the committee and showed them to the councillors, telling them the price, £3 each, or as a special offer to the committee they could have three for £10.

Three councillors took the three for ten pounds; my staff was trying to hide their laughter but I just smiled, for it was what I expected from politicians.

Three Weddings

We had three weddings in 13 months. Alison married a local policeman Stephen Smith in April 1981, Gillian married a chef Alan Barrington in December of the same year and Cath, who had been divorced from Mike, married an accountant Simon White in May 1982.

I had always promised to hold the ladder while all three eloped but they all decided otherwise.

Alison's wedding was at the old parish church at Woodchurch. At first Steve's parents offered to get involved and pay for part of the wedding; we soon found out that what they meant was that they would decide everything. After the first meeting we told them that we would arrange the wedding and pay for it, thank you very much.

Alison and Steve wanted "Top Hat and Tails" so this was the order of the day. It was a very nice wedding in the old church with the reception at the Bowler Hat Hotel. I felt so proud walking my daughter down the aisle.

All the proceedings went off without a hitch with the speeches and toasts going down well. We had finished and were about to leave the table when Hal Smith, Steve's father stood up and made a speech. Everyone looked round for it was not the usual thing for the groom's father to do, but that was Hal for you.

There was a disco at the hotel in the evening when more of Alison and Steve's friends were invited, but very many more people than the numbers invited arrived. We found out that Hal had invited so many of his friends without telling anyone that there was not enough food to go round: to help out Gill and I, Cath and Gillian and others did without.

Gillian and Alan got married at Hoylake Chapel 12th December on a cold, snowy morning but in brilliant sunshine. We had to dig the car out and only just managed to get out of the top of York Avenue. It made for good pictures with a foot of snow on the ground. The reception was at the Concourse; my staff had decorated the rooms with flowers from the parks department.

Gillian looked beautiful in her bridal gown, and all went well but little did we know that the photographs could not be printed. We were all extremely annoyed because they had hired a professional photographer. He promised to retake the photos later, and we got everybody together again in the spring, but by then Alison was sporting a bump as Jamie was on the way.

Cath was going out with Simon White, a lad she met at the sailing club; he was an accountant with the Mersey Docks and Harbour Company. There was a job with the company in Papua New Guinea (PNG) but the person had to be married. Simon got the job and they decided to get married in Birkenhead Town Hall at the registry office. There were only close relatives present, Gill and I, Alison and Steve, Gillian and Alan, and Simon's family. They left for PNG soon after the wedding. I promised them that the money that would have been spent on a reception would be there for them later when they came home on leave.

British Sports Association for the Disabled (BSAD)

During my time at Birkenhead I continued to promote disabled sport at all the centres in all its forms. I used to attend the British Sports Association for the Disabled (BSAD) meetings held at Stoke Mandeville, where Sir Ludwig Guttmann was the top consultant.

Sir Ludwig had started introducing patients with spinal injuries to take up sport as part of their treatment. This had begun during the Second World War and continued afterwards. When the 1948 London Olympics were finished he organised games for his patients and called it the Paraplegic Games.

Sir Ludwig was the most inspiring person I have ever met: he was so determined to achieve whatever he set out to do and no one or nothing would get in his way.

By the time I met him he was known throughout the world, and sport for the disabled was happening in many countries. He was so dictatorial that some people could not work with him; he did not suffer fools gladly. I thought he was a wonderful person, my sort of man, and yet we had many arguments on how things should progress. But I felt that he respected me for standing up to him and arguing my case, so we did get on well.

I had managed to get John Oxton, one of my managers, to get involved with BSAD. He and I would travel down to Stoke Mandeville together by car. One visit we stayed in a country pub outside Oxford; we booked in had a meal and as the evening wore on the pub filled up with students until it was packed. There was a retired major who owned the pub and he was not too sociable but his very nice 20 year old barmaid was most helpful.

When it came to closing time, 10.30pm in those days, the girl came up to us and asked if we would like to go into the dining room while the bar was cleared of students. We took our drinks into the dining room and half an hour later it was all quiet in the bar so we went back in; there was the major chatting up the barmaid who looked glad to see us. We sat at the bar talking to her while the major grunted and disappeared. An hour or so later the major shouted to the barmaid that it was time for her to go upstairs as it was just before midnight. .John and I still wanted to carry on drinking and because we were residents we could do so. A few minutes later the major shouted down again and the girl said she had better go up. We shouted up to the major that we would like to carry on, and when he said help yourselves we did, but we thought he was maybe having a better time than we were.

Development of BSAD

I was now a member of the Sports Council at both national level and the North West Region. I was also an adviser to Government Departments for both the Arts and Sports Ministers. John Oxton and I regularly travelled to Stoke Mandeville for meetings of BSAD.

One day I was approached by the Sports Council who told me that there was a problem with the allocation of funds for disabled sport. The Sports Council's charter did not allow them to give funds to organisations that were not constituted democratically along the lines of the Sports Council Regions which covered the whole of England.

They had been holding meetings with Sir Ludwig who would not change his organisation for anybody; they wanted me to help break the deadlock.

A meeting was held in the London offices of the Sports Council at which both Sir Ludwig and I attended, along with the director of the Sports Council and his senior staff plus a representative from the Government. After an hour we were getting nowhere and the temperature was rising. The Director told us that it was impossible for him to give BSAD any money unless it was constituted regionally inline with the Sports Council boundaries.

At this point Sir Ludwig banged the table and said he would phone the Palace and speak to the Duke of Edinburgh, (he had his personal number) and he then left the meeting. We knew Sir Ludwig would not budge. It was suggested that Sir Ludwig be promoted to President and that I should become Chairman to oversee the changes, which sounded good but would it work?

Sir Ludwig came back into the room slightly less uptight, he had spoken to the Duke of Edinburgh, so I put the idea to him stressing the fact that he would still be the head of BSAD and in charge and I would do all the admin work to regionalise the organisation. To everyone's surprise he agreed.

The Sports Council helped me with the paperwork so that we had a constitution to place before an annual general meeting, the venue yet to be arranged. Sir Ludwig had a word with his friend the Duke of Bedford who readily agreed that we could hold it at Woburn Abbey.

That is how we came to hold the First AGM of BSAD at Woburn Abbey.

I remember driving up the long approach drive to be met at the door by His Grace himself, who said, "Welcome to my home, I think you are going to have your work cut out this afternoon."

The meeting was well attended and all the proposals accepted. A committee was appointed and I chaired the first of many meetings which established the British Sports Association for the Disabled, on a formal basis. We could at last receive grants and other help from the Government through the National Sports Council.

The work of creating the regions progressed at varying rates within the country. I was determined that the organisation would never again be a one-man band and with that in mind I stepped down as national chairman and concentrated on the development of the North West Region. I was chairman of the region for the next six years.

The Vice Chairman, Secretary, and Treasurer were all disabled and in wheelchairs, a fact that I overlooked when I arranged for our first committee meeting to be held in my office at Byrne Avenue Baths, which was on the first floor. We had to carry all three of them up three flights of steps. I only made that mistake once.

The NW Region was a thriving success, and we held our first athletics meeting at Kirkby Stadium, where the council were so generous that we had more trophies than events, but we soon grew into them.

Bernard Manning, the comedian, owned his own club in Manchester and he offered to give the whole of the night's takings to NW BSAD.

The club was packed and various raffles were held just to make cash for us. Barbara our Secretary and Marge our Treasurer were both in their wheelchairs having a great time, having drinks sent up to them on a regular basis.

Marge turned to me and asked where the ladies disabled toilet was. I went to find out only to be told that there were no toilets for the disabled, just ordinary male and female ones. Marge said she was desperate so I took her to the ladies.

One of the club's female staff went into the ladies and asked them to vacate the place while I took Marge into the toilet. I had to lift Marge out of her chair and place her on the loo seat, and she helped me by placing her arms round my neck. After the deed was done the reverse procedure took place and then we left the toilet. Outside a queue had gathered, who were getting impatient, and after this they refused to empty the room and told me to get on with it, not caring one way or the other. The night was a success in every way thanks to the generosity of Bernard Manning and the people of Manchester.

Getting Things Done

When Birkenhead Market Hall caught fire it was replaced temporarily by a steel girder structure with a high roof with a large span. I immediately thought that this would make an ideal sports building and suggested that the building be bolted together not welded for ease of dismantling. Later when the new market was finished with the development of Grange Road, the old temporary market building was surplus. The Engineer Frank Rodget wanted it for a depot for the engineers, but I said it had always been earmarked for a sports building on the Woodchurch Estate - well it had been in my mind! In the end I managed to get the agreement of the Council.

Being on the Sports Council I put the idea forward that this would make an ideal cheap Sports Barn: a simple building without frills or heating, with an asphalt base which would stand up to anything at all. The existing offices and changing rooms at the centre would be used. I managed to get a grant to help with the removal and erection. That is how the Woodchurch Sports Barn came about.

Director of Leisure Services and Tourism for Wirral was the best job in Britain. No other City or Authority had placed together all the facilities and responsibilities that I had, 2200 staff and a budget of £16m and income of £6m.

I was an adviser to the Association of Metropolitan Authorities on both sport and the arts in which capacity I had advised three different Ministers for Sport and two Ministers for the Arts. I was also on the Arts Council. I had a lot of power which placed the department on the same footing as any other department for the first time ever.

All this involvement gave me great satisfaction but it took up a lot of time, and I felt that Gill and I should just go off and have a weekend somewhere quiet.

We booked in at the Wild Boar at Crook nr Windermere; it was exactly what we needed. It was spring and all the hedgerows were full of daffodils and it made your spirits rise just to drive past the miles of flowers. I was determined to have the same in Wirral.

On my return I called in the assistant director in charge of parks. How much we spent on bulbs and flowers, he did not know as it was all lumped in with trees and shrubs. I then asked Alec Bennet who was in charge of the departments finances if he could find me £10,000. He said that since I was the boss I could have what I wanted, out of a budget of £16m. I then told the parks section to purchase £10,000 of spring bulbs, daffodils and crocus etc.

The following spring the road verges and open spaces were a carpet of colour; the press commented on it and so did the public. At a meeting of the Leisure Committee Clr. Steve Whickham made a vote of thanks to the Chairman and the Department for the magnificent display of spring flowers. The Chairman turned to me and asked how it had come about. I replied, "Don't ask, and just accept the vote of thanks."

Because I had such a control of the finances I was able to get many things done that in the past would never have been passed. One of my favourite ploys was to get the committee to agree in principle to something if it could be done without going overspent which always worked. Everyone would agree to it except the Director of Finance.

Leasowe All Weather Pitch

All Governments keep some money back from their budgets and if there is any to spare, they announce schemes which will be given grants if the cash can be spent before the end of the financial year (April 1st)

As a member of the Sports Council I often got tipped off about forthcoming schemes early. In conjunction with the architects department we decided to have a few plans drawn up ready so that we could take advantage of any cash available.

My staff decided that there was a demand for an all weather football floodlight pitch which could be used for any outdoor activity, and if it was sited next to the Leasowe Sports Centre it could be staffed and managed without any extra recourse.

In December it was announced that a 100% grant was available to the value of £100,000 for outdoor facilities provision.

I put our proposal to the Sports Council who thought it was a very good idea and said they would support it.

At the next meeting of the Leisure Services and Tourism Committee I informed the meeting of the scheme and said that we had the full support of the Sports Council. The Committee were full of enthusiasm, and then I was asked why I had proposed that it should be built at Leasowe (a Labour area) and not in other (Tory) areas. My reply was that Leasowe had the best case based on need and not politics and it could be managed without extra resources.

A full blown row took place with the councillor from New Brighton saying that she could not support the scheme being sited at Leasowe. I could see that I could not get a positive decision in time for the money to be spent, so I informed the committee that I would tell the Sports Council to give its support to a different scheme on Merseyside, which it did. Wirral residents lost out due to political bickering once again. I did not win them all.

Because I had more control than even the finance department I was able to move money about. I knew every unit of electricity, every unit of gas, and water in every building throughout the department by getting the staff to read the meters every Monday morning and record it on the notice board.

Later on when the Director of Finance was making out his case for a new computer costing £2m he was asked what the Council would get for the money. He replied, much to my amazement, that he would have the same level of financial control as Brian Barnes has in Leisure Services.

By using the above described method I created the North Wirral Coastal Park, and at the Floral Pavilion I renewed the VIP room back stage, curtains, sound system and seats.

The first three costs for the theatre were met out of the yearly budget, but the seats would cost £30,000 which even I could not slip through. At the theatre row J was always kept for any VIPs such as the Mayor or the guests of the production company if the theatre was being hired; this row of seats had more leg room and was far enough back from the stage to give a very good view of the performers. I instructed the staff to remove all the seats from this row and replace them with the worst seats in the theatre.

The next time the chairman and the civic party attended the theatre they all complained that the seating was awful. I sympathised but explained that they all needed renewing. After a month or so with many more complaints about the seats I was asked at the Leisure Services Committee to report on the seating at the Floral Pavilion which I duly did.

When my report to the committee quoted a cost of £30,000 to renew the seats the Director of Finance said that there was no money available. Every member knew the situation and when I asked if they would agree to the renewal of the seating if the money could be found, it was a unanimous "Yes". At the end of the financial year we were still within budget and we had installed the new seating much to the annoyance of the Director of Finance. That's what financial control means.

Part of the job of being Director was to get things done, but sometimes the difficulty was the members themselves: their job was to make policy; mine was to carry it out. There were times when politics got in the way of common sense, such as in the balancing of the books: you can cut back spending but in my department we could increase income as well. Labour members thought that if you played rugby you were well off but if you played football you were poor, and if you sailed you had untold wealth.

To get over this problem I formed two organisations, one for the arts and one for sports.

The Sports Advisory Council and the Arts Advisory council, these organisations would look at my proposed scale of charges, make recommendations and then they would go to the Council. It was difficult to change charges that had been agreed by the sports bodies themselves, so common sense prevailed.

Staff and Trade Unions

There were five different trades union within the department and regular meetings were held at the town hall where I was represented by the appropriate assistant director. The unions had shop stewards and paid area officials. The union side wanted me to attend in person, and I did not mind this but the other directors did not go and did not want me to create a precedent.

Due to the fact that we seemed to have the largest share of any cuts that had to be made, I decided to attend. The meeting was due to start at 2pm and I was there at 1.50pm. At 2.05pm I was about to leave when all the union side walked in. I said that in future if the meeting did not start on time there would be no meeting, and they were never late again.

Some union leaders were better than others; I got on better with those that could deliver what we had agreed.

There was a Mr Davis from Vauxhalls who was known as a hard negotiator and had made his name in General Motors in America. We got on very well for when we made an agreement it worked.

But NUPE was the opposite. He took them out on strike the Sunday morning after we had been in a meeting for hours on a Saturday night when he promised me that I could go off on holiday the following morning because all was settled. I had to return home from London on Sunday night to sort it out.

I had a few run-ins with Bill Jones, and one Christmas I was informed that a member of my staff, a shop steward in Birkenhead Park, had taken a parks van, to take his mate to New Brighton to a night club, got drunk and smashed the van into one of the Four Bridges on the way back. He was charged by the police with taking and driving away a council van, drink driving and driving without due care and attention, to which he pleaded guilty. I had to interview him and as he admitted it I sacked him for gross misconduct. His union representative said he would appeal which he did. The appeal was to the councillors who felt sorry for him and reinstated him.

Another shop steward who was a regular malingerer was caught one night at 11pm on his hands and knees, drunk, crawling on the roundabout outside the Arrowe Park Pub looking for a bag full of woods (bowling bowls), which he had stolen from the park pavilion. The next morning I interviewed him with his union representative; he was off work sick and this is his story: "I have been off work for some time now and I was bored, so I decided to take the woods home to clean them. I met a pal who invited me to have a drink in the Arrowe Park Pub, I only had one pint. When I went outside I tripped and the woods fell out of the bag." I asked him if he expected me to believe that far-fetched story. He was off sick, should not have been out at night, had no right to go into the pavilion or to take the woods, and he should not have been out drinking or been drunk when off sick. I sacked him for gross misconduct.

He was charged by the police, went to court and managed to convince the jury of his story and then asked me to take him back. I did not believe him and he stayed sacked.

Many times Managers have wanted to dismiss someone and they have not given them a warning or followed the correct procedure. When it came before me it was always prudent to give them a further chance, because they either took and learned their lesson, or made the same mistake again when this time it justified dismissal.

I have personally been to the Industrial Tribunal on three occasions, and each time I have had my decision upheld. The last time was when a member was consistently off sick; he had been given warnings but it made no difference. He was a plant man, one of two at Livingstone Street Baths, and we could not operate without a plant man. It was costing the department a lot of cash in overtime to cover his shift. I decided I had had enough and decided to dismiss him.

I was told by the personnel department that an employee could not be sacked while on sick leave, but I did this. I was taken to the Tribunal in Liverpool, and the Council's solicitor was still advising me to withdraw even at lunch time. I gave evidence myself and read out all the time the plant man had been off sick over the last 18 months. I said that if he was so sick that he could not and did not do his job, the department could not go on paying out all the overtime.

The Chairman ruled that I could dismiss the man and he commented that it was a change for the Director to give evidence personally in such a case.

Flooding at the Cemetery

I had always said that any member of my staff could ask to see me personally if all else failed. One day I was taken up on this by a gravedigger called Jack at Pensby Cemetery. Beryl my secretary said he had asked to see me. He came in and apologised for coming in his work gear and said he had tried to tell his boss, the cemetery manager Frank Armstrong about his problem but nothing had been done about it. It appeared that Jack was concerned that the cemetery was flooding in the bad weather. I wondered what was going on since Pensby Cemetery is on the highest land in the Wirral, but Jack was insistent. I said I would go and have a look, but Jack said, "Not now, you have to come when it is raining hard." We left it: that he would phone me when the weather was bad enough.

When I phoned Frank Armstrong, the cemetery manager, he was so apologetic and said Jack was a little lacking but a good gravedigger. A month or two later it had been raining for days when I had a call from Jack who told me that the cemetery was flooded and would I go round, and to bring Wellingtons. I told Frank Armstrong to meet me at the site.

As I arrived at the cemetery I could immediately see the problem. Although the land was the highest in Wirral it was like a saucer with all the water running into the cemetery area. I got out of the car and I could hear the steady thump, thump of a 'donkey pump'. It was pouring down with rain which was flowing from the fields in streams. Jack was standing by the pump at a newly dug grave with the pipe from the pump at the bottom of the grave trying to empty the water, fighting a losing battle. Then in the distance I could see the funeral procession arrive. Jack stopped the pump, took the pipe out of the hole and covered the edge of the grave with plastic grass. We stood back to let the vicar and mourners gather round the grave, the rain continued to fall and I could hear the water running under the artificial grass into the grave.

The vicar seemed to take forever with the service; I had visions of the coffin floating when it was lowered down and still the rain continued. At last the time came to lower the coffin, and I held my breath until the funeral director released the straps and walked away followed by the mourners. As soon as they had gone a safe distance we started the pump again. I left Frank Armstrong and his staff to finish the burial and returned to my office, my first job being to have drainage installed to prevent the day's events ever happening again.

About this time when I was 43 years old something happened that was a milestone in my life. I used to regularly swim to keep myself fit, and I would swim 200yds of each stroke, a total of ½ mile, or more if

I felt like it. I often used to go on a Sunday afternoon to Livingstone Street baths.

The baths were closed so I had the pool to myself, and I would switch on the sauna cabin to get it hot while I did my swim. On this particular day I set out as usual to swim 200yds each, butterfly, backstroke, breast-stroke and crawl. I got over half way when I felt fed-up, not tired but fed-up. I said to myself, "Stop, you don't have to go on," but I had never stopped and not finished what I had set out to do. This went on for a couple of lengths, with me arguing with myself. Then I made the decision: I stopped swimming. I climbed out of the water and walked to the sauna where I cried. This was the first time in my life that I had given in and not finished a task that I had set myself, and yet no one knew about it but me. I will never forget that Sunday afternoon.

Each Christmas and on special occasions the Chief Officers Group (COG) which included all the directors and their deputies, would have a get together, and because I was in charge of leisure I got the job of organising the event.

We would hold it in one of the rooms in the department such as Bebington Civic Centre or Heswall Hall. My staff would provide the food and I could purchase the drinks at cost price. We paid the staff but had the premises free. It was always a very good evening and yet there would always be someone out of over 20 people who was not satisfied, usually it was a wife who thought she or her husband should have been the centre of attraction, but 99% of the time a great time was had by all.

I made some very good friends among the directors. Gerald Chapple was a true gentleman, and Roger Shaw, Bill Hughes, Norman Rothwell and Cliff Darley were great pals to be with and work with. Often after a meeting in Wallasey Town Hall we would all gather at the Magazines Pub in New Brighton, and one night Roger Shaw and Bill Hughes arrived first. A new barmaid was behind the bar, and she had a figure that could stop traffic; she was very proud of her assets and was wearing a white low-cut top which left nothing to the imagination. I walked in and just stared; Roger and Bill laughed, they had been waiting for me to react and I did. Roger decided to have a bit of fun when Norman Rothwell arrived; he asked the girl if she was willing to play along, to which she agreed. Roger and Gail the barmaid swapped names and pretended to be very good friends.

Norman entered the bar and stood looking at Gail with his mouth open. Roger said "Gail, would you get my friend a drink, love." "Yes dear," said Gail. Norman could not wait to find out how Roger knew the barmaid, and we all kept the joke going for a time before Norman realised that he had been set up. It was this sort of evening that helped to take the stress out of the job.

My police training and my experience of combating trouble-makers in Wombwell was used again when we started to experience trouble at the libraries which were often staffed by young women. Gangs of youths would descend on a library and terrorise the women; the police would be called but it took so long for them to arrive that the women had to lock themselves and the public inside the building for safety.

I complained to the police but they said they did not have the resources so I asked for volunteers from the young men in the parks section. I would pay them overtime if they would sit inside the library in Eastham after work. Sure enough the trouble-makers came and so did my parks staff: the youths were themselves given a lesson in terrorising and told that if it happened again they would be dealt with by us first then handed over to the police.

We only had to do this once at each library where we had experienced trouble for the problem to vanish. The same tactic was used at the West Kirby Concourse when we had trouble at the youth club with non-members trying to intimidate the members when they left; again it was soon solved.

1982 Jamie Stephen Smith 30th August

Alison was pregnant and went into Arrowe Park Hospital where Jamie was born on her birthday, 30th August; this was my first grandchild, a boy to even up the females in my life. Little did I know then just what very good friends we would become, and how sailing would change both our lives.

Sri Lanka

I felt that I would prefer to take a good holiday in winter when we were not as busy and the winter was dragging me down, or so it felt. Gill and I fancied somewhere hot in February, and Ray Wood played cricket with someone who came from Sri Lanka: I met up with him and after talking about his homeland we decided to have three weeks in Negumbo. We went back to the same hotel twice more spending a total of 16 weeks there; we really had very good winter holidays in Sri Lanka.

Caravan

I fancied a caravan to be able to get away from the hustle and bustle of work and I thought Gill would like it as well. She did but she was not as enthusiastic as I was. We purchased a five berth Swift caravan in 1983 and went to the south of France in it, but the weather could not have been worse. It rained very hard every day, and although it was September it was also cold, so we ended up making soup each day to keep warm.

We got as far as the Spanish border and decided to return home early, and when we arrived at the French port all the other caravans had cut their holiday short as well.

From then on I went by myself each year to Argeles-sur-Mer on the south coast, just north of the Spanish border. I had a Laser dinghy on the roof rack so that I could sail as well.

I used to take a week to get there and a week to return with two weeks sailing. I never used the motorways, only the back roads so that I took a different route each year.

I used to choose my way each night for the next day and I would write the names of the towns I would pass through on a pad which was stuck to the dashboard.

One Saturday somewhere in the centre of France I was making my way looking for the next town, St Etienne, but there were no signs so I kept going straight on. The day was very hot; it was midday with so many people walking in the road the traffic was stopped. I asked a man the way to St Etienne and he said first turning right. I thanked him and little by little I moved forward with the traffic.

Eventually there was a right turn which was a curved road lined by trees. I slowly moved along this road which was full of people walking in the road, then I saw a sight that frightened me to death: I was going into a covered market! Stall holders started shouting and waving their fists at me and I didn't blame them for I could not back out and could not go forward.

I sat in the car wondering what to do when the man I had asked for directions came up and started to explain what I had done. He told me to stay in the car while he persuaded the stallholders to dismantle some of the stalls to let me continue to the rear of the market and drive out. After a lot of shouting and swearing (I did not need an interpreter to know what they said) I got to the exit.

The man said, "I will guide you," and he got in the car. We went ¼ mile and he got out and said, "Allez, Allez," and off I went still shaking at the experience. I soon came to a T-junction without any signs at all: should I go left or right? I decided I would not go anywhere until I found out where I was.

I stopped the car and van and walked over to an open-air café to ask directions. All the vehicles behind me started to sound their horns and go mad, but I just walked across the road to some men sat at a table. "Which is the way to St Etienne?" I asked. "Mon Dieu!" (My God) was the reply, while the horns continued to sound. I was getting nowhere, but then a man said in English, "Follow me, that is my car over there I will take you." He went to his car and I followed him for about six miles to the other side of the town. He finally stopped near a sign pointing to St Etienne, I got out of my car went up to him and threw my arms round him and said, "Vive La France, merci merci." As I drove on I laughed at what had happened, and I could imagine telling the story when I got home. I loved my caravan and it was a great way to relax; later I would use it to take Jamie and Kate away to the lakes and abroad.

Tranmere Rovers

Back at work the Council decided to help the local football team Tranmere Rovers who were in financial trouble. I was told to look into how we could help them. I had a number of meetings then called everyone who was involved to a special meeting. Present were Tranmere Rovers board members, the Football League, Football Association, Professional Footballers Association, Sports Council and Wirral Council. I suggested that the club could sell their ground and we would let them have the use of an all weather pitch to be built at the Oval Sports Centre.

This was well received until John Smith, Chairman of Liverpool FC, who was representing the Football League, said that he was against the idea. He took me to one side and told me that as long as he was at Liverpool they would never play on an artificial pitch. Wirral Council ended up sponsoring Tranmere FC which they are still doing.

1984 Kate Alison Smith 13th May

The most important event in this year was the birth of Kate my second grandchild on May 13th 1984 to Alison and Steve.

Tall Ships

The visit of the Tall Ships to Merseyside was to be a major event. The Merseyside County Council was the main sponsor and all the publicity was about Liverpool which did not go down too well with me especially when I found out that due to the size of the ships all the large ones, which was the majority, could only be berthed in Wallasey and Birkenhead Docks.

The Chief Executive of the County and I had many friendly arguments over the arrangements, especially the civic arrangements. Ray Wood and I made our own plans for seeing that our Mayor was the leading VIP on our side of the water.

Ships arrived from all over the world and it was a wonderful sight, especially at night when the ships were dressed and covered by thousands of lights. Ships' crews were invited to various sailing clubs to be wined and dined and shown northern hospitality. West Kirby Sailing Club was host to the Russian ship. The crew were accompanied by a political commissar who was there to keep an eye on what the crew did and said. The club had given some members, including me, permission to order drinks for the crew for which the club paid. It was decided by some of us to get the commissar drunk so that the lads could let their hair down, so slowly we kept topping up his glass as well as doubling the whiskey drinks, and eventually he fell asleep propped up in a corner of the lounge and from then on the party got going.

The major event was to be the parade of sail when all the boats lined up in the Mersey and sailed in line out of the river on Saturday evening. The best place to see the parade of sail was from the Wirral side of the Mersey and the best view was from the Wallasey town hall steps. I presumed that the Mayor would hold the civic viewing from the town hall, but much to my surprise some of the Liberal councillors thought that the general public should have the best view not the council and that was what happened.

I said that I had made my own personal arrangements and left them to it. Everyone wanted to see the parade so I booked a room at the Floral Pavilion Theatre, arranged for food and drinks to be provided, for which I paid, so that my friends and family could watch from the flat roof of the theatre which was the best view of all.

The County Council had hired Fort Perch Rock for a reception for the County Council and all the Merseyside mayors, I was also invited. My department had arranged a funfair and helicopter rides during the Saturday afternoon, and all in all it was to be a great day out. I remember telling all my friends and family to be at the theatre early during the day, and we had arranged for parking by the theatre.

When I took Jamie and some of my family up in the helicopter you could see that the Wirral was filling up as all the roads were full of parked cars; little did we know just how full it would get. There was a show on in the theatre but it ended just before the parade was due to pass.

Ray Wood and I decided to walk over to Fort Perch Rock to see the arrangements and to say that we would not be attending; when we got outside we could not believe what we saw: every piece of pavement and all the road surface was covered with parked cars, one of which stood out from the rest as it was a gold coloured Rolls Royce.

Nothing could move in or out of New Brighton, it was even difficult to walk. The Fort was empty except for the organisers and caterers: nothing and nobody was going to get to the reception. I phoned the Mayor's office and was told that neither the Mayor's party nor any of the other guests could drive anywhere since there was complete gridlock. I smiled and returned to my own party at the theatre.

Alison had Jamie with her, who was 2 years old, and Kate who was a few months. Of course, as usual, Alison was prepared for every eventuality including world war three and it proved to be needed.

When you say packed like sardines, that is just what it was like, yet everyone was in a good mood. The first time I noticed a problem was when my staff asked if we could help a lady with a small child who needed to feed and change her baby. Alison came to the rescue and provided nappies and milk for a bottle. Then there was a man who needed to sit down and eat because he had diabetes. I decided to open the theatre to let people sit down and rest. The bar staff asked if they should close the bar as it was after closing time, I told them to carry on as no one could get to us to check anyway. The chip shop ran out of potatoes and other cafes sold out of everything edible.

It was 11.30pm and still no one could move, and people were starting to get restless. I telephoned Merseyside Police HQ and spoke to the most senior officer on duty: I told him what it was like, no one could move and people were worried how they would get home when the buses and trains stopped. I asked him to see if the local transport could be kept going all night if it was necessary. He phoned back to say that we could inform everyone that public transport would operate all night and could we pass the news on.

We fixed the public address system on the roof and passed on the information. Everyone relaxed, and it was similar to the spirit people had during the war. We distributed any food we had left as did Fort Perch Rock. Jamie and Kate just slept when they got tired, and the rest of us talked and waited. It was 1.30am before the Rolls Royce managed to get away and we left after seeing that all the staff got home safely.

The police enquiry into the traffic situation resulted in them being criticized for allowing the M53 motorway to become the largest car park in the UK. People had tried to get to New Brighton and when they could drive no further just abandoned their vehicles, including on the motorway, and walked leaving total gridlock throughout the Wirral.

John Anton – New Brighton

In the early 1980s a developer named John Anton, a local man, approached the Council saying he wanted to develop a theme park on the sea front at New Brighton, saying that he had £150m to spend. The Council set up a sub committee to look into the proposals with the following officers on it: Norman Rothwell, Director of Finance, Roger Shaw, Director of Development, myself, Director of Leisure Services and Tourism, and the Director of Admin and Legal Services.

The plans split the local population; those who lived overlooking the proposed development were naturally against it while others thought it was just what was needed. The New Brighton councillor was on the committee.

When the matter was voted on in the council chamber the local councillor voted against it and yet I knew that she was a strong supporter of the plans. After the vote had been taken and passed, I spoke with the councillor and said that I was very surprised that she had voted against the plans. She looked at me, smiled and said, "Well it got through didn't it?"

You see that way she could be all things to all voters, she voted against but it went through as she knew it would. Politicians; they are as two faced as you can get.

More of John Anton later.

Liverpool International Garden Festival 1984

Part of the Government's plans for the regeneration of Merseyside was the development of waste land at Otterspool Promenade to create the first International Garden Festival in the UK. It was a mammoth project and horticulturists from all over the country and abroad wished to be involved, but because it was a Tory Government, Derek Hatton the deputy leader of Liverpool City Council would have nothing to do with it and stopped any of his council departments from being involved, especially the parks department.

As the largest parks department after Liverpool, Wirral took over the work that would have, and should have, been carried out by Liverpool.

We were of course thrilled to be involved in such a prestigious project, we had people applying to come and work for us from all over, and we became the main supplier of plants and shrubs. In conjunction with Unilever who provided the cash, we provided the expertise, and we built the Victorian Garden which won a gold award.

The Queen opened the Festival which ran all summer and was an international success, which brought hundreds of thousands of tourists from all over the world.

At the end of the Garden Festival, Unilever held a dinner at Egerton House for all my staff who had been involved in the construction and upkeep of the Victorian Garden.

Great Granddad Gudgeon

Great Grandma Gudgeon

Granddad Pullich's Grave Stafford

Dad, Mum and me aged two months

1934 outside 8 Dorman Rd Preston
Charlie Barnes, Mum, Dad, Harold Dowling, Agnes Barnes, behind Joyce Dowling

Me at 8 Dover Street Preston

8 Dorman Rd Preston Now

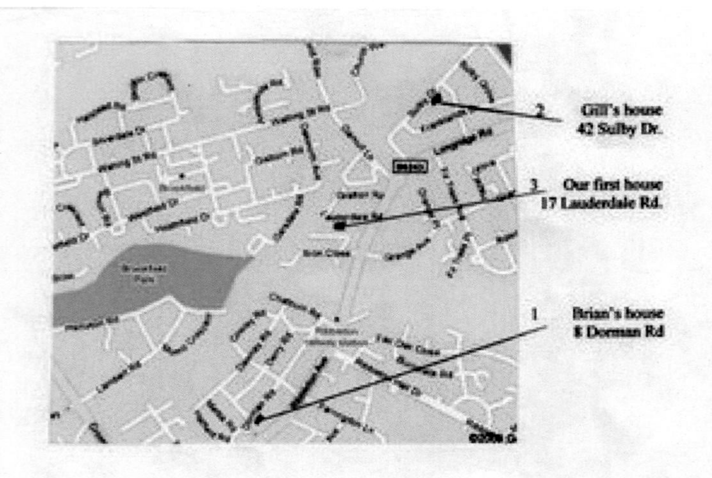
2
Gill's house
42 Sulby Dr.
3
Our first house
17 Lauderdale Rd.
1
Brian's house
8 Dorman Rd

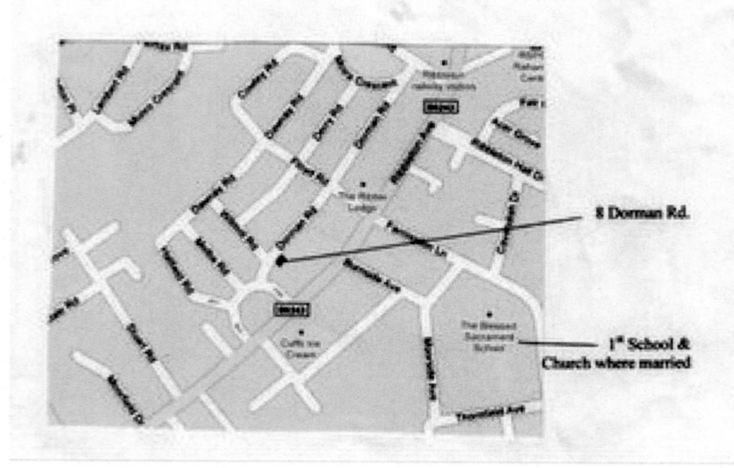
8 Dorman Rd.
1st School &
Church where married

1952 Olympic Games

TO CONTINUE AS SPORTSMEN. — Three Nort sportsmen discuss the next two years of their lives R.A.F with the recruiting officer Warrant Officer Prest, at Preston, this morning. They are left to Brian Barnes, Preston's Olympic swimmer; David Blackpool F.C reserve; and Alan Blan, Blackburn reserve.

Three sportsmen chose R.A.F.

THREE well-known names in local sport were signed on the dotted line at Preston's recruiting office to-da... Ther were: Brian Barnes, swimmer, of 8, Dor Preston, David Powell, reserve footballer, of street, Blackpool North Bean, Blackburn Rove team player, of 25, Infir Blackburn.

Among a batch of 44 Servicemen, they all step the office with one ho into the R.A.F.

David and Alan are year-old professional Brian, aged 18, a mem "Lancashire Evening advertising staff.

Said Flying Officer O.C. Recruiting office:

B. Barnes enters hospital

BRIAN BARNES has played no small part in Preston's success in the North Lancashire League Swimming and Water Polo League, yet few people knew that he has swam throughout the season with a hernia.

What is more important he travelled via the Northern Counties' Olympic trial at Atherton, and the final Olympic trial at Blackpool, to a place in the British team at Helsinki, where he registered the fastest time ever by a British swimmer in the 200 metres breast stroke. And all the time he was troubled with the hernia.

He then went to the A.S.A. championships at Hove and took second place in the 200 yards breast stroke. On Saturday, he helped Preston to a convincing win in the last league game of the season, and to-day he entered a Preston hospital for an operation.

Preston completely outplayed Accrington on Saturday, beating them 11-0 in the water polo event. Jim Bannister scored six, Barnes (2), and Cross, Langtree and Taylor one each.

The only swimming event won by Accrington was the 50yd. free style.

Results. — Schoolboys' squad: Preston; Junior women: Preston. Women's breast-stroke: Jean Burns; back-stroke: B. Simpson; 50yd. free style: C. Fisher; 100yd. free style: K. Bowen. Men's breast-stroke: D. Richmond; back-stroke: J. Bannister; 100yd. free style: B. Barnes Preston won the men's and women's squadron race.

Is there favouritism for athletes in Services?

LETTERS

I WAS interested in the photograph in the "Post" (January 7th) of three sportsmen who had chosen the R.A.F. for their National Service.

How does it come about that sportsmen can pick the service in which they would like to serve? Other National Service men don't have a look-in.

Ten months ago my son, along with several other Preston lads, was called up. Several asked to go in the R.A.F. but were told it was only possible if they joined the Regulars. They refused, and were put into the infantry along with two footballers. To-day they are in Korea, except the footballers, who are still here.—*FAIR PLAY ALL ROUND*

[Official reply is that these men, who had expressed a preference for the R.A.F., passed a high physical and educational test. Now that they have been accepted for the R.A.F. their Service job will be the main consideration and sport only secondary.]

1952 Gill and Me outside 8 Dorman Rd

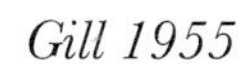

Gill 1955

WILLIAM
INN

Our first House 17 Lauderdale Rd. Preston

Mount Street Hospital where Alison & Cath were born

Three Musketeers Gillian, Cath, Alison

When manager of Wombwell Baths, Mr. Brian Barnes, heard how nine-year-old Gordon Martin was nearly drowned in the canal at Wombwell he invited Gordon to swimming lessons and after half-an-hour Go[...] almost swim. Here Mr. Barnes teaches the bre[...] his young pupil.

The boy from the canal

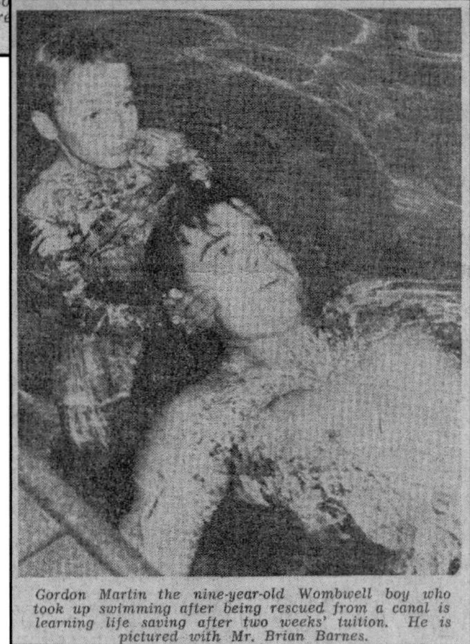

Boy from the canal life saving me

Gordon Martin the nine-year-old Wombwell boy who took up swimming after being rescued from a canal is learning life saving after two weeks' tuition. He is pictured with Mr. Brian Barnes.

Mum's old house Longridge 3 Generations of Barnes's

Bude Beach

1968Conway Castle - Growing up

1976 Christmas York Ave – Three beautiful girls

Alison

Alison Smith
Professional
Make-up Artist

59 Escolme Drive, Greasby, Wirral, CH491SF. Tel. 0151 604 1874 Mobile 07968358285
E-mail createthelook@btinternet.com

2005 Alison started her business

1986 Rita Rita Meter Maid – Beatle City

Miss Piggy and Me

1998 Circumnavigation

1998 Captain of Stratagem

1999 Salinas Ecuador Left on my 65th birthday

Panama Canal - a Tight Fit!

Sharing a Loch

STRATAGEM
WORLD VOYAGE
HALF WAY
TONGA, JUNE 1999

Cath arrives in Tonga

Start and Finish port in Palma

Jamie and Me – The start of a sailing career

Caravanning with the grandchildren

Cath and Me on Skye

1977 Alison's 21st - standing Gill and Pop, seated Brian, Alison, Dorothy, Great Gran, Edna, and Great Grandma

42 Sulby Drive, Preston. Gill's parents house

Prefabs at the end of the road built after the war 1950

2002 Helsinki reunion outside main stadium – Alison Brian Gill

Parading in the stadium

With Lillian Preece From Wallasey

2006 Danielle, Jamie Alison & Kate

Jubilee Torch Relay
Croydon, 2002

2006 August 30th - Alison & Jamie's birthday party

2006 Wirral Show – My Girls

Alison in St John's Hospice

Kate working at the elephant orphanage Sri Lanka

Lisa Cambridge for Degree Gillian, Lisa, Alan

Leon with degree

Leon in India

Lisa and Leon

2010 Jamie and Danielle wedding

2010 Kate and Chris wedding Perth

2012 Kate with Mia Alison Uusimaki born 6th July

2013 Mia first birthday

Mia eighteen months old walking

Paralympic Torch sponsored by Sainsbury

Paralympic Torch Relay Lords Cricket Ground to St Johns Wood

Friends & Neighbours – Jo, Joyce, Dorothy, Harold, Kath, & Lynne

CHAPTER TWELVE
Cutbacks and Savings

Cutbacks and Savings

Although the department was working very well the Government was cracking down on public spending, every year we had to make savings and keep within inflation which was romping on. I had had two people Peter Slater and Ralf Riley, working on research and forward planning, with their help we produced a Position Statement which listed in great detail everything the department did and managed, the objectives for each section, all the costs, manpower, income and estimates for the coming year.

I knew every unit of electricity, oil, gas and water that was used in each building, the number of man-hours including overtime and enhanced payments necessary to operate for each week.

On income I knew what a penny increase on each admission charge for swimming would bring in even allowing for an initial drop off, and the same statistics for each and every sport from squash to badminton. All this information was collated without the use of computers because we did not have them at the time. I had total control of my department's operational finances.

When at a Chief Officers, meeting the Director of Finance told everyone to increase the charges by the rate of inflation, I caused a stir when I challenged him and asked if he wanted the charges to increase or the income to increase? They are the same he said and everyone agreed, no they are not I replied, in some cases if I increase the charges, the income will go down, on others I can increase the income 100% by raising the charges, so which do you want?

Most of those present did not even understand what I was talking about that was the extent of their financial management expertise.

My problem was that I could see that the country could not carry on spending on services at the expense of manufacturing, and that it was up to local government to be as efficient as possible, many of my responsibilities were comparable with the private sector and should be managed the same way.

In 1983 the Tories were in control with a majority of one, they had set up a special committee to look into more savings. I was tipped off that this committee was meeting to discuss savings to be made in my department; I was extremely annoyed and marched into the meeting in the town hall. In the meeting was the Chief Executive, the Director of Finance and the members of the Tory group.

They were all very surprised to see me but I sat down and asked if they were discussing my department, without waiting for an answer I said that I could give them a professional management report but I did not think that they had the balls to deal with it.

That shook the room, some members asked what I meant by the remark? I told them that there were many things that the council did that were a complete waste of time but tackling it would require guts, which I did not think they had. That set them off, saying that I should not be saying things like that "Why not it's true" I said. OK then said one of them let's have the report next week.

That's what I mean you don't understand, I said a professional report, not a quick one page guess. "So how long will it take?" As long as is needed to do the job professionally, I told them. It was agreed that I could get on and produce my report.

The idea behind my thinking was simple, if the department was operated at the most efficient level no private organisation could be brought in to take it over, because there would not be any profit in it for them. Private business wanted a return on their capital of at least 15% to 20% at this time. In my heart I knew that we had too many staff in parts of the department which had been built up over many years.

I returned to my offices in West Kirby and went into Bryan Lucas's office, "Do you want to carry on working for me" I asked Bryan? "Of course I do what brought this on" he asked. I told Bryan that I intended to examine every one of the 2200 posts within the department; I was staying and now so was Bryan.

It was a simple evaluation I looked at each job and said to myself "what would happen if this post was not there?" Could we manage, if so how?

I had decided that there would be NO reduction in the level and standard of the service we were currently providing. Bryan and I did this with the top three tiers of the management tree; some of the assistant directors would not go along with my review so they were dropped from any further involvement in the assessment.

Those who did agree were asked "how few people do you need to carry out your departments commitments and still maintain the same service?" The best managers replied with the same question, "who will choose the staff, will it be last in first out?" When I replied that they would choose the staff they went off happy and when they returned I could not believe what they were telling me.

So long as they picked the staff they could and would manage with a lot less staff. When asked how? Easy we will get rid of the lazy buggers we have been carrying for years I was told.

It confirmed what I had thought all along the question was how to achieve it. I had been holding meetings with each of the unions separately; I told them that it was necessary to lose some staff to safeguard the majority.

Surprisingly each reluctantly agreed as long as all the union's members were treated the same, especially the senior managers,

I confirmed this but I was told they would still have to fight it when it was made public.

I now had all the reviews back and I went over them with Bryan and Alec Bennet my assistant director in charge of the finances.

The amount of proposed savings was staggering, so much so that I wanted any doubtful posts to be retained. Even so the amount identified was over £1,115,000, to be absolutely sure I kept the figure down to £1m.

The way I proposed to achieve the savings was to give everyone of the staff from the top to the bottom a notice of dismissal and at the same time give those I was going to keep on, a letter of their new appointment. I some cases it was an increase in salary due to the fact that because of the reduction in numbers they had to take on more work and responsibilities. I also knew that the most vulnerable part of my department was the Cemetery and Cremation side at Landican.

At the beginning of this exercise I held a meeting with all the funeral directors to explain that there was a possibility of strike action in the future, I did not explain my savings plan but just said it could happen. To my surprise they said that they would embalm bodies at their own expense if we provided an empty industrial building equipped as a temporary mortuary in which to store the coffins. They would start the embalming when necessary.

With this side of the potential problems covered I started to write my report.

There were only 14 copies printed, each one was numbered and marked strictly confidential.

The first page started at the top with two of the assist and directors posts going, then down through the admin section with a saving given against each post and a total saving at the bottom of the page. The next page gave the previous saving at the top with the new running total at the bottom. The grand total at the end was £1,100,000. Remember this amount was to be saved each year and with a guarantee of no reduction in the level of service.

I went to the meeting and said that there were conditions attached to the report.

1. I had to make all the appointments
2. The report had to be accepted in full. No picking and choosing.
3. 2 months to pass before the level of service was assessed.
4. Copies of the report had to be returned to me at the end of the meeting.

I will never forget the look on their faces as they read the report, they could not believe the amount involved. When I told them my decision to terminate everyone's employment, and then re-employ most of them, they said I could not achieve it without industrial action. I agreed and told them that I had taken that into account and made my plans accordingly, but I would not divulge what they were. The report was accepted but it had to be discussed by every member of the Tory party because of the potential row in the council chamber when the report was published. It was decided that there would be a special Council meeting to ratify the report so that there would only be one chance for the opposition to attack it.

The day of the special meeting at the town hall I got Gill to drive me to the town hall at 8-30am and to take the car home, the meeting did not start until 6-15pm. At lunch time the unions had started to picket the building with hundreds of people with placards, shouting at anyone entering the building, by 5-30pm the crowds were so big that the police had brought in mounted police to help to keep control. At teatime in the canteen I was asked by the leader of the opposition if this was in fact my own report or had it been pushed on my by the Tories? I told him it was my professional report and that I stood by every word.

The police let the protesters into the public gallery but that was only a tiny fraction of the people outside, the council agreed to let people into the council chamber itself and to sit all round the perimeter of the room, the atmosphere was electric it was like entering the arena as a gladiator with the lions roaring for blood.

The Council Chamber is set out in a horseshoe pattern with a table in the centre at which the Chief Officers sit; I decided to sit facing the public gallery so that I could see anything that might be thrown at me. The only other Director to attend was the director of Personnel, Bill Hughes a very good colleague.

It is customary to start the meetings with a prayer said by the Mayor's Chaplin. The Mayor's attendant shouted "all rise" as the Mayor walked in and took his place at the head of the chamber.

The Chaplin went to the front to say the prayers and started by saying "I call on Almighty God......" when someone in the public gallery shouted, "bloody hell he's even got him on Barnes's side" Laughter went all round the room and I tried hard not to smile.

The meeting started by Clr. John Hale setting out the report and saying that it was the report of the Director of Leisure Services & Tourism who would answer any questions, although I was ready and able to do so it was the perfect get out for the politicians. Questions came thick and fast but I had all the answers, I knew I was home and dry when the Leader of the Opposition Clr. Andrew Davis again asked me if I would comfier that this was my own report, which I did. He then closed all his papers and sat down, the rest of the council waited for the vote to be taken.

The Tories won the day and people started to disperse. I went to the bar for a well earned drink I saw a number of Labour Councillors and asked them why they had opposed the report but failed to ask what the savings of £1m would be used for. Not one of them had thought of that and yet the £1m was going to be saved each year, it could have been used for all sorts of things.

As predicted the unions called out on strike the staff at Landican Cemetery, this was the first time that a strike had been called which stopped the burial of the dead anywhere in the country. The press and TV soon picked up on this and we were on national TV.

I went down to the picket line at Landican to find only one member of my staff at the gates, he said I could not go in and when I asked were the rest of the union officials where he said they had just gone to a meeting. It was very convenient when they knew I was coming. I said to my staff who was a grave digger and a small man about 5ft 6ins tall " John I am going in and you know you can't stop me, I am going to make a cup of tea, why don't you come in and have one as well?" With that we both went inside.

The strike lasted two days and was broken when a new born baby died on the Woodchurch Estate. The parents and all their friends and neighbours decided to walk to the cemetery on mass with the police and press watching, as they reached the gates the picket line just parted and melted away. The strike was over.

The most amazing thing to me was the fact that so many supervisors and managers came up to me and said "I'm glad you got rid of that lazy bugger, we have been carrying him for years", but no one would say that to me before.

The department not only survived the cut backs but thrived so that I was able to maintain all the services at the same level as my report had promised.

The government was still cutting back on spending and introduced an excellent redundancy scheme, whereby staff could be given up to 10 added years on their pension payments if they left work voluntarily and were not replaced. Once I had turned 50 years of age I took the family out for a meal at the Kebab House in Hardman Street in Liverpool to celebrate the fact that if I was made redundant at least I could take my pension.

Marine Lake West Kirby

For a number of years the West Kirby lake wall had been failing, this meant that the lake was emptied and a stretch of wall had to be repaired, I was informed by the Engineer that the next time the wall was breached would be the last time, as it was not possible to repair it any more, it needed a new wall. The wall is 1000yds long and 50yds wide.

When I told Clr Hale that we would need £750,000 to fix it I was told that there was no way that the council would agree to spend that sort of money on the west side of the borough (Tory voting area) even though he was all for it.

Being on the Sports Council I was able to obtain the criteria for grants for capital projects, unfortunately there were none for replacement projects, but if we made the lake twice as big there were substantial grants available. I put this to the Engineers who said that to make the lake double the size it was only necessary to extend the side walls by 50 yds. To 100yds the length would be the same. The costs would be as follows

Lake as now 1000yds by 50 yds cost £750,000 no grant
Lake new 1000yds by 100yds cost £500,000 with grant

I still had to get the Council to agree. I asked for a list of all the lake users and found to my surprise that many organisations such as scouts and guides from Rock Ferry, New Ferry, and Birkenhead North area used the lake regularly (Labour voting areas). I was also told by the lake warden that many of the Social Services homes brought their patients by mini bus, parked on the promenade and walked round the lake wall.

With this information I sought out the labour members from these areas and suggested that their constituents would be the losers when the lake closed due to the council deciding not to repair the wall.

The councillor from Birkenhead and others areas were quite annoyed, so at the next Council Meeting they asked the leader of the council Clr Hale, what he intended to do about replacing the lake wall at West Kirby. This came as a complete surprise to John Hale who looked at me as I shrugged my shoulders as if I was as surprised as he was. "I will ask the Director to report to the next meeting" he said. After the meeting ended he asked me how this had come about but I said nothing. I presented the report giving the costs and it was agreed by the council to renew the lake and make it twice the size, which was the cheaper option.

The Engineer told me that there could be still more savings if the spoil from the old sea wall could be deposited outside the West Kirby Sailing Club frontage instead of taking it all the way to the Bidston Tip, it would give the club a very much larger boat and car park. The club would only have to pay a nominal sum for the land; I ascertained that the sports council would give a grant for the surfacing and lighting, as I was a member of the club I suggested that the negotiations should take place without me.

I told the Commodore of the scheme but he was not at all interested, I think it was because the idea came from me. At the time there were a few members of the club who felt that they were above most of the other members especially the younger ones.

I held a public meeting to inform the citizens of West Kirby of the proposals to increase the size of the lake, it was attended by about 110 people most of whom did not want any changes to West Kirby and certainly did not want to encourage more visitors to the town. At the end of the meeting a vote was taken and the only people to vote for the scheme were my family and one member of the sailing club, 5 in total.

The councillors were devastated and the scheme was almost lost. I contacted the sailing club and told them I was disgusted by their lack of support, it must have hit home because many of the younger members started a petition to hold a further meeting in which they packed the hall and those present voted 100% in favour of the new lake. I had managed to get the lake renewed and enlarged which was one of my last achievements; work started before I retired but was finished while Bryan Lucas was Director, which was fitting as he had been the Engineer and Surveyor at Hoylake for many years.

CHAPTER THIRTEEN

Early Retirement and New Life

Retirement

About this time I went to see a friend of Bert Butterworth, Bob Mura who had an office in Berkley Street in London: he was a financier. I had always provided Bob with Wimbledon tickets and Wembley tickets from my contacts on the Sports Council; he had told me that if ever I needed financial advice he would be glad to help.

I told Bob that I was thinking of taking early retirement so he invited me to his offices When I first entered he said I was too young to retire, but within 30 minutes of looking into my circumstances he said I was working for just £95 per month. This was the amount I would have less in my pocket each month if I took the redundancy being offered.

That made up my mind: I had always wanted to go into the commercial world, and in the past had turned down offers from the Rank Organisation, Mecca and others, but now I was financially able to risk it without placing my family in danger of losing out financially.

I talked it over with Gill and the girls and my mum, Gran and Pop, and then I asked Clr. John Hale to let me take early retirement under the government scheme. He was amazed and said he did not think the members would agree. I reminded him of what I had done for him and the council, saving £1m, so he put it to his members.

The reason I had kept Bryan Lucas as my deputy was so that I could be made redundant and Bryan would step up to my job as Director, giving him a much better salary prior to his retirement. It also meant that the Government would pick up the bill for my redundancy payment.

The Tories reluctantly agreed but when it was made public the opposition members thought that I had been sacked. When I explained it was my own request, it went through the council meeting easily.

For all my uncompromising dealings with the members, all three parties asked me to stand as their candidate for the council. All of which I refused with much satisfaction.

Politicians

I have worked with hundreds of politicians over twenty seven years, both local and national, and in all that time I can count on one hand the number that I could and would vote for. The standard of person entering politics has fallen dramatically over the years since paying them for their services was introduced in 1974.

I have always maintained that even the best of them are there solely for themselves, for a minimum of 90% of the time, then out of the rest, the political party gets 5% minimum; the rest of the time, if there is any left, is for their constituents.

My relationship with politicians was and still is one of distrust. If they accept as I do the division of responsibility between elected members and officers it is possible to work together.

Elected members are there to decide on policy, this of course will be based on their political beliefs, this policy should be set out clearly, and then it is the job of the chief officers to carry out this policy if it is within the law.

Problems arise when the politicians presume that it is their job to implement the policy and the officers let them.

In the past it was unheard of for a politician to tell the Town Clerk how to operate his department.

For myself I was always in charge of my department, the chairman was in charge of the committee. I had to remind a particular chairman who kept being quoted in the local press as the "Leisure Chief", that he was only the chairman I was the Leisure Chief, an appointment I had trained for over very many years.

Many councillors though are very nice people outside the town hall, I often had to travel to London with members on council business, the first time this particular lady and I were together she asked me if I would like a drink, (it was 10-30am), I got up to go to the dining car when she said just get some ice cubes.

On returning she had opened her bag, produced two cut glass tumblers, ½ bottle Gin and some tonics. The size of the drinks she poured was more than I have ever had, which made it difficult not to fall asleep, this was a regular thing each time we travelled together.

For many years now I have always voted in local elections by drawing a line through the ballot paper and writing the words "None of you are worthy of my vote."

I have been challenged a number of times about this statement but no one has been able to disprove it.

1985 March Retirement

I retired at the end of March, which was the last day in the offices at Riversdale Road. The department was moving to new offices in Westminster House, Birkenhead. We had a very good leaving party in the old offices on that last day: unknown to me all the secretaries had clubbed together to hire a strip-o-gram for me, but it was not a slim young girl; instead it was a roly-poly fat woman who made me take her garter off with my teeth. It was a great send-off and a night I shall never forget.

In the three months prior to my leaving I had written my own publicity article saying that I was setting up my own consultancy in Leisure and Tourism, as "Brian Barnes Leisure Consultants". While I was still at Wirral a firm of solicitors contacted me to ask if I would report on a company who were in financial difficulties with the bank.

It was a private squash club at 'Camelot' the theme park near Chorley. I told the solicitors that I wanted a guarantee of payment before I would take on the job; the banks agreed and so I commenced my first commercial assignment.

The squash club had been started by two teachers who were keen squash players. The idea was sound at this time as squash was a commercial enterprise and we had made considerable profits at Wirral. Prior to looking into the finances of the club I arranged to meet the owners on site at a weekend, the busiest period. The club was full with all the courts in action, and the café and bars were busy, but when I saw the prices I could see why. I took away the books and my suspicions were confirmed, the catering and bars were operating at a loss.

The membership although full, showed that most of the members were in arrears, some for more than a year. On Sunday mornings every breakfast sold made a loss - no wonder the place was full! When I pointed this out to the owners they told me that they knew all the members personally and did not like to ask them for their subscriptions.

I took them into the café and asked them to introduce me to some of the members. I asked why they were behind with their subscription and I was told by one man that he never paid anything until he received a red demand. I pointed out that the club was under threat of closing due to poor cash flow, and with that he pulled out his cheque book and paid his last year's and current subs.

I went through all the costs with the owners and explained that running a business was different from having friends round for a party. I reported to the bank that although I believed that the project was viable I did not think it could be managed by the two owners. I got paid but I did not follow up the future of the owners.

Nottinghamshire Sports and Safety Systems Ltd

In April I received an invitation from the owner of this company to meet with him; he told me he had a proposition for me. The company made artificial sports surfaces for football, tennis, cricket, bowls and playgrounds.

He wanted my knowledge and contacts within local government circles to get an introduction to council markets, as well as sports clubs. I was offered a job of Northern Sales Manager with a retainer of £500 per month and a percentage of all the sales on top. My area was from Aberystwyth in the west to Scunthorpe in the east and north to Scotland. I was still able to do my own work as well, so now I was earning more than I was prior to leaving Wirral. I had no trouble getting to see the appropriate chief officer in any authority, which is why they were paying me.

In 1985 **Lisa was born** on 31st October to Gillian and Alan, my third grandchild, the females were fighting back. She was yellow when she was born, a real Halloween baby, but sunlamps soon sorted that out. Lisa had Pyloric Stenosis (projectile vomiting) when she was a few weeks old, but the doctors and health visitors dismissed it as "babies are sick sometimes". After being sick in the surgery they admitted there might be a problem, and later after becoming dehydrated and very quiet, she was taken to hospital and operated on immediately, just in time to save her life. She soon gained her full weight and developed a healthy appetite.

John Anton "Transworld Leisure plc - Festival Gardens"

Also during this first year I had a call from John Anton asking to meet me to discuss a proposal he was thinking about. He asked me to join him at the Leasowe Castle Hotel for a meal, and with him were Peter Sergeant, a well-know-architect, and John Stanley, a former vice chairman of London Transport. John told me that he had taken over the site of the International Garden Festival in Liverpool and was going to turn it into a theme park by investing £150m; he wanted me to manage it.

I was amazed as he was supposed to be going to do the same at New Brighton. Anyway I did not want to go back into management and my business was doing well.

He asked me to get the project off the ground then he would set up a new company to develop New Brighton and I would be made Chairman. I said I was not interested; we never spoke about money or terms and conditions and after a few more drinks we parted on the friendliest terms.

When I got home Gill wanted to know what the proposal was. I told her that I was not keen to go back to managing staff again, but she asked what sort of salary would make it worthwhile. Eventually we agreed that I would not go for anything less than £12,000, a sum that I thought was impossible. I had no more contact with John Anton for months.

It was while I was with the engineer for South Lakeland in Windermere that I was handed a note from his secretary asking me to phone home. I drove to the banks of the lake at Bowness and used the red phone box (there were no mobiles at that time) to call Gill at home.

She said a Mr John Anton had called me and asked if I would call. I will always remember the telephone call: I was put through to John Anton who immediately said, "I want to offer you the job of Chief Executive of the Transworld Festival Gardens at a salary of £30,000 per year plus a bonus of £10,000 and a new Range Rover car. What do you say?"

I was shocked and could not say anything for a while. "Do you want it," asked John. I could not refuse such an offer and I said yes. "When can you start?" "I have to run down my current business, I have commitments," I replied. "Can you do it in a month? I want you to come down to London on Wednesday this week."

So for the next four weeks I commuted to London and wound up my consultancy. Money was no object, I travelled by first class on the train but it was then suggested I should fly down from Manchester, which I did.

I was taken to the site of the wooden offices used by the Festival management team at Aigburth. There was nothing in them at all: no desks, phones, kettle, nothing. John said to get whatever I needed. The first thing I needed was some temporary help, someone to be there when I was in London.

Cath my daughter was unemployed as she had just returned from PNG. Her ex-father-in-law, Russell White, was retired so I enrolled them both as temporary help. Cath went to WH Smiths in Liverpool with my credit card and purchased all the basic office tools from paper clips to an electric kettle: we were now in business.

John used to arrive on site in a large new Mercedes. The meetings with the Merseyside Development Corporation included all the people I knew and had been working with over the past few years, which made it easier for both John and me. The company secretary was Frank Cleghorn, Chairman John Stanley, Directors Peter Sergeant and Dick Lyon an American. I was given a company credit card, and I arranged with John not to take the new Range Rover but for the company to purchase my almost new Ford Granada Ghia at the price I paid for it, which suited me fine.

American Theme Parks

It was agreed that Frank and I should fly to Los Angeles to visit three theme parks: Disneyland, Magic Mountain, and Three Flags. We flew first class with Pan Am, hired a car in LA and stayed at Marina Del Rea.

It was the trip of a lifetime. Dick had arranged for us to be shown round each park by the Vice President, and I was very interested in how they managed crowds and potential troublemakers.

At Magic Mountain, which catered more for teenagers, the park staff identified coaches as they approached more than a mile away on the highway, then radioed into the control room who alerted the security personnel. As the coach unloaded the customers they were ushered into an entry point, surrounded by security guards who frisked everyone before they were admitted into the park. Once inside the park security cameras followed any groups who looked like possible troublemakers throughout their stay until they left.

All parks have "honey pots", that is a group of shops and catering places with toilets which attract customers, and these were set out in a circular fashion. In the centre was a custody cell, a real jailhouse like those you have in a western film, the idea being that any troublemakers could quickly and without making a disturbance be pulled inside and locked up until the sheriff arrived. I was most impressed, because it worked, and worked very well.

Another feature I noticed was a large electronic board outside the pay booths which notified the public if any of the rides or attractions were not available at the time of entry. The day I was there the weather turned very bad with strong winds and rain, and as I went round the park with the vice president he was constantly being asked on his mobile radio to authorise closures of rides due to the weather; this was immediately shown at the entrance site, so that no one could complain that they had paid for something that was not available.

The most impressive of the parks was Disneyland; the professionalism of all the staff, from the vice president to the cleaners could not be better.

I asked a 'litter picker' who was on roller skates about his job; he told me that he had worked part-time for seven years and had just been made a permanent member of the staff that year. He was so thrilled and you could see it in his cheerful manner as he told me that all the 'litter pickers' had been trained to be information officers as everyone asked them questions because they were so easily recognised.

I decided there and then that we would not employ anyone as 'litter pickers'; all the staff would pick up litter, from me and John Anton down. It worked a treat, and we never suffered from a litter problem.

While in America I had a phone call from Cath who told me that a press conference had been arranged by the London PR firm which was to be held at the site two days after we returned. Cath said the arrangements were non-existent and asked what should she do? I told her to take over and do whatever she felt was necessary to make the thing a success.

We returned home to find that Cath had arranged a first class event with plenty of drinks for the press (a must for a successful meeting).

John Anton and the board members were so impressed that they wanted me to take Cath on permanently. This is not something that I wanted, employing a close relative, and when I explained this to John he said that the board would appoint Cath and so she became the Public Relations Officer for Transworld, a position she deserved and did very well.

When I first met John he had a large Mercedes car, and not long after I took over at Liverpool he turned up in a new Bentley. "What happened to the merc?" I asked. "I thought that it was not the best idea to come to Merseyside in a foreign car," said John and I did not think anymore about it until ten months later when the bubble burst.

John had a property in New Brighton with a flat, above which he used when he visited, but he asked me to arrange accommodation on the top floor at the Atlantic Tower Hotel, in fact he took over the entire top floor so that he could offer investors and client's accommodation at any time.

We had some very good dinners at the Atlantic Tower when John was hosting visits from all over the country. Weeks later he said that the service was not up to standard and moved to the Moat House, again on the top floor. We did not find out until the collapse that John had not paid the Atlantic Tower for his stay.

Back to the opening of the site. One of the reasons for John wanting me to manage the site was for my contacts in the leisure industry. I appointed Simon Plumb as my deputy; Simon had worked for me at Wirral as did Peter McCloud, and we advertised for staff and used the local employment office to recruit 400 employees.

The catering was outsourced but everything else was my responsibility, including maintenance, security operation of the rides and all administration. It was a marvellous place to work, and the gardens were magnificent. Prior to opening I arranged for hundreds of school children to try out the rides free of charge to help us test our operational skills; they all had to arrive at the same time to see if the staff could manage to control large numbers. It worked well with only minor problems which we overcame.

The next job was to create a "Major Incident Plan" so that all the emergency services would know what to do if for example, a plane crashed on site after taking off from Liverpool airport.

At first the Police, Fire and Ambulance services were not interested in attending a meeting until I threatened to go to the press and tell the public of their apathy. A plan was put in place and was only used once when a ride collapsed trapping a maintenance man underneath, but at least everyone knew what to do and did it very well. The member of staff recovered and after a short spell off work returned to the site.

The opening of the Festival Gardens was a major event on Merseyside with the Press and Television covering the opening which was performed by Michael Heseltine MP, the minister for Merseyside. There was unprecedented security due to the ill-feeling against the Government of the day. Mr Heseltine arrived by helicopter at the onsite helipad and each of the site venues put on a special show which was repeated all day long for the people attending.

We had numerous television shows filmed at the site, including Blue Peter, James Last and others. Many visitors came from all over the world including Dr. S.E. Chua and Ho Cheok Sun from Singapore, J.R. Haywood, Hong Kong Government, Dr. Hosny Ali Kamel, Cairo, Egypt, Walt Wittmer, Minnesota, USA and Hans-Karl Winterfield, Bremen, Germany.

One of the main attractions was the Muppet Show – the real Muppets! This was very popular with my family.

Beatle City

One day I was with Terry Smith, the boss of Beatle City which was owned by Radio City, who told me that he had to leave early to attend a board meeting. The company were going to sell Beatle City, and this was the first I had heard about the sale. I said that I thought John Anton might be interested in purchasing it, if I could contact him. Terry said to go ahead and use his phone, and with that left the room for me to contact John. I told John that Beatle City was up for sale and he immediately said we would have it. I called Terry back into his own office and told him what John had said. He could not believe his luck saying that the board would be thrilled to sell it so quickly.

That was how John worked, but little did we all realise that he did not have any money.

The signing of Beatle City to Transworld Leisure was in all the papers; we were doing a photo shoot outside the building next to one of the publicity tour buses when I saw a female traffic warden approaching the bus as it was parked on yellow lines. I asked her if she would pose with me as Rita the Meter Maid giving us a traffic fine which she did. This became an iconic photo.

The Flower Arrangers

The site was in full swing when we started to experience vandalism in the gardens themselves; youths would trample on the flower beds and destroy them completely. It all came to a head when one of the gardeners remonstrated with a group of youths who set on him and beat him so badly that he was taken to hospital and kept in.

We called the police but they could do nothing even when a gang of youths stood by the police car shouting obscenities at them. I had had enough and said I wanted my own security people: John agreed to leave it to me.

I put the word out that I was looking for anyone who could sort out the problem of the gangs of youths. I was inundated with phone calls offering everything from shooting them to putting them in hospital.

I interviewed two men in their late 20s who came to my office on site. I explained that all I wanted was to stop the trouble. They asked me to walk round the site and they would follow at a distance, then we would meet up in the café.

I had been walking round for 20 minutes when a worried member of staff came up to me to warn me that I was being followed by a couple of murderers. I shrugged it off but told the two men about it when we had a coffee in the café. I asked them had they learned anything from their walk round. They replied that the four lads that we had passed in the Canadian garden had not paid to get into the site, and when I asked how they knew that I was told that those lads never paid to get in anywhere. "Can you sort out our problem?" I asked. "Sure, we will have a word with them." "Will that work?" "If it doesn't we will break their legs OK?"

I agreed that they would work every evening from 4pm to closing time around 8-9pm, and they would be paid cash in hand £100 per week. They were given site radios with a call sign "Flower Arrangers".

This was cleared by John and the board. I then informed the police who said they did not want to know but it was possibly the best thing I had done. We never had a single incident from that day on, so I considered it money well spent.

Due to opening in May we had missed many of the planned holiday coach parties but we were planning to get the next years booked well in advance.

We planned to close for the season at the end of September so that work could start on expanding the rides and installing new attractions.

On the last night Mike Burn, the entertainment manager, hired a Scottish piper to stand on a hill and play a lament. There was not a dry eye anywhere and something no one will ever forget. It was a wonderful experience and it had been a privilege to work with such a great crew.

We kept a small skeleton staff on with everyone agreeing to work at any and all of the tasks that needed doing.

On the 8th October I drove into work only to be stopped at the gate by security guards who were everywhere. I was given 20 mins to clear my desk and all the staff was locked out. Transworld had gone bust - or at least John Anton had!

It was a devastating experience which I never want to go through again. We all went to the Britannia Pub next to the site to get over the shock. Nobody got paid after that day; many had bills to pay and families to feed. Cath, Simone, Peter and Estelle came to our house and Gill raided our freezer to help and I gave them money as well: at least I had my pension. Although John promised me that he would pay me back the money I had given out he never did.

The way John operated was like this: he leased everything from cars and vans, to fairground rides, and all the equipment and computers. Because the amount of money was so vast - he was investing £200m - everyone was so impressed that good business practise went out of the window. Here is an example:

John said he wanted to purchase £100m of theme park rides from a Dutchman, Ronald Bussink, for the following year 1987, but he needed four rides immediately on site in 1986. One of the rides that were available was the "Santa Maria" at £100,000: John paid Ronald 10% down i.e. £10,000 and the ride was delivered.

John went to the leasing company who he had promised to do all his business with and said he wanted to lease the "Santa Maria" valued, by John, at £250,000. The company agreed to let John have 75% i.e. £187,500. Minus the £10,000 given to Ronald Bussink left John with a profit of £177,500 on one ride.

Remember he did this deal with everything on site

When we went bust in October 1986 the leasing company thought that at least they had the "Santa Maria" but Ronald was too canny for them: from the moment his rides came on site he had a member of his staff living in a caravan so that he claimed back all his rides. This was the only person I know who managed to salvage anything, including me.

When I went to see the Official Receiver to give evidence against John I said that I felt a fool; he put his arm round me and said, "If a British Bank can be taken for £2.5m cash and a Danish Bank for £1m cash you stood no chance." It did not help though, because I was owed £44,000 and Cath £8,000.

All in all, the experience was unforgettable and taught me a lot.

Small Firms Service

I was now out of work and looking for a job. There was an advert for an adviser in Leisure and Tourism by the Small Firms Service, a Government Department which advised small companies and people who wished to start up their own businesses.

It was right up my street and I got the job. I joined a group of 22 professionals who between us could advise on and solve any problem that arose. The pay was only £50 per day but the training was first class, and all included.

We went to the Inland Revenue for tax training, Institute of Marketing, Institute of Chartered Accountants, and Warwick University for training in Counselling.

Working with such a talented group of people was both exhilarating and informative; I learned what business life was all about.

We ran training classes every week in Liverpool and Birkenhead.

I also became a Business Adviser for the North West Tourist Board (NWTB). The NWTB had a special month-long help and advice session in Blackpool to help the small hotels and B&Bs to improve their efficiency and this was very successful.

By now I had purchased a small Amstrad computer to write all my reports. My pal, Joe Barnes, ran a training class for secretaries to convert from typewriters to computers and said I could attend a class anytime, all I had to do was to sit at the rear and follow the tutor. In theory it was OK, in practise when everyone else had finished I was still tapping the keyboard with one finger. I only went once.

1987 Gran Died - Gill's Mum

Gran died in Preston Royal Infirmary. She had not been well for some time and we had been going to see her regularly. It was a very sad time for Pop and all of us, especially the girls, for this was the first member of the family to die. To me she was the best mother-in-law I could ever have hoped for; we got on great and I missed her.

Offshore Sailing

Hayden Lockwood, a member of the West Kirby Sailing Club (WKSC) was a former captain for Shell. Hayden had a 30ft Ballad sailing boat which he used to take to the Mediterranean each year; various club members took two weeks holiday to sail with him, flying out to one port and back from a different one.

I arranged to sail with him back to Holyhead from the Channel Islands, and as soon as we left the island I knew that this was the life for me, especially sailing at night with millions of stars that you can only see when you are away from the lights that are on land.

We sailed to Southern Ireland, then up the coast to Arklow then Wicklow.

Hayden and Gwen knew members of the sailing club who invited them to a birthday party that night, a Saturday. I had to be at work on Monday morning so it was arranged that Hayden would set out the course to Holyhead and I would stay on board, get some sleep and then when Hayden and Gwen returned in the early hours I would sail the boat back to Holyhead while they slept.

I was woken at 2am when, Paddy their friend, fell from the harbour four feet onto the deck. He was so drunk that he did not hurt himself, just got up and laughed.

We cast off and I sailed the boat all night. There was an electric storm which I thought was a wonderful sight with all the lightning flashing around us.

Hayden got up about dawn and as the weather was poor and visibility bad he switched on the radio, but it did not work as the mast had been struck by lightning. It was a good job that Hayden knew the waters and was able to get us back to his moorings in Holyhead from where we got a lift back home.

I knew that this is the sort of sailing that I wanted to do but I realised that I would never be able to afford an offshore boat, with this in mind I decided to train to be a sailing instructor. I passed my exams and taught sailing at the club on the marine lake. I held classes for adult members every Wednesday which was appreciated by many parents of sailors and wives of sailors.

1990 Leon Luke Barrington 3rd August

It was also the year that I taught Jamie to sail. I was taking a class of 8 -12 year old children for the Royal Yachting Association (RYA) during the summer holidays. Jamie was too young to join the class but I gave him lessons during the lunchtime break.

By the end of the week he was the best sailor by far, he was a natural, he knew where the wind was at all times and his boat handling was superb.

The last session always ends with a race which Jamie won easily. Everyone took the RYA basic certificate which included climbing back into an upturned dinghy; they all did it except Jamie who could not pull himself back into the boat he was too young.

My next off-shore trip with Hayden was to Spain. We were towed from the boat yard to the beach then when the tide came in we set off for Spain via the Channel Islands to Lorient, our twin town in France, then across the Bay of Biscay to El Ferrol and La Coruña.

Arriving in La Coruña, where I was leaving the boat to fly home I was on the bow of the boat ready to step off onto the pontoon to secure the boat. I was dressed ready to go to the airport. The way a boat is moored in the Med is bow-on to the jetty: to do this you drop a stern anchor as you approach so that the boat is held about a foot off the jetty. I was just stepping off when the stern anchor caught hold so my stride was short of what was required and I went straight down. I could not believe it as I saw the wall going past my wide open eyes. I was still holding the rope in my hand. When I came up to the surface everyone was in tears laughing so much so that they could not help me out. Eventually I got out and had to unpack my case to get clean clothes in which to return home.

Later that year I took my Hilbre to the straits. Alan and Jamie came with me, and one day we could not get a third crew which is compulsory for racing so we decided to let Jamie helm the boat, less strength required, while Alan and I sailed it. We came in second and could have won if I had not made a mistake. That same race had Roger Glover's grandfather on board which meant that there was the youngest ever helm at 8 years old and the oldest crew at 80 years old. They were both given a memento of the race.

We decided to get Jamie an Optimist sailing dinghy so that he could practise regularly, which he did and became a very good sailor. Many is the time that Jamie was on the lake sailing, with Alison and Kate on the prom watching and waiting.

As I have already said we bought a five-berth Swift Caravan in 1983. My favourite place to go was to Park Coppice camp site at Coniston, and it proved to be a hit with the grandchildren as well because they could play in safety on the site. I joined the Coniston Sailing club so that I could sail as well as walk on the fells. Jamie and Kate used to love staying with me.

On one trip we had a problem with the car, a Ford Granada automatic, and we had to stop on the way to the lakes but the problem appeared to right itself. However on the M6 near Wigan the car overheated and we had to stop on the hard shoulder.

The Green Flag breakdown truck came and put the car on the back and towed the van home. We had sweets for the kids and yellow flashing lights on all the way back. As we stopped outside our bungalow Kate and Jamie ran in to tell Gran that we had broken down and that they had had a ride in a breakdown truck with flashing yellow lights.

The next day they both asked if we could break down again next time we went out.

1991 My Mum Died

My mum had been deteriorating for some time and we managed to get her into a nursing home in Morpeth Road, West Kirby. I took my mum out in a wheelchair along the promenade at Hoylake; it was March and a beautiful spring morning. We sat down as I needed a rest, and I told her that most of her furniture had gone to Cath's house in Skye; she was so pleased because she expected it to be thrown out. I took Mum back for her dinner and that is the last time I saw her.

Later that week Jamie and I went to Coniston for the weekend in the caravan. We pitched the van and then walked to the village for supplies. When we returned there was a note on the door of the van, asking me to contact the warden, and when I did I was told that my mum was in hospital after having a heart attack. We left the van and drove home. Gill said that my mum had died and we both cried. All the way back Jamie was comforting me in a way well beyond his years, something I will never forget. I promised him that we would go back to Coniston later and we did.

September that year brought devastating news. Alison had it confirmed that she had breast cancer. You just never think that it will happen to you or your family. We all rallied round as Alison had chemotherapy and radiotherapy; it was a terrible time for us all but especially for Alison. She was determined to last until her children were grown up and she did.

Jamie was now in the national sailing team of Optimists and was invited to compete in Holland at Braassemermeer, near Amsterdam. I took the caravan in which Steve, Kate Jamie and I slept while Gill flew with Alison and they both stayed in a hotel close by. Alison was determined to see her son sail for England; I don't know how she did it but she did.

Investors In People

While I was working as a business adviser a new national initiative was introduced to improve businesses by taking the best practise from successful businesses and making it a national award called "Investors in People".

To get this going there was a nationwide search for business advisers with plenty of experience in working with people, to train as advisers and assessors for the new award. I was one of those chosen.

After going on courses I was one of five assessors to carry out the first assessment at the Health and Safety Executive in Bootle. At the end of the first day we all met and decided that the organisation was not up to standard so we stopped the assessment.

The first assessment I did on my own was Unilever Research Laboratories in Port Sunlight. The Chairman of Unilever came up from London to be interviewed; I also interviewed a security guard who did not stop complaining from the time he came in, and after 20 minutes he took a breath so I asked him, "Marks out of ten - what is it like to work here?" "11 out of 10, it's bloody good really!"

I passed the company which meant that they were entitled to a feedback session. The entire board attended along with the staff who had worked on the award.

I seemed to get most of the larger organisations due to my background in local government. I assessed Cheshire Fire Service, Warrington General Hospital, Greenhalls Brewery, and Glaxo. All of them were the first of their kind to get the award.

There were many funny incidents like the person I chose to interview at random from the staff list who turned out to be half way through a sex change and no one would let him use the ladies' or the men's toilet so he used the disabled toilets.

Another company in Liverpool had a very hands-on Chairman who was getting in the way of every other director; he was holding them back unknowingly by getting in the way.

The factory shop floor was a typically Liverpool group of scousers, and I arranged to see them before they started work at 7am. When

I was introduced to them in the canteen no one looked up, and some carried on reading the papers. "What's it like working here?" I asked. No one spoke, then a voice said, "Hot in summer, cold in winter," and they all laughed. Progress, I thought so I asked the nearest man what he did: he told me he stacked the boxes. I asked what would happen if I stacked them, and quick as a flash he replied, "They'd all fall over 'cause you'd do it wrong." Again they all laughed but the ice was broken and from then on we all got on so I was able to complete my interviews.

The company was successful but I still had to give the feedback session which was held in the boardroom: every director was looking at me to see if I would raise the subject of the Chairman. I took a deep breath and said that although the company had been successful it would be even better if the directors could be left to make their own decisions without the Chairman constantly looking over their shoulder.

To everyone's relief the Chairman accepted the comments and the rest of my report. Some five years later I met the Chairman at a function in connection with the award when he said that my comments had changed and improved his management style.

When assessing the hospital I arranged to interview the night staff by working with them on a Tuesday night. The staff were very impressed that I should do this but I forgot to keep Wednesday free to sleep: you live and learn.

One of the most memorable assessments I carried out was that of "Nugent Care", a charity that looks after everyone and anyone who needs help. It was through Nugent Care that I met Sister Benedict who was in charge of Clumber Lodge, a very large Victorian house that has been adapted to enable them to care for young persons in small family size groups. I first assessed them in 1992; I was so impressed with the organisation that I recommended that they be used as an example of how to become an Investor in People. Every year I still call to see Sister Benedict and her staff, she is a remarkable person who just gets on with the job of looking after others, the world needs more Sister Benedicts.

My work on Investors in People was keeping me busy as well as bringing in a substantial amount of money. One day as I was driving to Wigan on the M58 I was thinking of changing my car when I had the idea of buying a boat instead. I asked Gill who said that as long as I did not want her to sail on it she did not mind. From then on every job was for a piece of the boat, sails, rigging, engine etc.

CHAPTER FOURTEEN

1992 - 1997

'Stratagem' Sadler 34

Once I had decided to buy a boat I knew that I needed to get my qualifications in navigation and seamanship. I knew that I would do better if I went on a residential course of one week. I enrolled with John Goodge at Southampton and passed both my Yacht Masters and Board of Trade certificates. I also did a week's sailing on the Solent with the same organisation to obtain the practical side of the qualification.

Finding the right boat was to prove more difficult than I thought. There were many boats available but when I went to inspect them I found that I could not stand upright as the internal height was usually 6ft. I am 6ft 2ins. After going up and down the country with Alan, Gillian's husband, we finally saw a Sadler 34 that was the right size, but it was under offer. However at least we knew exactly what boat we were searching for now. I finally found one at Newhaven on the south coast; it was out of the water.

The owner was only the second one in seven years. The boat was filthy: I could not believe how anyone could leave a boat in such a state. The oven was foul, the fridge was full of mould, and the sails were still wet and it smelt of damp. I was about to leave when Alan said, "If the boat and engine are OK we can easily clean the rest." I decided to have the boat surveyed; the result was a very dirty but sound boat. I made an offer that reflected the state of the boat and it was accepted. I now owned a Sadler 34 called STRATAGEM.

Alan and I spent days cleaning the boat from bow to stern, Alan up front and me at the back. We scrubbed everything with Flash and sent the sails to be laundered professionally.

The next project was to sail the boat to Liverpool Marina where I would keep it over the winter months and get the electronic equipment replaced, as well as new rigging.

A number of members of the sailing club asked if I was going to have the boat transported by road to Liverpool to which I replied that it was a sailing boat and I would sail it back.

1993 Sail to Liverpool

I asked Alan and Tim Dodd, who was an accomplished dinghy sailor, to join me on the sail home plus a non-sailing friend Steve Davis who asked to join me.

We set out from Newhaven with a plan to sail non-stop to Liverpool, and we arranged shifts to sleep and keep watch. The weather was great with good winds and clear skies. We passed the Isle of Wight going west but as we were off Falmouth the wind grew stronger and stronger.

We were going great guns but Alan was violently sea sick and was unable to help sail the boat. I asked Tim to take the helm but he was unable to cope, much to my amazement, so I was left to do it all myself.

We could not go on so we decided to go into Falmouth harbour for safety. This meant that we were sailing downwind with a very rough sea, so bad that we could not identify the navigation lights, which meant that we could not be sure of our position.

Everyone was tired and fed-up including me, and then I made a massive mis-judgement: I said, "I don't bloody know where we are". That brought panic to both Alan and Tim.

Alan somehow threw off his seasickness and began to help me navigate the boat. We knew we were sailing towards the land and when we managed to identify a navigation light we were able to confirm our position.

It was still a long, tiring, hard sail into the safety of Falmouth but at 1.30am we tied up alongside a fishing boat. The crew went below to sleep while I sat up to keep an eye on the boat. The next morning at dawn we called up the marina and sailed into a berth.

The crew had had enough and said they did not want to sail any further; they were going to hire a car and drive home. Steve the non-sailor said he would stay if I wanted him to but, as he could not sail the boat, I thanked him and said he should go with the others.

The truth was that both Alan and Tim thought that I had missed the gale warning the previous day, but there hadn't been one. I took all the crew to the marina restaurant for a drink and a meal and while we were there I saw a group of RNLI crew having a drink. I went over and asked if they would speak to my crew which they did.

They asked if we had been out last night because the lifeboat had been called out to salvage a much larger boat than ours, and said that we had done very well to manage the gale and survive as we did.

I asked about the weather forecast and the gale warning and was told that there was no gale warning and that it was not unusual for this to happen in this area.

I felt relieved that it was not my fault but understood why the lads did not want to sail with me any more, because they were not going to be much use if they could not cope or trust in the skipper. We parted on good terms.

I asked the marina manager if he could help me to find a crew. I was introduced to Bob Philpot who was working on a large sailing boat, the "Irene Jack". He said he had never been to Liverpool and would be willing to sail with me, so I agreed to pay his rail fare back to Falmouth.

The weather was still blowing a gale so we agreed to monitor the forecast and depart at the first lull in the wind. Two days later the two of us set sail for Liverpool.

It was simple for just the two of us the sail the boat because we had an automatic pilot that kept the boat on a set course. We agreed to a shift of three hours on and three hours rest.

Bob was a very nice bloke and we got on very well. I explained that as we approached Holyhead we would not get round the Skerries, a series of rocks, into Liverpool Bay until the tide turned so we entered Holyhead harbour to wait four hours.

I phoned home to keep the family informed, and Cath asked if she could join us on the leg into Liverpool. She got the train to Holyhead where I met her and introduced her to Bob. We set sail that night.

We had a good sail but as we approached Formby Point at the entrance to the Mersey smoke poured from the engine compartment. We stopped the engine and found that the water hose had burned through, so we dropped the anchor and the sails. We were in no danger, the boat was sound, the weather was fair, the sun shining, but there was no way we could get up the river against the tide.

We informed the coastguard and Mersey radio of our problem and asked them to inform our families which they did. My plan was to wait until the next tide and then sail up the river with the tide to the marina, about four miles, so until then we made a meal had a drink and waited. The tide turned about 1am when we could feel the boat swing on the anchor.

I called up Mersey radio to let them know that we were about to sail up the river: they were horrified, and said that we could not tack across the Mersey.

I said it was the only way we could get there, and after much deliberation they agreed on the understanding that we reported in each time we left each side of the channel.

The plan was that Cath and I would sail Stratagem while Bob kept the coastguard informed of our progress. We planned to sail across the river from buoy to buoy, which are numbered, so that it went something like this:

Bob "Mersey Radio, Mersey Radio this is Stratagem. We are crossing the river from buoy C9 over." Mersey Radio: "Stratagem, Stratagem all clear, go ahead."

After an hour of this with everything going so well Bob was told, "Don't call again until you get to Brazil." "Bloody hell, I thought we were going to Liverpool!" shouted Bob.

The airwaves were full of laughter, for Brazil is a very large buoy off New Brighton.

The sail was perfect as we passed by the Liverpool waterfront with the Three Graces all floodlit.

The marina entrance is about a mile further up river from the Pier Head, and Bob asked what our plans were. We had been told that the lock gates would not be open until 6am when the tide was right; as it was then 4am we had to wait. I decided to lower the headsail and go into the entrance under the jib alone: the problem was the incoming tide that was still running. The wind was from Widnes but as we got out of the tide we had to stop the boat before we hit the closed gates.

We had a practise and then made the decision to go for it. At 4.30am we were successfully tied up alongside the entrance to the marina.

All three of us got down fully clothed and fell asleep to be woken by the lockkeeper at 6am shouting, "How the hell did you do it?" to which I replied, "Seamanship".

We were towed into a berth and all three of us felt that we had achieved something by sailing up the River Mersey and berthing without an engine.

It was only as we had a cup of tea before Bob was due to catch his train home that he told me that he was an examiner for the RYA Yacht Masters qualification and that I had made the perfect sail home in spite of the engine failing. I felt very good about the trip in spite of the mistake at Falmouth. Stratagem was lifted out of the water so that improvements and new equipment could be installed.

Over the next two years I had the electronic equipment installed, Radio, GPS, Depth, Speed and Wind indicators, plus all new rigging. In order to try out the equipment Steve, Jamie and I sailed Stratagem to Fleetwood, the place where I had my first sail with my dad on the boating lake at the age of 4years in 1938.

!995 Optimist Training Officer

By now I was the Training Officer for the Optimist Association. The 1994 Nationals were to be held at Pwllheli so I sailed Stratagem round there to act as the mother ship for the competitors.

It was a great place to view the races, especially when Jamie was way out in front in one race. We had hot soup and drinks on board for any competitor who capsized and one little girl capsized every day so that she could come onboard for the loo and a hot drink.

I decided to sail Stratagem back single-handed, which I was insured to do: all went well, although going through Bardsey Sound was exciting.

It was while Stratagem was in the marina that Lisa came to look over the boat, and as she sat there on the deck she said, "Poppa, do you know that Stratagem spelt backwards says 'MEGATARTS', and from then on many people referred to us as Megatarts.

1995 Sail to Gibraltar

My plan was to sail Stratagem into the Mediterranean and on to Greece, to do this I would ask friends and sailing club members if they wanted a week or two holiday sailing with me. The following year 1995 the Optimist Nationals would be at Plymouth which would be a good starting point, so I sailed Stratagem to the south coast with Tony Tongue and Steve Davis. During this voyage I experienced my first Mayday call, but when we replied other boats were much nearer and so we were not required to assist.

Once again acting as mother ship to the Oppy sailors was great and very much appreciated. Sailing finished on Saturday and on Sunday morning the three of us set sail for Gibraltar. We were seen off by Jamie and Gill.

We had a gale warning in the Bay of Biscay but Stratagem coped with it very well which gave my confidence a boost. As we approached Cape Finisterre a dense fog came down which meant that to get into Muros, the nearest port. We had to use the depth sounder and GPS, just like we did for the exams, but we made it and the following day set off again, the next stop Gibraltar.

The approach to Gib was spectacular: it was 1am but the Rock itself was full of light, in fact there was so much light that we could not make out the navigation buoys or lights. We radioed in for advice and were told to tie up by the first jetty and report in next day. As we finished securing Stratagem we got out the drinks and had a wild celebration: it was my first long distance voyage in Stratagem. Next day we booked in and obtained a berth in the marina, and then I flew home to Liverpool feeling very proud of myself.

Gib to Majorca

As the weeks and months went by I gradually moved Stratagem east. On the first leg Arthur Kemp joined the boat which was a good job for just off Almeria the engine stopped working due to a dirty fuel filter. Arthur took it apart and sorted out the problem while I sailed slowly east.

We got as far as Torrevieja and booked into the marina for the night. It was a beautiful town so we stayed and flew home from Alicante a few miles north.

The next leg saw Howard Reynolds-Jones and Roy Jones fly out with the intention of making it to Palma, but the weather was terrible, so much so that Howard had to return to work leaving Roy and myself to make the trip alone. I wanted to sail overnight directly to Palma but Roy was not too keen on night sailing so we made it to Ibiza in daylight.

We berthed in the marina at San Antonio; I had been here before in 1973 with Gill and the girls. How the place had changed! We decided to go out for a meal and a drink. There was no one about and this was 9pm. By 10.30pm we were ready to return to Stratagem, and as we walked through the town it started to come alive.

The problem was that all the people seemed to be kids, aged about 12-14 years, and neither of us could believe it. We arrived at the marina with the sound of disco music throbbing in our ears, which went on all night. We both felt very old.

Next day we left and sailed up the west coast of the island to anchor in Portinatx, where we stayed overnight, and the following morning we sailed into Palma Bay to find a berth in Can Pastilla a small village five miles from the capital and two miles from the airport. This place was to be my home for the next year or two because there were so many ex Brits living on their boats who made me feel at home as well as looking after Stratagem when I returned home.

I made a lot of very good friends, especially Claire who ran a bar the "Gin Palace" where we all met each day and George who lived on his boat in the marina and spoke perfect Spanish.

1996 Palma Can Pastilla

I was in Can Pastilla for the Optimist European Championship. I was still the training officer and I had hoped that Jamie would be a competitor but he developed glandular fever and was unfit to compete. I took both Jamie and Kate out with me to stay on the boat; we had a great time apart from the time when we were anchored in the bay watching the races with some of the kids and parents swimming by the boat. Unknown to anyone, one of the dads used the toilet and flushed it while others were still swimming. The result was one embarrassed dad and a bunch of swimmers who moved quicker than they had ever done before trying to get out of the sea.

I was often asked at the sailing club why I had my boat berthed in Palma, but the facts were simple. I could leave my home in West Kirby, drive to Liverpool Airport, check in, take a 2 ½ hour flight, and be on my boat all in five hours. Plus the annual charge was less than at Liverpool or Pwllheli. The family used Stratagem as an apartment for holidays, all it cost was the air fare.

CHAPTER FIFTEEN

1997 Circumnavigation of the World

1997

My stay in Can Pastilla was superb and I enjoyed every minute there. It was in 1997 that I heard of the Blue Water Rally, which was an organisation set up to organise a sail round the world: not a race, but a rally over two years. I sent off for more information and asked my friend and colleague at the sailing club, Tony Tongue, if he was interested. He took all of two seconds to say he was very interested, and so began the greatest adventure of my life.

Blue Water Round the World Rally1998 – 2000

Three years earlier at the London Boat Show a group of sailors were having a drink at the Guinness stand talking about the new trend in racing round the world. Someone suggested sailing, not racing, round the world, and from this the group organised the first round the world rally.

When they returned they formed a company and called it "Blue Water Round the World Rally". The advert I had seen was for the second rally and the first Blue Water one.

The Rally would start and finish in Gibraltar, the date of departure being October 1998.

Once I had talked it over with Gill and the family I made the decision to book my place. Gill does not sail and is sick even on the Mersey Ferry, but she said that she would fly out to the places that she would like to see. The rest of the family thought it was a great adventure.

I told the gang at the Gin Palace and my friends in the marina what I was going to do. Everyone was full of admiration and so a farewell party was arranged as I set sail back to Gibraltar,

It was early morning about 6am when we called in at Almeria for fuel and milk. As we tied up to the jetty a voice from the far side of the water shouted, "Hi Megatarts." It was the crew of a boat we had met in Gibraltar two years earlier: it's a small world.

In Gibraltar we booked a berth for the next year so that we could prepare for the circumnavigation. Over the next six months other boats arrived and so we got to know many of our fellow rally members.

We made good friends with the marina staff who helped to keep an eye on the boats when we had to return to the UK where I was still running my business.

Back home everyone was excited about the trip. One evening I was having a drink in the sailing club when Steve told Toll Smith and others at the bar what I was planning to do. "If you do manage to sail round the world you will be the first club member to do so," said Toll Smith, something I had never thought about.

The Rally had a charge for each boat taking part of £7,500 plus £500 for each crew member. The money was to cover their expenses and included the cost of each boat passing through the canals, Panama and Suez, plus many free berthing places along the way. On top of this the rally organised a series of seminars in Warsash on the south coast to inform us of what to prepare for and equipment to purchase.

We were told that the three main problems we would face were

1. Personal Relationships
2. Power for the boat
3. Drinking Water

Problems 2 and 3 are dealt with under the heading Preparation Stratagem.

1. Personal Relationships did cause serious problems on Stratagem and also on many other boats.

I have spent much time thinking if I should record all the incidents and if so how and where. After consulting Cath who sailed with me and Gill who experienced some in port on her visits I have decided not to enter any details but to record that I should have employed a hired crew.

Tony left the boat in Crete when Cath came out to sail home with me; at last I began to enjoy sailing again.

There were many incidents but enough is enough, you live and learn.

Preparation - Self

The preparation was in two parts, me and the boat. It was a condition of the organisers that all boats had a short-wave radio, which meant that I had to obtain a certificate to operate it. All skippers had to pass the "Ships Captain Medical Course": this was to enable us to be in a position to take advice from doctors in the A & E department in the UK if we had a serious incident at sea. Tony thought that if I attended that would be adequate but I realised that if he did not do the course there would be no cover for me if I was injured. We both did the course.

It was the same with the Survival Course which was held at Fleetwood. As everyone else on the course was hoping to work on the North Sea oil rigs, it was compulsory for them: no pass, no work. The course was in a purpose-built pool, like a swimming pool but with very high sides about three feet above the level of the water, which enabled them to create very large waves in the pool. We had to practise righting an upturned life raft, then get inside it, which was not an easy task. There were many laughs as some could hardly swim and everyone struggled to climb into the raft.

We had a break for lunch and were told to put on our full sailing gear. As we sat at the table the lights went out and sirens started to sound; it was pitch black and very noisy. We were told that this was an exercise and that we had to go upstairs where we found ourselves high up over the pool with a ship's guard rail. It was the equivalent of a five metre diving board.

The pool was in darkness with flashing strobe lights, regular loud bangs, hose pipes showering us with water, sirens sounding and waves three feet high in the pool down below. We were told to jump, swim to the life raft, turn it over and get into it. Some panicked and did not jump, but I thought it would be safer to get in first and move away before anyone jumped on top of me. I got to the life raft and with others managed to right it, all the time feeling the full force of the large hose pipes hitting us with cold water.

I helped one chap into the raft and he pulled me in, then together we grabbed hold of each swimmer, bounced them up and down in the water a couple of times to get a rhythm, then pulled them up into the raft. We had this going so well that one bloke who was smaller than the others shot out of the water so fast that he went straight out of the other side of the life raft. After everyone was inside and the covers were closed we were left to sweat in the dark for 10 minutes to feel just how uncomfortable it was to be in one for hours at a time. We all passed in the end.

Being away for two years meant that I had to arrange for my credit and bank cards to cover the entire trip, I also took out extra cards such as American Express, Diners, as well as Visa and MasterCard. One of the banks said they could not cover the whole trip but they would send a replacement out to me. When I told them that at that time I would be somewhere in the Pacific Ocean they still refused to do anything so I changed banks.

I made a will and also gave Gill Power of Attorney; we were still trying to sell our house at the time. I wrote individual letters to all the family because I did not know what could happen over two years.

The rally advised everyone to take a number of photo-copies of our passport and have them laminated, so that we could hand these over in place of the real one when visiting foreign ports. We also duplicated copies of the ship's papers and took extra passport size photos of each crew member.

When I enquired at the doctors about vaccination I was asked which country I was visiting: when I replied all of them they thought I was being sarcastic. Some vaccinations required three visits to be fully covered; we thought that we had covered everything, then at the last minute Tony's daughter, a vet, asked if we had been vaccinated against rabies. We had not.

At one seminar we were asked what would we do if there was a death at sea. Someone said tow the body behind the boat until we reached port. I could imagine being followed by a group of sharks.

The answer was to take photos of the deceased and make a detailed account of how it had happened which was to go into the ship's log, and as soon as possible report it to the other ships and the authorities in the area where it happened. Then it was to be buried at sea. It was a sobering afternoon with no-one smiling at the thought.

All skippers were advised to have a questionnaire for each crew member stating what operations they had had, e.g. appendicitis, so that it could be ruled out as a problem. Other illnesses and medication would also be recorded. A recommended medical kit was ordered costing £880. I also started to collect small denomination US dollar bills as the American dollar is a universal currency. I left with $2000 in small change and ended up as a banker for many other boats who had not thought of this.

Scuba Diving

We were told that we would be visiting some of the best diving places in the world, and that it would be a great advantage to be qualified to dive and to have your own gear. I joined a class at Gibraltar to obtain my diving certificate but decided to purchase the gear in the Caribbean as it was much cheaper. It proved to be an excellent decision as the equipment also came in very handy for repairs to the underside of the boat as well as freeing the anchor from time to time.

Preparation – Stratagem (see list with costs appendix ii)

We had already renewed the rigging in Liverpool, but we needed a self-steering mechanism which would be wind-operated to save power. The best one available was a Hydrovane costing £2,500 fitted at Shepherds, in fact all the equipment was supplied by Shepherds of Gibraltar. This was the best piece of equipment that we bought, it saw us through all weathers, gales and light winds, and we could not have managed without it.

Power generation was a concern so we installed two solar panels, and a towed generator which we used when sailing but it could also be used when at anchor by placing the turbine in the rigging.

I then added three 100amp/hr batteries which proved their worth over and over again. The cold-box was converted into a freezer to help out the fridge; the rules of the boat were that if you took out a cold beer you replaced it with two warm ones. We had our priorities right.

The other concern on long journeys was drinking water. Stratagem had a built in water tank holding 60 gallons but I reckoned that we needed 100gals to be safe on the long trips. We solved this by purchasing ten 5 gallon plastic containers that we stored about the boat. It proved to be a smart move for we never got down to less than 50 gallons.

A new 6 man life raft was bought and as an added safety measure I bought a sea anchor for £350 which, although expensive and never used, gave me peace of mind which I thought was worth every penny.

An EPERB is an automatic electronic piece of equipment that sends out a mayday emergency call if submerged in water or switched on by hand. You register the vessel on which it is being carried so that anyone receiving the call knows who it is from. Ours cost £300.

I also set up with the GPO a radio/telephone account so that I could phone home from anywhere in the world from my new radio. Gill could also call me by the same equipment.

I decided to clean out the water tank on the boat, which proved to be more difficult than we thought because the entrance was so small that it was impossible to get a brush to all parts of the tank. The answer was to make two extra holes and from then on we had no problems.

The fuel tank was the next on the list. I asked Shepherds for a price for doing the job but they said that they did not want to do it so we took out the stainless steel tank and did it ourselves. The inside looked as though it was painted with bitumen, so we took the tank to some waste ground, placed ten stones inside, poured in some diesel, and shook it vigorously for five minutes, when we emptied it out it looked vile. We did this six more times and each time the diesel was cleaner until it was clean. It now looked like the outside, all shiny and clean. I dreaded to think what would have happened to the engine in a gale with the boat being tossed about if that sludge had blocked the fuel pipes.

After we told the other boats just what was inside our fuel tank they all did the same with theirs.

In some marinas and lagoons you are not allowed to discharge sewage from the toilet directly into the sea, though it is OK when you are miles from land in the middle of the ocean. We therefore had a stainless steel holding tank fitted to Stratagem. We could use the 'heads', as the toilet on a sailing boat is called, although I don't know why because it is the other end of the body that you are catering for. The contents are kept in the holding tank until it could be emptied out at sea, or it could be discharged directly into the sea.

I needed an extra anchor and Hayden had advised me to get the largest, heaviest one we could manage, which is what we did.

Charts were the next item on the shopping list. I bought a package of 269 second-hand charts and added to them; with the pilot books that we needed the cost was £1,000. (Appendix iii)

As we had to fly the courtesy flag of each country we visited we needed 50 flags at £300.

I also purchased a set of engine spares as advised by the makers Bhuke for £600.

At the last minute I ordered a new set of cruising sails, and I am very glad that I did - £1,800.

In order to pass through the Panama Canal each boat had to carry on board four ropes each 150feet long. I had made friends with a chap living on board his yacht who used to be in the army on the Rock. He said that it would be better to have two lengths of 300 feet and that he could get them for me cheap. He arrived at our boat one day with a large rucksack in which was 600ft of unused rope. I did not ask where it came from and gave him £50 cash; it was worth it.

For a year I was back and forth to Gibraltar or Warsash learning how to book in and out of countries, keep my ship's papers in order, and actually operate the new equipment on Stratagem.

Gill made a list of the places she wanted to visit and Cath said she would like to sail with me at some stage. Alison wanted to visit Australia with Kate so we arranged to hire an apartment for us all; things were progressing and the starting date in October getting closer.

A number of members at the sailing club said that they would love to sail round the world but when I offered to let them come and sail for part of the trip they all backed down except Arthur Kemp and Louis O'Sullivan, Tony's friend.

Departure 24th October 1998

I said goodbye to friends and family at home, and it was an emotional time for I did not know what the future held. Gill and the girls saw me off at Liverpool airport for my flight to Gib.

The last week at Gib saw all the skippers get together for a briefing on the weather we could expect over the next few days. It was then and only then that I began to wonder just what I had let myself in for. It lasted one night only: that was the only time I had ever had any doubts about the boat or the trip itself.

The last night ashore, 23rd October, we had a dinner at Bianca's Bar after which we sat out in the sun for a beer or two. All 110 of us were sitting drinking and I noticed someone who looked just like Gill, and no one spoke then as she moved round the group I said, "It's my wife!" and everyone laughed for I was the only person who did not know that Gill and Cath were coming to see me off. It was a wonderful surprise. The next morning I said goodbye to both of them and set sail to a point off the end of the Gibraltar rock where we all assembled and at the firing of a gun by the army set off on our circumnavigation.

The first leg to Tenerife was 750 miles and lasted 6 days. Arthur was with us for this first leg and proved a winner with the wind vane. We started and immediately the fog came down; I did not have radar and so I tucked in behind the French boat "La Billebaude" who did. As soon as we passed through the Straits of Gibraltar the sun came out and we had a wonderful sail down the Atlantic to Tenerife.

The boat performed very well but I realised that as the smallest boat I was also the slowest. I decided there and then that I would set off before the others so that I would not be at the end of the fleet on the longer trips.

We had a good steady wind with a clear sky. We cooked our first meal and arranged to sleep four hours on watch with eight hours sleep.

The morning saw a small bird had landed on the boat. It was a friendly little bird; it joined in with breakfast and had its own saucer of water on the stern of the boat. It stayed with us for a few days; at night it would fly off, catch a moth and then return to its perch on deck.

It took us six days to reach Tenerife. We arrived on Friday 29th October. Arthur left us to fly home. Gill my wife arrived for the 2 weeks we were in Santa Cruz.

The Rally organisers had arranged for us to use the Real Club Nautico de Tenerife which is more than just a sailing club, it is more like a grand sporting club with two Olympic-size swimming pools, tennis and squash courts and its own marina.

The waiting list for joining is 20 years and membership costs £20,000.

The Tourist Board organised many social trips around the island including a trip up the highest mountain Mt. Teide. Having Gill with me for two weeks was great and we had a very nice time.

Getting the boat ready for the next leg forced me to think about the 2600 miles across the Atlantic.

I knew that I was the slowest boat and while it was not a race I would rather be in the middle of the fleet than at the rear. Marc and Pauline Blomme, a Dutch couple sailing the second-smallest boat 'Samen II', had been quite depressed being at the back of the fleet coming down from Gibraltar. I made the decision to leave two days sooner than the rest of the boats. We left on Thursday 12th November 1998 and most of the other sailors waved us off as well as Gill.

The Atlantic

We soon found out that we had not finished all the little jobs that we had identified needed doing, so I decided that we would have a list made of all those little things we wanted doing and tick them off before we left Antigua.

We headed south towards the equator, the idea being that you go south until you reach the trade winds which are about 10 degrees north, then you use them to go west. In bygone times the rule was go south until the butter melts then turn west.

The first day out we both felt sick. I insisted that we took Stugeron tablets which enabled us both to keep going. Soon we were into our routine. From 6pm we kept watch for four hours each so that we had a lookout at all times, especially at night, not that we saw anything. It was 21 days before we saw another boat of any sort.

On day 6, or the night of Monday 16th November I saw the most spectacular display in the sky.

There were shooting stars all over the sky, and with no other lights to pollute the night it was superb. I started my stop watch to count the time when there were NO shooting stars. The longest was 19 seconds, and yet I could not see those behind me.

They were at all angles, speeds and colours. I was told when we reached Antigua that it was the remains of comet "Temple-Tuttle" which returns annually, with up to 5000 meteors an hour caused by particles no bigger than grains of sand. It could have been the start of world war III and I was listening to the radio to see if that was the reason for the display.

During the day we were escorted by dolphins, 20 or 30 at a time. They loved to swim at the front of the boat on the bow wave. They would knock each other off the wave then swim round and come back to do the same to the others. After days of watching them we took it for granted.

There was very little wind for the first two weeks. The other boats would ask us what the weather was like and because we had no wind they sailed further north and found better conditions.

On all long sea passages there is usually a radio net. This means that someone voluntarily broadcasts on a published radio frequency and asks any boat to radio in with their position and the actual weather they are having. This information is then given out as a factual state of the weather for the area, in this case the Atlantic.

A Canadian called Herb was the organiser for the Atlantic, as all who have crossed this sea will know. It gave you a feeling of someone else being about although you never saw anybody. The Rally also did a net for both safety and weather reasons but we still called in to Herb.

People often ask what it is like being at sea for weeks at a time. The first thing you realise is that a day is 24 hours, not 12 or 16 as it is at home. You are confined to your boat which in my case is 34 feet long or 11 meters: you can walk round the deck and you need to do so each day to check the rigging, that is the wire and ropes that hold up the mast and sails.

A typical day, breakfast to breakfast, would be like this:

Whoever was on the last watch at dawn woke the other up with a cup of tea. Then get up and wash and shave just as at home.

Breakfast was made, cereal and a fry up if that is what you felt like. Then wash up.

At 10am there was the roll call for the B W R followed by the report to Herb at 11am.

Ship's Log (see Appendix iv)

The ships log was completed each hour on Stratagem, the idea being that if we forget to do it we would only have lost one hour of records.

We recorded the wind speed and direction
The barometer pressure
The log, that is like a milometer for the boat
The ship's speed
The course
Whether the engine was on or not
The ship's position, longitude and latitude.

When we were in coastal waters we recorded the time of high and low water.

There was always one of us looking out for other boats or debris.

We had elevenses and thought about lunch.

Sometimes one of us would have a nap or go and read or listen to tapes.

Lunch was often a sandwich. We had a rule that whoever cooked did NOT wash-up.

Snacks again in the afternoon, and read or sleep or sunbathe - there was plenty of time.

I like cooking and so I did most of the main meals. We used tinned food, dried food and packet foods, especially soya mince to make bolognaise, chilli con carne, mince etc. Although we set off with fresh fruit it did not last long in the heat so we soon had to resort to tins.

After dinner, usually about 5pm, we would have a can of beer and start the three-hour watches. 6-9pm, 9-12, 12-3am, 3-6am.

Depending on the conditions you either had a good sleep or none at all, but we still changed over at the times above.

I liked the night watches best. This is what got me hooked on offshore sailing. The quiet night when you can see all the stars gives you time to think about life, the world, the universe and your little tiny part in it all. It is very humbling. You either love it or hate it. I loved it all.

It was day 19 before we saw any other vessel. It was a sunny clear day and we were both in the cockpit drinking a beer when I looked up and saw a large container ship crossing our bows about half a mile ahead. It then turned and passed us to port, it was obvious that he had changed course for us. I called up the ship on the radio to thank the captain for altering course, and he then asked us where we were going and told us he was going to Antwerp. We said our goodbyes and decided to keep a better lookout in future.

21st November 1998 Pop Died

I had the radio on which was unusual at that time of day when I heard a message for Stratagem was waiting. I called the operator and was put through to Gill who told me that Pop, her dad, had died that day. I knew he was at the end of his life before I left and I had said my goodbye to him but it was a sad day for me. Pop had been like a dad to me over the years. We flew the flag at half-mast for the rest of the day and raised a glass or two in his memory.

On 5th December, it was 24 days since we left Tenerife and at last we got the trade winds proper. The boat was going great now at 6/7 knots about 8/9 mph, our top speed, and we even reduced sail to make the boat easier to manage.

Monday 7th December 7.30am Tony sighted land: it was Antigua right on the nose. We were due to arrive on the far side that is the west of the island, at Jolly Harbour.

At 1.35pm we were alongside the customs office to be greeted by the BWR people with a beer. We had crossed the pond in 26 days.

It was hard to believe that it was December it was so hot. As soon as we had signed in we secured the boat and we went for a swim in the clearest warm water I have ever seen. It was all worthwhile.

Concert

During the crossing of the Atlantic we got to know more about the other sailors and their talents to play instruments, sing, or tell jokes. John Boyd from 'Athena' played the bagpipes and had full highland dress. It was decided to use this talent and put on a show in the harbour bar. I was asked to be the compère, I don't know why. All was going OK until we found out that the bar would be open to everyone. This meant that as most of my stories and jokes were in-house ones it was going to be a risky time.

However the night was a great success and very well received. Some of the acts were of a professional standard, especially Tony Manzi, 'Arietta', who was superb with his monologues which he composed as we sailed round the world.

On Wednesday 16th December we set sail to the south of the island to English Harbour. We dropped the anchor 20yds outside the apartments that Gill had booked for her stay in Antigua for Christmas. Antigua is a beautiful island and we hired a car to get around in. I also did some underwater diving. The equipment was so cheap that I decided to purchase my own so that I could dive anywhere as well as inspect the boat under the water.

Christmas Day was so unusual. We all met at Nelsons Dockyard where there was an old boat on the shore which was filled with ice and then topped up with bottles of Champagne at £5 per bottle. A party soon developed and ended up on the beach where some of the boys made a snowman out of sand and then sprayed it with "snow". We all swam in the sea, then went out for a traditional Christmas Dinner at Nelsons Dockyard.

Boxing Day was another set of parties going from boat to boat. It was a Christmas I shall never forget. The apartment, 30 yards from the boat, was brilliant and Gill and I drove round the island to make it a beautiful holiday.

Stranger than Fiction

Gill and I were having a cool drink in the local bar at about 11-11:30am. We were the only people there when a couple walked in hand in hand, ordered a drink then came over and asked to join us.

They looked about mid-30s, she was a very large person, he was tall and slim, and they told us that they had sailed north from Tobago on their 40ft wooden boat. Ann, the lady, had gone onto the foredeck to adjust the sail without a lifeline when she was swept overboard by a large wave. Her husband John immediately tried to turn the boat round but he first had to reduce the sails and the sea was rough with medium size waves which made it hard for him to see Ann. Eventually John stopped the boat and sailed back towards where Ann had gone overboard but he could not see her. Ann said she knew that John would return for her and she was a good swimmer even though she was without a lifebelt.

Ann saw the boat return and come back in her direction but then it started to sail left and then right without getting any closer. This went on for more than two hours: Ann could see the boat in the distance but John could not see Ann.

John put out a mayday call for help and continued to search for his wife but after a few hours he realised that he was not going to find her. He sailed into Dominica where he was boarded by police and arrested on suspicion of killing his wife. He was taken to the local police station and questioned, all the time he kept asking for them to continue the search for Ann. He told us that in the end he did not care what happened to him, he just gave up.

Ann saw John sail away in the distance but all the time believed that he would return. The water was warm of course and Ann was insulated due to her size, and her long skirt helped to keep her afloat. After a few hours she thought she saw John returning but as the boat got closer she realised that it was not John but another boat that was coming towards her. Ann shouted and waved at the boat as it got nearer then she realised that it was coming straight at her so she had to swim away to avoid being hit. As the boat passed by she shouted for help, and luckily someone heard her cry and raised the alarm. Eventually Ann was taken on board and she told her story.

The owner of the boat sent out a radio message to say Ann had been rescued. They were on their way to St Lucia which is where they left Ann. The police in Dominica got the message about Ann and let John go; he sailed his boat to Antigua where Ann flew in just minutes before they arrived in the bar. No wonder they looked like two love-struck teenagers. It proved to me that truth is stranger than fiction.

Louis O'Sullivan flew out to join us on the voyage to the Panama Canal. We had decided to set sail on New Year's Eve to go to as many islands as possible in the Caribbean prior to going through the Panama Canal.

Antigua to Colon – The Caribbean

We left Antigua on New Year's Eve 1998, three on board, with a good wind in the sails.

Gill waved us off as she was leaving in two days to fly home. The Caribbean Sea is full of islands laid out in a row from Cuba in the north to Trinidad & Tobago in the south.

Antigua is about half way down the line of islands. The appeal of the Caribbean is the closeness of the islands to each other. You can see the next island from wherever you are, yet each one is a separate country.

We could see the Island of Montserrat on which the volcano was erupting while we were there. One boat sailed too near the volcano, and when the wind changed direction the hot ash ruined his sails.

The prevailing wind blows in from the Atlantic Ocean between the islands and makes for a lively sail. This turned out to be too much for our newest crew member who was seasick until we slowed the boat down to give him a smoother sail.

The first of our intended stops was Basse-Terre on Guadeloupe but when we arrived all the berths were full and most were double or triple booked. We had no option but to sail on to the next island, Dominica.

The wind was now gale force and on the nose, and we had one of the worst sails so far. We arrived in a rainstorm so bad that we stopped the boat and waited for the rain to stop just outside Prince Rupert Bay. When the rain cleared we were met by Alex, a boat boy, who offered to guide us to an anchorage (for a tip).

The system is that at each country the skipper must take the boat's papers and all the crew's passports to Customs, Immigration and Port Health control to "book in", and only then can the crew go ashore.

As it was New Year's Day all three offices were closed. I was told that the staff were at a party in town so I got a taxi and went to try and find them.

The noise and music soon identified the flats where the party was but no one wanted to know about booking me in. I was told to come back the following day, but as we were only staying one night this was not going to help. I was finally told to return later that day.

I returned in the afternoon with the party still in full swing, and after much shouting and ringing of door bells I managed to persuade them to open the offices for me. Three men came down with drinks in their hands, and one for me; we walked down the road to the offices where they suggested that they book me in and out at the same time so that I did not need to return in the morning. When I got back to the boat the crew were enjoying beer and gin and tonics. Who wants to be the skipper?

The following day 2nd January we set sail for St–Pierre, on Martinique which was a poor island. We only stayed a day, and then sailed with a good wind to the next island.

St Lucia

We arrived 3.15pm on 3rd January at Rodney Bay Marina in St Lucia which was OK and gave me a chance to make repairs to the autohelm and stern leak while the crew toured the island. I liked St Lucia and would like to return without a boat. While we were in the marina we heard that bad weather was on the way so we decided to cut short our trip to St Vincent and Grenada and sail directly to Bonaire, one of the ABC Islands (Aruba, Bonaire and Curacao) off the north coast of Venezuela, and it is a marine nature reserve.

Bonaire

Bonaire is very low-lying and there are salt flats along the southern coast. You are not allowed to drop your anchor just anywhere. You must use the hundreds of anchor buoys which have been set all round the island in order to safeguard the coral reefs. Each buoy is numbered; you receive a map of them all when you book into the country. There is a marina at Harbour Village a mile or so from the town.

I went diving each day and sometimes twice; the water was the clearest and cleanest I have ever seen. With water temperature of 26C and sun all day long what more could you ask for.

One day as I was diving at the edge of an underwater cliff in about 40ft of water, I saw a ship's bell lying part way down the cliff. It was upside down. I signalled to Dave, my diving partner, that I was going to get it and swam down to it.

The bell was about the size of a bucket. I expected it to be reasonably heavy and got hold of the edge to pull it up. To my complete surprise it was soft and slippery. It was in fact a plant of some sort. Dave was in stitches laughing and had to go up to the surface in order to take off his mask to have a good laugh. I followed him up; we both saw the funny side.

On another day we hired a coach between a few of us and toured the island. It was very beautiful and well worth the trip. As there were a few of the rally boats in the marina we often booked a large table and had our evening meal together. Later Pat, from Windfall, and I would sit on my boat late in the night with a whiskey each and swap stories.

Pat had done the trip two years before in his own boat, and now he was crew to the largest boat in the rally.

What he told me was significant; he said that it was far easier as crew as he did not have all the worries of being in charge, yet he could do all the jobs that needed to be done. I was later to learn just how true that statement was.

San Blas Islands

We left after six wonderful days, to sail to the San Blas Islands off the north coast of Panama. These islands are home to the Kuna Indians who are small people, but not pigmies. It was very difficult to get to the islands and we had to have special charts blown up to a large scale to find our way through and behind the reefs which guard the small islands.

It was a case of having one person on lookout on the bow of the boat, another watching the depth gauge, and one steering the boat very slowly indeed. Only a few of the boats risked the sail into San Blas but it was worthwhile.

We anchored and went ashore to a small island full of mud huts with thatched roofs made out of palm leaves. It was like going back in time, that was until we saw the chief's hut which had a generator and a TV aerial.

The water was very shallow in places which meant that we had to be on constant watch, Stratagem needs 5ft 8ins and at times we only had 6ft, so not a lot to spare.

We visited a number of small islands before setting sail for Panama and the canal.

We had one more stop on the way, at Puerto Bello, a small bay where we went ashore with a number of the other boats for a meal together prior to sailing to Colon for our trip through the Panama Canal. It was on this leg that we caught our first shark; it was a young one about 30ins long. We managed to get it on board without getting bitten then decided to cut it into steaks and fry it. It was superb and went down a treat. It had been arranged that all the boats would meet at Colon and go through the canal at the same time.

Panama Canal

Colon is at the Atlantic or eastern end of the Panama Canal

Everyone had told me that this part of the rally would be the most memorable; it was.

We had arrived here on 27th February 1999 after some very hard sailing so I was glad to get alongside and get a good night's sleep.

It had been arranged that every boat would meet here to go through the three locks together: three up and three down. In between was the largest man-made lake in the world, Lake Gatun.

At each end of the canal by the three locks there was a viewing area with tiered seating where you could watch the ships pass through the locks.

We went to the area the day prior to our passage through to see what it would be like. What a sight; boats are made especially to pass through with the minimum of room to spare only 1ft 6ins at each side, 3ft in all.

When you consider that each lock is 1000ft long and 110ft wide it gives you some idea of the size of the ships.

The locks raise the ships up 85ft or 25.9m to Gatun Lake. The total length from the Atlantic to the Pacific is 50 miles.

The rally had arranged for us to pass through together without any of the large ships sharing the trip. Each boat had to be registered and have on board four 125ft ropes to tie two on the bow and two on the stern. Theses ropes would be taken to the sides of the lock and controlled by handlers to keep the boat in the centre of the lock.

This is because when the water is let in, it has such force that it can force the boats, even the largest ships, against the sides of the lock.

The very large ships are pulled in place by large electric engines called mules after the beasts that were used when the canal first opened. The trick played on all first time users of the canal is to get the crew to take carrots for the mules.

We were all made to assemble outside the first lock where each boat was allocated a pilot who stayed with you for the entire journey, and for which you paid.

We were to raft up in threes that is three boats tied together; I was on the right or starboard side of the raft.

We had to keep our engines running at all times and the outside boats had their ropes taken to the handlers on the lock side. The pilot in the middle boat was in charge; if he wanted to move the raft to the right or starboard he told me to put my engine in reverse and the left or port boat to put his engine in gear to move forward. That way we could turn right in a very small space. The opposite instruction made us go to the left. We entered the lock all tied together and were lifted to the next level, then again, and finally a third time. At the final lift we were free to motor out into the lake and hoist our sails.

As we could not sail fast enough to reach the other side of the lake, 23 miles, in daylight we had arranged to drop anchor out of the main traffic lanes for the night. Our pilot told us where to anchor and when we were settled a launch came alongside to take the pilot off home and it would return him in the morning next day.

After a good meal and a beer we washed the boat down in fresh water and then we had a shower and a swim in the lake. It was only after I had climbed out of the lake that someone shouted that there were crocodiles in the lake.

The next morning the pilots returned and we got ready to leave. Our pilot said not to hurry as there was plenty of time. The others had all started to sail off when he asked me to pull up the anchor. Then it happened: the anchor was stuck, and try as we could it would not come up. The anchor was attached to 57mts of chain and cost in all over £200 so I was reluctant to abandon it.

As time went by I decided to place a marker buoy on the end and sail off without it. I had a second anchor but no chain, only rope. We sailed off to try and catch up with the other boats but failed. Our pilot radioed the control office and asked for instructions.

The instructions he received were to have a great effect on me and the crew.

We were to pass through the three descending locks with a massive container ship coming up behind us. When we saw it I nearly died.

The pilot took me to one side and said, "Skipper this is going to be very tricky". He told me that as the tug pulling the container ship passed me going into the lock I had to get in behind the tug and in between the tug and the ship. When we were all in the lock I had to go alongside the tug and tie on to it as we descended.

All I could see when I looked back at the container ship was the large rusty bow towering over my boat. I felt like an ant looking up at a tall man's shoe just before he stands on the ant.

We managed to survive the lowering of the water level and sailed out to the next lock.

That was when the pilot took me to one side again and said that this next one was going to be even more difficult. I could not believe that it was possible, to be worse than the previous lock, and asked him why. He then told me that the next one was a double lock. That meant that we had to do the same manoeuvre again, that is to get in between the tug and the ship, but the tricky part was that after the first lowering we had to move forward into the second lock with the tug pulling the container ship. The wash from the tug could smash us under the bow of the ship if we got it wrong.

The plan was as follows. The pilot on the ship was in charge and I had to do exactly as I was told immediately he gave the order. My boat had been tied to the tug for the lowering of the first lock, and I had then to reverse my boat away from the tug as far as I could which was at the far side of the ship's bow until my mast was almost touching the ship.

At the signal from the pilot I was to put my engine on full power at the same time as the tug started to pull the ship forward. It was essential that I got it right as the wash from the powerful tug would smash me against the ship.

Boats are not made to go backwards, they are pointed at the front and blunt at the back, so reversing is at best a tricky manoeuvre. I prayed that I would be able to do it.

I untied the boat from the tug, pushed off and engaged reverse, and we began to go backwards in the right direction. I steered past the ship's bow to the other side of the lock away from the tug; we were up against the ship with the engine running in neutral. I was asked if I was ready, I indicated that I was and then heard the pilot shout NOW.

I put the engine in forward gear and pressed the throttle full open as far as it would go. All I could see was foaming white water from behind the tug rushing towards Stratagem and yet we did not seem to be moving. The noise was very loud with spray everywhere, the wall of water reached the bow of Stratagem and we appeared to be climbing up it, then we were on top of it. From then on we raced down the front of the wall of water past the tug. All I could hear was our pilot shouting to stop the boat as we were heading for the lock gates that were still closed.

I put the engine in reverse and opened the throttle. At last we slowed down, then stopped. We had done it with no damage other than to my nerves.

The tug pulled the container ship forward to the second lock and we once again tied up to the tug. The water lowered us down to sea level and we were able to sail out into the Pacific Ocean.

Our pilot put his arm round me and said, "You will make a canal pilot some day." I was shaking but very glad to be able to sail under the massive road bridge, the Bridge of the Americas, which links North and South America. As we approached the moorings at Balboa Yacht Club all the other rally boats cheered us in.

We were at Panama in the Pacific Ocean

While we were in Balboa we were able to get hauled out of the water to enable us to fix a leak on the propeller shaft, and at the same time I went back up the canal with one of the rally organisers to retrieve my anchor. We had to get permission to go on the canal in a small dinghy which we did after a lot of hassle, but try as we might there was no way that we could get the anchor up. As we were wondering how to proceed, a large tug was coming up the canal. We called them over and explained what had happened.

They let us go on board; all tugs have a flat deck at the back so that when they are towing nothing gets in the way. We all stood looking at the chain on the buoy then two very large men took hold of the chain wrapped it round a bollard on the tug and signalled to the captain to go ahead, up came the chain but it was still stuck fast. So they wrapped more round the bollard and did the same thing over and over until the anchor came to the surface stuck to a very large wire hawser which was used to hold the container ships when they anchored. The two men untied my anchor and let the hawser drop, we were free at last.

At first the tug captain did not want anything for helping but I gave the crew $50 so that they could have a few drinks when they got ashore. We returned triumphant to Stratagem, then to the Yacht Club bar to celebrate.

Balboa Yacht Club

While we were in Balboa I made friends with George the manager of the Yacht Club. He explained why the club house was in such a poor state of repair: it would appear that the club was waiting for the government to agree the plans for the new club house so that it could be rebuilt to modern day standards.

The original wooden building had been put up in the 1920s by the Americans when they were running the canal. It was now closed down except for the bar and toilets.

I told the manager that I could not understand why the government would not want a new building at the gateway to the country, if only for good public relations, then he told me that it was because the club would not pay the minister a large bribe in cash.

The trip by taxi into Panama City was an experience in itself. The driver locked the doors and took out a sawn-off shotgun and placed it on his lap, just in case the car was stopped at traffic lights he said.

The Rally had arranged a reception to meet the Minister for Tourism in the civic offices, and I could not resist the opportunity ask why the club house facilities were so bad as this reflected on the country. This did not go down at all well and the minister was hurried away by officials.

While we were still there in the city the minister visited George, the club manager, who was at school with him as a young boy, to ask again for his bribe. The manager told him he was not going to get anything and the minister left in a rage.

The following day we left for Ecuador, and that night the government had the club house burnt down.

It later sold the land to a hotel chain. I don't know what happened to the club.

CHAPTER SIXTEEN

1999 The Pacific Ocean

Sunday 7th February 1999 we left Balboa with very little wind.

The sail to Salinas in Ecuador was 650 miles during which we would cross the equator.

I have explained before that we had on board a GPS, that is Global Positioning System. This sends signals to 12 satellites which are bounced back. From these signal angles the exact position of the boat is fixed and it is accurate up to 30m so we knew when we were at the equator.

We stopped the boat and I was going to swim across the equator but the boat was surrounded by about 20 dolphins circling us.

I was reluctant to go in the water but one of the crew, Susan, was a vet and she went in and swam about. The dolphins just stayed round us but made no attempt to come right up to her so feeling brave, I joined her in the water and swam across the equator.

The sailing conditions were not as good as we would have liked. There seemed to be a current flowing against us and very little wind, which meant that we had to use the engine.

After a few hours the engine suddenly stopped. We managed to get it going but the same thing happened twice more. We decided to fit two new filters in the fuel line and this did the trick.

We saw many turtles as we sailed by, some within a yard of the boat. The weather was hot and we had frequent rainstorms. Due to the heat and humidity it was not easy to sleep, you had to get a quick nap when you could.

The rain was so heavy that there was no point in everyone getting soaked so when I was on the helm the others stayed down below. The storm got worse as the wind increased: we were steering a course of 175 degrees with very little sail yet the boat was going at top speed.

I could only just see the bow of the boat 30 feet in front of me; the waves that hit us came over the top of the boat and at times I felt I was under water. I had my harness and life jacket on and I was fastened to the boat. After 2 hours the wind died down to nothing but we were steering 105 degrees, and we were in the eye of the storm. Within a few minutes the wind started again and took us back to the original course of 175 degrees.

In all I was at the helm four hours, and my hands looked white and crinkly: I thought to myself that is how they will look when I am dead. After the wind was back to normal I went down to change my clothes, have a hot drink and a sleep.

The experience of this rainstorm proved to me that I had a very good boat that would look after me in all weathers. I was also pleased with myself.

Saturday 13th Febuary we arrived in Salinas Ecuador.

The marina was quite new with all the modern conveniences plus a first-class hotel and restaurant.

Gill, my wife, was flying out to stay with me here for 2 weeks. I had booked an air-conditioned room overlooking the water. What a change from living on the boat for so long.

We had planned to fly from Ecuador to the Galapagos Islands with an official tour because although you can sail there you are restricted as to where you can anchor and cannot visit any of the islands without permission.

The rally had arranged for us to visit a ranch which was so large that they took days riding on horseback to get from one side to the other.

The capital is Quito which is 11,000ft up in the Andes Mountains. We flew there from Guayaquil: I thought that I was ill the first night Gill and I went out for a walk, but it turned out to be due to the thin air at that altitude.

The town is surrounded by five active volcanoes; the road we travelled on to the ranch was called the avenue of the volcanoes.

People in Ecuador are either very rich or very poor; there were armed guards on all supermarkets and petrol stations. It was a country waiting for a revolution.

When we arrived the currency was 700 sucres to the £1 but when we left two weeks later it was 1400 sucres to the £1, a 100% increase in 14 days.

We visited a local market which was an experience in itself. The women all wear brightly coloured clothes and small round hats like bowler hats. When it rains they put an old hat on top of the best hat to keep it dry.

Ecuador was one of the special stops on my trip round the world for many reasons, one being the poverty I have mentioned already, and another the train journey on the highest railway in the world. Having seen Michael Palin's TV film of his journey, we just had to give it a go.

Train Ride

The train itself was old and looked unstable and that was when it was in the station. As we travelled out onto the mountain on a single railway track with over a thousand foot drop to the river below, the train felt even more unstable.

The train suddenly stopped and the driver and guards all gathered round the engine: it had derailed. The passengers including Gill and I got off as well and so did the locals who were sitting on the roof of the train.

There was no panic from the crew, only from the tourists when we were told, "Its OK, we have only derailed, we shall put it back on." With that the guard brought out a heavy metal object to place under the wheel that had come off the rail, and then he placed some eucalyptus leaves from the side of the track. A long handled crowbar was used to lever the metal object and the train driver was given the OK to start the engine.

With a mighty lurch the whole train moved forward and the engine was back on the rails. Everyone cheered and had to run to get back on the train as it began its journey once more.

That was not the end of the story: we derailed twice more, and it's apparently a common practice. I took the opportunity to ride on the roof along with the locals, and this is one train journey I will never forget. Why is it that in the UK the wrong type of snow, rain, or leaves stop the railways?

Using the toilet was an experience also. On entering there is a woman who will sell you a piece of toilet paper if you need it, then she stands with her hand out holding the paper waiting for the cash. As I did not need any paper I walked in and started to pee standing against the urinal: I looked to my right to see the female standing next to me holding out her hand with the paper waiting for her money. She was smaller than me and I was not sure if she was about to grab me or just hold on to what was there. I gave her some cash and she left.

Galapagos Islands

Of all the places I have been to this is the one place I would go back to time and time again; it is not cheap but it is unique. There is nowhere in the world that compares with it.

The area is designated a World Heritage Site: each island has a maximum number of days when visitors are allowed and limits the numbers per day. Animals and birds have right of way and take preference over humans, and they know it and exploit it.

We stayed on a small ship similar to a Mersey Ferry. Each day we visited a different island with a guide. We all carried binoculars and cameras, and one day Rommel, our guide, took us to see a pair of rare owls that were nesting close by. Rommel wanted everyone to see the bird which was on the ground about 100m away, but because they are well camouflaged it was not easy to spot, so Rommel spent time with each of us to point out the bird. This took some 20 minutes, then as we turned round to move on the mate of the one on the nest 100m away was perched on a post just behind us a mere 2m away. I felt sure that it was taking the mickey out of the bloody tourists.

None of the wildlife had any fear of humans, and we were told by Rommel not to touch or let the wildlife touch us, for this was to stop them getting used to the smell of humans. Even while swimming iguanas would come and swim round you and look you straight in the face, and it was the same with turtles and seals. It was like 'never never land', so wonderful.

We met Lonesome George, a 100 year old tortoise who had outlived his mate, hence his name. These creatures had been introduced to the islands by early sailors who kept them for food, and they really are so big you could sit on them.

The islands are still forming and moving with new lava flows and eruptions rising out of the sea. It is a truly great place to visit.

We flew back to the mainland and a minibus picked us up at the airport to transport us back to Salinas; the journey was at night with no lights and it was pitch black.

Suddenly there was a bang, the bus lurched to the right and everyone was thrown across the seats. After what seemed an eternity we slid to a halt on the wrong side of the road. Everyone looked round to see if we were OK and asked what happened. I saw that Gill was all right and the rest appeared to be in shock but not hurt so I opened the door and went out to see what we had hit.

It was difficult to see anything and no one had a torch but as our eyes grew accustomed to the dark I could see skid marks on the road. I traced them back to the other side where there were more tracks gong back to the side we had ended up on. There I saw a car off the road partly on the hillside and two men running away at great speed: at least they could not be too badly hurt.

Why had the car suddenly veered across the road on to our side, hit us and careered off the road?

Suddenly we realised that we were stopped on a bend in the road and did not see the next vehicle coming: it swerved, just missed us and carried on at great speed as all drivers in Ecuador do. We were in a very dangerous position. Tony had gone further down the road and found the cause of the accident, namely a donkey who lay dying on the road having been hit by the car which then swerved hitting our minibus.

Then the next vehicle came round the bend and almost killed the four of us looking at the donkey. I shouted to get back on the bus and drive away from the bend, but no one moved so I swore at them all in my very loud voice which did the trick and I ushered them all back on the bus.

Luckily the bus started although it was badly dented, and the driver was very upset because he said that he would be blamed for the accident and would lose his job. I took a list of the names of those on the bus who, like Gill and I, would go to the police and give evidence that it was not the fault of our driver. This we did and the driver, as far as we know, did not lose his job.

The time spent in Ecuador was an experience but for me not enjoyable since it reminded me of what it must have been like in Russia before the revolution. I cannot accept that some should have so much wealth while others starve and have nothing.

The Pacific Ocean 2nd March 1999

I left Salinas on my 65th birthday; Gill waved us off and she was flying back home the next day. Before us was a vast empty sea, 3,800 miles to the next land, an extinct volcano called Fatu Hiva in the Marquesas Islands, French Polynesia.

This was to be the longest voyage; we did not know how long it would take but my planning was based on 100 miles per day. We only had the wind to drive the boat, so if it blew we moved and if there was no wind we stayed put.

On any long voyage you have to study the charts, obtain as much local knowledge as you can from anyone you trust, but in the end it is down to you to make a decision. I thought it would be better to go further south to get the wind; Tony did not agree but we went south. For a day or two there was very little wind and we needed the engine to make headway.

It is difficult to sleep when there is little wind as the boat slops from side to side which did nothing for morale but eventually the wind arrived and we began to make good progress. I radioed other boats that were north of us and they were struggling to find the wind, so I had been right to go south.

This leg of the voyage I enjoyed the most. We soon got into a routine of three hours on and three off; we had tried other times but this seemed to suit us best. The nights under the Pacific sky were wonderful, and I had not realised just how many stars there were.

The first time we encountered a tropical storm it was both frightening and beautiful.

The entire sky from left to right on the horizon went black; we had no choice but to sail into it, then we saw the lightning striking down to the sea, followed by thunder, quiet at first but as we got nearer it got louder.

We could see forks of lightning hitting the sea a mile away and I was scared for the first time. I thought what would happen to the boat if we were struck by lightning? I decided to place the portable GPS and radio in the oven to act as a "Faradays Cage" just in case. We sailed straight through the storm and then it was back to normal, whatever that is.

Every night we had the same experience, so that after a few nights I stopped worrying about the storm and began to enjoy the beauty of it.

We had a meeting with whales, we saw them in the distance, and then as we were eating our evening meal one jumped out of the water immediately in front of the boat, about 20yds away. Neither of us could believe what we had just seen, then another one, or the same one again, did the same thing. Unfortunately we did not have a camera handy.

One of the other boats had a rather worse experience. They were just sailing along when a very large whale, longer than their boat, surfaced and lay alongside them. They had no idea what to do: if the whale had flipped its tail it could have seriously damaged their boat. This lasted for 30 minutes then the whale slowly sank below the water. What an experience.

We saw numerous turtles, as well as the regular dolphins who love to follow any vessel. The waves in the Pacific are so large that it can be half a mile between crests, so that the boat is slowly rising up to the top where you can see for miles then you slowly descend to the trough, all very sedately.

Flying fish were a constant sight. Eventually they take to flight when threatened by a predator, and they can fly for up to 100m and twist and turn while flying a foot or two above the waves. Each morning we would walk round the boat to find a number of fish who had not made it over the boat and crashed onto the deck. There is always something to check on a boat or records to keep which keeps you busy, and then there is the cooking which I enjoy. To save fresh water we cooked with sea water, and we also showered with it as well, in fact we were so well organised that we still had 50gallons of drinking water left when we arrived at Fatu Hiva.

1st April 1999 Fatu Hiva

We saw land on the evening of the 31st day; a large mountain with clouds covering the top, and as we approached the storm clouds appeared so we decided to wait until they had passed before trying to anchor.

It was about 1am when we decided to close in on the land mass; it was pitch black and there are no lights there. Slowly we approached the land and the radio came on: it was Dominique in 'La Billebaude'. "We can see you," he said. "Sail straight towards us and we will put our lights on." It was a very scary sail; we could hear the waves breaking against the rocks but we were unable to see where they were. At about midnight we dropped anchor in 20ft of water and went to bed.

The next morning we realised just what we had done: the mountain was like a very large cake with a slice taken out of it, and we had just sailed into the slice. The sides of the mountain were at least 1000ft straight up and it was awesome; two other boats were also anchored beside 'La Billebaude'.

We got the dinghy ready to go ashore; as we got near to the shore we could see children waving to us so we waved back. We were so taken with the reception that we were getting that we forgot to look behind us: because the inlet was wedge shaped, as we approached the land it was getting narrower, which meant that the waves were getting bigger. About 20yds from the land we were picked up and thrown into the water much to the delight of the children who did this every time a new vessel arrived. At least they ran into the water to help us out and retrieve the dinghy.

All the islands in Polynesia are under French control; the French have made them part of France, so that they get aid from the European Community. How very clever the French are. While we were exploring the island we were asked by a woman if we could fix her washing machine. We were surprised that she had a washing machine on such a small island, but she went on to say that she was the wife of the chief and they had a generator which powered the washer. Would we look at it? We decided to get our toolkit from the boat before going to her "house". Armed with the toolkit she took us to where she lived with two other wives and her husband. The chief, her husband, was lying on a straw bed on the floor where he remained throughout our visit.

On examining the washing machine we traced the problem to a broken switch which controls the opening of the door when the machine is working and prevents spillage.

We explained to the wife that we could not fix it but that we could bypass it, and then it would work, but that meant they must not open the door or else it would flood the floor. It was an easy job to bypass the switch, then we switched it on and it worked.

The wife jumped up and down then ran out into the garden and literally climbed up a tree which was full of what looked like footballs but were in fact giant grapefruit called 'Pamplemousse'. She called out the two other wives who brought a sack which they filled with the fruit, and continued to fill two more. It was an embarrassment and very difficult to take such a load of fruit which we only just managed to get in the dinghy.

When we returned to Stratagem we gave some away to the other boats in the bay; the fruit was delicious and very sweet. That night two other Rally boats arrived Ted & Gill Rogers on 'Genevieve' and Mark & Pauline on 'SamenII'. Ted held a party on Genevieve to which we were all invited. The following day we set sail for the largest island in the group, Nuku-Hiva 145 miles away.

All the rally boats were due to meet here and stay for a few days. We anchored in a large bay which meant that it was a long trip in the dinghy to get ashore. Here we collected mail and we were able to phone home, and that night the local people put on a show for us and everyone got "leid", that is we all received a garland of flowers placed around our necks. The wine flowed making it difficult to navigate back to the boat in a small dinghy.

The following day along with Joe and Doreen from 'Vitamin Sea' we hired a four-wheel drive car to tour the island. We saw all sorts of nuts growing as well as coca plants, coffee beans, limes, lemons and bananas; the scenery was magnificent.

We visited the remains of an old civilisation and could clearly see the sacrificial altar with the carved stone bowl that used to catch the blood, as well as a monument to the god of love which had the head of a turtle.

That night we were out having a meal with most of the other boats, when a message came through that Jamie, my grandson, had won the British Youth Laser Radial Championship back in England. I had to drink a toast with each and every boat which meant that I don't remember getting back to the boat.

The next morning I had a very bad hangover but did not remember anything, so I decided to go on the radio to the other boats to apologise for anything I may have done or said. Tony Manzi on 'Arietta' came on the radio to say that I ought to apologise to his wife Christine for what I had done.

I was mortified because I had no recollection of anything. Of course I apologised, I said I was extremely sorry, still not knowing what I was apologising for. "That's not good enough," said Tony, "you should do it in person." "I will, I will," I said, then he began to laugh and so did everyone listening in: it was all a joke, I had done nothing embarrassing, it was Tony sending me up and I fell for it.

The following morning we left to sail a few miles to Daniel's Bay, which is very well hidden so much so that during the First World War a fleet of German warships hid in the bay when being pursued by the British. It was a scary trip getting into the bay as you would never believe such a narrow entrance would lead into a perfect setting, surrounded by mountains with just one house on the shore, Daniel's. We stayed the night, some including Tony climbed the mountain; I stayed on board to plan the next part of the trip which was to the Tuamotu Group of Islands, in Polynesia.

We had been advised by Dominique, who had served in the French Navy in the Pacific, not to try and visit too many islands but to stay longer at a few. I picked two, Ahe one of the smallest and Rangiroa the largest; it was 400 miles to Ahe.

The problem with the atolls is getting in to the lagoon. Atolls are formed when volcanoes rose out of the sea many thousand of years ago, and then sank back into the sea leaving only the outer rim of coral which encloses a lagoon in the centre where the volcano had been. Sometimes there is only one entrance into the lagoon as in Ahe, and in others five or six entrances as in Rangiroa.

Thursday 15th April Ahe

There were no tide tables or indeed no tides on the equator, but the water in the lagoons flowed in and out according to the strength and direction of the wind. You had to sail to the entrance to find out if the water was going in or out.

Inside the lagoon the water is crystal clear and warm, about 28C to 30C, which is warmer than the public swimming pools. Because not many boats visit these small atolls the people are very pleased to see you and sail out to meet you in their small boats; the children love to swim out to the boat looking for sweets or other gifts.

We had a stock of notepads and pens with 'Stratagem' printed on which we gave out to the children who really treasured the gifts. Only about 100 people lived on Ahe; they lived on fish which was plentiful and grew all the food they needed because fresh water was available from wells on the island.

It was uncanny to be able to see clearly the anchor on the bottom when it was 20-30ft deep. The problem though was the growth of coral that sticks up like small towers throughout the lagoon, and if the anchor chain wraps round them you have to get the diving gear out to unwrap it.

Often one of the boats would invite the others to go on board for a drink. We had been invited a number of times so I thought it would be a good idea to invite the five other boats on to Stratagem.

Stratagem is the smallest boat so we called the night the "Stratagem Squash". We just about managed to get everyone on (15 of us) but it was a genuine squash. Everyone had a great time and the usual swim resulted in everyone getting wet before going back to their own boats. We stayed two days then set sail for the largest atoll, Rangiroa 100 miles further west.

21st April 1999 Rangiroa Wednesday

When we arrived at the atoll we could see two other boats waiting at the entrance to the lagoon. I called them up and found that they had tried but failed to get in against a strong current flowing out. After waiting with them we decided to try with both sails up and the engine on: slowly we advanced over the ground at 1 knot speed but at least we were making progress. Slowly we entered the lagoon and as the current slowed down we shot forward into beautiful blue, clear, warm water and dropped anchor. The others followed us in; over the next day many boats arrived.

Rangiroa is large, 10 miles long with a number of villages each by an entrance. There was a diving school close to where we were and I soon found out that diving there is classed as one of the 12 best in the world. I dived on four occasions, each a "drift dive", that is you descend to a depth and let the current take you in or out depending on its flow.

The first dive was down to 70 feet and we could see many sharks which did not bother us but I was apprehensive all the same. We adjusted the buoyancy so that we had negative buoyancy, not going up or down, just drifting with the current. It was magic: as I floated by the fish came to look me over then carried on doing what fish do. I had my arm round a turtle as it grazed on the coral; it was unreal but great. On one dive we went looking for sharks and found over 25 of them, interesting but frightening.

Joe and I each hired a bicycle to look round the place and came across a lady selling pearls, black pearls. I had never heard of black pearls but we listened as she told us that the men dive for them in the lagoon; she had a tray full of pearls, all shapes and sizes and she explained what made them valuable.

I asked her which was the most valuable so she brought out a pearl larger than all the others and told me that it was perfect in colour, lustre, and size. I asked her how much she would sell it for; she quoted in US dollars the equivalent of £600. I bought it not knowing whether or not I was being done. (It was valued back home at £2000).

On Saturday we set sail for Tahiti and two days later we approached the capital Papeete. It was a wonderful sight: as dawn broke the mountains seemed to change colour as we got nearer to the harbour entrance. The marina was alongside the main road in the centre of the town and we berthed Mediterranean-style stern-to. We could sit in the cockpit and watch the world go by, and we did, especially at night as the people walked by and some came on board to join us for a drink. When in port or harbour we all listen in on VHF channel 72, it is our own phone system.

Tuesday 27th April 1999 Tahiti

The rally organisers arranged a coach trip round the island which is truly beautiful. Next to our moorings was the area set aside for the berthing of cruise ships in front of which was a very large car park during the day but at night it was transformed into the "Roaches" where more than 75 mobile stalls, vans, carts and other contraptions set up vending of every type of food in the world, and it is all delicious, clean and reasonable. I have seen nothing like this anywhere in the world.

My dinghy used for getting to and from the boat had sprung a number of leaks so I went into town to a ship chandler to get a replacement. There were many available, but to my surprise the one that was the same size as mine cost more than one twice the size. After making certain that I had got the price correct I bought the larger but cheaper dinghy, much to the delight of Tony.

Not for the first time I was homesick and thought that I should have built into my schedule a trip home.

The next stop was the island of Moorea where the film "Mutiny on the Bounty" was filmed; we stayed for one night and then set sail for the place I had always wanted to see Bora Bora.

Friday 7th May 1999 Bora Bora

There is only one entrance into the lagoon: the approach is from the south, and you have to sail along the outer edge of the reef with the clear water crashing against it. Whilst it is beautiful it made me very worried about missing the small entrance even though the weather was perfect.

After checking and rechecking the chart we eventually went for it, passing boys fishing on both sides only 50yds apart; it made the adrenaline run faster.

Inside the lagoon it was a magical experience for me. The remaining section of the volcano covered with trees and brush stood dominating the island.

This was a holiday tourist destination for a lucky few who could afford to visit; there was a hotel, a marina and a small town with shops. You could cycle round the whole island in a couple of hours, which we did, Joe and me. I could not believe that I had sailed to Bora Bora.

The second day I went on a trip outside the lagoon to watch the feeding of sharks. About 20 people were taken by boat a mile or so from the island where we all put on scuba diving gear. We were told that we had to descend to the bottom of the sea, then settle down holding the rocks or coral to keep still.

A large steel cage was lowered down which contained pieces of fish. The man in charge had a steel sleeve on his arm and he took out a fish to feed the 50 or so sharks that had gathered round us. One by one the sharks swam round and then suddenly darted at the fish in the man's hand, taking it in one quick bite. I did not need to be told to stay still; I was petrified, especially when out of the blue appeared two very large sharks, three times the size of the others: as these slowly swam around, all the other sharks kept away. I am 6ft 2ins tall and each of these could have swallowed me whole, without chewing off any part of me. I tried to sink into the ground. The man took out some larger pieces of fish which these two monsters swallowed as if they were jelly babies. When the cage was empty they seemed to know it was over, and they disappeared as quickly as they had come.

I was missing Gill and the girls more than I thought I would. I will never go away for such a long time again. I phoned home and was told that Gill had sold the house in York Avenue at last, and I was able to wish Kate a happy 15th birthday at the same time. Cath was going to meet us at Tonga and sail with us to Fiji which meant that we had to be on time.

Bora Bora to Tonga 1400miles

We left on Thursday 13th May 1999 along with Mark on 'Samen11' and there was very little wind. Samen11 managed to get ahead by 10 miles but we kept in touch by radio, the next day we had good wind and made excellent progress. I cannot understand the weather: one day wind, the next none.

Saturday proved to be one of the worst so far with an electric storm all round us, lightning flashing like artillery guns at war, then the whole sky would light up for 40 seconds then turn pitch black until the next flash. It was all around us and there was nowhere to go; I even tried to go back east but we could not escape. In the end I thought we might as well be hit going in the right direction so I headed straight for the centre of the storm.

It was scary; Mark had gone north and missed the worst of the weather although he was still scared like me. Tony pretended to be OK but I knew he was not. I gave Tony precise orders on what to do and the courses to steer prior to having a rest; but when I came back on watch we were miles off course. I am not sure if he did not know what to do and would not ask, or if he was just stubborn and did nothing at all. At dawn the sky was blue and the worst was behind us so we had a good downwind sail. That night the storm returned again with bolts of lightning hitting the water all round us. Mark radioed that he was very scared and tired. I had a long talk with him trying to convince him we would both get through together.

Sunday 16th May

Dawn came; the sky was black but no wind. When the wind came it was from the east (where we were heading) along with a rain storm, the wind increased to 32kts and went from east to north to west to south, we realised that the wind vane was taking us round in circles. In order to get free of this we lowered the sails and started the engine, hand steering to keep our course. I have never seen rain like it, over two hours we had the engine on then at last we saw blue sky.

What a day I did not want to go through that again. The following day proved to be as bad as before once again I did two hours hand steering the boat with the engine on. Mark on Samen11 was really down in the dumps, no one was enjoying this trip. My other concern was fuel; we never thought that we would use the engine as much as we did, and we still had 900 miles to go.

Tuesday was different again, no wind and clear blue skies, so the engine went on again. On Wednesday we had a good wind from the east so twin headsails up and a very good sail with no engine, peace at last. With a good wind we could still be on time to meet Cath.

The next three days we had wonderful sailing wind and we were able to get back on course in time to meet Cath. We had the new sails up and were beginning to reef down due to the wind reaching 41kts as we stormed along at 6/7kts; the boat was going well, I felt safe and secure.

Sunday 23rd May day 11

We were still experiencing very strong winds but enjoying the trip when we turned on the radio and heard MAYDAY, MAYDAY. It was Patricia Landamore in 'Lucifero'.

It is every sailor's worst nightmare to hear this distress signal, and I immediately grabbed pen and paper to take down the message.

There are rules to follow when you hear Mayday because you may be the only person in the world who hears it and you must write down the position, type of vessel, the problem and how many are on board. We did this and Patricia told us that they had hit an object four hours ago and could not stop water entering the boat. They had inflated the lifeboat and were ready to abandon their boat as the water level was only inches from reaching the radio. Both Patricia and her crew, Will a 22 year old Canadian, were uninjured. Just as she said this the radio went dead.

I knew that the boat was going down, and with that other boats in the rally came on the radio to say that they had all heard and recorded the message.

We in Stratagem were the furthest away from the stricken boat, the nearest being Mike Smither on 'Akwaaba' 60 miles away. It was Mike who took over the rescue and turned round to help Patricia.

Terry on 'Tudor Rose' was just mooring in Niue, a remote island: he alerted the New Zealand authorities who sent up an Orion aeroplane as it was too far for a helicopter. As Mike made his way back to where Patricia was last reported to be, the Orion circled above the lifeboat to guide Mike to the spot.

Patricia and Will were in the lifeboat for 10 hours. We all met up again in Tonga for a celebration with the ladies donating clothes, underwear, and toiletries for Pat and the lads doing the same for Will because all they had was what they had on plus their passports and ship's papers.

We still had 240 miles to go with the wind still blowing at 35/40kts; we now felt that 30kts was fine and we continued to speed along although I wanted one of us looking out for debris so that we did not end up like 'Lucifero'. Tony did not like this but he had to take his turn with me.

Wednesday 26th /27th May 1999 Day 13 - Tonga

We crossed the International Date Line and added a day; we decided to slow down so that we would arrive in daylight. Only a few boats had arrived, most were still at sea. I was very pleased that we had completed this leg and was looking forward to Cath's arrival after weeks with Tony. A shower and a pint were the order of the day.

We had anchored in a bay at the Royal Sunset Island Holiday Resort until all the boats arrived. In the bar a man was placing a notice advertising a trip in a small seaplane to an active volcano 90 miles north of the resort. There were only five seats so I booked two, for Cath and me.

The next day Tony went ashore with a list of supplies that we needed but on his return he had no supplies and could not say why, but still Cath would arrive tomorrow. Gill had moved house and I felt awful leaving her with all the problems that moving entails, especially since Pop died; I will have to make it up to her when I get home.

Cath arrives, Volcano Trip - Tonga

Cath was flying in today; she does not like flying so I didn't know how she would feel when greeted with a trip in a very small seaplane. The chap with the plane was to bring her to the resort, and as soon as she arrived we were going to depart for the volcano.

It was great to see the seaplane land and taxi up to the jetty at the resort, and Cath's face was a picture: she could not believe that I had fixed up the trip. The other three were waiting on the jetty, Cath's luggage was offloaded and we got on. I was told to sit in the front, in the co-pilot's seat but with instructions NOT to touch anything. The other four including Cath sat behind.

I had never been in a seaplane and thought that we would never get off the water. We appeared to go for a very long time still on the water as we gathered speed then at last we were airborne. We were flying about a thousand feet above the sea and we could see the coloured water as the gas escaped under the sea from hidden fissures; the whole of this area is active with a line of volcanoes.

In the distance we could see two volcanoes, the most recent one was still growing and was a perfect cone shape; the older one, the one we were going to, looked as though the top had been blown off, which it had. We had to climb to 2000 feet to get over the rim of the crater which was covered in very dense trees and bushes, yet the other one was still only rock.

This volcano had blown its top hundreds of years ago and a fresh-water lake had gathered at the bottom. There was still a vent at one side which was bellowing smoke, and as we flew over it you could see the molten rock bubbling like a can of beans. "You can open the window to take photos," the pilot said, and we did as he flew round again for everyone to get their shots.

We then landed in the lake and drifted to the side where the pilot climbed out onto the float and tied the plane to a tree branch. "I don't think anyone will steal it do you?" he said to me, and we all agreed.

We scrambled ashore and were given our orders. If the wind changed direction we must get down quickly as the gases were poisonous; the pilot was staying with the plane as he had done the trip many times.

Off we all went in the hot sun with our cameras and cold drinks, not that they stayed cold long. Half-way up Cath said that her back was killing her and that this was as far as she could go. She sat down and the rest of us climbed up the side of the volcano.

It was a long way up so we had to keep stopping which gave us many chances to admire the unique view from the inside of a volcanic crater.

As we climbed closer to the top there was no vegetation at all, the stones looked like they had just been thrown out of the crater like thick custard which had splattered and set, because it had been molten rock.

You could hear the magma bubbling as we reached the rim of the volcano; steam was rising all the time so you could only catch glimpses of the bottom.

It was one of the best experiences of my life to stand by the rim, although I did not get too near. After a while we all walked down, collected Cath, and arrived at the lake edge to be told by the pilot that it was customary for visitors to swim in the lake before leaving.

No one had any swimwear but that did not stop us from jumping in the cool fresh water for a very enjoyable bathe.

It was time to go and the pilot told me that we had to go to the far side in order to get a long run for take off, but not to tell the others. He started the engine and we raced to the far side; it was obvious to everyone that we were still on the water and that we would not make it before we ran out of lake. At the last minute he slowed down, turned the plane round and said "This time we will get airborne," to the relief of the others.

In order to climb above the rim we had to circle round in a spiral, each time gaining height so that we eventually just flew over the tops of the trees, it was an awe-inspiring flight and one I will never forget or experience again. Cath feels the same but for different reasons.

When we arrived back at the resort we were told that it had been decided that we would put on the concert that we had performed in Antigua for the other visitors. I had only two hours to write the script, select new jokes, and prepare for a show in front of 100 people; the others had known about this all day.

The hotel staff had a ready-made show that they performed every week, which was excellent and we had to follow that. All I can say is that we had a tremendous round of applause from both visitors and staff of the resort; I was beginning to think of turning professional.

The following day we all moved to the main island and tied up to the jetty, which was much easier than getting the dinghy out. Cath went out to find a place to go for the evening dinner and came back having booked us a table where there was local entertainment thrown in. Other boats asked to join us and in the end there were 25 from three other boats.

The meal was good and was followed by a cabaret, with all the dancers dressed to the nines and looking really stunning. Tony could not take his eyes of the girls but no one had told him that they were all "Lady Boys." It was a toss-up whether to watch the show or Tony. The next day on the radio everyone was told not to go out with the Stratagem crew as they preferred transvestites.

Cath and I went diving in some really superb waters with underground caves that took a bit of getting used to when going through small tunnels with the risk of getting stuck.

Cath had had T Shirts printed with "Stratagem Round the World Trip - Half Way Tonga" on them which we wore with pride, and were the envy of all the other boats.

Fiji

It was a four day sail to Fiji which is made up of hundreds of islands, the capital is Suva on the island of Viti Levu. The Royal Suva Yacht Club had a suitable anchorage which we headed for, and behind us was Tommy Tomasek, in 'Tipolo' sailing on his own. There was a large breakwater guarding the bay and we could see Tommy heading straight at it: we could not believe what we saw as he sailed into the rocks and was fast on them. We had been calling Tommy on the radio as soon as we had realised that he was about to hit the rocks but there was no response.

Tommy was not hurt, he had been asleep, but the boat had to be towed off and needed repairs to the bow.

We anchored, got out the dinghy and went ashore to the clubhouse. There was only one person in the lounge, but as soon as we walked in he said "Cath?" and Cath said "Colin what are you doing here?" It seems that the last time they saw each other was six years ago in Papua New Guinea where they had sailed together when Cath was the Vice Commodore of the Royal Papua New Guinea Yacht Club.

This meeting proved to be very helpful to us as Colin took us round the town and fixed it for us to dive in some fabulous places.

We enjoyed our stay immensely in Suva especially when Colin took us out for a meal to a club which again was full of gay people, and Tony still did not realise until we told him after an hour or two.

We left Suva for the short trip to Musket Cove 30 miles away on the next island, and this is where Cath was to fly back home.

As we approached the island we had to negotiate a reef which totally surrounded the entrance to the bay. We lowered the sails and went in on the engine alone; you could see the reef quite clearly in the water, the rocks being only just below the surface.

When we were half way through the reef the engine just cut out. We were only moving slowly but fast enough to damage the hull if we hit the reef. I dropped the anchor and got poles to fend us off the rocks, and then we tried to start the engine but to no avail. I called up Muscat Cove Marina on the radio to ask for assistance, but a rally boat which was following behind us agreed to tow us in. We berthed alongside the other boats at 12 noon

22nd June 1999. Muscat Cove

This was the best place we have visited so far. The owners, Dick and Carol, were so helpful and arranged to get a mechanic to see to the engine for us. We did some fantastic diving here and Cath even took her Rescue Certificate, which I think was so that she could look after me.

Cath was to fly home from here but we were to leave for Port Villa in Vanuatu the day before she left. We had a good party the night before leaving and Cath and the others waved us off.

As we got to the reef the engine stopped again, so we radioed the marina and were towed back to our berth. Once again the mechanic looked at the fuel line but could find no reason for the failure; we stayed the night and set out in the morning. I could not believe it when the engine stopped in the very same place and we had to be towed back by Tudor Rose.

We were now christened 'Boomerang' because we kept coming back. At last the mechanics found the fault in the fuel lift pump, which was something to feel pleased about.

That day Cath left and we were able to see her off. The next day we left Muscat Cove for the third time and managed to sail past the spot where we had stopped before, much to my relief.

It was 400 miles to Port Villa which we anticipated would take four or five days; we arrived on 8th July to be met by customs officers who took food and vegetables off us and charged us $30. We met up with Mark and Pauline 'Samen11' for a meal and a drink; it is a beautiful place and should be on the rally list in place of Tonga. I sent out my usual 26 cards home and went to the launderette to get a proper wash for some clothes and towels.

The following day we left with 'Samen11' for Cairns, Australia, and as we were leaving the harbour 'Merlin' was just arriving from Muscat Cove; they had a parcel for Pauline which had arrived after they had left. They sailed alongside and threw the parcel to Mark. Within minutes the customs boat came up and boarded 'Samen11' thinking the package contained drugs. It did not, but they went all over their boat before leaving.

The trip to Cairns was about 1600 miles over 13 days; it proved to place an intolerable strain on the relationship between skipper and crew which lasted until we arrived in Australia.

The engine was giving off funny noises which we could not identify; this also caused me to decide that I must obtain a new engine before we leave Cairns.

We also had trouble with the rudder on the Hydrovane which came loose: it took both of us hours to fix it when the wind subsided. In the end we stopped the boat and I put on my diving gear, fixed a safety line round my body and went underneath the boat to inspect the rudder and propeller.

Both appeared to be OK so we went on our way, but every night I was listening to any unusual noise thinking the worst every time.

One evening we had all the sails up with the pole goose winging the Genoa when the wind suddenly got up. It took us both to reduce the sails and get the pole down. 'Samen11' was days ahead of us and Joe and Doreen in 'Vitamin Sea' the same behind.

CHAPTER SEVENTEEN

1999 - 2000 Australia to the Red Sea

Australia

Tuesday 20th July in the evening we sighted Australia for the first time. It was an emotional time for me, to think I had sailed Stratagem to the other side of the world. I remembered being on the sands at Blackpool and asking my mum where would I be if I kept digging the hole in the sand?

It was the same question my three girls asked me when we were on the beach; the answer was Australia to all of us.

As we approached Cairns we could hear on the radio that the Australian Sail Training Ship Endeavour was leaving harbour, we could see this vessel, a replica of Captain Cook's ship Endeavour. As we passed by we lowered our red ensign, the ship's flag, in salute and we got a reply from Endeavour acknowledging our gesture.

It was a superb entrance to Australian waters, and as we approached Cairns we informed the authorities who we were and that we required to be booked in.

The Immigration, Customs and Port Health authorities were all waiting at the dock side, but just as we were six feet from the jetty the engine finally died. I threw a rope to the officers who pulled us alongside and we tied up in Cairns: we had arrived. After inspecting the boat and taking away food which we were not allowed to bring in they charged us £60 to dispose of it.

The arrangement for our stay in Cairns was to berth in the marina at Yorkeys Knob, 10 miles north. I had booked an apartment for Gill, Alison, Kate and me for three weeks. Because of the problems with the engine Stratagem would have to stay in Cairns.

This was not as bad as it sounds, the marina was literally next to the new Shopping Mall which contained every type of eating place you could imagine plus some extras, and next to the Mall was the Cairns Yacht Club.

After agreeing a price for Stratagem to stay where she was I walked up to the sailing club for a drink and a look round. It is the custom for all visiting yachts' crew to be made temporary members; I introduced myself and my boat and went to the bar which was the length of the room. I'll have a pint of beer please I said to the girl behind the bar, and two blokes drinking next to me said, "We don't have pints here mate only stubbys." "OK," I said, "give me a stubby." The girl gave me a half-pint glass, I drank half of it in one go and said to the chaps next to me, "It's a good job my club members back home can't see me drinking halves." The locals said, "Out here mate it's so hot it would get warm if it was a pint." "Not at the rate we drink it in the UK," I said.

That set the tone for the rest of my day in the club.

I later found myself at the end of the bar sitting next to a very nice chap who turned out to be the Regional Salesman for Nissan Cars in Oz. We both bought each other drinks as we swapped tales about each other.

At 2pm the girl serving us said it was now "Happy Hour" so the drinks were cheaper. I can remember being told that happy hour lasted for two hours in OZ. About 4.30pm we were back on normal prices, each taking it in turn to pay, and around 6pm I was talking and the words did not sound right: the more I tried to make them sound right the worse they got. I then decided it was time to leave and go back to the boat.

I do not remember going back or getting into my bunk but there I was the next day, safe and sound. Once again no headache, only a very large thirst for which I drank pints of water.

At lunchtime I thought I had better return to the club to make sure that I had not offended anyone or made a fool of myself, and as I walked into the bar some of the regulars who had been in the night before said, "Gooday, you and your mate can certainly drink beer." I asked around and everyone was OK so I had lunch and left to go shopping in the Mall.

New Engine

I contacted the Marine Engine people who came out to examine the engine and told me that I would have to have the boat taken out of the water. Stratagem was lifted out and it was decided to replace the engine with a new one with more power if it would go in the same space. I settled on a Yamaha which had to come from Sydney and it would take a few weeks.

Tony was making his own arrangements for his stay in OZ.

Gill, Alison and Kate

I had booked an apartment at Yorkeys Knob for three weeks as Gill, Alison and Kate were coming out for a holiday, and I also hired a car.

Meeting my family at the airport was a magical moment; it took quite a time to give all the hugs and kisses to each of them.

I had not realised just how much I had missed them all. The three weeks that we had together passed all too quickly; we had a trip to Ayres Rock where the weather was cold then we went down to Sydney and did all the sights.

One of the highlights of the trip for Alison was seeing the Flying Doctor Service museum which Alison had always been interested in. We had a number of meals with John Downs and his wife Sandie; John was going to sail with me to Darwin. We visited the Barrier Reef as well as all the functions arranged by the Rally.

Soon it was time to say goodbye to them, and I took them to the airport and saw them off. The journey back to Stratagem was the worst time so far on the whole trip. I phoned Mark who was staying in Cairns until the baby was born and we downed many beers until I felt that I could face the boat alone. Tony returned but the new engine was still not available when the rest of the Rally set off for the sail to Darwin.

It was another three weeks before we had the new engine fitted and tested before we could follow the other boats. I had decided that we must catch up with the rally at Darwin which meant that we would sail non-stop round the north of Australia.

Going north from Cairns we sailed inside the Barrier Reef which is classed as restricted waters as far as commercial vessels are concerned, and means that they have right of way. I had been given some very practical advice when I was told to call up on the radio any vessel that we saw and ask them which side they wanted to pass us on.

It worked a treat; most Aussie Skippers are a friendly, talkative lot and we had many a great conversation with the captains of ships that we met. It was a great pity that we were unable to spare the time to stop at the superb places that we passed, but I felt that we must catch up with the rally at Darwin.

Cape York

I had been advised by Robin Woodall, the ex-captain of the QEII, that passing the northern tip of Australia, Cape York, through the Torres Straits would be a challenge; he said it was a challenge to the QEII.

It is because the Straits are a constriction between two seas of dissimilar tidal ranges which makes the tidal prediction difficult.

As we approached the northern tip of Australia we met an Australian warship coming south. It had obviously sailed through the Straits, so I called them up on the radio to ask what the weather and the tides were like. I received a pleasant reply but the information was not available to me. I never thought that the Aussies were so insecure that they could not share tidal information with a 34ft British yacht.

We approached Cape York as darkness fell but we had a clear sky, and as luck would have it, it was also low water. You could see all the rocks above the water on either side of the channel which was well lit with the port (red) and starboard (green) lights. The actual navigational channel is between many small islands named by Captain Cook by the days on which he discovered them: Monday Island, Wednesday, Thursday, and so on.

We did not sail through but used the engine all the way and we were making very good progress but at about 12.30 am we saw a large cargo vessel in the channel behind us approaching very fast relative to our slow speed.

You never know if the lookout has seen you at times like this but I was hoping that we would be turning left out of the channel into the shallow Bay of Carpentaria before he caught us up. It was touch and go but we made it: as we turned to port into the darkness and leaving the brightly lit channel behind we all cheered, hoisted the sails, set the self-steering gear and had a few beers and a gin and tonic each.

The trip to Darwin was uneventful but when we arrived after nine days at sea we were informed that we could not enter the marina until the boat had been sterilised as there were growths in the water.

This did not go down at all well with me and a stand-up row took place with the rally organiser. Knowing quite a bit about water sterilisation I knew that it was all a waste of time, effort and money to do what was being proposed. Eventually the marina people agreed and they did a very cursory job and let Stratagem through.

East Timor War

The plan was to sail to all the Spice Islands starting with East Timor and working our way to Bali, but there was a war being fought in East Timor against Indonesia, with the Australians on the side of East Timor. This did not go down too well, so we were advised by everyone not to visit the islands but to sail directly to Bali.

Indonesia is a string of islands thousands of miles long, from just north of Australia to Thailand in the north.

As we approached the island of Bali from the south of the string of islands we had to sail north through the narrow channel between Bali and Lombok. The tide rips and overfalls are so violent that the fishermen believe there is a monster lurking in the depths. The tide was so strong that we had to have the engine on and the sails up to stop us going backwards, in fact we only made 1kt over the ground, but we managed eventually to enter the marina.

Monday 11th October 1999 Benoa Harbour Bali

Two days after we arrived we went on a site-seeing trip round Bali. The weather was not great and I could feel tension everywhere. It was not the friendly place you see and hear about in the brochures.

Tony took the time to fly home to the UK, and I arranged for him to collect some spares which Gill would get for us and the other boats.

There was a Presidential election taking place and the MP for Bali was expected to win, but unfortunately she did not. Everyone said it had been rigged and rioting started in the towns. We were on the boat but we could see the fires that had been started a few miles away; we also had radio calls from some of the boat crews who were still in town saying they could not get back to the marina.

A number of skippers had a meeting and decided to put to sea if the rioting got any closer. Eventually the army placed barricades across the road which stopped the mobs. The following day the Indonesian Government and the new President made the Bali MP the Vice President which appeared to satisfy most people, but it still left a strange feeling about the place.

All the crews returned and we then decided to sail in groups of two or three boats as we had been told of single boats being attacked along the coast.

26th October we left Bali to sail the 900 miles to Nongsa Point where we would leave Indonesia to enter Malaysia and Singapore. Every fishing boat we saw that approached us made everyone uneasy; although nothing happened we did not feel safe until we left Indonesia.

I had always phoned home whenever it was someone's birthday, so when it was 31st October, Lisa's 14th birthday, I called into a very small island, Bawean, to see if there was a telephone.

The other boats thought I was mad visiting such a small island. We dropped anchor and went ashore by dinghy. Immediately the dinghy was surrounded by children, then the head man appeared who to my surprise spoke a little English, enough for me to understand.

He told the kids to guard the dinghy and took me inland, past mud huts with thatched roofs and pigs, chickens and babies everywhere. We walked on until we came to a hut with an aerial; inside was a wooden counter with a radio on it and a straw cubicle opposite. The young girl was told I wanted to make a call, then the man left.

The girl's English was not so good so we had a job trying to find the country that I wanted to speak to. Then I remembered that at the Olympic Games in Helsinki it was announced that I was swimming for "le Royaume-Uni" (United Kingdom), which was the name she wanted and I was told to use the phone in the booth.

When Lisa answered the phone she was so surprised and wanted to know where I was. "Bawean," I said. "Where's that?" said Lisa. "Indonesia," I replied. "Where's Indonesia?" she said. "A long way away in the far east." After that we got on to a normal conversation about the trip and everyone back home.

Back on the beach no one would believe that I had managed to phone home, but you never know until you try. We left Bawean and sailed without stopping again, day and night; I did not feel like going ashore anywhere in Indonesia.

One day with a calm sea and a fresh wind I saw a large local wooden fishing boat coming straight towards Stratagem, so I woke Tony up and told him to keep watching the boat through the binoculars as it got closer. I changed course and so did the fishing boat, I changed course again and again they followed us. I was beginning to believe he was going to ram us, and if he did we would sink due to the fishing boat being much larger and heavier. It came at us but just before we collided it veered away with the crew laughing at us.

I found out weeks later that the local fishermen believe that if their catch is poor it is due to a bad demon being on the boat, and the only way of getting rid of the demon is to flip him off the bow of their boat onto someone else's, which was us, Stratagem.

Other problems were huts on stilts used by fishermen which did not have any lights on so you could just sail into them. These huts did not have permanent families living in them but were used intermittently as and when the fishing was good, the idea being that a large net was lowered into the water about a metre down then at night an arc lamp was lit which shone down into the sea, and this attracted the fish to come and see what was going on. When there were enough fish over the net it would be raised to catch the fish.

This meant that it was not too bad if it was being used but impossible to see when not in use.

We made our way north to Nongsa Point which was the place where we had to book out of Indonesia prior to sailing to Singapore.

We decided to sail between the mainland South Sumatra and the large island of Bangka, though others wanted to sail to Borneo.

The weather was very unsettled and changeable; one minute you could be sailing in clear skies and then the gale-force winds would appear from nowhere making it impossible to see even the bow of the boat. This sort of weather was dangerous because you could very easily be swept into another yacht or a fishing platform.

Some of the other boats decided not to sail at night and found small anchorages in which to shelter. One such night we had a very difficult job to find a secure place in a very small bay in a little island. We had to get all the chain and two anchors to secure the boat which still kept dragging the anchors. I stayed up all night in case we had to slip the anchors and leave the bay; the wind was blowing 34-37kts which is a good gale in any language.

We crossed the equator on our way to Nongsa Point which was now only 100 miles away. The trip was still unpleasant for many reasons but we arrived at 10.45am Friday 12th November 1999; I was so glad to be able to leave Indonesia.

Singapore Straits

We had a night out with the other boats prior to crossing the Singapore Straits which is the busiest stretch of water in the world. We had arranged to be hauled out of the water again at Kipples Marina for more attention to the stern gland.

Crossing the straits is dangerous because of the two shipping lanes, one going east the other going west. We had to cross each lane at right-angles although we could change course in between them. Waiting to cross we counted 125 ships crossing east and west in front of us. It was like walking across the motorway at rush hour.

We made straight for the marina but after a few miles as we approached land we had a very clear message from the Singapore Navy informing us to turn round immediately as we were in restricted waters.

We got out as quickly as we could and had to sail miles back the way we had come to go round a small island then we could once again make toward, the land. By this time it was dark but all the land and the sky was lit up with lights and advertising hoardings.

I called the marina on the radio for directions but they just said we should keep heading towards the city. I was getting really bothered that we were lost as far as finding a specific marina was concerned, then Tony said he could see a green light so we sailed towards it. However as we got close, we could see it was an advert for Carlsberg Larger. My heart sank and I called up the marina again. "That's OK," they said, "we are under the sign," and they were.

Monday 15th November we were hauled out next to 'Bella Rosa' which belonged to Smiley and Doreen, who had been there for many years and lived on the boat.

The engine was taken out and repositioned on two-inch thick aluminium bearers in place of soft wooden ones; I hoped that they would do the trick.

Smiley had had a number of cancers removed from his face and body over the years, and he said that I had a mole on my back that should be looked at: he gave me the name and number of the specialist that treated him.

I made an appointment to see the specialist who asked me why I had contacted him so I told him about Smiley. "Is he a doctor now?" he said. I told him that it had been said in all good faith and he examined my back.

He said it was all OK. When I asked him what it was he said "They are barnacles that you pick up on the sea of life," a phrase that I have repeated to many doctors who like the sound if it.

Two days later we were back in the water and set sail for Sabena Cove in Malaysia. This was up a river which was lined with tropical trees, and we were going along quite nicely with Tommy Tipalo when the monsoon came. We could not see each other or land so we just circled round for an hour until the rain passed, and by then we were fed-up and very wet so we asked for a launch from the marina to guide us in, which they did.

While we were at Sabena Cove a trio composed of two girls and a boy performed at a dinner laid on for the Rally. They were top class;

the girls could sing like Whitney Houston and they would have had a great future in the UK. I was so impressed that I bought them a drink in the bar after the dinner finished, and as we talked I found out that they were from Thailand. Each night they performed in the bar until closing time and when one night they sang just for me everyone wanted to know how I managed to get on so well with them.

It was from here that I took the ferry to Singapore City and lost my camera in the process, which contained film from Australia and Indonesia.

Thailand - Phuket – The millennium

Monday 29th November we left for Phuket up through the Straits of Malacca, this proved to be a very tiring journey. We had fishing boats with no lights on all around us at night, and as we got close they switched on their lights so we changed course, then others switched on their lights so that we were going round in circles. After an hour of this I called up the other boats and said we should go straight for the fishing boats and make them change course. The others only agreed if I went in front which I did, and as the lights were switched on I shone my main light at them and kept going straight at their nets. That did the trick and they soon moved out of the way. From then on that was the plan: play them at their own game.

Straits of Malacca - Port Dixon

Each afternoon we had bad storms as if they were following us from Singapore. During the day we had to avoid many large cargo vessels in the shipping lanes, so I decided to go into the next harbour wherever it was, and it turned out to be Port Dixon, a small marina with only 6 foot of water to get in: I needed 5ft 8ins.

We tied up and went for a shower, and then to the bar. There was a man sat at the bar with a beer and as I asked the barman for a local beer, he (Paul Humphrey) said, "That's a good northern accent. Where are you from?"

It has been easier to reply to this question by saying Liverpool which is better known than Wirral. "Liverpool," I replied. "I used to work at Camel Laird's," he said. When I told him I was from West Kirby, it turned out he knew Toll Smith, and from then on we drank the night away together. It is a small world.

We left to go north to Lumut another small town and then to Langkawi where we could book out of Malaysia. I was now totally fed up with the trip, if I could have sold the boat and flown home I would have done.

The previous night Tommy Tipolo almost ran us down: he was asleep with the boat on autopilot and did not hear us calling him. We just managed to keep clear. It was a close thing since he missed us by two metres.

9th December 1999 we arrived in Phuket at 9am and anchored in 3am about half a mile off-shore in a shallow bay. We booked in and arranged for another lift-out, to try and fix the stern gland which was again leaking. The following day we left for a marina which had all the facilities but was at the end of a two mile long winding shallow channel. We made it OK but Tommy Tipolo ran aground and was later pulled off.

I met a number of very nice people in the marina. Andy, an ex-airline pilot, lived on his own boat with a very nice local girl who was his crew, girlfriend, and soul mate. After having a meal he told me that he could not understand how I managed and suggested that I would be better off with a hired crew.

The other friend I made was an Aussie called Monty who had been crewing for a Frenchman with his fiancé and a Scots lad. They were sailing his boat back to France and hired Monty for his experience.

They had got as far as Madagascar when the Frenchman decided to sail up the east coast of Somalia. This was pirate water even then in 1999. Monty had refused to sail along this coast and had agreed to be paid off and was making his way back to Oz when we met in Phuket.

A few days later Monty had a reporter from the Sunday Times fly out to meet with him because the Frenchman's boat had been attacked and the Scots lad shot and killed. There was a TV programme made about this incident a few yeas later.

Gill came out for two weeks so we hired a Jeep and stayed in a super hotel on the west coast. Joe and Doreen also stayed with us. It was just what I needed to lift my gloom: no crew, a superb hotel, but most of all, my wife with me for 14 days.

The hotel put on a great show at Christmas with a cabaret. Everyone received a present and the children sang carols, but it was strange for it to be so hot at this time of year.

The celebrations for the Millennium were held outside in the hotel grounds, with a large clock counting down to midnight. I will never forget where I was at the start of 2000.

Gill and I went into Phuket town where I bought her a pair of black pearl earrings to match the black pearl from Rangiroa, which caused quite a stir when we produced it in the shop.

The two weeks gave me hope and lifted my spirits for the journey home which could not come quickly enough. We used the Jeep every day and yet when we filled to tank up to hand it back the fuel came to less than £5.

Gill left to fly home and we had the boat put back in the water after a new prop shaft had been made and fitted: hopefully this would do the trick.

Thursday 6th January we left for Sri Lanka with Joe and Doreen in 'Vitamin Sea' at 9am. 1100 miles to go.

The following day we were motor sailing in clear weather and not a thing in sight when I noticed a line of white on the horizon from east to west as far as I could see. I got the binoculars out but all I could see was a wall of turbulent water about 2-3ft high. There was no way round it; we were doing about 5kt travelling at right angles to the "wave". As we got closer I could see calm water behind the "wave" but the turbulence was about 200 yards wide. It was a very strange feeling as we approached the front of the water: would we sink or sail over it?

We sailed through the turbulance and carried on. Four years later there was an underwater earthquake which triggered a landslip causing the tsunami which devastated the entire area, and we were in the same area but did not know what was yet to happen in the future.

The sail from Phuket to Galle was supposed to be the best sailing of the whole circumnavigation, with good winds and blue skies, but someone forgot to tell Him Upstairs. We experienced some of the worst weather so far, heavy rain storms and fierce winds, but at least we were getting closer to home every day.

One morning at 5.55am I went to relieve Tony who had been on watch only to find him fast asleep on the floor of the cockpit. How long he had been asleep I did not know or care; he had not just dozed off, he had made himself comfortable. This was the cardinal sin of sailors, failing to keep a good lookout; it places the boat and each of us in danger.

I woke him up and sent him to his bed but I could not bring myself to say anything.

Later that day I asked him if he had anything to say but he said nothing, not even an apology or an excuse. That was the final straw: I could not trust my crew and we both knew it.

The autohelm had been giving us trouble for some time but in the bad weather it packed up altogether, so at times we had to steer by hand.

15th January 2000, we arrived in Galle ten days after leaving Phuket. I booked into a hotel to have some peace and quiet; the place looked familiar from my last holiday with Gill. Tony went off for a few days, and on his return we found that the wind vane rudder had been stolen. We informed the police and made arrangements for a replacement to be shipped out, and in the meantime 'Rainbow Spirit' lent us their spare. I had to go by car to Colombo airport to collect the spare which was not a pleasant trip, but at least we were able to return the one we had borrowed.

One night while having a drink in the hotel we were told that a turtle had come ashore and was laying her eggs in the sand. We all rushed out and I was privileged to watch her lay 60 or more eggs in the sand then cover them over before she returned to the sea. A truly remarkable experience that I shall never forget.

Sri Lanka to Djibouti – Pirate Country

Our next big journey was to Djibouti, at the entrance to the Red Sea, 2340 miles, but we intended to stop overnight somewhere in the

Maldives, en route for this was pirate country and we had to sail in convoy of at least three boats.

As an extra security we were told not to give out our normal position when checking in with Rally Control, instead two positions "Z" & "A" was known to everyone on the rally and we gave our position relative to these. For example we would report that we were 200 miles south west of "A". An added bonus was the fact that the French Navy was supposed to be in the area and monitoring our progress. Many of us could remember how ineffectual they had been during the war, and were not surprised when we neither saw nor heard from them.

The Maldives Government had a policy of repopulating many of the small islands such as the one we stopped at, Uligamu. There were only 420 people on the island; the government had provided a well, radio facilities and accommodation for the families. It was paradise, the water was pristine, warm and full of fish, and the beach was white sand: the entire population walked round the island every week to pick up litter and flotsam.

We were made very welcome and could use the radio facilities to call home which I did. We were allowed to hold a BBQ on the beach provided that we cleared up any mess the following day and did not drink any alcohol since it is a Muslim Country.

I felt that this was my idea of paradise and due to the many problems I have recorded I felt compelled to balance the record by saying just how much I was enjoying my short stay in Uligamu.

Because the water was so warm, clear and clean, I took the opportunity to dive under the boat to clean the hull and the propeller while Tony checked the mast and rigging.

4th February, we left for Djibouti. Next day we had to sail in convoy and I got lumbered with two single-handed sailors, Tommy on 'Tipolo', and Ray on 'Lady Rosemary'. Joe on 'Vitamin Sea' and others were staying a day or so longer to avoid the two single-handers. The reason was that they required help during the time they slept and someone, us, had to keep watch for them and alert them to any danger.

Neither Tommy nor Ray should have been sailing on their own.

Tommy had told the rally that his crew were on the way but they never materialised, while Ray, who had fallen out with everyone at some point, had two lads who refused to sail with him after the Panama Canal leg.

Night sailing was the most dangerous, with both Tommy and Ray sleeping at some point; it was easier when you could see them than it was if they drifted away. The worst time was when they got too close and we could not wake them on the radio; this was a frequent occurrence which did nothing for my peace of mind.

We had good sailing conditions for our boat but because the other two could not manage with full sails they kept falling behind. This resulted in us stopping the boat in order for them to catch up before darkness each day.

At one time we not only lost sight of them both but we were unable to contact them on the radio. It was made more difficult due to the radio restrictions on giving out our position.

Ten days out I got up in the night to use the toilet and found Tony once again flat out asleep in the cockpit. I said that I would do three 3hr. watches and he would do two 1½ hour watches so that he should be able to stay awake.

We should have been close to Djibouti by now but the wind had dropped so we started the engine and motor-sailed to keep going at a reasonable speed. Ray who did not purchase any extra fuel in the Maldives, even though Joe had offered him the money to do so, was getting low on fuel: he had got further and further behind as he would not start his engine. He could have waited for the other boats that were approaching from astern but he wanted us to go back and give him the fuel. I could not refuse the request so we turned about and told Ray to stop his boat and that I would go alongside with 50 gallons of fuel and five AA batteries for his GPS which he also needed. There was no sight or sound of Tommy on 'Tipolo'.

Sunday 20th February we arrived in Djibouti at 8am; dropped anchor 200 yards from the club house, went ashore for a shower and a pint. Ray, Tommy, Joe and others all followed us in that morning. It was typical Arab country, hot and dirty, but it was land and only 1100 miles to go to Eilat.

I walked into the town and on one side of the road was a long high wall. As I walked an armed man appeared on top of the wall shouting at me that I had to walk on the other side as this was the Palace and I was an infidel. I crossed over and continued into town with the guard watching me all the way.

I bought my customary 27 cards which I posted at every port; I later found out just how much they had been appreciated.

I did not like Djibouti and decided to leave for Eilat before any other boat, and not therefore be available to nursemaid Tommy and Ray.

I thought that the 1100 miles to Eilat would take us two weeks; in fact it took three and a half weeks.

CHAPTER EIGHTEEN

Three Weeks of Hell Djibouti to Eilat

Djibouti to Eilat

t this stage of my story I feel that I should explain some of the rules affecting sailing and the terminology for those who do not sail. I will keep it simple, so sailors please be patient.

- Normally power gives way to sail, i.e. motor driven vessels keep out of the way of sailing boats, except in restricted waters and shipping lanes.
- Boats pass each other in opposite directions with the ports side (left and red) showing to each other.
- Boats on a collision course both turn to starboard (right and green).
- Sailing boats cannot sail into the wind; they can only sail up to 20 degrees to the wind.
- The Red Sea for the purpose of this demonstration runs north to south & is 1400 miles long.
- Sailing boats therefore cannot sail straight up north and must keep crossing the width east and west to get north, which is called tacking, and changing tack is called going about.
- The sea can be very choppy with short steep waves which can in some cases stop a sailing boat especially when trying to go about.

The sail to Eilat was to be the worst leg of the Rally, every skipper agreed and not one was ready for it.

Wednesday 23rd February we left at noon; we soon had gale-force winds and sailed with just the gib. The first disaster could have been fatal: we were leaving a light on a ship to port when at the last minute we noticed that it was a lighthouse on shore and managed to turnabout with less than 100 yards to spare.

That night we heard on the radio that every boat at anchor in Djibouti had been burgled by swimmers climbing aboard at night and stealing money, watches, equipment and anything valuable without anyone knowing. At least we missed that one.

The Red Sea is a 1400 mile long narrow stretch of water only 200 miles wide, but there are oil rigs just off shore and islands which forces the international shipping lanes to take up the rest of the sea room. The Red Sea is a very busy route for ships going to Japan, China and the Pacific.

The wind was getting stronger and gale force, the sea was very choppy with short sharp waves that made it difficult to go about. We had only 30 minutes sailing between the oil rigs and the shipping lanes before we needed to tack. It took two of us and the engine on to make a tack. We were both wearing harnesses and could only sleep for 20 minutes: we managed this for 24 hours and then I knew we could not continue so I decided to cross over the shipping lanes and find an anchorage with some shelter on the Sudan side. We steamed across at maximum speed and found a small bay, dropped anchor in 8 metres of water and slept for 12 hours.

After a good meal we set off again to try and make headway north. The wind was still gale force and the sea difficult. We had two near-misses with other boats, the first being a fishing boat which was coming at us on starboard: I was asleep when Tony woke me, so I rushed to the cockpit to find this boat two lengths away. I turned to port and the fishing boat continued alongside us just metres away. I shouted to the fishing boat and at last they saw us and turned to starboard. When I asked Tony why we had let them get so near without taking any action he could not, or did not answer. I took over and he went to bed.

I decided that we would not go to Port Sudan as planned, which would save us 100 miles. At 10pm we were buzzed by a US military helicopter, and then there was a radio call to say that four US Navy ships were heading south and that all vessels must keep clear. I wished I had had a torpedo.

We were struggling to make any headway over the ground as the wind was head on. We heard on the radio that many of the rally boats were having gear failure.

Last night, 29th February, we were once again almost rundown by a large vessel; we had all our lights on and a radar reflector working but this ship just came straight for us. I called the ship on the emergency channel 16, but got no reply. All the time this vessel was getting closer and closer, so I decided that we should put the engine on and turn round, and by the time we finished the turn the boat was only 50 yards away. We flashed our light at the bridge but there was no-one there, the boat was on automatic pilot. I swore at the boat and a passing Dutch Captain came on the radio to say he had witnessed the whole thing but said it was common practice for some ships to go the entire length of the Red Sea on autopilot.

We heard more news of gear failure on 'Lady Rosemary' and 'Tudor Rose'; the weather was still bad although the wind had eased to 29 knots. We were running out of dry clothes and towels.

Saturday 4th March Tony saw the starboard rigging fail so we immediately lowered the sails and tried to secure the mast with rope. I could have cried, we could not sail again until we had replaced the rigging and the only way we could do that was to return 80 miles downwind to Jeddah. I called up Jeddah but they did not want to let us in: I told them it was an emergency and that we could lose our boat. They sent out a patrol boat to check us out and then let us enter harbour under guard.

Jeddah

There was only one other boat in this particular dock, 'Frolic' an American boat; John was the skipper and Sue and Christian the crew. They had been there for three weeks waiting for a new engine.

The guards sealed the drinks cabinet and asked if that was all the alcohol we had on board. Tony was about to say we had more under the floorboards when I kicked him hard on the shins. We were also told that we could not use the radio. Then we got a shock to be informed that they were going to charge us $2000 US, to stay and $33 US each for a pass to allow us to take a taxi into town to get repairs and supplies.

When the guards left the boat one stayed on the quayside all the time day and night. We went aboard 'Frolic' to introduce ourselves and invited them back to have a meal with us, and they were so pleased to find that we had a large stock of beer and spirits especially so when we helped them to "smuggle" plenty back to their boat under our clothing.

We needed to inform the other boats about our problems and where we were, but we could not use our call sign STRATAGEM because we were not allowed to use the radio. I had a nickname for one of the lads on another boat, I called him "Snowball" and he and everyone called me "Weetabix" because I was always shopping for Weetabix cereal, so I went on the radio as Weetabix calling any of the Rally boats. This did the trick and I was able to inform the Rally just what had happened and that we were alright. I also asked for a full set of rigging to be available in Eilat.

The following day Tony and I took a taxi into Jeddah where we met a chandler who would come out to the boat and renew the broken rigging. We also went into a supermarket to get fresh supplies of food. As we were shopping with a full trolley there was an announcement which we did not understand and the lights went out. We were bungled out of the store onto the pavement; we still had the trolley but had not paid for any of the contents. We asked a passer-by what was happening and he told me that it was time for prayers.

We did not dare move in case anyone thought that we were stealing the food, but it was two hours before they reopened the supermarket and we were able to pay for the supplies. We could not wait to get away and back to the boat.

Later that day the chandler arrived and made emergency repairs to the rigging so we were able to leave the next day.

Other boats had overtaken us while we were in Jeddah and radioed to say how bad the weather was. I was told that as the smallest boat they did not think I would make it through the Strait of Tiran, the seas were that bad.

We continued to sail over to the Sudan side of the sea on port tack: we passed 'Rhythm' on the opposite tack, whilst 'Matata', 'Nikita' and 'Rain Again' were all 60 miles north of us but still experiencing very bad weather.

The boat was full of water which we had to continually pump out, sometimes the floor boards floated about. We were wet and so was everything in the boat. The wind was still between 32 and 39 knots.

Some of the larger boats had taken down their sails and were going directly north on engine alone, we tried it but our engine could not get us to do more than 1 knot over the ground.

It took both of us plus the engine to go-about in between the waves, which was very tiring yet we would have many more days of this before we got to Eilat.

I thought I had broken my arm the previous night when I was thrown against the sink but thankfully it was only bruised.

Forestay Fails

As we approached the Strait of Tiran the wind was still gale force when the stainless steel forestay parted. We immediately took down the sails and started the engine. We used the spinnaker halyard to keep the mast secure, but there was no way we could consider trying to navigate the straits now in this wind. I decided to get under the lee of a mountain on the Saudi side of the Strait and out of the wind. I set two waypoints which we went back and forward to all night. We could just make out the lights of Sharm el sheikh on the other side of the water.

The following morning as dawn broke the wind appeared to have lessened so I decided to venture out from under the mountain to literally test the water and the wind. It went from 30 knots to 20 knots and then under 10 knots. An Egyptian patrol boat was tied up to a marker buoy with the rope trailing in the water, the wind had vanished. With only the engine we slowly passed through the Straits in calm water: in days gone by they would have claimed a miracle.

We now had 90 miles to motor to Eilat and I radioed Gill who was getting messages from the other boats who were already in Eilat to tell her the good news that we had entered the Gulf of Aqaba.

On Friday 17th March the sea was flat and the going was good: for the first time in weeks I felt that we had weathered the storm. That night at about 2am a very strong bright light shone on us from both sides and a loudspeaker called to us, "This is the Israeli Navy. Identify yourself!" they shouted. I was woken up, angry, and pissed off, and we had already had to copy all our ship's papers and our passports to send to Israel prior to leaving Phuket months ago, and also in very large letters on both sides of the boat was our name 'STRATAGEM'. What more could they want?

I got on the radio and told them to look up the papers that we had sent to them and asked them to turn off the searchlights. They did and I calmed down, to the relief of Tony who had been on watch but they had crept up on us in pitch-black uniforms. They said they would escort us into Eilat which they did. We arrived at 7am, we booked in, then I saw Gill waiting and I gave a very big hug and a lot of kisses: never again will I do that trip.

Saturday 18th March, Eilat

The hotel we were booked into was superb, overlooking the marina. After such a long, lousy journey it was good to be in an air-conditioned room which was not moving about and yet if felt as though it was moving for a day or two. After a good shower and a rest Gill and I went to find the other skippers and crew: there were two groups drinking at the bar, one of which was the skippers who all agreed that it was the worst trip anyone had experienced. The other group consisted of crew who, now it was over, thought it was not all that bad. It just goes to show who had the responsibility and worry.

The new rigging and roller reefing had been delivered and was fitted; I had upgraded the size and strength of all the rigging just to be on the safe side.

Gill and I booked a trip to Petra which was amazing; I could imagine just what it must have been like when it was in use.

We then went to the Dead Sea and had a swim in the very salty water in which you floated so high it was so difficult to swim. When we came out of the water we got plastered with Dead Sea mud, which is supposed to be good for the skin. Later we visited the old Jewish fortification at Masada which was accessed by cable car. The whole experience was worth the sail from Djibouti.

The new rigging and roller reefing cost me £3000 which I hoped to claim off the insurance. I felt that there was only a relatively short sail to Suez (250 miles) and another to Crete (450).

We left Eilat with Joe Dormer on 'Vitamin Sea' and it was an easy sail until we reached the Straits of Tiran where the wind got up and was right on the nose. We could not get round the corner to the Gulf of Suez so we decided to spend the night in the harbour at Sharm el sheikh. It was a good decision because no other boat managed to get round.

Once again the following day the wind had dropped and off we went north to Suez and the Canal. Believe it or not we had to motor most of the way, because there was no wind. The following day was just the opposite again we had 41 knots of wind and a bloody awful sail, as I wrote in the ship's log.

Wednesday 12 April, Suez

We arrived at 11am where we saw John from 'Frolic' who came on board with two large crates of beer, as a thank you for our help in Jeddah.

A reception had been arranged for all the boats at the Yacht Club that evening and we were all asked to attend as the Minister would be attending. The reception was held in the afternoon, we all waited and waited and waited, but nothing happened. There were seats and tables but nothing was being served, no water or drinks, nothing.

After two hours we were all getting fed up with the lack of food and drinks especially. I asked an official looking person why we were not being served any drinks and was told that the Minister was late and we could not have anything until he arrived. I went back to the Rally sailors and agreed that we would all leave, but as we got up to go the officials panicked and said we would be insulting the Minister. I said that the Minister had insulted us by being late and that we were going. I was asked to stay and we would be served drinks and food if we sat down again. We did and we got served, but once again my contact with Arabs did nothing to make me feel any better towards them.

When in Suez we had to have a pilot on each boat for which we paid. The canal is a ditch, no locks but with a lake just over halfway along the route where we had to moor for the night. We motored through the canal so the larger boats got ahead: as they were leaving the canal they were accosted for extra money and cigarettes. We could hear them on the radio arguing with the pilot boat. I radioed that we did not have smoking on board and that we would NOT pay anything extra to anyone.

We also got out large wooden stakes which we said we would use if anyone tried to get on board the boat. I said all this in front of our pilot so that he knew exactly what we would do if there was any trouble.

As we approached the end of the canal the pilot boat came alongside; our pilot was shouting in Arabic all about what I had said, I assume, and he jumped off 'Stratagem' into the pilot boat as soon as he could.

I was never so glad as to leave the canal and sail into the Mediterranean; it was as if we were back in civilisation and home waters. The sail to Crete was the best yet, no more problems, and soon to be sailing with Cath.

The Last and Best Leg

19th April 2000 we arrived in Achois Nikolaos at 8am, where Gill was waiting and we had another good hotel on the sea front. We hired a car to go to meet Cath at the airport; she was staying in the hotel with us until we left for home.

While we were there it was Easter which was earlier than it is at home and the colourful processions and celebrations were great to get involved in; we had a truly great time. Both Cath and I had Greek salad at least once each day. Tony moved out of the boat and Cath moved her belongings in.

Jamie had just won his second British Youth Championship in Laser Radials, which added to the celebrations.

I had a very good feeling about the rest of the trip: it was going to be enjoyable for the first time since Antigua. We had a good wind as we waved goodbye to Gill on the harbour wall, and we rounded the headland and set sail for Malta 532 miles west. I was enjoying the sail, and then I looked at Cath: her face was white and she felt sick. I should have realised that I had my sea-legs and Cath had not sailed for some time. I reefed the main sail and brought the boat upright, which gave us a smoother sail. I should have known better, but I was so pleased to be with Cath.

It was a pleasure to sail again, and it must have been infectious because we were joined by eight birds who wanted a lift. We fed them and placed water on the deck, and they stayed with us for two days then left without saying goodbye.

Friday 5th May we entered Valletta Harbour and stayed the night after stocking up on milk, bread, and fuel.

The last leg of my circumnavigation was 625 miles to Palma, because it was from Palma that I sailed back to Gibraltar to start the Rally, so I had completed my round the world trip when I docked in Ca'n Pastilla, Palma, Majorca.

The sail was typical of the other legs; we either had no wind or gale force winds. We also had some violent electrical storms which once you get used to them appear as things to wonder about and enjoy.

Cath is a good cook so I was able to sit back and enjoy being looked after for a change. Cath and I have always had something: we had worked together and sailed together, and we could argue but never fell out.

On the night of 9th May we experienced every type of weather including electrical storms all round us, gale force wind and then hailstones, and on top of this we had $1^{1}/_{2}$ knots of current against us.

It was 4.30pm Thursday 11th May when Cath first sighted Majorca and it was at 9am the following day that we tied up in the same marina that I had left to sail round the world.

I had completed the circumnavigation of the world.

11th May 2000 (Extract from my diary)

Tomorrow morning at this time I will have completed my circumnavigation of the world, I never thought that this day would come. It is an achievement I am proud of and I find it hard to believe that I have done it, "Sailed Stratagem round the world".

I would not do it again and I do not think I would have started if I had known what I know now. Dick Allen said that personal problems would be the worst problems and also personal hygiene.

The boat has looked after me and the crew very well even when equipment failed; I never thought that we would NOT make it.

The one person I owe it all to is Gill, she encouraged me to go and when problems surfaced and all else failed, and it was Gill who came up with the goods, literally as well as morally. I could not have done it without Gill; her visits were superb morale boosters.

It was a lot harder both physically and mentally than I ever imagined but I did it.

Olympics at 18 years

The world at 66 years

And all the time with my wife Gill. Now I will spend all my money and time on Gill and have a very good time.

Bry

0830 11th May 2000 off the coast of Majorca with Catherine my daughter. We arrived OK and tied up at the same place we had left years before, and what a party we had at the Gin Palace.

Circumnavigation Complete

We decided to leave the boat there and fly home. That person who wanted to purchase 'Stratagem' had bought another boat. We packed our things and got a lift to the airport, it never occurred to either of us that we would receive such a superb welcome home.

At Liverpool Airport Gill, Alison, Kate, Patrick and Diane had placards welcoming me home with the local press in attendance. It was overwhelming but very much appreciated.

I later paid a firm to sail 'Stratagem' back to Liverpool where she stayed until I sold her. The last I heard she was sailing in the Mediterranean. She was a very good boat who looked after me as I looked after her. I never felt that my life was in danger at any time I sailed her.

CHAPTER NINETEEN

2000 - 2004 Home to Reality and Family

Talks

The first talk I was asked to give about my trip was to Greasby Junior School where the children had followed my journey for two years: they had written to me and I had sent them cards from every port that I stopped at. The headmaster, Mr Moss, had all the pupils sat on the floor in the hall; I asked how long should I speak for, about 20 minutes he told me otherwise they get restless.

I started and after a short time looked at my watch - 40minutes had gone by and I was only three-quarters of the way round. "Carry on," the head said. I spoke for one hour and fifteen minutes and only one little girl left to go to the toilet: they loved it and so did I. That was the start of hundreds of talks I have since given, with slides and now a computer to make it all a professional event. All the money raised has gone to either St Johns Hospice or Claire House Children's Hospice.

The new bungalow which Gill moved into while I was in the Atlantic was superb, and it was the best decision we had made when we moved from York Avenue; it was smaller and half a mile closer to the shops and railway station.

South Africa

Jean used to live next door to Gill in Sulby Drive, Preston when they were both little girls; her parents emmigrated to South Africa after the war. Gill and Jean kept in touch but did not see one another until 1997 when Gill visited Jean in Johannesburg for a three weeks, holiday.

The highlight was a visit to the Kruger National Park and Cape Town to see Jean's daughter Mandy. The photos Gill brought back and the tales she told me of her visit inspired me to plan a trip with Gill on my return from sailing round the world.

In 2002 Gill and I booked a flight to Johannesburg to stay with Jean, her bungalow is in Santon a few miles outside Johannesburg, in a private estate called Four Ways. I felt that I had known Jean for many years due to the telephone conversations that we had regularly. Jean had Freelander Land Rover which we found excellent especially as the roads outside the built up towns could be little more than tracks in the Kruger Park.

Kruger Park

The Kruger Park is 100 miles north west of Jean's and is as large as Wales is wide but in length it would extend from Anglesey in the north to the south coast of Cornwall. There is a tarmac road running down the length of the Park from north to south, with four roads connecting with this coming in from the west, 70 to 50 miles apart. The rest were just tracks or nothing at all.

In the centre there were one or two hotels as well as one in the north, and south. The accommodation that we used, there were only five of them, were Bushveld Camps.

Bushveld Camps

These camps were always near to water, either by a river or a water hole and consisted of bungalows with thatched roofs, very basic but clean. Some had two bedroom others three or four, all had electric cooking facilities, and toilets. Each had its own BBQ with loungers for watching the sun go down with a drink in your hand. The entire camp was enclosed with an electrified fence to keep the animals out. The warden had a generator to supply the power and there were a number of freezers for the tourists to store their food. (Everyone carried a large freezer box). The camps closed before sunset and did not open again until sunrise.

We had decide to enter the Park at Punda Maria the northern gate and spend four nights at each camp, working our way south.

The first camp Sirheni was on the banks of the river Mphongolo; we had our first taste of the African Bush. We could not wait to get the BBQ ready and a cold beer as we prepared our first meal outside in the cool night air. It took a few days to get used to the different sounds especially at night, we each had our own camera and binoculars always ready so that we did not miss a chance to see the animals coming down to drink or bathe and in some cases to hunt for a meal.

The following day we decided to go out to see what was in the area, the dirt track was just wide enough to take our vehicle with the trees and bushes at times touching the car. We had been travelling about an hour when we came round a corner to see a very large Bull Elephant standing in the middle of the track eating the leaves from the trees at the side of the road. We stopped and he turned to look at us with a look that said get out, this is my space. I thought that we would watch him for a while but he did not want to be watched, he turned to face us and bellowed as he shook his head from side to side. I put the gear into reverse, he stood his ground then he started to come towards us. Time to go, I am trying to move faster than the elephant while reversing round a corner not the easiest manoeuvre. I retired about 400yds then waited to see if he would follow us but he did not, after another ½ hour we ventured forward and the elephant had gone, but we had to stop again when we saw a large herd of Water Buffalo crossing the road. There were 25 in sight as they crossed and this went on as we counted over 100 animals, after the last one entered the bush we moved on and could not see any of them even though we knew they were there.

On returning to camp we told the warden about the elephant, "that would be Titan" he said; he loves to chase tourists.

Bateleur was the next camp at the junction of two rivers, Shingwedzi and Mashokwe, on the way we had to stop to let a herd of Zebra cross the track, a truly real Zebra Crossing. That night we were wakened by the sound of lions who had killed an Impala and were fighting over the right to eat first, although the Lionesses killed the prey the male Lion had first go.

Shimuwini Camp on the banks of the Letaba was our favourite camp; we have stayed here on all three visits. The boundary fence is only one yard from the river bank, Hippos, Crocodiles, Elephants and small game all visited the river. We spent over one hour watching a very large Croc contemplating how to get from the water to a rocky ledge about four feet above him. Eventually he stood on his back legs and with the help of his tail pushed his body up onto the ledge, and then he lay and waited for something to appear for lunch.

Just outside the camp was a hide by the side of a tributary of the river, the branches of the trees were within touching distance, and about seven feet above the water. Kingfishers used the branch to wait for a suitable size meal to swim past, and then they dropped down into the water like a stone, caught the fish and returned to the branch. We watched as it manoeuvred the fish in its mouth so that it could hold it by the tail and hit the head hard on the branch until it died, and then it swallowed the fish head first. We saw this remarkable event three times all happening less than an arm's length away.

Talamti

Every journey each day brought something new, something different, to see animals in their true environment, free to wander where they pleased made me realise that animals should not be in captivity in zoos for humans to look at, even when we claim to be doing it for their own good. I shall never again visit a zoo.

We stopped our car to watch a Dung Beatle fly to a recently produced pile of dung; it climbed all over it selecting a suitable size of dung three times its own size, to push along the road to the side of the track and into the grass. It was fascinating to watch how it managed to roll it along with its legs.

You do not realise just how tall a Giraffe can be, we could drive underneath its stomach if it stood still. Most of the time they are graceful and slow but they can be violent and aggressive when they have young with them.

Just an hour or so later we saw to our delight and amazement a Leopard calmly walk out of the bush onto the track a few yards ahead of us; we stopped as he looked at us and carried on walking. We slowly followed the Leopard for a few hundred yards taking photos as we kept a safe distance behind.

You are constantly warned not to get out of your car as all the animals are wild and some think you really are meals on wheels. Earlier that year a couple had stopped on a bridge over a river, after looking to see if it was all right to get out to take photographs. As they were concentrating on photography they were taken by surprise by Lions and killed.

Biyamiti was the last and most southerly camp that we stayed at. It was here that we found out as we booked in that we had picked up a thorn in the front tyre which was deflating. It was spotted by one of the staff, who changed the wheel for us and fixed the puncture as well. So many times on the journey we thought we could see a particular animal but when we stopped and looked through the binoculars it was usually a boulder or a bush, these sightings became known as "Coudabeens", they could have been Elephants, could have been Rhino, could have been Waterbuck.

That night we were invited to our next door neighbour's BBQ for a drink and a chat, Ben and his family had just entered the park that day and where excited about what they had seen so far. I asked Ben if he had seen any Coudabeens, he was not sure, but reluctant to admit that he did not know what they were. We kept on about how we had seen them almost every day, in the end we explained and everyone laughed. Ben said he would use that story the next day.

That night we went out with the warden on a night safari for a different experience. There were two guards with guns ready just in case, but they were not needed.

Of all the places I have visited in the world The Kruger National Park is the one I would go back to time and time again.

We did visit Cape Town and went to the top of Table Mountain by cable car, the view and experience is magnificent, we also went to the most southerly tip of Africa where the Indian Ocean and the Atlantic Ocean meet. We took the car onto the shore and I got out taking photos. On turning round I saw a very large Baboon sat watching me, it was in-between the car and me. I gathered a number of large stones and made a lot of noise. Jean started the car engine and we managed to scare off the Baboon.

Jamie Sailing

That summer Jamie was asked by the RYA to sail a catamaran, a twin hulled boat, because they did not have any good sailors in this class of boat. They lent Jamie a Hobie 16 and a crew. Jamie walked away with the race so he was entered for the European Youth Championships in Jersey.

Gill and I went to watch him sail and on the last day he was leading the race, the closest other boat being a French boat.

On the final race it was between Jamie and the French lad. The TV commentator on the shore was asking who this Jamie Smith was, they had not heard of him. When I told them that he was sailing in a borrowed boat and this was only the second time he had sailed it, no one would believe me. Jamie finished second in the championship beaten by half a point by the French lad.

Jamie went on to sail and win in the catamarans and was asked to sail in the Olympic Boat, a Tornado.

The cost of this would be too much for him or us to find so I approached Toll Smith at the club to see if he could help with sponsorship. Toll asked for all Jamie's past records and a breakdown of what was required. I said I would manage his sailing if sponsorship was forthcoming. To our delight Mercedes agreed to sponsor Jamie. They provided a new boat, road trailer, Vito van, "employment" and expenses. A marvellous deal! I was also included on the insurance for the van but I paid all my own expenses.

Over the next three years Jamie sailed all over Europe with me often accompanying him, and then joined the Olympic Squad and sailed in New Zealand, Australia, and America. I was so proud of him.

He towed the boat all the way to Athens for the Olympic training; he did not make the team as only one boat would be chosen but he was the training partner for the successful boat.

The only problem he had was finding the right crew, someone who was as committed as he was. I could see that no one was.

I suggested to Jamie that he should go back to sailing single-handed; he spoke to Toll and agreed to sell the Tornado and get a Laser.

Jamie and David Hivey from Southport, a former Laser champion, often trained together. On one occasion I hired a RIB from the sailing club at Pwllheli so that the two lads could train in good conditions in Cardigan Bay. I had my hand-held radio plus drinks and we all had lifejackets on so off we went. The conditions were perfect and we practised starts and tactics. Both were international sailors and none of us noticed that the wind was getting up: it only added to the testing conditions, which was why we were there.

With the seas getting rougher David's mast broke. There was no danger, and I went alongside to assist David to prepare his boat for towing while Jamie just sailed around.

David got into the RIB but we could not start the engine, try as we might. We then noticed just how far we had drifted south, a few miles. I decided to call the sailing club to come out with a boat to tow us both back to the marina, informing them that we were in no danger but we had just lost a mast on a Laser.

To our horror we saw the RNLI lifeboat approaching us at high speed. Jamie said that he was not getting involved in this embarrassing incident and started to sail home. I called up the lifeboat but they insisted that they wanted the experience and continued towards us. At this stage we once again tried the engine and to our surprise and embarrassment it started. The lifeboat continued to follow us back to the marina, enjoying the fact that an international sailor and coach had been forced to ask for help. Both lads took a terrible ribbing from their fellow international sailors.

2002 Helsinki Reunion

It was the 50 year anniversary of the 1952 Olympic Games in Helsinki and the first of what has become a regular event for the other Games.

All competitors were invited to attend with their families the celebrations and Gill and Alison came with me. We had a truly wonderful time. I am so glad that it was Alison who came as you shall see why later.

We were treated like royalty and visiting all the places again after 50 years was very nostalgic especially when we visited the flats were we had stayed. The fact that the buildings and the stadium and swimming pool were still in use surprised me: at home we would have pulled them down in the same timescale.

One night in the lounge I was asked why I had given up swimming in 1954. I told them the story of how I had been treated by the governing body, the ASA, and then to my surprise others started to say how badly they had been treated by officials in other sports. Some of the tales related by the ladies were far worse and more serious than mine.

2004

In January we decided to extend the garage and convert it into an en-suite double bedroom, never thinking that it would play such an important role in Alison's life.

I have written this as it happened because so much happened over the next two years. The first blow was when Mercedes decided to stop all sponsorship other than car racing. When Toll told Jamie and myself we were both shattered even though they said they would honour their commitments for a further year. Toll said that he would try and find another sponsor but we both knew that the end was in sight. Jamie kept sailing but it was not the same, he said, and I agreed, that he was not going to sail at a lower level than he was currently at, so if he could not find anyone to replace Mercedes he would quit sailing.

In December Jamie bought his first house, 7 Scotia Avenue, New Ferry, Birkenhead. A semi-detached property near the site of the old New Ferry pool. I said I would decorate for him while he was away sailing in Australia and America in January and February 2005. It was a very big decision for Jamie but he wanted to get onto the housing ladder, although one of the main reasons was the problems with his dad. There were constant arguments at home which affected both Jamie and Kate, who both told their mum to leave their dad.

I enjoyed working at Jamie's: it was much easier painting with no one there; I could leave the mess and go back home. While I was at Jamie's there was a lot of mail addressed to a Mr Joynson, which I opened, I found that every letter was demanding money. The house had not been purchased from this man so we had no knowledge of him. I was concerned that Jamie would get a bad credit rating if this continued so I answered each letter and told them all to stop harassing my grandson. I never told them Jamie's name.

I also informed each one that if I had to write to them again there would be a charge of £50 per letter. Most stopped but Barclays bank did not so I sent a second letter with an invoice for £50, a second letter arrived so I sent a letter direct to the Chief Executive at Barclays Bank with another invoice now for £100. This did the trick and I received a cheque for £100. I regularly use this method to get results every time.

We then started turning the garage into an en-suite double bedroom. Steve did the electrics and while he was working on them he said he was not going to leave Alison to go to New Zealand and could I convince her. I didn't really understand this and never said anything to Alison but told Gill about the conversation.

2004

This year was the start of Alison's move to find a career for herself. She enrolled at Birkenhead College for a hairdressing course, and she was the oldest of all the girls. Most of the others just spent the time messing about as they had no interest in the course they had been sent on.

It was also Kate's 21st birthday, by this time there was an uneasy atmosphere between Steve and me as well as one between his parents and the rest of us. I was not going to attend Kate's birthday so as not to create more tension, but Alison said that Steve's parents had not been invited by Kate so I decided to go; I had never wished to upset either Kate or Alison.

It was a very nice day: Jamie and Danielle cooked on the barbeque and we all sat outside in the garden. I was talking to Kate's friends who were asking why I was drinking water; I told them that I had not been drinking alcohol for 12 months. Steve, who was sat a few yards behind us stood up, came over and said, "I have not had a drink for 18 months".

We had not been talking to him and there was no need to get involved, especially to lie, because I knew that he had only managed to stop drinking for eight months at best when he was attending Alcoholics Anonymous. I surprised myself in that I said nothing and the day passed off very well. Kate I believe had a very good 21st birthday.

Jamie returned from sailing abroad to the news that Toll had not been able to find another sponsor, I also new that this was the end of his competitive sailing at the top level. Jamie was down in the dumps.

To help with the costs of attending college Alison took a part-time job as a waitress at Brimstage, for three days per week.

At the end of May Jamie asked if I would like to go with him to France and have a week at a motel we had stayed at in the past. It is at the foot of Mont Ventoux near Carpentras. We motored down in my car with Jamie's bike in the back. Gillian had printed in French a notice which I had in the rear window which said "Cyclist Escort keep clear".

Each day we went out, Jamie on his bike with me following behind. It was a super holiday, the weather was superb, the views stunning and we got on great together. On the second day Jamie decided to go up Mont Ventoux. I could not believe just how fit he was: I got tired just sitting in the car driving, but he just kept going. I would go ahead and take pictures as he passed by, never stopping.

It was a super time, I enjoyed being with Jamie, the weather was good and the accommodation was great. We had two rooms and a kitchen so we could cook or eat out. There was a small pool in the grounds of the motel as well as a café. Each day we went out and at night we talked and talked. Jamie was getting a lot of worry off his chest.

He was concerned about his future but agreed that he should put more hours in working for his dad; he needed to in order to pay off his mortgage and personal loans. While we were in France Jamie had a phone call asking how many days he was prepared to work for his dad and he said he would work seven days per week from now on. We both felt that things were looking up and did another trip up Mont Ventoux.

The day after we arrived back home Steve informed Jamie that he had better look for another job as he had sold the business and was leaving for New Zealand. Jamie was lost for words: I could not believe it, for it was only in February that Steve had asked me if I could convince Alison that he was not going to abandon her and go to New

Zealand. I had said nothing to Alison, the only person I told was Gill, yet four months later he was doing just that.

CHAPTER TWENTY

2005 - 2008 The Worst Time of My Life

In June 2005 Steve walked out on his family taking all the money from the business, leaving Alison and Kate with the house and £33,000 of debts but with no money other than the part-time work Alison had as a waitress.

Soon there were threatening letters arriving and banks and credit card companies sending bailiffs to the house. Alison was desperate. I wanted Alison to go and see a solicitor but Steve had said that she should not do so or even talk to me about it.

After much persuasion by Gill, Cath and Gillian we got Alison to let me help with the bank and seeing a solicitor.

I did three versions of her financial situation:

1 Where Steve paid off everything,

2 Steve paid nothing,

3 Steve left Alison with his police pension of £781 a month.

Even with the pension the current outgoings were £2200 per month so we had to drastically cut her spending. The bank manager was a friend of both Alison and Steve; he was appalled at Steve's actions and told us both that the business had been making good profits over the years, so Steve must have taken the money with him.

The solicitor told Alison that she was "too nice a lady" and must fight for what she was entitled to and file for a divorce.

I took on the job of fending off the bailiffs and credit companies as we all tried to comfort Alison, Kate and Jamie. I would have hurt Steve if I could have got my hands on him and I told him so.

In October Alison broke her toe while working at the café at Brimstage and could not work at all; Gill and I kept the finances going even when Alison managed to get accepted into college for a

Theatrical Make-up Course: we promised her that finance or lack of it would in no way stop Alison from doing the course, something that she had always wanted to do as long as I could remember.

Gill and I took Alison each day to Liverpool to the college off Seal Street, in the morning rush hour, returned home, then returned again at rush hour to bring her home, but it was worth it.

At the end of the course Alison was presented with a prize for Best Student. She was now qualified as a Professional Theatre Make-up Artist.

Create the Look

Alison formed her own business called "Create the Look" and registered the name. She started to get work locally and the highlight was applying for and getting the job with the BBC Production of Casualty 1906 but reluctantly she had to withdraw prior to starting as her health deteriorated.

The winter of 2005/06 was difficult for us all but things were to get much worse in June 2006. Alison had not been feeling well and had been in hospital a number of times due to difficulty with her breathing and she had to have her chest drained.

2006 Alison's Cancer

On 12th June Alison, Gill and I went to see the consultant, Mr Errington, who told Alison that she had terminal cancer. When Alison asked how long she had he said about 18 months. That was, up to then, the worst day of my life and yet there was an even worse one to come two days later. Jamie was having an interview for the police the following day; Alison decided not to tell Jamie and Kate or anyone else apart from Cath and Gillian.

On the 15th June 2006 Alison asked Jamie to come to her house in Escolme Drive, Kate was there along with Danni, Gillian, Gill and me. Alison, in a very calm manner told her children that she had terminal cancer with only about a year to live. I was so proud but upset as everyone in the room started to cry. Alison was the strongest of us all. I only hope that if ever I am in the same situation I will be able to be as strong, and calm as my daughter.

Alison said that she wanted to enjoy every minute of every day that she had left and instructed us all to help her to do so.

The house was up for sale, but although we reduced the price there were no buyers. The hospital arranged for Alison and the family to meet the staff at St John's Hospice, who proved to be the most important people who would help us all to get through the next year.

We immediately told Alison that money would be no object in anything she wished to do and gave her £1000 in cash and subsequently paid for many of the household bills. This enabled Alison to give Jamie and Kate the sort of birthday and Christmas presents she wanted to give but in the past could not afford to.

The first big problem for Alison was the fact that she had to stop driving immediately, which meant that Kate or Gill and I had to take Alison everywhere. Although we did not mind, Alison felt she was a burden which was understandable.

Kate took over the car and was able to use it for travelling to work at Ellesmere Port; we found it gave us an opportunity to be helpful, because there was nothing anyone could do medically.

In the summer Cath and Gillian took Alison to the Wirral Show in a wheelchair, it was a wonderful time and the pictures taken are invaluable.

Alison and Jamie have the same birthday, August 30th. Jamie decided that he wanted it to be very special and arranged to have all Alison's friends he could contact to come to his house in New Ferry. We did a montage of photographs of both of them from birth to this year and stuck them on a large sheet of wood which was placed on the wall at Jamie's house. The weather was great and the friends came from all over: it was a super day for everyone.

Taking Alison home in the car she said that she did not expect many people to be at her funeral, little did any of us know just how wrong that would be.

One of the hardest things to come to terms with was knowing that Alison was dying but not knowing when it would be. We always asked the doctors at the hospice but they told us that it was impossible to tell;

they did say that Alison would gradually get more tired and her body would gradually close down.

We all tried to keep optimistic, especially Alison who was determined to keep going as long as possible. With Catherine living in Skye we needed to know how fast she could get to our house so we planned for car and plane journeys.

Alison's breathing deteriorated and she had to go into Arrowe Park Hospital to have her chest drained. It was terrible seeing her in such discomfort, and she was terrified of needles.

St John's Hospice

Over the last year Alison was in and out of hospital as she deteriorated. At one time she was taken from Arrowe Park to the Hospice where she was given a room to herself because the doctors thought that she was going to die. She recovered and was able to go for "walks" in the wheelchair round the grounds.

Kate was with her mum every night straight from work, Gill and I were there every day and Jamie visited either during the day if he could, or at night. Cath came down from Skye and Gillian often visited after work.

One evening we were in the room with Alison when a nurse came in with a trolley full of bottles of spirits and wine. "Would you like a drink Alison?" he asked. "What about the tablets I am on?" asked Alison. "I don't think they matter now, do you?" he said. "I'll have a whiskey then," said Alison, and from then on she had a drink each day and enjoyed it.

Alison was moved to a bay with other patients which was not as good so we asked if she could come out to our house, which she did for a few hours each day. With Christmas approaching we were all hoping that Alison would be fit enough to have lunch with us at home.

Escolme Drive was still not selling although there was some interest being shown by a potential buyer. Alison wanted to purchase a house for herself and Kate and used to get the details sent to her from the Estate Agents. This worried Gill and I so we talked it over with the consultant who agreed that moving house was one of the most stressful things after divorce and death.

We began to try and convince Alison that she could move in with us in the bungalow which would enable her to leave the Hospice.

After a lot of discussion Alison agreed to move in with us when she was able to leave the Hospice.

The staff at St John's Hospice, from the consultants to the nurses and reception staff, were exceptional in every way. You have to experience the warmth, comfort and care that everyone gives freely in order to be able to believe such actions exist.

We had no idea that this is how a hospice works: we all, Alison especially, thought that you went into the hospice to die; instead they made living bearable and enjoyable.

All the family were treated, not only Alison, which was a tremendous help. I could not have managed without the help I was given by everyone at the hospice, especially Catherine Lewis Jones the consultant, who always saw each of us after she had seen Alison.

My problem was that for the first time in my life I could not solve Alison's problem: as her father I felt I had failed my daughter. It took a lot to get over this feeling, but eventually I managed to do so.

We wanted Alison to be home with all the family on Christmas Day if it was at all possible. Jamie, Kate, Gillian, Lisa, Leon, and Gill waited for me to bring Alison from the Hospice, so that eight of us sat down to dinner. Alison was tired but managed to stay until the afternoon when we had opened all the presents. Cath, who had to go to work back in Skye, telephoned Alison which completed the family reunion.

We took Alison back to the Hospice; the staff were all pleased that she had managed to cope with the excitement of the day.

Alison Moves in with us

We were now planning to move Alison into the "East Wing" as we called the double en-suite bedroom we had created from the garage conversion.

Over the Christmas period Kate and Jamie spent most of their time with Alison; she was never without someone from the family although so many friends such as Jade and Kelly from College, Judith Price, Evelyn, Adam and his family. Liz and her mum and dad, Cathy, Gabrielle, Sandy and John neighbours, Danielle and her mum, as well as Diane and Patrick.

We had Alison home for a full day on Saturday 6th January 2007. This was so successful that it was agreed that Alison could move to our house permanently, which she did on

Friday 12th January 2007.

The West Kirby Concourse District Nurses had been to see the room and arranged for a special hospital bed and other equipment to be supplied in order to help with her care. District nurses attended in pairs three times each day.

The number of tablets Alison had to take each day was unbelievable, 22 different tablets some four times per day resulted in a total of 44 tablets. (See appendix viii).

I had to print the doses and times on a spread sheet so that we gave the right medicine, just like the hospital nurses, rounds.

We soon got into a routine, it was superb having Alison home and far easier to look after her. Jamie had the idea of having a bell for his mum to call us if she wanted anything; we bought an electronic door bell which plugged into a socket in the house. All Alison had to do was press the button and the bells chimed in the house. It worked brilliantly and the district nurses passed on the system to many other patients who needed to call for assistance.

Alison was able to go out in her wheelchair. We went shopping to Sainsbury's and the local West Kirby shops, and we would walk up the promenade on good days.

One Sunday I suggested that she might like to visit the Sailing Club. Alison got dolled up and off we went. She was nervous of the reception she would get since she had ceased to be a member some years earlier due to the money situation. I booked Alison in as a non-member and we sat down with a drink each.

Everyone who came in said they were glad to see her, friends she had not seen for ages came over to chat, the Dransfields, Reynolds-Jones's, Toll, the Riley's, the Cheshire's and many others made it a day she would always remember.

Kate visited every day after work and used to get on the bed with her mum. Jamie came on a regular basis but his work made it more difficult for him, plus he lived 11 miles away. Gillian brought her bags of the little penny sweets they used to eat when they were children. The number of visitors to see Alison grew and grew, but it was what she wanted. We had to visit the hospital from time to time to see the consultant but we all knew that they could not cure Alison, but just keep her comfortable.

At least Alison had all her music and Sky TV with DVDs. Kate also had the task of clearing out Escolme Drive and all her mum's things and this she did every night after Alison had got down to sleep. Jamie also helped when he could but Kate had the difficult task of disposing of all that was home to her and her mum.

Eventually Kate was sleeping on the floor in her bedroom. Getting rid of all the things that could not be stored in other people's houses meant many trips to the tip; it was a very sad time for everyone but especially Kate.

The Final Week

On 6th February 2007 we had to visit the Oncology unit to see the consultant but he was not there, the Registrar was not at all helpful which made Alison more depressed.

Monday 12th February the following week, we saw Dr Errington the Consultant, who apologised for the previous week but then went on to give us all the bad news that Alison only had a few days to live. He apologised for letting Alison down but Alison replied "You have not let me down; you gave me an extra 13 years." We all began to cry.

That week we made sure that everything Alison wanted to do and wanted done for her was achieved. Cath came down from Skye, Lisa came home from Cambridge, and Kate was as usual here every day as were Jamie and Danni, Gillian and Leon.

Alison was getting weaker each day: a moving scene I will always remember was when Jamie picked up his mum in his arms and turned her on to her side to make her more comfortable as if she was a little doll. Jamie and Kate spent very many hours alone with Alison which she liked.

On the Thursday night I lay on the next bed to Alison and read her the story of my life that I had started writing two years ago. I had got as far as the birth of Catherine, 1957. She enjoyed the reading and made me promise to finish the story and print the book, which I will.

Friday 16th February Alison slipped into a coma from which she never recovered. There were two beds in her room and at all times day and night one of us was with her, taking it in turns to sleep by her side with another one sleeping in the lounge on the floor to be ready if needed. The rest went to bed as normal. Alison looked as if she was asleep but her breathing was getting difficult.

Alison Died Monday 19th February 2007 at 4.49am

I was in the next bed to Alison when Gill popped in to see if I was OK, at that point Alison stopped breathing. She was at peace at last.

We called Cath who was in bed in the back room, and Kate and Jamie and Gillian; we had all agreed to these arrangements days before.

They all came to see Alison who looked as beautiful and peaceful as I have ever seen her. We sent for the doctor at 8am and then the undertaker Quinns came to take Alison away. As they placed her in the vehicle Jamie said he hoped that they had put the seat belts on, as his mum would not be happy without. We all laughed for it was very true.

Jamie informed his dad later that day, when I believe he immediately stopped payment from his pension so that Kate had to find the last mortgage payments on Escolme Drive until it was sold.

The funeral was to be held at St John the Divine in Frankby; Alison had made all the arrangements when the vicar came to see us a few weeks earlier.

I was surprised that the vicar did agree to the type of service that Alison wanted: she had chosen all the songs and we would provide the CD or tape. The vicar asked if anyone wished to take part in the service by saying anything about Alison, and Kate and Jamie said they would like to do so. I said I would not be able to do it so the vicar said if I wrote it down he would read it for me.

Tuesday 27th February 2007 was the day of the funeral. We had to decide how many order of service booklets should be printed; Gill and I thought 50 would be enough, then Jamie and Kate said it should be 75 and we agreed. Jamie, his pal and I wanted to carry the coffin which was arranged.

When we arrived at the church I could not believe what I saw: the church was packed to the back, people standing as the pews were all full. I thought of the conversation Alison had with me last summer when she thought that there would only be a few family members present; there were over 190 people in that church.

People came from the college in Liverpool, the Hospice, Concourse staff attended, the sailing club (they flew the flag at half mast, even though she had ceased to be a member), friends from Greasby school, neighbours from Escolme Drive, many of my staff at Leisure Services who knew Alison, old school friends who now lived far away, all Jamie's friends, all Kate's friends, as well as relations on all sides.

It was unbelievable and wonderful, and Alison deserved it. It was fitting that the Smiths were at the other side of the world; she was free of them at last.

Before the start of the service the vicar, Ken Owen, said that this would be unlike any other funeral that anyone had seen: it was organised by Alison herself. The songs by Olivia Newton John, Whitney Houston and Elton John all meant a lot to Alison and the family.

Kate went to the front of the church and read out her tribute to her mum, her best friend. Jamie followed but was only able to get part way through his tribute so the vicar finished it for him. Then he read my tribute to my daughter Alison. The vicar by this time had to stop because he was crying himself.

(Appendix v, vi, vii)

The service then concluded at Landican. All the people attending were then invited to The Country Mouse at Brimstage for refreshments, the place Alison used to work as a waitress.

The numbers just kept arriving and the Country Mouse managed them all very well. The whole event was a success, stage-managed by Alison, and performed by her family. I will never forget that day, neither will all those who attended; it was a tribute to Alison which she deserved.

Soon the house in Escolme Drive was sold and Kate moved in with Jamie in New Ferry. We had to dispose of most of the furniture but at the time Kate could not bring herself to part with her mum's personal stuff, so we packed as much as we could to be stored at our house, Jamie's loft, next door's garage, Diane's and so on. Kate had the worst of it: she was working and coming home to an empty house to throw things away.

Kate had been using the car that Steve had "bought" for Alison when he left. When Alison was diagnosed with terminal cancer she could not drive. At the time Steve heard about Alison's death he also stopped paying for the car: he had not "bought" it at all, he had only put down the minimum deposit on it. Now the finance company wanted it back. Kate was so upset she could not pay for it as it was all in Steve's name.

The bailiffs came to repossess the car which I had arranged should be left at my house. I would not let them take it until they had paid Kate for the petrol she had put in the car, and after much argument with me threatening to charge them storage they finally gave Kate the cash in £20 notes.

Kate summed up how she felt when she cried and said, "I have lost my mum, my dad has gone, my home has gone, and now they have taken my car".

A month later in March 2007 I was suddenly taken ill in Tesco's with very bad stomach pain. I was taken to Arrowe Park Hospital where I was given every test possible and kept in for six days. They still did not know the cause when I was discharged so I had to have further scans over the next few months. I was finally given the all-clear in the summer, but they still did not know what had been the cause of the problem.

The week before Alison died I asked her where she would like to have her ashes scattered, and she said that she would like them to be scattered in the walled garden in Royden Park if it was possible. I promised Alison that we would do that even if we had to climb over the wall to do it: she laughed because she knew we would if we had to. One cold day in April Kate, Jamie, Gill and I took the casket to the walled garden and scattered the ashes among the flowers. All the family go back regularly to have a quiet word with Alison as if she is still with us, and it helps a lot.

Summer 2007 saw Kate carry out her mum's wish to go travelling again. She had four weeks in Sri Lanka at an elephant orphanage, and then she went to Canada, USA, and Hawaii with her friend Lynn. On her return we suggested to Kate that she move in with us at Madeley Drive as Jamie's house was getting crowded now that Danni had moved in.

In September Kate moved into the East Wing.

We had possessions stored all over the place. Jamie had a loft full, Diane Bentley had some, there was some in Gabrielle's garage, we had some in our garage, a hell of a lot in the loft, but it is all worth while.

Kate was intending to go to work in Australia for two years, but Rob, a chap she worked with at LMS, was going to Thailand in June 2008 which was a place Kate also wanted to visit, so she put back her departure until 3rd June 2008.

At this time Lisa was at Clare College, Cambridge 2005-2009, reading for a BA in Oriental Studies (Arabic and Russian). For part of her studies she lived in Syria, before the war began, and her mum Gillian and brother Leon visited her in Damascus.

CHAPTER TWENTY ONE

2008 - 2012 Grandchildren and Torch

2008

In May I started to get sore in my left groin as well as a red swelling: I was determined not to go back to hospital so I ignored it. The red swelling spread to my hip and got much worse. Gillian and Gill insisted that the doctor should be called out, and when he came he sent for an ambulance to take me back to Arrowe Park.

This time they operated to drain an abscess which had turned nasty. Once again I was in for eight days. I cannot remember having to spend so much time in hospital in all my previous 72 years, and on top of all this in November 2006 I had been diagnosed with glaucoma which meant regular trips again to Arrowe Park.

It was a good job that we had converted the garage since it gave Kate some space that she needed. June soon arrived and with Rob's parents we saw Kate and Rob off at Manchester airport. Due to the internet Kate could send all her photographs to Facebook and then we could download them onto my computer. Kate was having the time of her life which she needed to have.
We were back to normal again at home

Jamie's electrical business was doing well and he took the final necessary qualifications with a mark of 96%. He was so busy that he asked me to do his accounts for him which I said I would.

2009

I was now fully involved with helping Jamie and Danielle as well as Kate. I had internet control over Kate's cash and was able to make sure she had the right amount in the right account when she needed it while she was away travelling.

Jamie kept me busy with all the paperwork as well as ironing out the flow of cash for his business; I was the bank of Poppa.

I also "helped" with the re-wiring on jobs: I had the title of "Temporary, acting, part-time, apprentice electrician's assistant, unpaid"

Lisa was doing very well in Syria and Leon went on his travels to India much to our surprise and admiration. He kept in touch through e-mail and Facebook, which was great from our point of view.

Jamie rewired Cath's house which was a big job so we all helped including Leon who was the only person who could get under the floor joists. Jamie and Danni were engaged and planed to have the wedding in March the following year.

I was now getting more trouble with my hips which cut down my weekly walks considerably as well as my cycling. I went to see Dr George who said that I had arthritis and that I would have to have both my hips renewed at some time when the pain got worse. I thought that that was a long time in the future, but by the end of the year I had to see the orthopaedic surgeon who said that I needed two new hips.

In October Gill and I went for our flu jabs and we were both asked if we would be willing to attend a meeting to set up a Patients Participation Group (PPG). We did and I was voted Chairman of the group.

2010 Lisa and Leon

Lisa had finished her studies at Clare College, Cambridge where she achieved a BA Oriental Studies (Arabic and Russian). She was now working and living in London at the Ministry of Justice but then moved to a permanent job also in London with a firm doing business throughout the Middle East and Russia. (What a girl).

Leon had managed to get into Staffordshire University reading Computer Science, and was making a great job if it.

Weddings

Jamie and Danielle's wedding took place on 6th March at Inglewood Manor; it was a perfect day even though many of us were very apprehensive due to the fact that Steve, Jamie's dad was invited.

He kept out of the way so that I only saw him at the meal and the actual ceremony.

I had told both Jamie and Kate that if they could, and wanted to forgive their dad, they should do so but I, Gran, Cath and Gillian never would.

Kate brought her boyfriend Chris, an Australian, when she came for the wedding. They both stayed with us for three weeks. Chris is a very nice lad who thinks the world of Kate, which he proved when he took Kate to Paris and proposed to her there. We were all very pleased that they were engaged.

Chris's Gran died so Kate and Chris decided to return home for the funeral. We were not at all surprised to get a phone call from Kate saying that they were going to be married on 25th April and would we both attend. I could not travel due to my hips but I booked Gill a business class ticket for her to go and stay with Kate for a month as a stand-in mum which made Kate and Chris so pleased.

My hips were getting so that I could only walk a few hundred yards. Doctor Sudlow sent me to see Mr Carol who told me that he would renew both hips but one at a time with a three-month interval in between operations.

I had the first one done on 24th June and the second on 23rd September, both at Murrayfield Hospital.

Within a week I was walking to the shops: it was the best thing I did, having those operations.

2011

The work of the PPG was progressing all the time with the formation of an area body called the Patients Forum which again I was involved in and then made Chairman.

The work I was involved in through the PPG meant that I was now on the main NHS Committee for Wirral. I found myself attending meetings once or twice each week which meant that I did not have time to spend with my family, visit Cath in Skye, or Jamie in Manchester.

Lisa was doing very well, now doing a MA in Middle Eastern Studies at the University of Lund, Sweden and she went to Bahrain for six months as part of her studies – Mum Gillian went to visit her there.

Leon has fixed himself up with a job in Crawley for his work year then he finishes with a last year at Uni.

Cath went into hospital in Inverness to have a knee replaced, Gill stayed with her for six weeks until she could drive again. Cath is now able to walk again.

We heard about being able to donate your body to the University, so after discussing it with all the family both Gill and I have made all the arrangements to donate ours to Liverpool University Hospital

We will arrange our own funeral just like Alison did, but I doubt if it will be as good.

2012

Cath has at last sold her house on Skye after years of trying and at the same time bought a small bungalow on the main road at Broadford, just down the road. It all works out in the end.

I am able to sail again helping with the Wirral Disabled Marine Association which is great news for me; I have missed it a lot.

Paralympic Torch

This year turned out to be one of the most significant in my life. I was chosen to carry the Paralympic Torch for the London Games.

Gill and I were also invited to London to a reception at the Mansion House by the Lord Mayor of London, a former Olympian, along with 600 other Olympians. We had a great time meeting up with some of my Olympic colleagues from1952.

We stayed with my cousin, Jane Handley, at her house in Horsham, travelling in to London by tube.

Returning from the Mansion House we were sitting in a full carriage when a man noticed my Olympic tie. "Is that an Olympic tie?" he asked. When I told him it was he asked if he could have his photograph taken with me: his friend took the picture and then others in the carriage joined in asking about my event in Helsinki. The rest of the journey revolved around the London Games with me having my photo taken many times over.

Normally in London no one speaks to anyone but the Games changed all that.

The Paralympics were sponsored by Sainsbury's; I was asked to go to the local store to have promotional photos taken. What a thrill it was to hold the Torch.

We were all given a special uniform and allowed to keep our own Torch, Sainsbury's arranged transport to London for Gill and I along with four others from the area, and they put us up at the Holiday Inn. When I told Cath she immediately said she wanted to attend the event and I arranged for her to stay at the same hotel as us.

The Torch relay was to go from Stoke Mandeville Hospital, the birthplace of the Games, to the Stadium non-stop overnight, in teams of five.

The team I was in had to be at Lords Cricket ground at 5.15am to take over from the English Ladies Blind Cricket Team.

A coach collected us with our families to take us to Lords; there was a delay due to the crowds of people who came out to cheer the torchbearers throughout the night.

We had breakfast in the new pavilion then went out to meet the Ladies Team.

The Metropolitan Police, who were in charge of all the arrangements, were superb in every way; they turned on the gas cylinder for each Torch in order to light the flame from the other Torch then turned off that Torch.

As I was the fittest one in our group I carried the Torch the longest distance, which I was very pleased to do. It was a marvellous feeling with crowds of people cheering, clapping and taking photographs all along the way. I will never forget that feeling.

I handed the Torch to the next group, who were made up of members of the International Paralympic Committee; we were then taken back to our hotel, then back home by coach holding the Torch all the way.

Prior to the relay I met the members of the International Paralympic Organising Team. We were all asked to introduce ourselves. When I said that I had worked with Sir Ludwig Guttman and was the first Chairman of the British Sports Association for the Disabled they could not believe it.

Even though things have progressed so much since then they said it was like listening to the history of their movement.

Because of how I felt every time I held the Torch I decided to let as many other people as possible share the same great feeling.

The first visit I made was to St John's Hospice, where Alison had been looked after, and Claire House, the children's hospice. The patients and staff all had photos taken with the Torch, it was so worthwhile for me as well as them.

I took the Torch to the Disabled Sailing Club (WDMA), the club that I had started in 1982, where the disabled sailors sailed round the lake holding the Torch; it was difficult to get it back from them. Then we allowed anyone passing on the Promenade to have their photo taken with the Torch for a small donation to the club.

Ron, a member of WDMA asked if I would be willing to take the Torch to a bedridden lady who turned out to be a former member of my Library staff.

I will always remember seeing her face as we showed her the Torch and let her have her picture taken with it, even though she was in bed.

This visit gave me the idea of taking the Torch to anyone who wished to see it; I got the names and addresses of all the nursing and residential homes in the area and asked them if they would like me to visit their residents with the Torch. Eventually I called on every one of them; it was just as effective for me as it was for them, a real spirit lifter.

I also took the Torch to Barrow-in-Furness where my "Aunty" Joyce lives in a nursing home. She had her picture with two other residents over 100 years old which made the local newspaper.

I did this on my way to see Cath in Broadford on the Isle of Skye; again we visited the local hospital and residential home. The nearest Hospice is in Inverness so we went over to the east coast; it was one of the most moving visits that I have made. They were so pleased to think that we would go out of our way for them; they all joined in, staff and patients, and they even baked me a cake. But the most memorable visit with the Torch was to the village school at Elgol where Cath's very good friend Lorna worked. All the children at the school, all 22 of them, had studied the history of the Paralympics and took it in turn to run round the playground with the Torch in their own relay.

It was also the year that I did something for the first time in my life; I stood down from all my commitments with the NHS, except for my involvement with the new Health Centre Building project. I decided to put my family first.

Mia, Alison Uusimaki 6th July 2012

But the most important event was the birth of our first great-granddaughter, Mia Alison Uusimaki, a beautiful little girl. Kate had a difficult time but it was all worth it for both Kate and Chris.

Friends

Where I live there are a number of very good neighbours who keep in touch with each other, all are over 80 years and some over 90 years. We had our photo taken with the Torch and a few drinks to celebrate, prior to opening the garden to everyone in the area to do the same.

These very good friends tell me that I am just a child, not yet being 80 years old. They keep me young trying to catch them up: Dorothy, Joyce, Kath, Lynne, Harold, and Phil, then Arthur, Rose and John a generation down. Also our previous neighbours in York Avenue, Diane and Patrick, as well as Peter and Pat Finney. To you all thanks for your friendship, it makes life a pleasure.

2013

I formally stood down at the PPG annual general meeting, but as I said I continued with the planning of the new Health Centre. The plans were finally passed by Wirral Borough Council after some objections.

Gill received an invitation from Kate and Chris to spend Mia's first birthday with them, Gill was so thrilled. She had a month in Perth and was able to get to know Mia and Mia to know her Great-Grandma.

Gill was experiencing a lot of pain in her right knee, the original one. Mr Parkinson who had replaced her left knee said it had to be replaced because it would only get worse. Gill was given a date in September but at the last minute it was cancelled and put back to 24th October.

While Gill was in Perth, Leon had his graduation at Stafford University. He achieved a First Class Honours Degree in Computer Science. Gillian, Alan, Lisa and I attended. I was so proud to see my youngest Grandson receive his deserved reward.

I now had plenty of time to finish my book, every day I would sit at the computer and remember the journey through the Pacific home. It is taking longer than I anticipated but it would appear to be looking all right.

I met with Jeane Emerson, a publisher in Birkenhead who will help me with the final editing and presentation.

CHAPTER TWENTY TWO

Still Looking Forward

The Final Chapter

I have decided to start this chapter in 2006 because I will never know when it is due. I will update it at regular intervals depending on how long I have from now.

Already there are disappointments: family members wanted me to start this and as of now no one has read it and given me feedback. It could be because it is unreadable or just plain boring. I will continue at present and see how I feel later.

The one thing I must stress over and over again is Gill's input into my life. I cannot imagine life without her; I know I would not have done or achieved any of the things I have if she had not been my inspiration, guide, trouble shooter, listener, therapist, wife and mother of my girls. I did not deserve her, she deserved better.

Then there are my girls, no dad could ask for better loving children than Alison, Catherine and Gillian. We have had some very wonderful times together, and still do. As a family we are "The Best."

From them came my grandchildren, Jamie, Kate, Lisa and Leon. They all take after their mums, they have given me so much love and pleasure and this is growing as they get older.

I do listen to what they say because most of the time they are right and I am out of touch, I feel and hope that they will always say what they think and not what they think others may want to hear from them.

At the time of writing this page I have one great-granddaughter, Mia. I have only seen her on video but she looks and acts like her mum. I hope that when she is older she will read this because I do not think that I will ever see her in person, but this does not stop me from loving her.

Mentally not much has changed over the years, and as I remember things it seems like yesterday. Physically though I feel old, and remembering does not help; to think of how fit I was makes me into an old man, which I am.

Yet I don't think of myself as an old man. When my mum and Pop and Gran were my age I was looking after them, yet now I am still looking after my own family. So perhaps I am not such an old fart as I am made out to be.

Looking back I have very few, if any, regrets. I have done all the things that I have ever wanted to do, there are no achievements left to do.

I wish I could have made a better job of my marriage. Somewhere along the line I let things go down the wrong road, but I don't know where. I know when it was, it was in the late seventies early eighties that things changed and never got back on track. If it is anyone's fault it is mine, for once my planning let me down. I would give anything to be able to put this right but it will never be.

Looking back there are so many changes in the world, most for the better. There are of course problems. I have tried to summarise the problems to see how they came about, I believe that most if not all, stem from a lack of respect leading to a lack of discipline which in turn affects law and order.

I am the first to point out that it was my generation that let this happen. We stopped corporal punishment, capital punishment and allowed children and young people to commit crimes without an effective sanction.

Park keepers, bus conductors, teachers, even parents, are not allowed to administer a slap at the time of the incident, so that now they get away with it or go to court and get a criminal record. I would have been punished on the spot, which was far more effective and I speak from personal experience.

I was taught at school that justice involves punishing the guilty as well rewarding the innocent, and as I write this the morning paper lists a number of convicted murderers who have committed a further murder while out on bail.

All through my life I have learnt that no one likes to be physically hurt. At school, national service, teaching swimming, policing, managing public events, in all these I have been prepared to apply this rule and it has always worked.

It is about time the Government did the same.

There are lessons to be learned, some of which I have picked up from others, but I only use those that I have proved to myself to be true.

- If you love someone tell them over and over again.
- If you want something bad enough and work at it hard enough, you can achieve it.
- Always be strong and courageous enough to say sorry. (but the word it is not always enough).
- Be nice to people on the way up for you will meet them again on the way down.
- If you want to do something go ahead and do it. You never know how much time is left.
- Don't put off until tomorrow what you can do today, for if you enjoy it you can do it again tomorrow.
- Religion has been the cause of all the wars and troubles in my lifetime.
- Religion is OK if it is kept to individuals and they keep it to themselves.
- Unless you want to, do not believe in any God or Religion. It is just not true.

I am only now realising just what my mum meant when she said getting old was not very nice. At 79 years I am finding that people, the system and almost anyone you speak to, automatically assume that you are not as intelligent as you once were.

I never felt this years ago especially when I was working. I commanded respect and got it; people asked for and listened to my advice, but not now.

I realise that some things are now out of date compared with 12 years ago but not as much as others think.

It is sad because everyone hopes that they will grow old, but they are in for a shock when they do.

It is said that you can't put old heads on young shoulders but if you could for even just a day, attitudes would surely change for the better.

The media is one of the worst offenders: newspapers, TV, and Radio all go on about there being too many retired people in the country, forgetting that they all worked and paid taxes from the age of 14 years and some 12 years.

The income tax that I pay on my pension is equal to the OAP pension that I get from the state so I am not costing the country anything.

But the one thing that upsets me most is the fact that the state will not allow me to die when I chose to do so, even though they keep on telling me that I am past my sell-by date and a drain on the country.

I have informed all my family that I do not intend to live until I am sat in a chair in an old people's home, and I shall decide when and how I die.

I am not morbid about this. I will make all the plans, as I have always done since I was very small, on my own. I shall plan the last sentence of my book.

It is also harder than I thought it would be to stand back and let the younger members of my family take over the reins. I know I should do so but it is not at all easy.

The girls are all capable of taking over; even Kate and Lisa are now looking after me instead of the other way round. Jamie and Leon are now self-sufficient in everything and giving me advice which I want to take and do, although it still feels strange.

I do not want to get to the stage like my mum and then Pop where I have to sit in a chair all day in a home with other old people. I will not allow that to happen, but I have not yet figured out how to do it. I have been in touch with Dignitas the Swiss organisation which helps people to die.

It is strange that because I think like this and talk about the end of my life, people, especially those who should know better, like doctors, automatically assume that you are depressed. I am not. I like to be able to plan my life and my death: it is my life and it should be my death.

When I look back on my life I am pleased with the way it has gone: I have never had a job that I did not enjoy doing from the first to the last. Not many people I know can say that. I have achieved all that I have wanted to achieve except that I should have made a better job of being a husband.

Gill has been my life, my reason for living and everything I could wish for. Without Gill I would be nothing.

Even so I would not like to be starting out now, in the 21st century. Jamie and Kate, Lisa and Leon, have a far harder time than we had when we were their age, and it is getting worse not better. But perhaps that's what Pop and Gran thought about us in the 1950s.

Life is worth living when you have a wife, children, grandchildren, great-grandchildren and good friends.

Thank you all for making my life perfect, I would not change any part of it.

Brian Barnes

TO BE CONTINUED …

GILL'S (GEESS) CONTRIBUTION

From GILL the Wife of Brian

fter injuring my leg in 1950 doing high jump at school I gave up my favourite games and started to swim.

I joined the swimming club in 1951 and eventually got into the team swimming back crawl. As Brian and I lived near each other he used to see me home, we only had bicycles in those days.

We got married in 1955 and our three daughters, Alison, Catherine and Gillian came along just as we wanted.

Brian's work changed from policeman to schools swimming instructor and he studied hard to work in Baths Management.

By the time Gillian was 3 weeks old Brian had his new job in Leek, Staffordshire and our "wandering" life began. (This is where you should read Gillian's Typhoo Gypsy.

Our first move to Leek was quite an adventure and hard work with 3 little ones, my dad was recovering from a major operation, but my mum was able to help.

After a year we moved regularly for Brian to climb the ladder work wise. It was never boring and always had an air of excitement.

Sometimes I had not seen the house we were going to and my chest full of curtains were put up wherever they fitted. No removal expenses in those days.

The girls settled into various schools as we went along and when we eventually got to Hoylake they loved the house because they each had their own bedroom, a luxury after some of the houses.

I taught swimming along the way but I worked for Sefton Education Authority for eleven years teaching school classes.

I never found the moves a chore it was exciting. In fact I got quite good at packing and labelling and only unpacked the boxes really required at each move.

We are proud of our girls, they adapted well as we moved around. I am also very proud of Brian; he planned, worked, and looked after us wherever we moved to. He is truly a hands on dad.

When we lost Alison it was very hard but we had two daughters Catherine and Gillian and four grandchildren, Jamie, Kate, Lisa and Leon, plus Danielle now Jamie's wife to fill the very large gap.

Brian's sail round the world was a wonderful experience and I went to meet him where I chose to visit. He did a great job when you think he couldn't sail at all in 1975.

We are settled in our in West Kirby bungalow, again planning by Brian (with me helping of course) and life is good.

Our daughters and grandchildren still give us lots of pleasure and we are proud of them all. Kate and Chris married and produced Mia, a great granddaughter, a long way away in Australia but I have visited and she is lovely.

So far I or should I say WE have worked hard and in spite of some sad times we have a great life, hopefully with more to come.

Thank you Brian and all our family for a good interesting life.

CATHERINE'S CONTRIBUTION

'My Father My Hero' – they were the words I saw on a fathers' day card earlier this year. I bought the card and sent it to the man who has always been there for me and all my family.

I have so many wonderful memories of a man who has been the head of the family since the beginning, and still is. I am very proud of all his achievements, not least the way he has studied and worked to be able to provide a better life for us all. I clearly remember the moves we made to a new town every couple of years each time he was appointed to a better job. I remember being excited to see our new home and surroundings, especially when we moved to the Wirral in 1967. It was a time of the Beatles and Ferry Across the Mersey, and living by the seaside for the first time.

I had a wonderful childhood with days out in Southport and London; Christmases spent with grandparents in Preston and summer holidays in Bude, Cornwall. We built sandcastles with moats for the incoming tide to fill and surfed on a home made surfboard. We didn't need much money as we had a loving and happy family life. It is only as I became an adult that I began to realise just how hard my parents worked to provide for us.

I know I was a difficult teen and moving out at just 17 years old caused arguments and heartache. Dad was the one who gave me a lift the bed-sit I was to share with a friend. He was the one who asked me if I wanted to come back home when he could see my marriage was in difficulty and he was the one who drove up to Skye and gave me his precious caravan to live in, even though he could see I was close to a breakdown.

I was so proud to fly out to Tonga to meet him on his circumnavigation and was only too pleased to cook one of 'my curries' for him in the tropical heat of Fiji. Being with him on the boat for the last leg from Crete to Majorca was incredibly special. Just the two of us and the dolphins that joined the bow wave at dawn each morning. I remember when we crossed the finish line wishing we had some champagne to celebrate with. In the end we settled for a warming cup of tea. It was hard to believe just what he had achieved.

Seeing him carry the Commonwealth Games torch was just the precursor for watching him carry the torch for the Paralympics in 2012. It was only the night before that he told me the full story of his involvement with the development of the Games from the beginning. It's not often I am stunned into silence! I remember elbowing people out of the way to get a photo, shouting 'that's my Dad!'

The Real Life of Brian Barnes is just that – the real but extraordinary life of a man who was determined to make a better life for all his family and one who did it like no other. A few may not agree but I know that the world is a better place for him being in it and that he has touched so many peoples' lives in a positive way. Thanks Dad.

GILLIAN'S CONTRIBUTION

The Typhoo Gypsy

1959

(So I'm told)

The sun was shining on Lauderdale Road
And the tea-chests all were packed.
The removal van was ready to go,
But what was it the Barnes's lacked?

Alison had Rupert on stand-by,
For the adventure they knew was in store.
Cath was crawling in innocence, and Brian was pacing the floor.

The focus of all this activity
was Gill getting bigger and hotter. Then the 19th June produced a result:
two weeks late, but a big bouncing daughter.

No. 3 had three weeks to get used to the world,
Then her wandering childhood began,
Her carrycot landed in Leek for a while.
But soon the tea chests were back in the van.

They nearly forgot her the day that they moved,
left behind in her pram unaware.
But the next stop was Leicester, then Leicester again,
There were Baths to be Managed out there!

1962

(Now I remember)

My world was Wombwell where the washing came in black.
New concrete on the kitchen floor, steps and gooseberries at the back

Ice-cream vans and "Kayligh" (?), winters in the snow.
My photo in Dad's wellies: Carol friend and foe.

Learn to swim on Saturdays: dances in the hall.
Grandpa performing on roller skates: Mum hurt her wrist in a fall.

Norman and Shirley, Robin and Gail, lemon-cheese sandwich for tea.
Cherry cake, hotpot, Mum always around, and Dad walking home I still see.

1964

(The little blue scooter arrived safely)

"Don't you have tea-chests" I said to my friend,
"They're where you find all the things you once had"
Moving was normal, we never unpacked:
Baths were waiting to be bossed by my dad.

Eastcote was sunny, the pavements were smooth,
A roller skate heaven I'd found.
A jungle of garden was quickly transformed
With a car tyre for hanging around (who needs a climbing frame anyway)

Julie and Pat, chicken pox, Doctor Who,
Steve and Mo and a big trampoline.
Riding a bike (ouch!) and learning to skip (not quite)
But on roller skates I was the Queen!

Dad with his cine, and Alison's Kodak
Recorded my first days at school,
I soon learnt 3Rs with my slate and my chalk
But my accent was really uncool.
Summers in Cornwall and Christmas in Preston,

Lewis and Eileen, the dogs, Catherine Tann.
But our life in the south had come to an end:
It was "tea chests" and "follow that van"! (isn't there a song about that)

_1967_

(The roller skates arrived safely but one later suffered a terrible fate under Dad's car)

Home no.7, me not yet eight years old,
By the seaside, a real dream come true.
The accent amended, I soon fitted in,
Lots of friends and a room with a view. (top of the slide at Hoylake Baths)

Here Dad really excelled in the Baths that he Bossed,
Managed parks and sports centres too.
We went sledging in winter, in the road before school,
and our house had a neat outside loo! (Complete with spiders)

I played my guitar and Mum's violin
while Alison dreamed of the "stars",
Cath had a coat that crawled round the hall,
And we sure had a mixture of cars!
(five in a mini to Cornwall, just a bit too much)
Christmas was fun with a house full of Crinklies,
Auntie Dorothy on the home-brew.
Johnnie Ocko's cheese toasties, I'll never forget
And queuing all night for the loo!

A midnight swim in the phosphorous with Scott's of all sizes,
Bertie Jones and his bottle of wine.
Gran dancing "Charleston" and me in that cozzy:
Why grow up? We were doing just fine.

Then the Frenchmen arrived and my life soon changed course,
a linguist I just had to be.
Thanks for the chance, Dad, to meet them and travel:
I wonder why there's this gypsy in me?

1976

(guitar and dictionaries delivered intact)

I didn't see the tea chests, you moved while I was in Spain,
Which left me feeling cheated but I suppose I can bear the pain?
Two out of three had moved away so the mansion had to go.
No more 16ft Christmas trees in the West Kirby bungalow.
(though we did manage some rather wide ones)

1981 & 1984

(my own set of tea chests made their was to Moreton then , back to West Kirby between houses)

The bungalow seemed very small,
Like a much loved garment outgrown,
Thanks for putting us up, Mum and Dad,
But your littlest the nest now has flown.

The Crinklies for Christmas got fewer,
But new faces soon came through the door.
Paddling pools in the garden, tiny washing and prams.
You were telling your stories once more.

2000?

Now you no longer shout "Girls, fall-in in threes"
And your grandkids are bigger than me.
You moved to a Tardis to stop us returning,
but you can bet we'll be back for our tea

Now I'm settled in Greasby with a Minx and a Boof,
And Alan who just spoils me rotten.
Thanks for the childhood of smiles, tears and wonder
And the tea chests which won't be forgotten.

So that's my little offering for your book Dad. I wrote it a good while ago and could maybe add a few more verses now. Reading through your book I can see quite a few connections between my early life and where I am now:

-Moving house around the country was an excellent opportunity to learn to copy accents, which I think helped me to learn languages. Being exposed to a house full of foreigners and being offered free holidays also helped!

-The camper van that I sometimes park on your path is your fault: when I was little you told me 'tales of the Dormobile' which you sold before I was old enough to remember it, so I had to try it for myself.

-Some of the best memories are family holidays, and we have had plenty of good ones. They don't have to be expensive or exotic and this tradition has been carried on.

-I firmly believe every child should be given the opportunity to ride a bike. We never had new ones but we had a lot of fun and freedom with them. I think I am now in my second childhood as I park my bike in your hall again. Roller skates were good too, but I'll pass on that for now......

have now finished trying to proof-read your book (remaining errors now my fault), and Alison ('Bossy Boots') will be proud of you for writing it all down. Maybe we will be of historical importance some day, like fossils????

APPENDIX I

People

Dorman Road

Hall No.5 Dorman Road. Mr. Hall was a French Polisher, Mrs. Hall used to look after me when I was young. They had two boys Bobby and Billy who were both younger than me but I used to play with them. Billy ran out of our garden and was knocked down by a corporation bus and broke his arm. The buses that used to go down the road were re-routed after the accident.

Walton No.6, next door. Mrs. Walton was very old, she had two grown up sons, Sydney, who was disabled and was not called up and Joe who was in the army but used to run away. He was caught by the Red Caps (army police) and taken back but he kept going AWOL. (Absent without leave). They were all very strange.

Robinson No.4, Mr. Robinson was a sailor at sea and was killed in the war. Mrs. Robinson did not work but always had a lot of men visiting the house, called "Uncles." There were three girls and one boy. **Freda** the oldest, **Marie** a year older than me, **Anne** younger than me and then **Graham** the youngest. The house was dirty all the time; they used to keep chickens in the cupboards and in the large drawers next to the fireplace. My mum did not like me to go round to their house but I played there a lot and had lots of fun. It was Marie who taught me how to cook because she did cookery at school.

Shaw No. 1 Mr. Shaw worked at the GPO. They had two children **Eric** and **Marian**, both were older than me, but we played together.

Roberts No. 10 next door, **Alf** was in electronics at the Post Office Telephones. His wife was a good friend of my mother's and used to go to the river with us. They did not have any children.

Taylor Later moved in here. Mr. Taylor was a toolmaker; Mrs. Taylor was not up to much. She sat in the house all day in front of the fire. They had two boys **Robert** the eldest and **Stan** who was seven years older than me. Stan used to go to Blackburn on a Wednesday and buy an old car at auction, such as a Ford 8 for £5. He would bring it home and get us to help him clean the wire spokes on the wheels, then he would take it to the Blackpool auction and sell it for £7-£10. He made himself a lot of money when he went to India soon after the war.

Swain No. 12, **Alf** was a male nurse at Whittingham Mental Hospital, a large man. They had 2 boys **Roy** the eldest and **Frank** both older than me but I used to play with Frank.

Mitchell No. 9, Mr. Mitchell was an insurance agent and the first person on the estate to get a car after the war

Wilmot Road

Rosebottom No. 1, Mr. Rosebottom was a worker for the Saint Mary Magdalene Church. Two boys **Bobby** older than me and **Billy** younger than me, we all played together. Billy and I played a lot of football in the street.

Tatford No.3, a boy and a girl both older than me **Frank** and **Doreen**

Leyland No.2 Mr. Dick Leyland drove the council cleansing truck and his wife worked in a shop. Two lads both a lot older than me, **Bob** a pilot in the RAF was killed in the war and **Dick** was convicted of murdering his wife when he found her in bed with a man. He was let out after many petitions from neighbours and friends.

Derry Road

Price No.1, Mr. Price was a Police Constable who used to catch us by the ear and take us home for playing football in the street. Two boys **Clifford** who was older than me and **Derek** who was younger. Derek and I went to Butlins Skegness, together.

Brown No. 7, Mr. Brown was a postman. Two boys **Percy** a lot older than me and **Jackie** my best friend at school for a long time. He played in my football team and was always round at our house. Jackie went to play football for Plymouth Argyle FC as a professional footballer.

Hatfield Road

Eccles Ian was at school with me and very clever, and a good runner.

Cowley Road

Sergeant Terry Was a good pal at school. But nobody who did not live in this road went there. If you did there would be a fight. Even when I was a policeman it was not an area I liked to go to.

Ribbleton Avenue

Yates Michael Was at school with me. He wore glasses and was a thin frail lad. His dad had a large Austin car garage and dealership in Fishergate, Preston near the railway station. They had a large house and had a lot of money compared with the rest of us. I used to go and play at their house. Michael always had the best toys and even a new bike.

Greenlands Crescent

Brewer Keith A year older than me, he had red hair and he used to chase me. My mum used to say that if I did not eat my dinner Keith Brewer would come and get it.

APPENDIX II

Stratagem Costs

No.	Item	Cost	Paid By	B.J.B.	T.T.	Others
1	Entry Fee to Rally - Boat & Capt.	7500	B.J.B.	7500		
2	Entry Fee to Rally - 1st. Crew.	500	T.T.		500	
3	Entry Fee - Subsequent crew	500	Shared	by all	four	Per week
4	Preparation of Boat for world cruise	15000	B.J.B.	15000		
5	New Sails	1800	B.J.B.	1800		
6	Courtesy Flags	300	B.J.B.	300		
7	Charts & Pilot Books	1000	B.J.B.	1000		
8	Lower shroud	100	B.J.B.	100		
9	2 Hatches	600	B.J.B.	600		
10	Repair to rigging - Jeddah	666	B.J.B.	666		
11	New Roller Reefing and Rigging	3000	B.J.B.	3000		
12	New engine	4000	B.J.B.	4000		
13	New Autohelm	375	B.J.B.	375		
14	Engine spares	600	B.J.B.	600		
15	Osmosis Preventative Treatment	2500	B.J.B.	2500		
16	Leaking Stern Glands & lift outs (5)	1700	B.J.B.	1700		
17	New Bilge Pump	100	B.J.B.	100		
18	New GPS	300	B.J.B.	300		
19	Hydrovane Rudder Replacement	110	B.J.B.	110		
20	New Dinghy	800	B.J.B.	800		
	TOTALS	41451		40451	500	500

APPENDIX III

Chart Lists

Pack A			**Number**
GIBRALTA TO CANARIES			
	Chart No.	***Name***	
1	1448	Gibraltar Bay	
2	144	Gibraltar	
3	142	Strait of Gibraltar	
4	773	Strait of Gib. to Adra	
5	92	Cabo de St. Vincent to Strait of Gib.	
6	4104	Lisbon to Freetown	
7	1228	Cabo St. Vincent to Gap Ghir	
8	3133	Casablanca to Canaries (including Madiera)	
9	1229	Cap Ghir to Bajador	
10	3132	Strait of Gib. To Madiera	
11	1831	Madiera	
12	1870	Lanzarote to Gran Canaria	
13	1858	Santa Cruz de la Palma & Santa Cruz de Tenerife	
14	1856	Plans of Canaries	
15	1869		15
CANARIES TO ANTGUA			
16	5124	Routing chart North Atlantic Ocean	
17	4102	North Atlantic Ocean Southern Part	
18	4402	Caribbean Sea	
19	2064	Antigua	
20	2065	Northern Antigua	5
Pack B			
ANTIGUA TO PANAMA			
1	1480	Tobago to Tortuga	
2	B5	Martinique to Granada, Tobago & Barbados	
3	A281	Leeward Isles – Anchorages in Guadaloupe	

4	A4	Guadaloupe – St Lucia	
5	B30	St Vincent – Mustique	
6	955	Sombrero – Dominique	
7	762	West Indies & Carabbean Isles	
8	A30	Martinique	
9	494	Plans in Martinique	
10	2600	Dominica up to Mona Passage	
11	A28	Leeward Islands – Guadaloupe	
12	A3	Anguilla – Dominica	
13	B31	Bequia – Cariagou	
14	B30	Granada	
15	B1	St Lucia	
16	D14	Islands of Venezuela	
17	D12	Venezuela	
18	D22	Los Roques	
19	1412	Plans of ABC Islands	
20	D232	Curacao	
21	D231	Bonair & Aruba	
22	1966	Tortuga to Cabo la Vela	
23	2417	Harbours on N Coast of Central America	
24	26065	Approach to San Blas	
25	26061	San Blas	
26	26063	San Blas	
27	396	Barranquilla to Mesquito Bank - Columbia & Panama	
28	1300	Approaches to Panama canal	
29	3111	Colon & Chrystabol	
30	1299	Panama Canal	30

PANAMA TO GALAPAGOS

31	1929	Gulf of Panama	
32	3318	Punta da la Santa Helena – Golfo Dulce	
33	21606	Los Perlas	
34	4811	Mexico to Ecuador	
34	2257	Gulf de Guayaquil to Bahia	
36	2799	Ports on coast of Columbia & Ecuador	
37	1375	Galapagos	7

Pack C
GALAPAGOS TO MARQUESAS

1		Atlas of charts to South Pacific	
2	4618	Galapagos to Marquesas	
3	4619	Galapagos to Marquesas	
4	1640	Plans of Marquesas	
5	3931	Nuka Hiva	
6	5989	Marquesas	
7	5990	"	
8	5988	"	
9	5991	"	
10	3997	"	10

MARQUESAS TO TAHITI

11	6597	Marquesas to Tahiti	
12	4061	South Pacific Western Part	
13	4607	South East Polynesia	
14	6689	Tuamotos	
15	1382	Approaches to Tahiti	
16	1436	Plans of Tahiti	
17		Various photos of charts of Society Islands	
18	1060	Huahini to Maupatu	8

Pack D
TAHITI TO TONGA via Cook Islands

1	1174	Nive (Cook Islands)	
2	1264	Cook Islands	
3		Various photos of charts of Vanuatu	
4	2366	Approaches to Nuku Alofa	
5	1421	Tonga	
6	3097	Tonga Anchorages	
7	3099	Tonga – Haapar Group	
9	3100	Haapai - Group	
10	473	Tonga - Lefuka	
11	1385	Tonga Anchorages	
12	474	Tonga - Nomuka	
13	8259	Tonga – Nomuka	13

TONGA TO FIJI

14	845	Fiji	
15	1670	Plans of Fiji Viti Leiri	
16	1829	Fiji Islands to Samoa Islands	
17	4605	New Zealand to Fiji showing Tonga to Fiji	
18	745	Kadavu to Suva	
19	441	Fiji Islands	
20	440	Fiji Islands	
21	1244	Fiji – Levuka	
22	905	Fiji – Suva to Levuka	
22a	746	Navula Passage to Beqa	
23	1682	Fiji – Beqa Passage	
24	381	Fiji – Blighwater	
25	845	Fiji – Kamadra Passage	
26	F5	Fiji – Lautoka	
27	1670	Fiji – Lautoka Harbour	
28	1660	Fiji – Suva Harbour	
29	1670	Fiji - Musket Cove	
30		Various Photos of charts of Yasawa Islands	
31	1673	Approaches to Suva Harbour	32

Pack E
FIJI TO AUSTRALIA (Including passage to Darwin)

1	4060	South Pacific Fiji, Australia & Indonesia (2 charts)	
2	780	Pacific Ocean – Eastern Australia	
3	4602	Pacific Ocean – Tasman & Coral Seas	
4	4604	Coral & Soloman Seas and adjacent seas	
5	2907	New Caledonia	
6	6687	New Caledonia	
7	3033	New Caledonia	
8		New Caledonia	8

QEENSLAND

9	820	Queensland
10	1024	Fraser Island to Cumberland

11	74230	Magnetic Island to Whitsunday Island	
12	74210	North Reef to Pine Peak Island	
13	74220	Percy Island to Whitsunday Passage	
14	819	Bustard Head to North Reef	
15	375	Cape Sidmouth to Cape York	
16	374	Bathurst Bay & Nawick Group	
17	262	Approaches to Cairns	
18	427	Cunberland Islands to Cooktown	
19	830	East Coast 16° 25 – 17° 15	
20	74293	NE Corner 9 ° 50 – 11° 20	
21	74340	East Cost 17° 40 – 19° 20	
22	373	Frankland Island to Lizard Island 14° 30 – 17°	
23	374	Part 13° x 13° 50	15

TORRES STRAIT

24	73552	Arden Island to Bramble Cay	
25	377	Bligh Entrance to Eastern Fields	
26	292	Dolphins Channel to Prince of Wales Channel	
27	74295	Prince of Wales Channel	
28	299	Part – Thursday Island	
29	376	Torres Strait	6

NORTHERN TERRITORY

30	715	Cape Arnheim to Cape Wessel	
31	410	Booly Island to Cape Wessel	
32	20	Clarence Strait	
33	18	Port Easington	
34	308	Gourbourn Island to Melville Island	
35		Part of chart – Cape Fourcroy to Arnhim	
36	309	Darwin	
37	28	Darwin	
38	1044	Geve to Darwin	
39	722	Clarence Strait to Darwin	
40	4603	Australia – North Coast & adjacent waters	11

Pack F
AUSTRALIA TO INDONESIA & SINGAPORE

1	2683	Australia to Bali Route Planner
2	4508	South China Sea
3	5126	Routing Charts – Indian Ocean
4	2149	Indonesia - Selat Bangka – Selat Gelasa
5	3948	Selat Durian
6	2137	Selat Gelesa
7	2056	Selat Sunda & approaches
8	414	Rowley Shoals to Lombok
9	3706	Selat Lombok & Selat Aloa
10	3756	Linta & Molo Straits
11	9421	Eastern Archipelago Kupang
12	3296	Kupang
13	2776	Strait between Flores & Lomblen
14	895	Sunibawa & Flores
15	1697	Flores to Timor
16	2466	Plans of Flores
17	2757	Straat Banka to Singapore
18	1653c	Jawa Eastern Part
19	946	Plans of Bali & Lombok
20	1789	Sumatra East Coast
21	3949	Selat Rian
22	945	North Coast of Jawa
23	1066	Jawa Sea
24	3731	Jawa North Coast
25	941b	Eastern Archipelago
26	2160	Karmaki Strait
27	941a	Eastern Archipelago
28	3937	Parts of Burtan & Batau
29	3726	Bali
30	2589	SW Corner of Singapore
31	1312	Singapore to Kalinantan
32	40	Indonesian Chart of Singapore & Indonesia
33	3833	Singapore Strait Western Part
34	3831	Singapore Strait Eastern Part

35	SC5	Raffles Marina Approaches	
36	SC10	West Jahor Strait Entrance	
37	2014	South Singapore	
38	2015	Singapore Part – Western Roads	
39	SC21	Singapore Eastern Approaches	
40	2023	Keppel Harbour & Cruise Bay	
41	1995	Part of Singapore Eastern Roads	
42	3833	Singapore Strait Western Part	
43	2570	Western Approaches to Singapore	43

Pack G
SINGAPORE TO MALAYSIA & THAILAND

1	1353	Malacca Strait	
2	792	Malacca Strait Sungaidinding	
3	3947	Singapore Strait to Malacca Strait	
4	5419	Northern Approaches to Selat Dinding	
5	3944	Malacca Strait Penang	
6	3946	Part Klang to Malacca	
7	1358	One Fathom Bank to Singapore Strait	
8	71271	Port Klang	
9	71272	Approaches to Port Klang	
10	2152	Photo of Port showing Port Klang	
11	3737	Penang Harbour	
12	1366	Approaches to Penang Harbour	
13	843	Approaches to Bows Harbour Lankawi	
14	3453	Approaches to Port Klang	
15	2585	Sungan Vahor & Approaches	
16	3943	Penang to Lankawi	
17	5416	Le Mut	
18	3942	Thailand West Coast	
19	333	James Bond island	
20	3942	Lankawi to Phuket	
21	3941	Phuket	
22	308	Thailand	
23	3942	Thailand Lankawi North	
24	3941	West Coast of Thailand	
25	307	Thailand – Adaman Sea	25

THAILAND TO SRI LANKA – MALDIVES - DJIBOUTI

26		Pilot Charts of Indian Ocean	
27	4071	Indian Ocean – Northern Part	
28	830	Adaman Sea – Bay of Bengal	
29	3941	Sinulan Islands	
30	307b	Sinulan Islands	
31	841	Nicobar Islands	
32	819	Gall Harbour	
33	813	Colombo	
34	2738	Northern Part of Lakshadwell Sea	
35		Several Photos of Charts of Maldives	
36	N06	Gulf of Aden & Southern Part of Red Sea	
37	2954	Gulf of Aden Eastern Part	
38	262	Approaches to Djibouti	
39	253	Gulf of Tadjoura	14

Pack H

1	143	Red Sea 12° - 15°	
2	141	Red Sea 14° - 18°	
3	82	Outer Approaches to Port Sudan	
4	3492	Port Sudan & Approaches	
5	138	Red Sea 18° - 22°	
6	63	Red Sea 22° - 26°	
7	No8	Gulfs of Suez & Acabar	
8	2374	Red Sea 27° - 28°	
9	2373	Red Sea 28° - 29°	
10	801	Detailed Entrance to Acabar	10

EILAT TO CRETE THROUGH SUEZ CANAL

11	5501	Ronking Guide – Gulf of Suez
12	2375	Gulf of Suez
13	3215	Suez Bay
14	2098	Approaches to Port Suez
15	233	Suez Canal
16	2681	Alexandria
17	2574	Alexandria
18	2573	Port Said to Alexandria (part)

19	234	Approaches to Port Said	
20	183	Port Said to Crete	
21	1091	Crete	
22	1707	Harbours in Crete	12

CRETE TO MALTA

24	1439	Crete to Malta	
25	1800	Crete to Malta	
27	207	Crete to Zante	
28	206	Channels of Corfu	
29	203	Antipaxos	
30	1685	Pelipones	
31	1518	Greek Islands – Spetsei & Hydra	7

Total Charts (274)

APPENDIX IV

Ships Log

DAY ________________ **MONTH** ________________ **YEAR** ____________

PASSAGE from ___________________________ **to** _______________________

Time	HW +/	Wind	Force	B/Pres	Log.	Engine	Speed	Course	Position
100									
200									
300									
400									
500									
600									
700									
800									
900									
1000									
1100									
1200									
1300									
1400									
1500									
1600									
1700									
1800									
1900									
2000									
2100									
2200									
2300									
2400									

Comments

____

____

____

____

____

____

____

____

On Board____

Signed ___________________________ Captain Ref. Shiplog2

APPENDIX V

Kate's Address

Every person hear today has a warm memory of Alison, whether it be of something she has done or something she has said.

She was a quiet but strong woman that we all respected, admired and looked up to.

My memory of Alison is as my mum, she was also my best friend. I had a very close relationship with my mum; she was very easy to talk to and never judged.

My mum taught me to follow my heart and be true to myself. She helped me grow and appreciate the little things in life that count, like watching a sunflower grow, or watching the birds in the garden.

Mum liked to take time out from the rat race and go and sit in the walled gardens at Royden Park. Mum believed in taking the time to talk and understand people and made plenty of time for hugs and cuddles.

Mum and I did a lot of things together. We were both part of the Theatre Group, Mum always said she would have liked to have done the performing but never had the confidence or opportunity. Then she performed in "Role Em", she had so much fun playing "Morticia Addams". She later directed the show "Young Ones 2000"

We often went to see shows and concerts. Mum would run to the stage door before the end of the show to get autographs. In 2001 we went to Dublin to see Westlife.

Our weekends away always ended with a tale and this was no different, Mum fell head over heels and we spent the night in hospital. Mum broke her nose but didn't mind as she preferred the new shape; she said it was cheaper than a nose job. She was more gutted that Westlife didn't come and visit her. She did fall for them after all.

Out of everything my mum has had thrown at her, she could still make the hardest times bearable; she would turn them into a light-hearted time. She looked on the possible not the negative and still had time to laugh and smile.

One of the messages I know Mum wanted you all to know, is that life's to short and so so precious. You only get one chance in this life, so slow down and look at the friends and family you have got.

We had the chance to tell our mum just how much we loved her, not everyone is so fortunate, even if you go home tonight and tell just one person how much they mean to you, think what that will mean to them.

Dear Martha, Mum

You are my mum and my best friend, which was unusual
Somehow our characters still blend, your wisdom and my will
I turned and you were there for me
I spoke, you understood
I felt cared for, but also free,
You loved and I was good.
I'm fortunate that I was born to someone just like you,
I love you still, though you're gone
You live in what I do.
You've always been the perfect mum
And I will always love you

Kate27th February 2007

APPENDIX VI

Jamie's Address

This is undoubtedly the hardest thing I've ever had to do, not only because of the circumstances, but more due to, well, how do I put so many happy thoughts and speak about how loving, caring, strong, brave, and generous but most of all proud person Mum was?

You see in the last moments that Mum was alive; I asked her if she was happy with the life she had lived. Mums response was "Jamie all I ever wanted, the only job I ever enjoyed was being a mum".

Now, there are no words out there to fully justify a lot of Mum's qualities but one last example that stuck with me, was when she apologised for being so ill and the fact that she was leaving Kate and me behind.

Mum always found time for others, whether it was a letter to wish someone well, remember a birthday or in my case make sure I've got some words of wisdom and a good luck charm for a competition.

Mum made me smile a lot too; we had a close yet humorous understanding. We could spend weeks apart but she would have prepared a note for each day I was away.
When the chips were down or I needed some inspiration, although thousands of miles away, I always felt she was by my side.

She has been my greatest inspiration in life and I enjoyed making her proud.

Even though sport was not Mum's thing, she preferred music and theatre, she became interested because I was interested, and that meant so much to me.

Mum made me smile because back in June on the 16th, she wrote me a letter explaining about her terminal illness, and that everything will be OK. To end it Mum wrote "now must go, got a Tour de France to prepare for. Lance Armstrong has retired, so someone's got to keep the record going"

This to me just proved how much a fighter and positive thinker Mum was. What an inspiration. I love you Mum.

I would now like to finish by reading a poem that Mum stood by in her fight against cancer. It's called "Don't Quit"
Thank the sailing club for flag at half mast & Dr Errington for giving Mum 13 years and the chance to beat cancer twice

Jamie 27th February 2007

When things go wrong, as they sometimes will,
When the road you're trudging seems all up hill,
When the funds are low and the debts are high,
And you want to smile, but you have to sigh,
When care is pressing you down a bit,
Rest! if you must; but don't you quit.
Success is failure turned inside out;
The silver tint of the clouds of doubt;
And you never can tell how close you are,
It may be near when it seems afar;
So stick to the fight when you're hardest hit;
It's when things seem worst that you mustn't quit.

APPENDIX VII

A Tribute to ALISON a person in her own right

From her Mum &Dad

Earlier in the year Alison wondered how many people would remember her as Alison, a person in her own right. Someone who was not only a mum, a daughter, a sister, but also a person, - Alison.

The number of letters, cards, and the people here today prove that she was loved for being herself.

Alison is the loving mum of Jamie and Kate, the eldest daughter of Brian and Gill and sister to Cath and Gillian.

Due to Brian's work she attended 4 different primary schools, in Leicester, Wombwell, Ruislip and Greasby, while Cath went to 3 and Gillian 2.

All three girls attended Upton Convent.

Alison wanted to be a nurse and began training at Sefton General Hospital. Due to a back injury and poor health she had to give it up. Alison has never been out of work although she did many different jobs from Office Work, Barmaid at the Moby Dick to Classroom assistant at Greasby Primary School.

It was during the last two years that she had the freedom to do the work that she really wanted to do.

First she qualified as a hairdresser

Then she enrolled at the Liverpool Community College to train as a Professional Theatrical Make-up Artist.

To help with costs she took a part-time job as a waitress at Brimstage, where she had an unfortunate accident and broke her big toe. Even so with the help of daily chauffeuring by Mum and Dad she kept up her studies in Liverpool.

It was during this time that Alison was told she had terminal cancer.

Alison was first diagnosed with breast cancer in 1994 and thought that she had beaten the disease but it came back seven years later in 2001.

Again Alison fought the disease saying that she would not let it win. But it did in the end.

Alison not only qualified as a Theatrical Make-up Artist but was the top student.

She started her Business "Create the Look" and registered it at Company House.

Although she was ill she still managed to do some work on Film, Television and Theatrical shows.

When Alison got work on The BBC programme "Casualty1906" it was the best news she could have received. Sadly she was too ill to commence work and had to decline the offer.

The number of times the word "amazing" as been used by doctors, nurses, fellow students and friends, to describe Alison, says much about the person she was.

An early example of things to come was in 1959.

The family lived in the flat over the local swimming pool at Leek in Staffordshire, where Brian was the Baths Manager. One Sunday afternoon when the baths were closed Alison who was 3 years old and Cath her younger sister, were playing on the side of the pool when Alison fell in the deep end of the baths. Dolls pram with teddy where at the bottom of the pool when Mum and Dad ran in after hearing Cath screaming.

Even though she could not swim Alison had worked her way to the side of the pool and along to the shallow end steps, and was climbing out.

As a result of this, the fear of water did not go away, but because of her dad's job she had to learn to swim.

At Ruislip in 1965 aged 9 she asked how many lengths was it to swim a mile. 56 she was told.

With that Alison swam 56 lengths then said to her dad "I can now swim a mile and I am not going to swim again."

She then left the water.

It was that sort of determination that showed throughout her life.

Alison collected autographs so when a telephone call came from the White House in America, to check if an Alison Smith lived at that address, it was so that The President, Ronald Regan could send Alison his autograph, which he did.

As did The Prime Minister Mrs Margaret Thatcher.

When asked how she managed it she said "Dad always said to go straight to the top if you want to get anything done"

But of all her achievements the greatest was that of being, "the best mum in the world" to Jamie and Kate.

Throughout the last 13 years, against all the odds, Alison has maintained that title.

She always said that it was her job to live long enough to see Jamie and Kate grow up. And she did.

When Alison left the Hospice she moved to live with Brian and Gill in their bungalow so that all the family could look after her. At no time was she alone day or night.

They were all with her on her last day.

It was a privilege to look after her.

A super mum

A loving daughter

A great sister

A good friend

That was Alison

Brian and Gill February 2007

APPENDIX VIII

Box no.	Medicine	Feb. Mon 12	Tues 13	2007 Wed 14	Thurs 15	Fri 16	Sat 17	Sun 18	
	Morning								
1	Adcal-D3 (1)								
2	Anastrozole (1)								
3	Colpermin (2)								
4 b	Cyclizine (1)								b = bottle
5 b	Dexamethasone (2)								
6 b	Diazepam (1)								
7	Doxycycline (1)								
8	Frusemide								cancelled
10	Gelclair (mouthwash)								
11	Ketoprofen (2)								
12	Merbeverine (1)								
13	Omdansetron (1)								
14	Omeprazple (2)								
15	Oxycontin (1)								
16	Paracetamol (2)								
17	Symbicort 1 puff								
	Lunchtime								
3	Colperine (2)								
5 b	Dexamethasone (2)								
6 b	Diazepam (1)								
10	Gelclair (mouthwash)								
12	Mebeverine (1)								
16	Paracetamol (2)								
	Evening								
1	Adcal-D3 (1)								
3	Colpermin (2)								
4 b	Cyclizine (1)								
10	Gelclair (mouthwash)								
11	Ketoprofen (2)								
12	Mebeverine (1)								
13	Omdansetron (1)								
16	Paracetamol (2)								
6 b	Diazepam (1)								
	Bedtime								
2 a	Co-Danthramer (1)								
6 b	Diazepam (1)								
9	Gabapentin (1)								
18	Haloperidol (3)								
15	Oxycontin (1)								
16	Paracetamol (2)								
	Extra for pain								
19	Lorazepam 1/2 tab.								
20	Orthana oral spray								
21	Oxynorn Sugar 2mls.								
22	Salbutanol 2 puffs								